Rosenbaum, Julius

The Plague of Lust

Inktank publishing

Rosenbaum, Julius

The Plague of Lust

Inktank publishing, 2018

www.inktank-publishing.com

ISBN/EAN: 9783747750674

THE
PLAGUE OF LUST,

BEING A HISTORY OF VENEREAL DISEASE

IN

CLASSICAL ANTIQUITY,

AND INCLUDING:—DETAILED INVESTIGATIONS INTO THE CULT OF VENUS, AND PHALLIC WORSHIP, BROTHELS, THE *Νοῦσος Θήλεια* (FEMININE DISEASE) OF THE SCYTHIANS, PAEDERASTIA, AND OTHER SEXUAL PERVERSIONS AMONGST THE ANCIENTS,

AS CONTRIBUTIONS TOWARDS

THE EXACT INTERPRETATION OF THEIR WRITINGS

BY

Dr. JULIUS ROSENBAUM

TRANSLATED FROM THE SIXTH (UNABRIDGED) GERMAN EDITION

BY

AN OXFORD M.A.

THE SECOND OF TWO VOLUMES

Paris
CHARLES CARRINGTON
PUBLISHER OF MEDICAL, FOLK-LORE AND HISTORICAL WORKS
13, FAUBOURG MONTMARTRE, 13
MDCCCCI

CONTENTS OF THE SECOND VOLUME.

FIRST SECTION.

SECOND SECTION.

INFLUENCES WHICH HINDERED TO A GREATER OR LESS DEGREE THE INCEPTION OF DISEASES CONSEQUENT UPON USE OR MISUSE OF THE GENITAL ORGANS.

THIRD SECTION.

RELATION OF PHYSICIANS TOWARDS DISEASES CONSEQUENT UPON THE USE OR MISUSE OF THE GENITAL ORGANS.

DEFINITIONS.

Irrumare: Penem in os alienum inserere, ut sugatur, itaque voluptas quaedam libidinosa paretur; to put the penis into another's mouth to be sucked — a form of vicious indulgence.

Fellare: Penem alienum in os admittere, ibique eo sugere ut voluptas quaedam libidinosa paretur; to allow another's penis to be put in the mouth and to suck it — the active form of the above vicious practice.

Fellator: Is qui pro habitudine fellat; one who practices this vice.

Cunnilingus: Qui mulierum pudenda lingit; a man who licks women's private parts.

THE PLAGUE OF LUST

IN

CLASSICAL ANTIQUITY.

SECOND PART.

II.

§ 21.

Irrumation and Fellation.

(Irrumare, Fellare).

VERY much more abominable and repulsive still is the habit of Irrumation [1] (*penem in os arrigere est irrumare*—to erect the *penis* and insert it into the mouth of another person) and the practice of the

[1] *Festus*, p. 135., says: *Rumen* est pars colli, qua esca devoratur (The *rumen*, or gullet, is that part of the neck, where food is swallowed). *Nonius*, p. 18.: rumen dictum locus in ventre, quo cibus sumitur et unde redditur (rumen was applied to the locality in the belly to which food is taken in and from which it is given back).—*Isidore*, Etymolog. bk. XII. 37., Ruminatio autem dicta est a *ruma*, eminente gutturis parte, per quam dimissus cibus a certis animalibus revocatur (Now rumination is so called from the *ruma*, or gullet, the upper portion of the throat, by which food after being swallowed is brought up again by certain animals). It is true *Varro* gives another explanation: ruminare propter *rumam*, id est prisco vocabulo mammam (to ruminate so called on account of the *ruma*, that is in old Latin the breast); and so one might equally well understand by *irrumare* the custom of voluptuaries, one that is still practised, of employing the space between the bosoms as *vagina*. At any rate *Dr. Hacker* of Leipzig assured the author he had on several occasions observed cases where prostitutes had chancrous swellings between

Fellator[1] (*si quis vel labris vel lingua perfricandi atque exsugendi officium peni praestat*—one who with the lips or the tongue performs the office of rubbing and sucking another's *penis*). This the Greeks called **λεσβιάζειν** (to follow the Lesbian mode), because the vice was especially practised by the Lesbian women, though in common with all others of the sort it came originally from Asia. *Lucian* in his *Pseudologista*[2], in which he severely criticizes the the dissolute Timarchus, who had taken the expression **ἀποφρὰς** (unmentionable) in ill part, says: "By the gods, what should make you fly into a passion, since it is a matter of common report that you are a *Fellator* and a *Cunnilingus*[3]. Are you

the bosoms, as well as under the arm-pits,—for these also are employed with the same object.—Does *ruma* possibly stand for *rima* (a chink)? In any case we should compare what *Suidas* gives under the words **ῥῦμα, ῥύμη** and **ῥύμματα**. Synonyms are *comprimere linguam, buccam offendere*, etc. (to compress the tongue, to hit against the cheek).

[1] The etymology of *fellare* is still obscure. *Vossius*, Etymolog., derives it from the Æolic **φηλᾶν** for **θηλᾶν** and **θηλάζειν**, to suck the breasts. *Pliny*, Hist. Nat. bk. XI. 65., says of the tongue of cats: imbricatae asperitatis ac limae similis, attenuansque lambendo cutem hominis (of a ridged roughness of surface, like a file, capable of wearing through the human skin by licking). The meanings which *Suidas* gives under **φελλά**, etc. would seem to point to an old stem **φέλλω**,—to roughen, to file.

[2] *Lucian*, Works, edit. Lehmann, Vol. VIII. pp. 56—84.

[3] **πρὸς θεῶν, εἰπέ μοι, τί πάσχεις, ἐπειδὰν κἀκεῖνα λέγωσιν οἱ πολλοί, λεσβιάζειν σε καὶ φοινικίζειν**; (for translation see text above); as to **φοινικίζειν**, this will be discussed later on. The word **λεσβιάζειν** occurs in Aristophanes, Frogs 1335; and he also uses **λεσβιεῖν** in the same sense, Wasps, 1386., **μέλλουσαν ἤδη λεσβιεῖν τοὺς ξυμπότας**· (a girl standing ready to **λεσβιεῖν**—love in the Lesbian mode,—the revellers). On this passage the Scholiast remarks: **ἵνα μὴ τὸ παλαιὸν τοῦτο καὶ θρυλλούμενον δι' ἡμετέρων στομάτων εἴπω σόφισμα, ὃ φασι παῖδας Λεσβίων εὑρεῖν.** (this ancient

as much in the dark as to the meaning of these words as you are about that of ἀποφρὰς (unmentionable)? and do you take them for titles of honour? Or is it that you are now accustomed to them, but not to

trick, a matter of common gossip to any in our mouths, which they say the children of the Lesbians invented).—*Suidas* s. v. Λεσβίαι· μολύναι τὸ στόμα. Λέσβιοι γὰρ διεβάλλοντο ἐπὶ αἰσχρότητι. (under the word Λεσβίαι—Lesbian women, to defile the mouth. For the Lesbians were reproached for foulness). *Hesychius:* λεσβιάζειν· πρὸς ἄνδρα στόμα στύειν. Λεσβιάδας γὰρ τὰς λαικαστρίας ἔλεγον. (to play the Lesbian; to use the mouth to a man for an obscene purpose. For they used to call wanton courtesans Lesbians). *Eustathius*, Comment. ad Homeri Iliad. p. 741., εἰσὶ βλασφημίαι καὶ ἀπὸ ἐθνῶν καὶ πόλεων καὶ δήμων πολλαί, ῥηματικῶς πεποιημέναι· ἐθνῶν μὲν, οἷον κιλικίζειν καὶ αἰγυπτιάζειν, τὸ πονηρεύεσθαι, καὶ κρητίζειν, τὸ ψεύδεσθαι· ἐκ πόλεων δὲ, οἷον λεσβιάζειν, τὸ αἰσχροποιεῖν· εἶτα παραγαγόντες Φερεκράτους χρῆσιν ἐν Ἰάμβῳ τό δώσει δέ σοι γυναῖκας ἑπτὰ Λεσβίας· ἐπάγουσιν ἀμοιβαῖον τί· καλόν γε δῶρον ἑπτ' ἔχειν λαικαστρίας· ὡς τοιούτων οὐσῶν τῶν Λεσβίων γυναικῶν· ἐκ δήμων δὲ βλασφημία, τὸ αἰξωνεύεσθαι, ἤγουν κακολογεῖν. Αἰξωνεῖς γὰρ δημόταται Ἀττικοί, σκωπτόμενοι ὡς κακολόγοι, καθὰ καὶ οἱ Σφήττιοι ἐπὶ ἀγριότητι. (And there are many reproaches applying to nations, and cities, and demes, implied in the use of certain words; for instance in the case of nations, to play the Cilician, and to play the Egyptian, i. e. to be a rogue, and to play the Cretan, i. e. to be a liar; again, in the case of cities, to act the Lesbian, i. e. to act filthily; further we may bring forward a passage of Pherecrates in Iambic verse, viz. the line, "And he shall give thee seven Lesbian women," to which the answering verse is, "Verily! a noble gift, to get seven harlots," implying that such was the character of the Lesbian women. Lastly an example of such a reproach applying to demes, to play the Æxonian, in other words to be foul-mouthed. For the Æxonians were Attic demesmen, ridiculed as being evil-speakers in the same way as the Sphettians were on the ground of rusticity). The word σόφισμα (trick) in the passage of the Scholiast to Aristophanes explains the word "dogma" in Martial,

ἀποφρὰς, and so wish to erase it as something unknown to you from the list of your Titles? (ch. 28).—I am well aware what were your practices in Palestine, in Egypt, in Phoenicia and Syria, as well as in Hellas and Italy, and above all just now in Ephesus, where you set the crown on your extravagances. (ch. 11).—However you will never persuade your fellow-citizens that they ought not to regard you as the filthiest of all men, the very refuse of the whole city. Now it may be you rely on the belief of the generality in Syria, that you have never been accused (there) of any guilt or vice. But by Hercules! the city of Antioch looked on at the whole history, when you carried off the young man who came from Tarsus, and—but there, it would not become me to go over such ground again. All who were there know the facts and remember it all, that time when they saw you sitting at his knees (*καὶ σὲ μὲν ἐς γόνυ συγκαθήμενον ἰδόντες*), and doing you know very well what to him, that is if you have not utterly and entirely forgotten the whole matter. (ch. 20).—But when they caught you lying at the knees of the son of Oinopion the Cooper (*τοῦ μειρακίου.... ἐν γόνασι κείμενον*—lying at the knees of the stripling), what make you of that? Did they not surely take you for a man of the sort to be expected, when they saw you doing such a thing? (ch. 28).—How, by Zeus! after such a deed, have you the effrontery to give us the kiss of salutation?—Sooner kiss an adder or a viper? The danger and

bk. IX. 48., Dic mihi, percidi, Pannice, *dogma* quod est? (Tell me, Pannicus, what is the trick of the paederast?). *Theopompus* in "Ulysses" says: *δι' ἡμετέρων στομάτων εἶτω σόφισμ' ὃ φασι παῖδας Λεσβίων εὑρεῖν*. (a certain trick common in our mouths which they say children of the Lesbians invented). *Strattis* in "Pytisus": *τῷ στόματι δράσω ταῦθ' ἅπερ τοῦ αἰσχροῦ τάττεται* [*ταῦθ' ἅπερ οἱ Λέσβιοι*]. (with my mouth I will do those things that are reckoned as obscene,—those things that the Lesbians do).

pain of the bite a Physician may yet remove, if called in. But after your kiss and with such poison on his lips who dare draw near to Temple or altar? What god would listen to the suppliant? how many vessels of holy water, how many lustrations, would be needful? (ch. 24).—In Syria you are known as **ῥοδοδάφνη** (rose-laurel) [1]; why, a man cannot explain for very shame, great Athené!—But in Palestine as **φραγμὸς** (the hedge) [2], on account of the prickles of your beard, I suppose. In Egypt again as **συνάγχη** (sore throat),—and this is a well known business. It must have been a close thing with you not to be choked, that time you came across the sailor of a three-master, who fell upon you and stopped your mouth for you (**ὃς ἐμπεσὼν ἀπέφραξέ σοι τὸ στόμα**)."

This passage brings us next to a gloss of the *Pseudo-Galen* [3], on which *Naumann* [4], after laying

[1] Haud scio an Rhododaphnes cognomine a Syris isti tradito tecte sugilletur cunnilingus, ita ut rosa lateat cunnus, in lauri folio lingua lingens, (I cannot say for certain whether by the surname of "Rhododaphne"—rose-laurel—given the man by the Syrians it is covertly suggested he was a *cunnilingus*, as much as to say that while a *cunnus*—female organ—is suggested by the rose, a licking tongue is the same in the laurel-leaf), says *Forberg*, loco citato p. 281. *Suidas*, s. v. *ῥοδωνία· ἔστι μὲν ὁ τῶν ῥόδων λειμών· ἄλλοι δὲ καὶ τὴν ῥοδοδάφνην οὕτω φασὶ καλεῖσθαι* (under the word *ῥοδωνία*—rose-garden: it is the meadow of roses; but others again say this is called *ῥοδοδάφνη*). *Pliny*, Hist. Nat. XVI. 33. *Hesychius*, s. v. *ῥοδωνία* says: *δηλοῖ δὲ καὶ τὸ ἀνδρὸς αἰδοῖον αὕτη*. (under the word *ῥοδωνία* — rose-garden: this signifies also *the human genitals*).

[2] The explanation of this is to be found in the Priapeia Carmina, 75.:

Barbatis non nisi *summa* petet.

(With bearded men will touch but the extremities).

[3] *Pseudo-Galen*, Works, edit. Kühn, Vol. XIX. p. 142.

[4] Handbuch der Klinik (Hand-book of Clinical Medicine), vol. VII. p. 88. Also at a yet earlier date in Schmidt's Jahrbuch 1837., Vol. XIII. p. 101.

down his view as to the *Morbus phoeniceus* (Purple Plague),—a subject to be discussed presently,—goes on to express himself thus: "However we must go yet farther. In the above cited work of the Pseudo-Galen is included an Index of words, *which with a high degree of probability we may conclude to refer to Venereal diseases, so far as known to the Ancients* (loco citato, under word **στρυμάργου**, p. 142). We read there that *Dioscorides* called **στρυμάργους** or **στομάργους** (evil-mouthed) men in whom the longing for sensual indulgence had risen to frenzy. Of similar meaning to this would seem to be the expressions **μυοχάνη** (*maxillarum hiatu insignis*—conspicuous for the wide opening of the arm-pits) or **μυσάχνη** (*meretrix*—prostitute), **μῦσος** (*facinus abominandum*—an abominable act), **σαράπους** (crura ambulando divaricans—straddling the legs in walking), and **γρυπαλώπηξ** (from **γρύπος** *curvus*—curved, hooked, probably denoting the erection of the *penis*; at any rate a dissolute man is called in Aristophanes **κυναλώπηξ** (fox-dog). But most notable is the added observation, to the effect that Erasistratus called such persons **ῥινοκολοῦροι** (*i.e. qui mutilati naribus sunt*—men who have been mutilated in their noses). Just at the time of the Greek occupation of Egypt, *Rhinocorura* or *Rhinocolura* was the name of a wretched sort of "Botany Bay" situated at the North-Eastern extremity of the country, lying in the desert on the shores of the Mediterranean between Gaza and Pelusium, and serving as a place of residence for lepers (*Pliny*, Hist., Nat., Bk. V. ch. 4. *Livy*, Hists. Bk. XXXV. ch. 11). Now if we bring together all the information given here, and especially if we consider the various shameful forms of indulgence of the sexual impulse and the mutilation of the nose that is connected with them, *there cannot be much doubt left that these ancient and fragmentary notices refer to Venereal evil,* whether in conjunction with leprous affections or not."

But to test the correctness of these explanations

and conclusions, it will be necessary first of all to quote the gloss itself in full: **στρυμάργου. οἶδε καὶ ταύτην τὴν γραφὴν ὁ Διοσκουρίδης, οὐ μόνον τὴν στομάργου, ἀλλὰ καὶ τοῦτο οὐχ ὡς κύριον ὄνομα ἐξηγεῖται, ἀλλὰ τὸν μανικῶς ἐπτοημένον περὶ τά ἀφροδίσια δηλοῦσθαί φησιν· εἰρῆσθαι γὰρ παρὰ τῷ Ἱπποκράτει καὶ ἄλλα πολλὰ κατὰ τὸν αὐτὸν τρόπον ἐπίθετα, καθάπερ μυοχάνη, σαράπους, γρυπαλώπηξ· ἀλλὰ καὶ παρ' Ἐρασιστράτῳ φησὶν ὁ ῥινοκολοῦρος,** that is to say:—**στρυμάργου**: Dioscorides knows this form also, not merely that of **στομάργου,** but this too he regards not as a proper name, but says that it signifies one who is madly set upon love-indulgences; for that in Hippocrates as well many other epithets of the same sort (which refer to the same sort of vice) are mentioned, e. g. **μυοχάνη, σαράπους, γρυπαλώπηξ;** also he says that in Erasistratus (the expression) **ῥινοκολοῦρος** is found.

The reader sees in the first place that it is not merely expressions peculiar to Dioscorides that are here cited, as we might be led to suppose by Naumann's statement, but that they are every one of them found, as we shall presently prove more particularly, in *Hippocrates*, the **ῥινοκολοῦρος** of Erasistratus of course excepted. *Dioscorides* mentions them only in his commentary on the Second Book of the "Epidemia", when laying down the passages to be cited immediately, and declares them not to be proper names, but adjectives which all refer to insane indulgence in the pleasures of love; accordingly there can be no question here of *bodily disorders*, let the words in themselves signify what they will. Now if we examine into this more closely, we shall find first of all that we must obviously read **στυμάργου** in place of **στρυμάργου,** for not only is this form given by the author of the gloss (under **στομάργου** [1]), quoted on the preceding page, but

[1] *Στομάργου, ἐν τῷ δευτέρῳ τῶν ἐπιδημιῶν ὁ Διοσκουρίδης οὕτως γράφει, καὶ δηλοῦσθαι φησὶ τοῦ*

the text also of Hippocrates[1] offers it in both passages; whereas **στρυμάργου** gives no sort of sense.

The word **στυμάργος** in fact is derived either

λαλοῦντος μανικῶς· οἱ δὲ ἄλλοι στυμάργου γράφουσι καὶ ὄνομα κύριον ἀκούουσι. (Στομάργου: in the second Book of the Epidemia Dioscorides writes the word thus, and says it signifies such as talk insanely; others however write στυμάργου, and understand it as a proper name).

[1] *Hippocrates*, Bk. II. sect. 2. edit. Kühn, Vol. III. p. 436., Καὶ ἡ Στυμαργέω ἐκ ταραχῆς ὀλιγημέρου πολλὰ στήσασα, λ. τ. λ. (And the female slave of Stymargeos having after a few days' disturbance re-established much, etc.)—The same passage occurs in *Galen*, Comments on the Epid. bk. II. edit. Kühn, Vol. XVII. A. p. 324., with an explanation of the subject-matter, and also has Στυμαργέω.—*Ibidem*, p. 458., ἡ Στυμάργεω οἰκέτις ἡ Ἰδουμαῖα ἐγένετο, κ. τ. λ. (the female slave of Stymargeos, the Idumaean, was, etc.).—*Galen* cites the passage, *loco citato* p. 467., without comment, but he likewise reads Στυμάργεω. In two other passages, in which he comments on the statements last quoted from Hippocrates, the text is obviously corrupt. In "De tremore, palpitatione, convulsione et rigore" (Of Trembling, Palpitation, Convulsion and Rigor), edit. Kühn, vol. III. p. 602, it reads: Ἐστυμάργεω οἰκέτις, ᾗ οὐδὲ αἷμα ἐγένετο, ὡς ἔτεκε θυγατέρα, κ. τ. λ. (a female slave of Estymargeos, in whose case flowed no blood at all, when she gave birth to a daughter, etc.). Alao *Assmann* in his Index to Kühn's Edition of Galen, pp. 232 and 307., represents it by *Estymergi ancilla* (a female slave of Estymergus). However there can be no doubt Ἡ Στυμάργεω οἰκέτις (The female slave of Stymargeos) ought to be read in Galen; on the other hand we see clearly from this passage that the text of Hippocrates is quite wrong in giving the Proper name ἡ Ἰδουμαῖα (the Idumaean), and this, as indeed the sense too requires, must be changed into ᾗ αἷμα οὐδὲ (in whose case not even blood); and one is more especially convinced of this on reading the explanation given by *Galen*, *loco citato*. Besides this, following Galen's lead, we should read **δεῖ ἐλθεῖν** for **διελθεῖν** and **προφάσεως** for **προφάσιος**. Also he has ἀφορμὴν instead of ἀχήν.—The *second* passage of *Galen*

from **στῦμα** [1], the act of erecting the penis, and and **ἔργον** (work), so signifying anyone who performs the work of causing an erection of the penis,—or else from **στύω** [2], I erect the penis, and **μάργος** [3],

occurs in the "De venae sectione" (On the opening of a Vein) adv. Erasistrat., ch. 5.: *ἐκεῖνο δέ πως εἴρηται; ἐκ τοῦ μαργέω οἰκέτιδος οὐδὲ αἷμα ἐγένετο, ὡς ἔτεκε θυγατέρα, ἀπέστραπτο τὸ στόμα πρός [τῆς μήτρας καὶ ἐς] ἰσχίον καὶ σκέλος ὀδύνη, παρα σφυρὸν τμηθεῖσα ἐραΐσε [ἐῤῥήισε], καίτοι τρόμοι τὸ σῶμα περικατεῖχον [πᾶν κατεῖχον]· ἀλλ' ἐπὶ τὴν πρόφασιν χρὴ ἐλθεῖν καὶ τῆς προφάσεως τὴν τροφήν.* (Now how is this account given? from a female slave of Stymargeos not even blood flowed, when she gave birth to a daughter; the mouth was distorted from (the womb, and in) loin and leg there was pain; on being cut (bled) on the ankle, she found relief, though shudderings ran down the (whole) body; but we must go to the cause, and the origin of the cause). Here too it is evident, besides the emendations already pointed out as necessary, we must read *ἐκ Στυμάργεω*, as the edition of Kühn, vol. XI. p. 161., does actually and rightly read. *Dioscorides* may be right so far, that the word, *strictly speaking*, is not a "Nomen proprium" (Proper name), but in the passage named it stands for one, if only, as is likely enough, for a nickname, as it is called.

[1] *Athenaeus*, Deipnos., bk. I. ch. 8., quotes from the "Phaon" of the Comic Poet Plato: *τρίγλη—καὶ στύματα μισεῖ.* (a mullet,—and hates erections). Comp. bk. VII. ch. 126.

[2] The verb *στύω* (I erect the penis) occurs often in *Aristophanes*, e.g. "Acharnians" 1218., *στύομαι* (I have an erection), "Peace", 727., *ἐστυκότες* (men with penes standing), "Lysistr." 214., *ἐστυκὼς* (a man with penis standing), 598., *στῦσαι* (to make the penis stand), 869., *ἔστυκα γὰρ* (for my penis was standing); always in the sense of to make, or have, an erection.

[3] *Suidas* explains *μάργος* by *μαινόμενος* (being mad) and *Hesychius* also by *ὑβριστὴς* (recklessly insolent), a word we have already learned from repeated examples to recognize as signifying unnatural lust. *Clement of Alexandria*, Paedag., bk. II. ch. 1. p. 146., says: *καὶ ἡ λαιμαργία, μανία περὶ τὸ λαιμόν, καὶ ἡ γαστριμαργία, ἀκρασία, περὶ τὴν τροφήν· ὡς δὲ καὶ τοὔνομα περιέχει, μανία*

(mad), i. e. one who erects, uses, the penis in a madly lascivious fashion, so an *Irrumator*, and with this *Hesychius'* interpretation agrees: **λεσβιάζειν,—πρὸς ἀνδρὸς στόμα στύειν,** (to lesbianize,—to erect the penis in a man's mouth). **Στομάργος** on the other hand is formed by a combination of **στόμα,** the mouth, and **ἔργω** or **ἔργον** (work, I work), a word constantly used to express the employment of the genital organs [1], in fact indulgence in love generally, and signifies a man who performs the work (of love) with the mouth, so a *Fellator* [2]. Now

ἐπὶ γαστέρα· ἐπεὶ μάργος, ὁ μεμηνώς. (And gluttony, i. e. madness in connection with the gullet, and greediness, i. e. intemperance in connection with food, in other words as the name implies, madness as to the belly; for μάργος means a madman).

[1] *Lucian*, Pseudologist. ch. 21., uses ἔργον (work) of the *Irrumator* and *Fellator*. Similarly *Horace*, Epod. VIII. 19, says:

fascinum
Quod ut superbo provoces ab inguine,
Ore allaborandum est tibi.

(a member .... that needs, for you to provoke it to rise from the unsympathetic groin, to be worked with your mouth). *Ovid's* phrase "dulce opus" (sweet task) and *Horace's* "molle opus" (gentle task) are familiar. Comp. *Hesychius*, s. v. ἀῤῥητουργία,—αἰσχρουργία, κακουργία, τὰ ἄῤῥητα ἐργάζεσθαι, (under the word ἀῤῥητουργία, infamous action,—base action, evil action, the performance of infamous tasks).

[2] The word στόμαργος is found in *Sophocles*, in a passage where Electra says to Clytaemnestra (581):

Κήρυσσέ μ' εἰς ἅπαντας, εἴτε χρὴ, πλέαν,
εἴτε στόμαργον, εἴτ' ἀναιδείας πλέαν.
Εἰ γὰρ πέφυκα τῶνδε τῶν ἔργων ἴδρις
σχεδόν τι τὴν σὴν σύ καταισχύνω φύσιν.

(Proclaim me to all, if need be, an evil woman, *foul-mouthed* and full of shamelessness. For if I am cunning *in these tasks*, it is but that I am not far from sharing your own character). *Suidas* under the word interprets στόμαργος here by φλύαρος (prating). *Philo*, De Monarchia bk. I. edit. Mangey, vol. II. p. 219., says: στομαργίᾳ χρήσασθαι καὶ ἀχαλίνῳ γλώσσῃ, βλασφημοῦντας οὓς ἕτεροι νομίζουσι θεούς. (to indulge in *loose talking* and an unbridled

since only the most abandoned lust, lust that has really grown into a form of insanity, is capable of undertaking such obscenities, the interpretation of *Dioscorides* μανικῶς ἐπτοημένον περὶ τὰ ἀφροδίσια (one that is insanely, madly, set on the pleasures of love) is quite satisfactory, assuming a hesitation on the part of the author to set forth the actual fact more explicitly, especially as we have already proved under the head of Paederastia [1] how unnatural sexual desires were commonly regarded as a *Mania*

tongue, blaspheming such as other men hold to be gods). The *Etymologicum Magnum* s. v. γλώσσαργον, στόμαργον ἢ ταχύγλωσσον, (under the word idle-tongued,—*foul-mouthed* or loose-tongued). Whereas *Aristophanes* has the word στοματουργός, "Frogs" 848.,

ἔνθεν δὴ στοματουργὸς ἐπῶν
βασανίστρια λίσπη
γλῶσσ' ....

(So thence a *phrase-making* word-sifting, smooth tongue...).

[1] Comp. p. 172 above. *Lucian*, Pseudolog. ch. 31., calls it παροινῶν (acting drunkenly). *Athenaeus*, Deipnos. bk. XIII. ch. 80., φιλόπαις δ' ἦν ἐκμανῶς καὶ Ἀλέξανδρος, ὁ βασιλεύς. (And he was a lover of boys, *to an insane degree*, was Alexander the King). *Dio Chrysostom*, Tarsica I. p. 409., says of the ῥέγχειν (snorting of the Cinaedi: ἀλλ' ἐστὶ σημεῖον τῆς αἰσχάτης ὕβρεως καὶ ἀπονοίας (but it is a sign of the most abandoned insolence and *infatuation*), and again p. 412.: ὡς ἤδη μανιά τὸ γιγνόμενον ἔοικεν αἰσχρᾷ καὶ ἀπρέπει (so now the resulting condition resembles madness, disgraceful and unseemly madness). *Clement of Alexandria*, Paedag. bk. III. ch. 8., περὶ τὰ παιδικὰ ἐκμανῶς ἐπτοημένοι (men set upon enjoyments with boys *insanely*). But above all is the following passage from Juvenal (Sat. VI. 299) apposite in this connection:

.... Quid enim Venus ebria curat?
Inguinis et capitis quae sint discrimina nescit.

(For of what does drunken love take heed? What are the differences betwixt groin and head, she ignores). *Seneca*, De ira II.: *Raptus* ad stupra et *ne os quidem libidini exceptum*. (Carried away into obscenities and not even the mouth held secure from lust). *Lactantius*, VI. 23., Quorum teterrima libido et execrabilis *furor* ne *capiti* quidem parcit. (Whose most foul lust and abominable *frenzy* spares not even *the head*).

or form of insanity. Even if we were not in a position adequately to explain the rest of the words, yet the phrase that comes next to them **καὶ ἄλλα πολλὰ κατὰ τὸν αὐτὸν τρὸπον** (and many others of the same fashion) at once shows that they bear the same signification as **στύμαργος** and **στομάργος**, or at any rate that they must all alike refer to unnatural satisfaction of the sexual impulse, for **τρόπος** (fashion) is the very word particularly appropriated to imply such-like practices, as we see from the expressions **Κρῆτα τρόπον, Ἑλληνικὰν τρόπον** [1], (Cretan fashion, Greek fashion) used to indicate paederastia.

In relation to the word **μυοχάνη** the readings differ greatly in the different MSS. of Galen. Franz in his edition of the Glossaries to Hippocrates gives **μιοχάνης** and **μυοχάνης**, while the Pseudo-Galen explains it under the word **μυοχάνη** as **ἐπίθετον χασκούσης· εἰ δὲ μυριοχαύνη γράφοιτο, ἡ ἐπὶ μυρίοις ἂν ἔιη χαυνουμένη** (epithet applied to a woman who gapes; now if **μυριοχαύνη** were read, it would mean "the woman who gapes wide for ten thousand men"); besides, various readings are found here,—**μηοχάνη** for **μυοχάνη**, also **μιριοχάνη**, and **μυιοχάνη** for **μυριοχαύνη**. Erotian says **μη-**

[1] *Xenophon*, Cyropaed. II. 2. 28. Hence too *Cicero*, Tuscul. V. 20., Haberet etiam *more Graeciae* quosdam adolescentes amore coniunctos (he would keep also, *after the fashion of Greece*, sundry young men bound to him in ties of affection); of course it is a question here of Paedophilia merely, but we have seen how readily this was confounded with Paederastia. *Aristophanes*, Eccles. 918.,

ἤδη τὸν ἀπ' Ἰωνίας
τρόπον τάλαινα κνησιᾷς·
δοκεῖς δέ μοι καὶ λάβδα
κατὰ τοὺς Λεσβίους.

(Now, wretched woman, you itch after the fashion of Ionia; and you appear to me to long even for the *Lambda* (licking) of the Lesbian mode). Hence *motus Ionicos* (Ionic movements) in *Horace*, Odes III. 5. 24. and *Plautus*, Stich. V. 7. 1., Quis *Ionicus* aut cinaedus qui hoc tale facere posset. (What *Ionian* or cinaedus is there could show himself capable of such an act as this).

ριοχάνη ὄνομα γυναικὸς (Meriochané—a woman's name). In the text of Hippocrates [1] is found *Μυριοχαύνη*, and the same form is given by the editions of Galen [2]. Inasmuch as *χάνω* and *χαύνω* both have the same meaning of gaping wide, that is with the mouth, it will practically make no difference which we choose as the end of the word; hence we have merely to consider the first part *μου-* or *μυριο-*, all the rest of the forms being obviously erroneous. If we read *μουχάνη*, we must suppose it compounded of *μύος* and *χάνη*; but inasmuch as *μύος* is merely a mistaken variant for *μῦσος*, the word must be read *μυσοχάνη*. *Μῦσος* in its turn we must derive either from *μύζω*, I suck,—so a woman who sucks with open mouth [3], or from *μυσιάω*, I snort through the nose, particularly in the act of coition, and consequently read *μυσιοχάνη*, i. e. a woman who with mouth open snorts through the nose, precisely what the fellatrix undoubtedly does when at her work. This emendation certainly makes better sense, and is all the more likely from the fact that *μυιοχάνη* and *μυριοχάνη* are also found as *variae lectiones*. Naumann would seem desirous of reading *μυσάχνη* (*μυζάχνη*), in which case it must be formed from *μύζω*, I suck, and *ἄχνη* (froth), in fact the secretion that adheres to the surface (of the *glans penis*) [4]. This last reading

[1] *Hippocrates*, Epidem. bk. II. sect. 1. edit. Kühn, Vol. III. p. 435.

[2] Comment. in Hippocrat. Epidem., bk. II. edit. Kühn, Vol. XVII. A. p. 312.

[3] *Martial*, bk. XII. 55., Nec clusis aditum neget labellis. (and refuse not access by shutting the lips).

[4] *Μύζουσις* is cited by *Eustathius* on Homer, Odyssey XVII. p. 1821. 52. and XIV. p. 1921. end, as also *ἀπομύζουρις* on Iliad XI. p. 867. 44., in the sense of *fellatrix*, *παρὰ τὸ μυζᾶν, ἤγουν θηλάζειν οὐράν*. (connected with *μυζᾶν*, to suck, that is to say to suck like an infant a man's member). *Suidas* says: *μυζεῖ καὶ μύζει, θηλάζει λείχει μῦ, μύζει· ἀπὸ τοῦ μῦ παρῆκται τὸ μῦζειν, πολλοῖς ἄλλοις ὁμοίως· μύζειν δέ ἐστι τὸ τοῖς μυκτῆρσιν ἦχον ἀποτελεῖν. Ἀριστοφάνης τί μύζεις,*—(*μυζει*

is all the more admissible, as according to Suidas [1] the word also occurs in Archilochus. Possibly however we must regard as aqually correct the form **μυριοχαύνη,** and take it in the meaning given by

and *μύζει*, — sucks like an infant, licks with a *mooing* noise, *moos*; from this *mooing* noise is derived *μύζειν*, as is the case with other similar words; now *μύζειν* is to produce the noise made in the nostrils in the act of sucking. Aristophanes has *τί μύζεις*; (what is the mooing noise you make?) On this passage of Aristophanes (Thesmoph. 238.) the Scholiast observes: *τοῦτο δὲ φώνημα σημαίνει ἔκλυσίν τινα ἀφροδισιαστικήν· ὅθεν καὶ μύται ἐλέγοντο το παλαιὸν ἀφροδισιασταὶ καὶ γυναικομανεῖς*. (Now this sound proclains a certain dissoluteness in lovemaking; whence of old voluptuaries and men mad after women were called also *μύται*). *Μῦς*, the mouse, also comes from the same stem, from its picking and gnawing; so does *μυῖα*, the fly, and as *Aelian*, Hist. Anim. bk. XV. ch. 1., says of a fish, *ὑποχανὼν κατέπιε τὴν μυῖαν* (it gaped its mouth and swallowed down the fly), we might perhaps read *μυιοχάνη* after flies, as if she wanted to catch flies, a fly-catcher, fly-trap, unless indeed we prefer to take *μυιοχάνη* as being a compound-word expressing a high degree of lecherousness. The lecherous nature of the fly is well-known, as well as their habit of licking, which makes *Varro*, de Re Rust. III. ch. 15., say: Non ut muscae *liguriunt*. (They do not *lick*, like flies). Ligurire (to lick) is used in the sense of *fellare* and *cunnilingere*. *Aelian*, Hist. Anim. bk. IV. ch. 5., mentions a fish, *χάνη*, which is particularly lustful: *χάνη δὲ ἰχθὺς λαγνίστατος* (Now the *χάνη* is a most lustful fish). Again *μυσαροχάνη* (*μυσαρὸς*, filthy) would be a significant word for a *fellatrix*.

[1] *Suidas*, s. v. *μυσάχνη, ἡ πόρνη παρὰ Ἀρχιλόχῳ· καὶ ἐργάτις καὶ δῆμος καὶ παχεῖα. Ἱππῶναξ δὲ βορβορόπιν καὶ ἀκάθαρτον ταύτην φησίν. ἀπὸ τοῦ βορβόρου καὶ ἀνασυρτόπολιν, ἀπὸ τοῦ ἀνασύρεσθαι. Ἀνακρέων δὲ πανδοσίαν καὶ λεωφόρον, καὶ μανιόκηπον· κῆπος γὰρ τὸ μόριον. Εὔπολις εἰλίποδα, ἐκ τῆς εἰλήσεως τῶν ποδῶν τῆς κατὰ τὴν μίξιν.* (under the word *μυσάχνη*; this means "the prostitute" in Archilochus; also in same sense *working-woman*, and *commonalty*, and *brawny wench*. Also Hipponax calls an unclean woman of the sort *filthy-eyed* (**βορβορύπις**) from *βόρβορος*, mire, and

the Gloss, viz. *in millibus hians!* (gaping in a thousand openings!), bearing in mind *Lampridius*'[1] expression about Heliogabalus: *Quis enim ferre posset principem per cuncta cava corporis libidinem recipientem!* (For

town-exposer (ἀνασυρτόπολις) from ἀνασύρεσθαι, to pull up the clothes. Also Anacreon uses *all-giving* and *public thoroughfare* and *mad in the privates* (μανιόκηπος); for κῆπος (a garden) means a woman's private parts. Eupolis uses *walking with a rolling gait*, from the rolling of the legs, the result of sexual intercourse).

[1] *Lampridius*, Life of Heliogabalus ch. 5. *Clement of Alexandria*, Paedag. bk. III. p. 254. edit. Potter, ἀβροδίαιτος περιεργία πάντα ζητεῖ, πάντα ἐπιχειρεῖ, βιάζεται πάντα· συνέχει τὴν φύσιν· τὰ γυναικῶν οἱ ἄνδρες πεπόνθασιν καὶ γυναῖκες ἀνδρίζονται παρὰ φύσιν· γαμούμεναί τε καὶ γαμοῦσαι γυναῖκες· πόρος δὲ οὐδεὶς ἄβατος ἀκολασίας. (delicately-living idleness searches out all things, attempts all things, forces all things. It constrains Nature. Men have come to endure the treatment proper to women, while women act as men contrary to nature; women are both given in marriage and themselves take men in marriage, and *no way of impurity is left untrod*). Again of a similar significance are perhaps the words μυριοστόμος (ten-thousand-mouthed) and ἀθυροστόμος, ἀθυροστομία, ἀθυροστομέω (unrestrained of mouth, unrestrainedness of mouth, to be unrestrained of mouth), and εὐρόστομος (wide-mouthed). *Epicrates* said of a lecherous girl, ἠδ' ἀρ' ἦν μυωνία (she was a regular mouse-hole, and *Philemon* called another μῦς λεύκος (white mouse), while *Aelian*, Hist. Anim. Bk. XII. ch. 10, gives yet another similar expression, μυωνίαν ὅλην ὀνομάσας (having named her a complete mouse-hole); she is a perfect mouse-hole, in other words she has as many entrances as a mouse-hole. Instead of μυριοχαύνη we might also read μυριομήχανος (of ten-thousand devices), referring to the *fessus mille modis* (fatigued by a thousand modes of pleasure) in *Martial*, bk. IX. 58. and on the analogy of Δωδεκαμήχανος (of a dozen devices), a name borne by the "fille de joie" Cyrené, because she had contrived twelve different *postures of Love*. Comp. *Suidas*, under word δωδεκαμήχανος, and the Scholiast on Aristophanes, "Frogs" 1356. Also μιαροχάνη (μιαρὸς, polluted) might be defended, on reference to *Aristophanes*, Acharnians 271—285.

who could endure a Prince *that welcomed lustful pleasure by every opening of the body!*)

The readings also vary as to **σαράπους** (turning out the feet); *Franz* gives **ἀγράπους** and **ἀράπους;** in the text of Hippocrates [1] on the other hand, as well in the Commentary of Galen it appears as **ἡ Σεραπὶς,** the latter also giving it in the genitive—**τῆς Σεράπιδος.** But inasmuch as the name of the goddess occurs sometimes as **Σέραπις,** sometimes as **Σάραπις,** and as the genitive ending—**πιδος** easily admits of change into—**πόδος,** it may very likely be that after all **Σαράπους** stood originally in Hippocrates' text. The author of the Gloss (loco citato p. 136.) explains the word by **ἡ διασεσηρότας καὶ διεστῶτας ἔχουσα τοὺς δακτύλους τῶν ποδῶν** that is, a woman who has the toes drawn apart and separated. But how are we to bring this explanation into agreement with the **κατὰ τὸν αὐτὸν τρόπον,** (after the same fashion), that is to say, with one of the modes of Love that are under discussion? Think of the *fellator* or *fellatrix*, we are told, cowering down (**ἐν γόνασι,**—on the knees) according to *Lucian's* picture (p. 229 above), and you will see the stress of the body's weight must always fall on the front part of the foot, and to widen the point of support he is instinctively compelled to spread the toes. Well! but who can fail to see how very forced such an explanation is? still we do not in the least know how we are to deal with it further. Of course we might leave the author of the Gloss his interpretation and proceed to look about for another of our own, though we have in many cases to confess the fact that our investigations undertaken with this end in view have not exactly led to any definite results. With the reading **Σεραπὶς** we really do not know how to deal. Perhaps the common representation, or else some particular quality, of the

[1] *Hippocrates,* Epidem. bk. II. Vol. III. p. 436. Galen, vol. XVII. A. p. 322.

goddess so named gave occasion for a comparison which we now fail to understand, one that might possibly suggest an explanation of the *Harpocratem reddere* (to recall Harpocrates) of Catullus (69.) implying *irrumare* [1]. Whether the reader will take

[1] Perhaps the word was σαπερδίς, which in *Aristotle*, Hist. Anim. VIII. 30., signifies a certain fish, for in *Athenaeus*, Deipnos. p. 591., σαπέρδιον (the diminutive) is the nick-name of a *hetaera*, and when *Diogenes* (Diogenes Laertius, VI. 2. 6.) made a scholar wear a σαπέρδης, the latter threw it away (ὑπ' αἰδοῦς ῥίψας), (having cast it from him in disgust). Note at the same time that the word *Sarapis* also occurs in *Plautus* (Paenulus V. 5. 30 sqq.), where Anthemonides says:

Ligula, i in malam crucem
Tune hic amator audes esse, hallex viri?
Aut contrectare, quod mares homines amant?
Deglupta maena, Sarapis sementium,
Mastruga, ἅλς ἀγορᾶς ἅμα; tum autem plenior.
Allii ulpicique. quam Romani remiges.

(Thou mannikin, go to and be crucified! Dost dare to play the lover here. thou Tom Thumb of a man? or to meddle with what male men love? Skinned sprat, *Sarapis* of the corn-crops, sheepskin, common salt of the market; and yet reeking worse of garlic and leek than Roman bargees!). To restore this undoubtedly corrupt text is beyond our powers, but this much at any rate results from the passage as a whole that *Sarapis* or *Sarrapis* here too signifies a vicious man. Anthemonides certainly takes Hanno, to whom this speech is addressed, for a *cinaedus*, for he says later on: "nam te cinaedum esse arbitror magis quam virum" (but I reckon you to be a cinaedus rather than a man), and he had previously said: "Quis hic homo est *cum tunicis longis*, quasi puer cauponius?" (Who is this fellow *with the long tunics*, like a waiter at a cookshop?) and "Sane genus hoc muliebrosum est tunicis demissitiis." (Surely this is a womanish sort, *with his trailing tunics*). Similarly *Turnebus*, Adversar. bk. X. ch. 24., mentions the fact that *Hesychius* explains σάραπις by περσικὸς χιτὼν (a Persian tunic). However he prefers to read, instead of *Sarrapis*, *arra pisa ementium*, (pledge of such as buy at the price of one pea) in reference to the vice of Bacchus, "obscoenum et mollem virum, qui pro arra dari possit vilis mercimonii." (a foul and deboshed man, fit only to be given as pledge at the value of any cheap commodity).

within his purview the ***Σεραφίμ, ἐμπρηστάς· ἔμπυρα στόματα· ἢ θερμαίνοντας*** (Seraphim: kindlers; fiery mouths: or, making hot) of *Suidas*' Lexicon, we must leave to him; in that case *Martial's* (II. 28.) *calda Vetustinae nec tibi bucca placet* (nor does Vetustina's hot mouth please you) might afford an analogy. Proceeding to consider ***σαράπους,*** we find *Hesychius* has ***σαραπίους,*** which he explains by ***μαινίδας*** (mad-women), and *Dioscorides* is at one with him in regarding the vice as something done ***μανικῶς*** (madly). In *Diogenes Laertius* (I. 4.) we read Pittacus was called: ***σαράποδα καὶ σάραπον διὰ τὸ πλατύπουν εἶναι καὶ ἐπισύρειν τὼ πόδε.*** (*turning out the feet*, because of his being flat-footed and trailing his two feet). It would be hardly credible to suppose that the author of the Gloss borrowed his explanation cited just above from Diogenes Laertius or Suidas, in whom the passage occurs as well. Further, the MSS. of Diogenes give also ***συράπους,*** a word found several times in the sense of "to stand with legs apart," and Naumann too must have understood this in our passage, for he gives as his rendering *crura ambulando divaricans* (straddling the legs in walking). Now leaving altogether out of the question the fact that the feminine form is found in Hippocrates, and assuming the word to be used of men, it might perfectly well signify the *irrumator*, who takes the *fellator* between his opened thighs [1], a posture that was generally

[1] Comp. the passage of Lucian quoted on p. 229 above. *Suetonius*, Tiberius ch. 44., "Majore adhuc et turpiore infamia flagravit, vox ut referri audirive, nedum credi, fas sit. Quasi pueros primae teneritudinis, quos pisciculos vocabat, institueret, ut natanti sibi *inter femina versarentur* ac luderent, lingua et morsu sensim appetentes, atque etiam quasi infantes firmiores, necdum tamen lacte depulsos, inguini seu papillae admoveret; pronior sane ad id genus libidinis et natura et aetate. Quare Parrhasii quoque tabulam, in qua Meleagro Atalanta ore morigeratur, legatam sibi sub conditione, ut si argumento offenderetur,

decies pro ea sestertium acciperet, non modo praetulit, sed et in cubiculo dedicavit." (He was guilty of a yet more flagrant and abominable villainy, so much so it hardly admits of being related or listened to, let alone believed, to this effect. He arranged that boys of tender years, whom he called his little fishes, should move about between his thighs, as he swam, and play there making darts at him with tongue and mouth and biting him softly; also infants of somewhat stronger growth, but still not yet weaned, he would put to his member as if to their mothers' teat, being indeed both by natural disposition and time of life more apt to this form of indulgence. So when a picture of Parrhasius, in which Atalanta is represented *gratifying* Meleager with her mouth, was willed to him with the stipulation that, if he objected to the subject, he should have a million serterces instead, not only did he choose the painting, but actually enshrined it in his bed-chamber). *Theophrastus*, Charact. ch. 11., ὁ δὲ βδελυρὸς τοιοῦτος, οἷος ὑπαντήσας γυναιξὶν ἐλευθέραις ἀ ν α σ υ ρ ά μ ε ν ο ς δεῖξαι τὸ αιδοῖον. (But he was such a filthy wretch, that on meeting free women he would *pull up his clothes* and show his private parts. — *Dionysius of Halicarnassus*, Excerpt. de Legat. ch. 9. says of the Tarentine Philonis, ἀ ν α σ υ ρ ά μ ε ν ο ς τὴν ἀναβολὴν καὶ σχηματίσας ἑαυτὸν ὡς αἴσχιστον ὀφθῆναι, τὴν οὐ λέγεσθαι πρέπουσαν ἀκαθαρσίαν κατὰ τῆς ἱερᾶς ἐσθῆτος τοῦ πρεσβευτοῦ κατεσκέδασε. (*raising his mantle* and throwing himself into the most disgusting posture to be exposed in, he bespattered the Ambassador's sacred robe with the unspeakable filth).—*Galen*, Exhortat. ad artes ch. 6., ἀνασυράμενοι προσουροῦσι. (lifting up their clothes, they make water over it).—*Lucian*, Cataplus 13., καὶ σὺ δὲ ὦ Ἑρμῆ; σύρετ' αὐτὸν εἴσω τοῦ ποδός. (You too, Hermes? drag ye him within your leg). *Clement of Alexandria*, Protrept. p. 13, mentions an Ἀφροδίτη περιβασίη Aphrodité protectress,—or otherwise, Aphrodité that stretches the legs apart), known also to *Hesychius*, and explained by some Commentators as "stretching the legs apart". In *Suidas* σαίρειν is explained by *hiare* (to gape open); and the Lexicographers give σάραβος as meaning γυναικεῖον αἰδοῖον (a woman's privates) and the word is found in *Dio Chrysostom*, De regno IV. 75., as the name of a Tavern-keeper,—also if we are not mistaken, in Plato. σάρων too *Hesychius* explains by γυναικεῖον (woman's parts). He also has ἀρρενώπες (masculine-looking), which

regarded as obscene [1]. Indeed if we think of the *fellator* as sitting on the ground at his work, the word of course can be equally well used of a woman, or *fellatrix*.

As to **γρυπαλώπηξ** we read in *Hippocrates* (loco citato p. 629.) as follows: "Satyrus in Thasos bore the nick-name of **γρυπαλώπηξ;** when about twenty five he suffered from frequent nightly pollutions, and yet by day the same happened him even more constantly. When he was thirty years of age, he got consumption and died." From this we see at once the question is of a dissolute man, who in consequence of his vicious practises had brought on such a weakness of the genitals, that he suffered from continual evacuation of seed, the result being that eventually Phthisis was set up, to which he succumbed. As variations of reading we find noted in *Franz's* Gloss **ῥυπαλώπηξ** and **τρυπαλάπηξ;** Schneider in his Lexicon renders **γρυπαλώπηξ** by "griffin-fox", so he must evidently have derived it from **γρύψ** (a griffin) and **ἀλώπηξ** (a fox). The Ancients depict the fox as a cunning, crafty animal and assign several characteristics as marking his behaviour that must probably be taken into consideration in the present connection,—and particularly the way he seizes and kills the hedge-hog. According to *Aelian* [2] he endeavours to throw the creature on

some interpret by Androgyne (man-woman) or *fellator*. The reading ἀγράπους occurring, we might also read γυρόπους (crook-footed); *Suidas* under word γραῦς (old woman) cites: ἡ γρῆϋς, ἡ χερνῆτις, ἡ γυρὴ πόδας. (the old woman, the spinster, the *crooked of feet*).

[1] *Catullus*, Carm. 35. 64.,

An continentes quod sedetis insulsi
Centum, aut ducenti, non putatis ausurum
Me una ducentos *irrumare sessores?*

(Think you, because you sit there side by side, a hundred fools, or two hundred, think you I shan't dare to *irrumate* two hundred *sitters* at once?).

[2] *Aelian*, Hist. Anim. bk. VI. ch. 24., ἡ δὲ ἡσύχως καὶ πεφεισμένως τοῦ ἑαυτῆς στόματος ἀνατρέπει αὐτούς. (but the fox, quietly and so as to forbear biting with its mouth, turns them over). ch. 64., ἤδε χανεῖν τε καὶ ἐνδακεῖν οὐ δυναμένη, κᾆτα οὔρησεν αὐτοῦ ἐς τὸ στόμα.

ita back, so that its mouth comes uppermost, and then discharges its urine into it. Now in order to signify the *irrumator*, the Ancients really could hardly have invented a better expression, when they, firmly convinced of course of the fact as stated, compared him to a fox. But what is a **γρυπαλώπηξ**? *Hesychius* under the word **γρυπός** (hooked, curved) explains it as **τὰ ἔξω τοῦ στόματος καμπυλόῤῥις· ὁ ἐπικαμπῆ τὴν ῥῖνα ἔχων.** (hook-nosed outside the mouth; a man having his nose bent down). *Suidas* again says **γρυπός, ὁ καμπυλόῤῥιν** (**γρυπός**,—a hook-nosed man); so a man with a nose bent down crooked over the mouth. Now this we might very well understand as applying to the *fellator*, inasmuch as his nose, when the *irrumator* presses down hard on him, as the sailor does to *Timarchus* (p. 230 above), is of necessity compressed and bent down towards the mouth; **γρυπαλώπηξ** would according to this be a man who, like Timarchus in *Lucian*, is at once an *irrumator* and a *fellator*. Of yet another word, **κυναλώπηξ** (fox-dog) cited by Naumann, we propose to speak under the head of the *Cunnilingue*, who as we shall see might likewise be signified by the expression.

Finally, as to **ῥινοκολοῦρος** (nose-docked), for which the MSS. also have **ῥινοκλοῦρος**, it is certainly the case that in Antiquity the man who practised vice with strange women (*Moechus*,—adulterer) had his nose cut off [1], and as *Moechus*

(but she—the fox—being unable to open her mouth and fix her teeth in, finally made water into its mouth).

[1] Virgil, Aen. VI. 494., says of Deiphobus, Helen's paramour:

Atque hic Priamiden laniatum corpore toto
Deiphobum vidit, lacerum crudeliter ora,
Ora manusque ambas, populataque tempora raptis
Auribus, et truncas inhonesto vulnere naris.

(And now Deiphobus he sees, the glorious Priam's son;

But all his body mangled sore, his face all evilly hacked,
His face and hands; yea, and his head laid waste, the ear lobes lacked,
And *nostrils cropped unto the root by wicked wound and grim.*
WILLIAM MORRIS's translation).

equally signifies the *fellator* [1], the latter also may very well have been obliged to forfeit his nose. Following this hint, it would be quite legitimate to suppose the punishment to have been put for the vice, and a *fellator* called **ῥινοκολοῦρος** (nose-docked) on this ground; in the same way as the loss of the nose might be looked upon as a consequence of vice, and anyone seeing a man in this case would at once think of his dissolute past life, as indeed frequently happens at the present day amongst ourselves.

The town of Rhinocolurus,—and its history is more than problematical,—would seem to have nothing whatever to do with the question. The passages from *Pliny* and *Livy* which Naumann quotes give absolutely nothing beyond the name; and the mere

Martial, bk. III. Epigr. 85.,

Quis tibi persuasit nares abscindere moecho?
Non hac peccatum est parte, marite, tibi
Stulte, quid egisti? nihil hic tua perdidit uxor,
Cum sit salva sui mentula Deiphobi.

(Who persuaded you to crop the adulterer's nostrils? 'Twas not with this part the offence was done you, sir husband! Foolish man, what have you done? in this your wife has lost naught, so long as her Deiphobus' member is safe and sound). *Martial*, bk. II. Epigr. 83.,

Foedasti miserum, marite, moechum:
Et se, qui fuerant prius, requirunt
Trunci naribus auribusque vultus.
Credis te satis esse vindicatum?
Erras! Iste potest et irrumare!

(You have mutilated, husband, the unhappy adulterer: and his face cropped of nose and ears asks itself what it was like before. Think you your revenge is complete? Nay! you are mistaken; the fellow can still *irrumate!*)—a passage that might very well be made to prove our point.

[1] *Martial*, bk. XI. Epigr. 61.,

Lingua maritus, *moechus ore* Maneius.

(Maneius is a husband with his tongue, a debaucher with his mouth). Bk. III. Epigr. 84.,

Quid narrat tua *moecha?* non puellam
Dixi, Tongilion. Quid ergo? *Linguam!*

(What tale is it your harlot tells? Nay! I did not say *girl*, Tongilion. What then? Why, *tongue!*).

existence of the name *Diodorus*[1] certifies, in his story of how Actisanes proceeded against the Robbers in a way of his own: "He did not wish to put the guilty to death, nor yet to leave them unpunished. So he had the accused brought up out of the whole country and inquired into each case most scrupulously; such as were found to be guilty all had their noses cut off by his orders, and were banished to the most remote spot in the Desert. The town he founded for them there received in remembrance of the punishment inflicted on its inhabitants the name of Rhinocolura. It lies on the borders of Egypt and Syria, not far from the sea-shore that borders the desert in that region, and displays an almost complete absence of all requisites for comfortable habitation. For the surrounding district possesses a soil thoroughly saturated with salt, while inside the town very little water is to be found and that positively tainted and of quite a bitter taste." Diodorus relates further that these Colonists lived by catching quails; but of *Leprosy* there is no mention either here or in Strabo or Seneca, so that Naumann's statement to the effect that it served as a dwelling-place for Lepers lacks entirely, up to the present and at any rate so far as we know, any historical foundation, though the character of the place is not against such a hypothesis. Nor is any question raised in any author as to the vicious life of the inhabitants of Rhinocolura,—in fact in later times it was actually famous for the number of its *men of piety*[2].

[1] *Diodorus*, Bk. I. ch. 60. Same is related in *Strabo*, Geogr. bk. XVI. p. 759.—*Seneca*, De Ira bk. III. ch. 20.

[2] *Sozomen*, Hist. Eccles. bk. VI. ch. 30., Rhinocolura vero illo tempore viris piis non aliunde advocatis, sed indigenis floruit, quorum optimos sapientiae sese studio hic dedisse intellexi. Novi Melanam, tunc ecclesiae episcopum et Dionysium, monasterium ad septentrionem urbis moderantem, ac Solonem, Melanis fratrem ac successorem in episcopatu. (But Rhinocolura at that time

Though the explanation of **ῥινοκολοῦρος** given just now might very well at a pinch be regarded as satisfactory, still we think it hardly answers sufficiently well to the **κατὰ τὸν αὐτὸν τρόπον** (after the same fashion), while the variant **ῥινοκλοῦρος** seems to point to **ῥιναύλουρος** or **ῥιναύλουρις** as the true reading. In *Tatian* (Orat. ad Graecos p. 83.) in fact we read: **ῥιναυλοῦσι τὰ αἰσχρά, κινοῦνται δὲ κινήσεις ἃς οὐκ ἐχρῆν, καὶ τοὺς ὅπως δεῖ μοιχεύειν ἐπὶ τῆς σκηνῆς σοφιστεύοντας αἱ θυγατέρες ὑμῶν καὶ οἱ παῖδες θεωροῦσι.** (They flute their obscenities through the nose, and make movements that in decency they should not make, while actors who teach on the stage the whole art of how to debauch a woman are the spectacle your daughters and your boys gaze at.) The Scholiast observes on this **ῥινοκτυποῦσιν, οἱονεὶ τὸ πνεῦμα τοῖς ῥώθωσι, συνέλκοντες ποιὸν ἦχον ἐπὶ καταγέλωτι ἀποτελοῦσι,** (they make a noise with the nose, a sort of breathing with the nostrils; by drawing in these they produce a certain sound by way of mockery), and in *Lucian*, Lexiphanes ch. 19., we find **ἔοικα δὲ καὶ ῥιναυστήσειν,** (and I am like to go nose-playing), of which the Scholiast gives the following explanation: **ἀντὶ τοῦ ταῖς ῥισὶ καταυλῆσαι, ἐποίουν γὰρ τοῦτο ῥιναυλοῦντες, ἤτοι διὰ τῶν ῥινῶν ψοφοῦντες ἐπὶ διασυρμῷ τινῶν καὶ χλεύῃ.** (put instead of *fluting with the nostrils*; for they used to do this when they nose-fluted, or in other words,

abounded in *men of piety*, not invited thither, but *natives*, the most eminent of whom I have been informed devoted themselves in that place to the study of Wisdom. I knew personally Melanas, then Bishop of the church there, and Dionysius, governing a monastery lying to the South of the City, and Solon, brother of Melanas and his successor in the Bishopric.). The same is affirmed by *Nicephorus* as well, (Hist. Eccles. bk. XI. ch. 38. Within the last two years there has appeared a Tract or Occasional Paper, dealing with the Colony at Rhinocolura, but unfortunately we cannot put our hand on the more precise memorandum of its contents.

made a noise with the nostrils by way of mocking people and joking). Now if we take **ῥιναυλεῖν** (to nose-flute) in these passages,—and all this confirms what has been previously said (above p. 144.) on the word **ῥέγχειν** (to snort) in the Speech of Dio Chrysostom,—for *fistulam canere per nares, to play the flute with the nose*, and at the same time remember that *Eustathius* (as was noted above, p. 236. Note 2.) derived **ἀπομύξουρις** and **μύζουρις** from **μυζᾶν-οὐράν** (**οὐρά**,—the tail, the penis), the Greeks would seem to have said **ῥιναυλεῖν-οὐράν**, *penem pro fistula canere*, (to play on the penis instead of a flute), and we should have the adjective or substantive **ῥιναύλουρις**, *qui penem pro fistula canit per nares*, one who plays on the penis instead of a flute with the nostrils), which admirably expresses not only the action of the *fellator*, but also the music he makes to accompany it, as he is compelled to snort, drawing his breath heavily through the nose.

Which explanation the reader will choose, we must really leave to him, for interpretations of words of this sort can never be brought to the absolute test of evidence, inasmuch as nick-names as a rule take their origin only too often in external circumstances. Still this much we think we may pronounce with certainty, that the words of the Gloss have to do simply *de rebus venereis*, with matters of love, and not with Venereal complaints, and thus Naumann's propositions [1] at least are devoid of foundation. Perhaps it may be possible by means of a comparison of the licentious representations on old Vases, of which the late *Hofrath* Böttiger would seem to have possessed a choice collection, and some examples of which are preserved also at Berlin, in connection with one or other of the words given in the Gloss, as generally with the embodiments in Art of the *Venus ebria* (drunken Venus), to afford a

[1] As to his views on the *Morbus Phoeniceus* (Phoenician Disease), this will be discussed under the head of the vice of the *Cunnilingue*.

better explanation, one that may indeed be of no particular value to the student of Antiquity pure and simple, but nevertheless is indispensable to the Physician for the correct understanding of sundry diseases of the Ancients, or at any rate one sufficient to avoid incorrect assertions and false conclusions, and to refute such.

We are not in a position to give a systematic history of the spread of the vice of the *fellator* and *irrumator*; but at any rate this much is certain that in Imperial times the Vice was most widely indulged in, as the Epigrams of *Martial*, and what *Suetonius* relates in his Life of Tiberius (chs. 44, 45.) sufficiently bear witness.

Diseases of the Fellator.

§ 22.

Now to pass on to the medical point of view, no one presumably will deny that the mouth of the *fellator* must necessarily be exposed to various complaints as a consequence of his Vice. Nevertheless there prevails universally, so far as our studies up to the present have enabled us to judge, complete silence among the Physicians of Antiquity as to the practice of **λεσβιάζειν** (to Lesbianize, to practise *fellation*) as a cause occasioning morbid affections of the mouth and the contiguous parts. This is the more surprising, as we find that non-professional Writers are not entirely unacquainted with such effects, as we shall show directly. For our purpose this silence is doubly unfortunate, depriving us as it does of all means of submitting such affections of the mouth as are described by Physicians to any proper appreciation in regard to their ætiological relationships,— an appreciation that in any case must naturally have been in view of our knowledge of the vice of the *fellator* one of extreme difficulty. The difficulty is this: *fellator* and *fellatrix*, equally with the *Cunnilingue*, the fornicater and fornicatrix, were liable to suffer from ulcers of the throat, for example, as a result of their peculiar vice, but in the former case these ulcers were primary, in the latter secondary,—now how is an inquirer to discover any diagnostic sign here, whereby to distinguish the one class from the other? Yet all the while, certainty on this point is of the very highest importance in view of the question as to the existence of Venereal disease in Antiquity, the chief argument always alleged against accepting the fact of such existence being the absence of secondary symptoms such as are nowadays commonly met with, especially about the throat [1].

It is remarkable that not one, so far as we know, of the authors who have studied the history of Venereal Disease makes any mention of this circumstance; neither do the Pathologists ever bring forward the vice of the *fellator* as an ætiological factor. *Clossius* [2] it is true speaks of *Irrumatio*, relying on *Perenotti di Cigliano* and *Fabre*; but these last are really speaking of the *Cunnilingue*, not of the *fellator*. Probably they are of Erasmus' opinion: *λειχαζειν ni fallor tale quiddam est Graecis, quale fellare Latinis. Nam vox etiamnum manet, tametsi rem iam olim e medio sublatam arbitor.* (λειχάζειν—to practise licking,—if I am not mistaken, is a similar practice with the Greeks to that of *fellation* with the Romans. The word indeed still remains, but the thing I believe to have long since entirely disappeared). On this however *Forberg* (loco citato p. 304.) very justly adds: *Vereor ut vere: certe audio, ne ab nunc hominum quidem moribus plane abhorrere id schematis, quid viderint ii, quibus magnas urbes adire licet.* (I fear this is not true: at any rate I am told

[1] *Bonorden*, "Die Syphilis" (Syphilis). Berlin 1834., p. 19.

[2] *Clossius*, "Ueber die Lustseuche" (On Venereal Disease). Tübingen 1797., p. 49. — *Perenotti di Cigliano*, Of Venereal Disease, p. 92. *Fabre*, Treatise on Venereal Disease, p. 5.

this sort of practice is not entirely repugnant to the habits of some men even of our own day, to judge by what those see who have the opportunity of visiting large cities). How many primary ulcers of the throat, especially in the case of common Prostitutes, may have been mistaken for secondary ones, and have been treated accordingly, in fact are treated so still, without the Physician having a suspicion of how they were actually incurred! But what the Physicians of our own times are ignorant of, though familiar enough to many of the Laity, this knowledge we cannot reasonably demand from the Physicians of Antiquity. Yet supposing they did actually possess this knowledge, it was very excusable if they looked at what lay nearest before their eyes and regarded all throat ulcers as being primary,—in just the same way as any Practitioner of to-day finds it excusable in a Colleague that he thinks only of secondary ulcers, inasmuch as what in Ancient times happened very commonly is practised at the present day at any rate much less frequently. Consequently the absence of mention on the part of the old Physicians of secondary ulcers of the throat in connection with complaints of the genital organs cannot be considered as any sort of proof of their non-existence.

Among the maladies to which the *fellator* was exposed, we have in the first place to reckon the *foul smell from the mouth* [1], which is mentioned as

[1] *Martial*, XI. Epigr. 30.,

Os male causidicis et dicis olere poetis:
Sed fellatori, Zoile, peius olet.

(The mouth you say smells ill with pleaders and poets; but Zoilus, it smells worse with the *fellator*). Hence the expressions, os male olens, anima foetida, gravis, graveolens, graveolentia oris spiritus ieiunio macer, ieiuna anima, hircosum osculum, basia olidissima. (evil-smelling mouth, fetid breath, foul, ill-smelling, fetid smell of the breath from the mouth—hungry and lean, fasting breath, goaty kiss, most smelly embraces). Possibly too this was the origin of the Lemnian women's punishment. Comp. above p. 148.

especially prevalent among the Romans. The Physicians as a rule derived it, if no local symptoms, of ulcers, etc., were apparent, from some fault of the stomach [1],—an instance surely where the Laity were cleverer than the Profession! The sympathy between the mouth and the genitals and anus makes it evident why at the present day we notice, particularly in immoral women, an evil smell from the mouth, which they endeavour to conceal by chewing burned coffee and the like. No doubt this was the case in Antiquity [2] as well, so we are by no means justified in attributing every instance of foul breath in harlots and *cinaedi* to the practice of *fellation*.

Yet another consequence of *fellation* was *pain in the mouth* (**στομαλγία,** mouth-ache; only we must remember as to this that *Pollux*, Onomast. III. 7. 69., cites **ἀλγεῖν,**—to suffer pain, as a synonym of *to love*), *tongue-ache* (*γλωσσαλγία* [3]) and *tooth-ache* [4], and generally pains of the palate and

[1] *Galen*, Comment. on Hippocrates' De Humor. bk. II., edit. Kühn, Vol. XVI. p. 215. Different means of counteracting this evil are given by *Galen*, De parabilib. bk. II. ch. 7., Vol. XIV. p. 424. of Kühn's ed., where amongst other matter we read: *διαμασῶνται δέ τινες καὶ τῆς πίτυος φύλλα, ὅταν ἐκπορεύωνται, καὶ ὕδατι διακλύζονται*, (but others chew up even leaves of the pine, when they go abroad, and *wash out the mouth with water*), the Latin *lavare, aquam sumere* (to wash, to take water)?—as to which later.

[2] *Martial*, VI. 55.,

Quod semper cassiaque cinnamoque
Et nido niger alitis superbae
Fragras plumbea Nicerotiana,
Rides nos, Coracine, nil olentes,
Malo, quam bene olere, nil olere.

(Because forever scented with cassia and cinnamon and smeared with spices from the nest of the proud phoenix, you are fragrant of the leaden caskets of Niceros, you laugh at us that are unscented; I had rather even than smell sweet, not smell at all).

[3] So *Euripides*, Medea 525., joins together *στόμαργον γλωσσαλγίαν* (busy-mouthed tongue-tiresomeness, i.e. wearisome talkativeness).

[4] Perhaps there is an allusion to this in *Martial*, bk. XI.

throat, rendering voice and speech indistinct. Hence *Martial* says [1]:

> Qui recitat lana fauces et colla revinctus,
> Hic se posse loqui, posse t a c e r e negat.

(The man who reads aloud his works, his throat and neck bound about with wool, declares he cannot speak, yet cannot hold his tongue).

But the evil by no means stopped here; there more often occurred as the result of the habit of *fellation* acute no less than chronic inflammations of the palate (sore throats, quinseys). In the passage quoted a little above from *Lucian's* Pseudologistae, it is said of Timarchus: "In Egypt on the other hand they called you **συνάγχη** (sore throat),—as everybody knows." In explanation *Lucian* adds: "It must have been a close thing with you not to be choked, that time you came across the sailor of a three-master, who fell upon you and stopped your mouth for you." Without in any way detracting from the importance of what we are told here, it still appears to us, on full consideration, that Timarchus

[1] *Martial*, Bk. VI. Epigr. 41. Also bk. IV. Epigr. 41.,

> Quid recitaturus circumdas vellera collo?
> Conveniunt nostris auribus illa magis.

(Why do you when going to read your verses aloud wind woollen wraps round your throat? The wool were better in our ears). The *tacere* (to hold his tongue) in the first Epigram stands for *fellare*, as in *Martial*, VII. IX. 5. 96. Perhaps too the verse of Epicharmus given in *Aulus Gellius*, Noct. Attic. I. ch. 15. is applicable in this connection, *οὐ λέγειν δύνατος, ἀλλὰ σιγᾷν ἀδύνατος*. (Not able to speak, yet unable to be silent). Comp. *Martial*, VI. 54. VII. 48. XII. 35. — "*Harpocratem* reddere (to recall *Harpocrates*" in *Catullus* 74. 4. Again *Minutius Felix*, In Octav., says: "Esse malae linguae, etiamsi *tacerent*" (To be of a *foul* tongue, *even if they kept silence*). *Priapeia*, 27. 4., "altiora tangam" (I will touch higher things). In part we may have to look for the same allusion also in *Ausonius'* Epigrams 46, 47 and 51, and several other very similar ones in the Anthology.

was not merely a *fellator*, but an *irrumator* as well, and this is the more probable as he no doubt acquired this nickname, because he, *bene vasatus* (well provided with a big *member*), frequently brought on sore throat, that is to say in those who served him as *fellators*!

Moreover this reveals to us the real meaning of a passage of *Aretaeus*, one that has often been quoted before as connected with Venereal disease. This occurs in the 9th Chapter of the Book [1], which would certainly seem to admit only of a direct application; still we are convinced that much of the pathological description of sore throat (Ch. 7.) and many symptoms of the complaints of the uvula (Ch. 8.) owe their origin to *fellation*. Undoubtedly we have nowadays much fewer occasions to note affections of the uvula, which were of very common occurrence among the Ancients [2], as is shown by their own accounts,—a circumstance hardly to be wondered at if we consider the particulars told us about Timarchus. *Aretaeus* in Ch. 9. makes a distinction between **κίων** (pillar, uvula) or columella (little pillar, uvula), when the whole uvula is inflamed and swollen, **σταφυλὴ** or uva (bunch of grapes), when only the lower part is affected, and **ἱμάντιον** (little strap), when the palatal membrane is attacked. "**Κίων**", he goes on, "occurs most frequently with old men, **σταφυλὴ** with young men and such as are in the prime of life, affection of the palatal membranes (**τὰ ὑμενώδεα**) in those who are at the age of puberty and in boys." The ninth Chapter runs as follows:

[1] *Aretaeus*, De causis et signis acutorum morborum, (Of the causes and symptoms of Acute Diseases). Comp. De Curatione acut. morb., (Of the treatment of Acute Diseases), Bk. I. ch. 9.

[2] *Martial*, bk. X. Epigr. 56.,

Non secat et tollit stillantem Fannius uvam.

(Fannius does not use the knife, yet removes the dripping uvula).

Of Ulcers of the Throat.

Ulcers arising in the throat of a benignant and harmless nature are common, the malignant and dangerous rare. Benignant ulcers of the sort are clean, of slight extent and superficial, neither inflamed nor painful. The malignant on the contrary are broad, hollow, lardaceous, with a white, livid, or black covering. These ulcers are known as *aphthae*. But if the covering is very tough. then the malady is an eschar, and is so called. At the edge of the eschar are set up an intense redness, inflammation and a congested state of the veins, as in *anthrax* (carbuncle, malignant pustule), while small, distinct and unconnected, elevations of the mucous membrane appear, which are continually uni'ing with fresh ones that successively follow, and so an extensivė ulcer is established. If this extends from the outer mouth too far inwards, in fact once it has attacked the uvula and relaxed it, the disease spreads over the tongue, gums and lips, while the teeth become loose and blackened. Further the inflammation attacks the throat. Patients so affected die in a few days after the inflammation and fever are set up, of the evil odour and of hunger; the ulcer propagates itself by way of the wind-pipe to the chest, so that very likely suffocation supervenes the same day. For lungs and heart can tolerate neither so foul an odour nor the ulcers themselves nor the ichor (puriform, septic matter) coming from them, but cough and difficulty of breathing supervene. Origin of this affection of the throat is the swallowing of cold, pungent, hot, sour, or strongly astringent, substances. Now these parts serve the chest on behalf of the voice and the breathing, as also the abdomen for sifting the nutriment, and the stomach for swallowing food. But when these inward parts, viz. abdomen, stomach and chest, are attacked by a disease, the disease is in turn conveyed and carried to the œsophagus, the tonsils and neighbouring regions.

Children up to the age of puberty suffer most in this way, for children have the very greatest and most marked desire for coolness, because with them the natural heat is at its greatest; the longing for foods of various sorts and cold beverages is boundless; while they shout loudly both in quarrel and at play. This is equally true of girls up to the commencement of menstruation.

With regard to locality, *Egypt* gives most numerous examples of the disease, for this country has at once a dry air to breathe, and many sorts of comestibles,—roots, herbs, garden vegetables, pungent seeds; while the drink is either thick, being Nile water, or artificially made pungent with barley or with grape-skins. In *Syria* the disease is also found, especially in Coelesyria. For this reason the ulcers in question are known as *Egyptian* or *Syrian* ulcers.

The mode and fashion in which death occurs in these cases is deplorable. The pain is a cutting and burning pain, as in anthrax (carbuncle, malignant pustule), the breath foul-smelling, the patient exhaling an intensely offensive breath, and re-inhaling into the chest another no less so. Patients are so loathsome to themselves they cannot tolerate their own smell; the face is pale or livid, the temperature excessively high, the thirst as distressing as in fever. Yet they reject drink when offered from dread of the pain of swallowing; for they undergo great agony both by the compression of the palate and by the return of the liquid through the nose. No sooner have they lain down than they spring up again; then finding they cannot bear an upright posture, no sooner have they sat down than they are forced by their agony to lie back once more. Most commonly they move about in an upright attitude. For as they are unable to sleep, they avoid all rest, as though they were fain to drive away one torture with another. Inhalation is deep, for they long for fresh air to cool themselves; exhalation on the contrary short and hurried, for the ulcers already burning like fire are heated yet further by contact of the feverish breath as it streams out. Hoarseness comes on, and loss of voice, and this goes on continuously increasing, until suddenly coming to the end of their resistance they give up the ghost."

In the portion of the work devoted to Therapeutics (Bk. I. ch. 9.), which bears the title: **Θεραπεία τῶν κατὰ τὴν φαρύγγα λοιμικῶν παθῶν,** (Pestilential Affections of the Throat Regions, their Curative Treatment), caustics are especially recommended, as the actual cautery cannot be employed, and finally we read: "In some cases the uvula is destroyed right back to the bones of the palate, and the throat to the root of the tongue and the epiglottis, and in consequence of this destruction they can get down neither solid food nor liquid, for liquids return through the nose, and so the patient dies of hunger."

Now if we examine these statements more closely, we cannot first of all help wondering how the ætiological factors named by *Aretaeus* could possibly be regarded by him as sufficient to account for such dangerous ulcerations,—ulcerations which he himself even calls **λοιμώδεα** (of pestilential character), though of course they are perfectly adequate to explain simple ulcers of the throat. Indulgence in pungent comestibles and beverages is as little adequate to cause such symptoms as are the shouting and greediness of children, not to mention the fact that these are in no way peculiar to Egypt or Syria. The whole account shows us clearly that while *Aretaeus* was well acquainted with the forms the disease took, the ætiological factors were obscure to him and it was merely in a spirit of ill-timed speculation he subjoined them, proving once more how right *Appuleius* was when he exclaims: *Dii boni! Quam facilis, licet non artifici medico, cuivis tamen docto Venereae cupidinis comprehensio.* (Great gods! how easy it is for any educated man, *always excepting a medical practitioner*, to understand the passion of love).

We have already more than once in the course of these investigations proved how Egypt and Syria must be regarded as the nursery of licentiousness in Antiquity, and the passage quoted from *Lucian* (above p. 229.) directly establishes the fact for us; again, a little further on (p. 240. Note I.) it was mentioned how boys particularly, (but also young girls), were used and specially trained as *fellators*. Hence *Martial*[1] wishes he had a boy,

> Niliacis primum puer is nascatur in oris:
> Nequitias tellus scit dare nulla magis.

(In the first place my boy must be born on the banks of Nile: no other land can produce more finished wickedness). From all this, as well as from a comparison of the passage in Lucian, we believe we are amply justified in concluding that Aretaeus' ulcers of the throat, these *Αἰγύπτια καὶ Συριακὰ ἕλκεα* (Egyptian and Syrian sores) were not unfrequently a consequence of *fellation*[2]. That this should be so is readily intelligible, when we consider the liability to corruption and the acrid quality of secretions from the *glans penis* in hot countries. Again the *βουβαστικὰ ἕλκεα* (Bubastic sores), which *Salmasius* cites from *Aëtius*[3] as being identical with

[1] *Martial*, Bk. IV. Epigr. 42. Bk. XI. Epigr. 14.: Urbis deliciae salesque Nili. (Darling of the City, savour of the Nile).

[2] The fact that, according to *Prosper Alpin* (De Medicina Aegypt.—(Of Egyptian Medicine, Bk. I. ch. 14.). gangrenous sore-throat prevails all the year round among children in Egypt, need not prejudice our conclusion; in fact it rather helps to explain how the sore-throat brought on by *fellation* was able so readily and quickly to assume the malignant type described.

[3] *Aëtius*, Tetrab. I. Serm. IV. ch. 21. Perhaps the "Cancer oris" (cancer of the mouth) in boys, of which *Celsus*, VI. 15., makes mention, belongs to the same category.

the Egyptian and Syrian ulcers, find a satisfactory explanation on this hypothesis, for *Herodotus* [1] tells us in his time of the licentious worship of Bubastis, daughter of Isis, at Bubastos. In this expression (*βουβαστικὰ ἕλκεα*) the malady is named from one particular place, where it was probably specially prevalent, whereas in Aretaeus it is spoken of as general throughout the country.

In this connection we must not pass over the fact that Casaubon commenting on the passage of Persius (V. 187.) to be quoted directly is inclined to regard the *ἕλκεα Συριακὰ* (Syrian sores) as a punishment of the Dea Syra (Syrian goddess). In this he relies on a passage of *Plutarch* [2] that runs to this effect: "But of the Syrian goddess the superstitious believe that, if a man eat a sprat or anchovy, the goddess consumes his shin-bones, fills his body full of sores, melts down his liver." The legend must at any rate be of great antiquity, for we meet with it in *Menander*, in a fragment which *Porphyrius* [3] has preserved,—

παράδειγμα τοὺς Σύρους λαβέ·
Ὅταν φάγωσιν ἰχθὺν ἐκεῖνοι διά τινα
Αὑτῶν ἀκρασίαν, τοὺς πόδας καὶ γαστέρα
Οἰδοῦσιν· εἶτα σακκίον ἔλαβον· εἰς δ' ὁδὸν
Ἐκάθισαν αὑτοὶ ἐπὶ κόπρου καὶ τὴν θεὸν
Ἐξιλάσαντο τῷ ταπεινῶσαι σφόδρα.

[1] *Herodotus*, Bk. II. ch. 60.

[2] *Plutarch*, De superstitione II. 170 D., *Τὴν δὲ Συρίαν θεὸν οἱ δεισιδαίμονες νομίζουσιν ἂν μαινίδας τὶς ἢ ἀφύας φάγῃ τὰ ἀντικνήμια διεσθίειν, ἕλκεσι τὸ σῶμα πιμπλάναι, συντήκειν τὸ ἧπαρ.* (for translation see text above). We may add that *μαινίδας* is the *maena* (sprat) of the Romans, for which *Hesychius* has *σαραπίους*, while *Plautus* uses *deglupta maena* (skinned sprat) as a contemptuous name for a vicious debauchee (above p. 238. Note 1.). By the Dea Syra some have understood the goddess Derceto, who was worshipped at Ascalon under the image of a maiden, whose lower half ended in a fish. To her the fishes were sacred, and for this reason the Syrians were forbidden to eat fish. Comp. *Lucian*, De Dea Syra p. 672. *Diodorus Siculus*, II. 4.

[3] *Porphyrius*, De Abstinentia bk. IV. ch. 15.,

in which however swelling of the belly and the feet is in question. To this also would seem to refer what *Persius* (loco citato) says:

> Hinc grandes Galli et cum sistro lusca sacerdos,
> Incussere Deos inflantes corpora, si non
> Praedictum ter mane caput gustaveris alli.

(Then the tall Galli, and the one-eyed priestess with her sacred rattle, instil terror of *the gods that make men's bodies swell*, unless three times at dawn you have eaten the prescribed head of garlic). True we cannot from the passage of Plutarch directly conclude that ulcers of the throat also were ascribed to the anger of the Syrian goddess in consequence of indulgence in a fish diet; rather should we expect what is said to apply primarily to external skin-ulcers, occurring on other parts, as just on the shin-bone. Still we shall be quite justified in making the reference general, more particularly as liver-complaint is also ascribed to the goddess's interference, and we shall see that in Antiquity the cause of all ulcers was supposed to lie in some fault of the liver. Now as the fish had necessarily to be put into the mouth to be swallowed, and as it was always supposed the punishment of the goddess followed immediately on the offence, and affected the immediately active part, throat-ulcers might very naturally be taken to be a result of such punishment. This again only further confirms our explanation just above to the effect that ulcers of the throat were a consequence resulting from vicious indulgence. For the Temple-

(As an example take the Syrians: These people, when they have eaten fish, in consequence of some unwholesome quality in themselves, swell in feet and belly. Then they take quickly a wallet; and down they sit by the road-side on dung, and so appease the goddess by their exceeding humbleness). At Athens ἕλκη ἔχειν ἐν τοῖς ἀντικνημίοις (to have sores on the shin-bones) would seem to have been a usual thing, according to *Theophrastus*, Charact. XIX.

service of the Dea Syra was of course connected with every sort of licentious practice.

Taking into consideration this marked prevalence of *Corrosion of the Shin-bones*, we might argue with considerable probability that it pointed to the existence of a disease of the bones following as a result of vicious indulgence. On the other hand the observation that the precise time the body became covered with ulceration was after indulgence in fish-eating cannot help being of weight in connection with the doctrine of Leprosy; for to the present day we note as very frequent among peoples whose chief nutriment is fish various forms of Leprosy. And again, we may very likely see in this prohibition of a fish diet, which is also mentioned by *Athenaeus* [1], a sanitary regulation justified by experience as necessary in Syria, where skin-diseases and ulcerations were so common.

But not alone in Egypt and Syria did *fellation* lead to suchlike unhappy results; we find the same to have been the case at Rome, as is proved by the following passage of *Martial* [2], a passage that has hitherto been completely overlooked in this connection, but which is none the less of great importance:

[1] *Athenaeus*, Deipnosoph. bk. VIII. p. 346. d. Indeed it would seem that the Stoic *Antipater* of Tarsus related how a Syrian Queen Gatis was excessively fond of eating fish, and accordingly forbad anyone ἄτερ Γάτιδος (except Gatis) in the whole country to indulge in it, and from this circumstance came the name of Atergatis—the Syrian Venus!

[2] *Martial*, Bk. I. Epigr. 79. Possibly also the passage in *Hippocrates*, Epidem. bk. VII., Vol. III. 691 of Kühn's ed., ὁ τὸ καρκίνωμα τὸ ἐν τῇ φάρυγγι καυθεὶς ὑγιὴς ἐγένετο ὑφ' ἡμέων, (The patient who was cauterized for cancer of the throat recovered under our treatment), which Jöhrens in a quotation to be given presently (below § 25.) refers to Venereal disease, as is also done by him in the case of the throat-ulcers mentioned in the Tract of *Hippocrates*, De Dentitione (On Teething), Vol. I. p. 484. of Kühn's ed.

Indignas premeret pestis cum tabida fauces
  Inque ipsos vultus serperet atra lues:
Siccis ipse genis flentes hortatus amicos
  Decrevit Stygios Festus adire lacus.
Nec tamen obscuro pia polluit ora veneno,
  Aut torsit lenta tristia fata fame:
Sanctam Romana vitam sed morte peregit,
  Dimisitque animam nobiliore via.
Hanc mortem fatis magni praeferre Catonis
  Fama potest: huius Caesar amicus erat.

(*When corrupting disease began to sorely afflict his unworthy throat and black contagion was creeping to his very face*, Festus, himself with dry cheeks, comforted his weeping friends, and determined to seek the pools of Styx. But still he never disgraced his dutiful lips with darkling poison, nor brought on a painful, miserable end by slow hunger; nay! rather by a Roman death he completed his holy life, and dismissed his soul the nobler way. Such a death fame may well exalt above great Cato's end; Caesar was his friend).

The words *indignae fauces* (unworthy throat) obviously point to the practice of *fellation*, whereby he had brought on himself the *pestis tabida* and *atra lues*, (corrupting disease, black contagion), and so we have here a clear statement of the cause by one *doctus venereae cupidinis* (learned in the passion of love), which cause was quite unknown to the *artifex medicus* (medical practitioner). The *pia ora* (dutiful lips) are therefore to be taken merely ironically, as also the *sancta vita* (holy life). Even the Cinaedus, as well as the maidens who prostitute themselves in honour of Astarté, are invariably, as we have seen, described in the Old Testament as *sanctus* (holy), and we read e. g. in Job. Ch. XXXV. 14., of a good-for-nothing, how he will die like such a *sanctus*. It was precisely this signification of *sanctus* that led us to the idea of taking the throat affection for a secondary consequence of paederastia, especially if we understand a *double entendre* to underlie the last words *huius Caesar amicus erat* (Caesar was his friend). The Commentators it is true take them merely as said by way of contrast with the death of Cato of Utica, who was forced by Caesar's enmity to take his own life, and as implying this was not the case with Festus, consequently that his suicide is so much the more remarkable [1]. However it is

[1] A striking analogy to this suicide is to be found in the well-known passage of *Pliny* (Epist. bk. VI. epist. 24.), one of much importance in connection with affections of the genitals, which may therefore very well be quoted here by anticipation:

C. Plinius Macro Suo S. Quam multum interest, quid a quo fiat! Eadem enim facta claritate vel obscuritate facientium aut tolluntur altissime, aut humillime deprimuntur. Navigabam per Larium nostrum, quum senior amicus ostendit mihi villam, atque etiam cubiculum, quod in lacum prominet. Ex hoc, inquit, aliquando municeps nostra cum marito se praecipitavit. Causam requisivi. Maritus ex diutino morbo circa velanda corporis ulceribus putrescebat: uxor, ut inspiceret, exegit: neque enim quemquam fidelius indicaturam, possetne sanari. Vidit, desperavit: hortata est, ut moreretur, comesque ipsa mortis, dux immo et exemplum et necessitas fuit. Quod factum ne mihi quidem, qui municeps, nisi proxime auditum est; non quia minus illa clarissimo Arriae facto, sed quia minor est ipsa. Vale. (Caius Pliny to his friend Macer, Greeting.—What a vast difference it makes, by whom a particular thing is done! For the very same actions in virtue of the fame or obscurity of the doers are raised to the topmost pinnacle or brought down to the lowest depth. I was sailing along our Lake of Larius, when my companion and elder pointed out a certain country house to me, nay, a particular bed-room, which projects into the Lake. From this chamber, he said, some time ago a fellow-countrywoman of ours threw herself, along with her husband. I asked the reason. *The husband, it seemed, in consequence of a disease of long standing was rotting with ulcers on the private parts of the body. The wife demanded a right to look; for she thought no one else likely to give a more conscientious opinion than herself as to whether he could be cured. She saw, and despaired of recovery; so she urged him to die, and herself was com-*

doubtful which Caesar is meant, whether the word is merely a Title or a proper name. In the second —and certainly this at first appeared to us to be the more likely,—view we were of course bound then to turn our attention to his character for dissoluteness. However as both *Catullus* [1] and *Suetonius* [2] represent him merely as a *Cinaedus* in regard to the male sex, if that is to say we subscribe to the accepted opinion, we afterwards came to the conclusion it was rather the *Emperor* generally that is spoken of here, and consequently that any other Emperor, e. g. Tiberius, or Nero, or another, might be intended. It is true that if *pathicus* (pathic) and *omnium virorum mulier* (wife of all men) are taken in a wider sense, there would be nothing to make the supposition impossible that Julius Caesar is pointed at. Only that perhaps another passage of *Martial* would seem to go against this, a passage where he seeks to excuse the several excesses and vices of a certain Gaurus by instancing an exalted personage as patronizing each of them, and says finally (Bk. II. 89.):

panion of his death, giving in fact at once incitement, example and compulsion to the deed. This achievement I had never, though a man of the country, heard of till that moment; not because it was a whit less glorious than Arria's renowned exploit, but solely because the doer was less famous. Farewell).

[1] *Catullus*, Carm. 57:

Pulchre convenit improbis cinaedis
Mamurrae pathicoque, Caesarique.

(An excellent understanding exists between the vile *cinaedi*, the pathic Mamurra and Caesar).

[2] *Suetonius*, Vita Jul. Caesaris chs. 49, 51, 52., where Curio, the Elder, calls him (Caesar) "omnium mulierum virum, et omnium virorum mulierem" (husband of all women, and wife of all men). The same indeed was said also of *Alcibiades*. In *Athenaeus*, Deipnos. bk. XII. p. 535., we read in a fragment of the Comic Poet *Pherecrates:*

Οὐκ ὢν ἀνὴρ γὰρ Ἀλκιβιάδης, ὡς δοκεῖ,
ἀνὴρ ἁπασῶν τῶν γυναικῶν ἐστι νῦν.

(For not being a man at all, Alcibiades, it seems, is now husband of all our women).

Quod fellas; vitium dic mihi cuius habes?

(But for your *fellation*: tell me whose vice you follow in this?) Still against the *cinaedus* view the words *indignae fauces* (unworthy throat) speak clearly. Probably in this connection the following passage of *Martial* should also come in,—where the Poet says of his servant (Bk. I. Epigr. 102.):

Destituit primos virides Demetrius annos:
  Quarta tribus lustris addita messis erat.
Ne tamen ad Stygias famulus descenderet umbras,
  Ureret implicitum cum scelerata lues,
Cavimus et domini ius omne remisimus aegro:
  Munere dignus erat convaluisse meo.
Sensit deficiens sua praemia, meque patronum
  Dixit, ad infernas liber iturus aquas.

(Demetrius left us in the first years of his bloom; the fourth summer was but just added to his three lustres. We took all means to save our faithful house-slave from descending to the shades of Styx, when he was consuming under a malignant contagion that had fastened upon him, and remitted all my master's rights for the sick lad,—who indeed well deserved to win recovery at my hands. On his death-bed he recognized what I had done for him, and called me his *master*, though so soon to go forth a free man to the streams of the neither world.)

Was this *famulus* (house-slave) the same person as the *puer* (boy, slave), who is mentioned by *Martial*, bk. XI. 95.?

That not boys only, but girls too, had to suffer in this way among the Romans, and lost their lives from the complaint in question, is shown, we think, by the following Epigram of *Martial*, Bk. XI. Epigr. 91.):

Aeolidon Canace iacet hoc tumulata sepulchro,
  Ultima cui parvae septima venit hiems.
Ah scelus, ah facinus! properas quid flere viator?
  Non licet hic vitae de brevitate queri.

Tristius est leto leti genus: horrida vultus
Abstulit et tenero sedit in ore lues:
Ipsaque crudeles ederunt oscula morbi;
Nec data sunt nigris tota labella rogis.
Si tam praecipiti fuerant ventura volatu,
Debuerant alia fata venire via.

(Canacé of the Aeolians lies buried in this tomb, who died a child,—her seventh winter was her last. Oh! the shame and horror of it! haste, a tear, thou that passest by. Here is no occasion to lament the short span of human life. Sadder than death is the way of her death; a dread contagion ate away her face, and settled in the tender little mouth. Cruel disease infected her very kisses; and her lips were half gone when they were consigned to the grim pyre. If death must needs have come to her with a flight so swift, at least he should have taken another way. Death so hasted to close the issue of her persuasive voice, that her tongue might not have time to bend the cruel goddesses to mercy).

Besides the passages quoted, there are several others to be found in *Martial*, that must be taken as referring to the *fellator*; but since the maladies that occur are equally prevalent in the case of the *Cunnilingue*, it will be more convenient to adduce them under that head. Further, we only require to mention the fact that *pale lips* seem to have been regarded as a mark of the *fellator* [1].

[1] *Catullus*, Carm. 80.:

Quid dicam, Gelli, quare rosea ista labella
Hiberna fiant candidiora nive,
Mane domo cum exis, et cum te octava quiete
E molli longo suscitat hora die.
Nescio quid certe est. An vere fama susurrat,
Grandia te medii tenta vorare viri?
Sic certe clamant Virronis rupta miselli
Ilia, et emulso labra notata sero.

(Would you have me tell, Gellius, why those rosy lips grow whiter than the winter's snow, when you sally out from home in the morning, and when the eighth hour of the long summer day wakes you from gentle sleep? Nay! I know not what it is for sure. Does report say true, that whispers *you mouth the swollen member of a man's middle?* So at any rate declare the deboshed

The Cunnilingue.

§ 23.

But the vice of the *fellator* is far surpassed in baseness by that of the *Cunnilingue* (*qui opus peragit linguam arrigendo in cunnum, eumque lambit,*—one who works by putting his tongue up into the female organ, and licking it). The Greeks called this practice **σκύλαξ** (a puppy), because it is a habit of dogs [1], and Hesychius explains it by **σχῆμα ἀφρο-**

vigour of poor feeble Virro, and *your own lips marked by the humour you draw out*). *Martial*, Bk. VII. Epigr. 94.:

Bruma est, et riget horridus December,
Audes tu tamen osculo nivali
Omnis obvios hinc et hinc tenere,
Et totam, Line, basiare Romam.
Quid possis graviusque saeviusque
Percussus facere atque verberatus?
Hoc me frigore basiet nec uxor.
Blandis filia nec rudis labellis.
Sed tu dulcior. elegantiorque,
Cuius livida naribus caninis,
Dependet glacies, rigetque barba,
Qualem forficibus metit supinis
Tonsor Cinyphio Cilix marito.
Centum occurrere malo cunnilingis,
Et Gallum timeo minus recentem.
Quare si tibi sensus est pudorque,
Hibernas, Line, basiationes,
In mensem, rogo, differas Aprilem.

('Tis winter time, and the shuddering chill of December is upon us. None the less, Linus, you dare to greet with your frosty salute all men you meet here and there, and to kiss all Rome. What more disagreeable or more cruel could you do, if you had been struck or thrashed? With an embrace so chilling may no wife kiss me, or unripe maid with wheedling lips. But you, —you think yourself more attractive and more pleasing, you from whose dog-like nose a blue icicle hangs, whose beard is frozen stiff, such a beard as the Cilician shearer crops with his upward-pointing clippers from the chin of a Cinyphian he-goat. I had rather meet a hundred *cunnilingues;* I am less afraid of a Gaul new come to town. Wherefore, if you possess any sense or any shame, I do beseech you, Linus, defer your wintry salutes till April is come). Now *Linus* is designated by *Martial*, bk. VII. Epigr. 9, as a *fellator*, and bk. XI. Epigr. 26., as a *cunnilingue.*

[1] Whence also the proverbial saying in *Suidas:* *κύνα δέρειν δεδαρμένην· τὸ τοῦ Φερεκράτους· σχῆμα δέ ἐστι ἀκόλαστον εἰς τὸ αἰδοῖον· εἴρηται δὲ ἐπὶ τῷ, ἄλλο πασχόντων αὖθις ἐφ' οἷς πεπόνθασιν ἡ παροιμία.* (to

διϭιακὸν, ὡς τὸ τῶν φοινικιζόντων (a method of love, resembling that of those who phoenicize). We have already, in the passage of *Lucian* quoted a little above, found **φοινικίζειν** and **λεσβιάζειν** put

skin the skinned bitch; expression of Pherecrates; is an abominable practice In connection with the private parts; the proverb is spoken of such as suffer something a second time over, after having suffered it once already). Similarly *Plautus*, Trinum. II. 4. 27., Edepol *mutuum* mecum facit (By my faith, he plays give and take with me). Again *κυνάμυια* (shameless fly) is found in *Suidas*, which he explains by *ἀναιδεστάτη· παρεσχημάτικε τὸ ὄνομα ἀπὸ τοῦ κυνὸς καὶ τῆς μυίας· ὁ μὲν γὰρ κύων ἀναιδής, ἡ δὲ μυῖα θρασεῖα,* (a most shameless woman: name borrowed figuratively from the dog and the fly; for the dog is shameless, and the fly audacious)—probably with a reference to *Homer*, II. XXI. 394., where *κυνόμυια* is found, and the Scholiast observes: *ἀναιδής ὡς μυῖα, ἐκ δύο ἀναιδῶν τελείων, τοῦ τε κυνός καὶ τῆς μυίας, διὰ τὸ ὑπερβάλλον τῆς ἀναιδείας.* (shameless as a fly; from two completely shameless creatures, the dog and the fly; on account of the excessive degree of their shamelessness). Further there is in this connection the word *κυναλώπηξ* (fox-dog), which was a nick-name of *Philostratus*, as we see from *Aristophanes*, Knights 1078., on which passage the Scholiast observes: *λέγει δὲ αὐτὸν καὶ πορνοβοσκὸν καὶ καλλωπιστὴν* (now he calls him both brothel-keeper and dandy). If we derive the word from *τὸν κύνα* (frenulum praeputii,—ligament of the prepuce,—Paulus Aegineta, VI. 54.) *ἀλωπίζειν*, it would designate the *fellator*, as *ἀλωπὸς, ἀλωπίζειν, ἀλωπηαίζω*. is formed from a privative (negative) and *λῶπος, λώπη* (the covering, skin, wool; and *ἀλωπηκία* is to be explained in the same way,—but not from the scab or mange of the fox, nor yet as the Etymologicum Magnum would have it, because the places where the fox discharges his urine die, the grass e.g. dries up and withers. Hence *ἀλώπηξ* might be taken as *bald-headed*, and then the further meaning of licentious dissoluteness given to it, for in Antiquity baldness was very usually looked upon as a consequence of sexual excesses, and as every one knows, Caesar was called by his soldiers *moechus calvus* (the bald-headed adulterer). But old men, who in particular are bald-headed, especially practised, owing to their lack of the power of erecting the

side by side; *Galen* moreover [1] does the same in the following passage, a noteworthy one for our

penis, the vice of *irrumation* and of the *cunnilingue*, which makes *Martial* say (IV. 50.) *Nemo est, Thai, senex ad irrumandum* (No one, Thais, is too old a man for irrumation). κυναλώπηξ would then be a *bald-headed cunnilingue.* Possibly however this idea was also partly due to a reminiscence of the fox's habit, when desirous of following up a scent, of sticking his head to the ground (*Aelian*, Hist. Anim. VI. ch. 24.),—a manœuvre he also adopts, as is generally known, when dying. In evidence of this view may be quoted what *Cicero*, Orat. pro Domo ch. 18., says to Sextus Clodius: *ligurris* (you are a licker), and ch. 31. Quaere hoc ex Sexto Clodio, iube adesse, latitat omnino; sed si requiri iusseris, invenient hominem apud sororem tuam (Publii Clodii) *occultantem se capite demisso* (Require this of Sextus Clodius, bid him appear; he lurks entirely out of sight. But if once you order him to be sought out, they will find the man at your sister's house (Publius Clodius's) *hiding himself with head held down.* Comp. *Catullus*, 87. In *Martial*, Bk. IV. Epigr. 53., *canis* is used in same sense as κύων in Greek, —apparently? Perhaps the women of Antiquity made use of dogs as well to serve as *cunnilingues.* According to *Brockhusius* on Tibullus I. 7. 32., II. 4. 32. they were usual companions of "ladies of pleasure" at Rome, whence too *suburanae canes* (bitches of the Subura) in *Horace*, Epod. V. 58. and *Subura vigilax* (the watchful Subura) in *Propertius*, IV. 7. 15. During the Middle Ages at any rate such an employment of dogs was nothing unusual. This is stated by *Panormita*, Hermaph. Epigr. XXX., Epitaphium Nichinae Flandrensis, Scorti egregii:—

Pelvis erat cellae in medio, qua saepe lavabar,
Lambebat madidum blanda catella femur.

(Epitaph on Nichette the Fleming, a famous Harlot:—There stood a basin in middle of the chamber, in which I would many a time wash myself, the while my fawning bitch-pup licked her mistress's dripping thigh).
and Epigr. XXXVII.,

Te visot Jannecta, sua comitante catella,
Blanda canis dominae est, est hera blanda viris.

(Jeannette shall visit you, her bitch-pup accompanying her; complacent is the hound to its mistress, the lady complacent to men).

[1] *Galen*, De simplic. medicament. temperamentis ac facultat. Bk. X. ch. 1., edit. Kühn Vol. XII. p. 249.

purpose on several accounts: "The drinking of sweat, urine and the menstrual blood of women is vicious and shameful, and not less so when a person, as Xenocrates proposes to do, smears the regions of the mouth and throat with excrement, and swallows it down. He speaks also of taking the wax of the ears. For my part I could never bring myself to take this, even though by that means I were never to be ill again. But excrement I consider yet more disgusting, and it is for a man of any decency far more shameful to be called an Excrement-Eater [1] than an **αἰσχρουργὸς** (worker of obscenities) or a *cinaedus*. But of **αἰσχρουργοὶ** [2] (workers of obscenities),

[1] **κοπροφάγος** (Excrement-Eater). To this *Martial*, bk. III. Epigr. 77., seems to allude, when he says:

Nescio quod stomachi vitium secretius esse
Suspicor, ut quid enim, Baetice, saprofagis?

(I suspect there exiasts some secret vitiation of the stomach; else why, Baeticus. do you *eat putrid meat?*)

[2] It is evident from this that *Meier* in his above mentioned Article on Paederastia is wrong in citing the expression *αἰσχρουργὸς* (worker of obscenities) as being used for the direct equivalent of *cinaedus*. Incidentally we would take this opportunity of further cbserving that the word **παιδοκόραξ** (boy-raven, i.e. a person ravenous after boys), which is also mentioned in the same Article as synonymous with *cinaedus*, is wrongly referred to paederastia, for it really, like the Latin *corvus* (raven), signifies a *fellator*. Its true explanation is given in *Pliny*, Hist. Nat. bk. X. ch. 15., Corvi pariunt cum plurimum quinos. *Ore eos parere aut coire vulgus arbitratur*. (Ravens produce at most a brood of five each pair. *The vulgar believe these birds produce or copulate with the mouth*).—Aristoteles (De gen anim. Bk. III. ch. 6.) negat, — sed illam exosculationem, quae saepe cernitur, qualem in columbis, esse. (Aristotle denies this,—but adds that there is the same billing, which is often noticed, as with doves). Hence also *Martial*, bk. XIV. Epigr. 74.,

Corve salutator, quare fellator haberis?
In caput intravit mentula nulla tuum.

(You raven that salute your mate, why are you thought to be a *fellator?* No member ever penetrated into your head). Greek Anthology, bk. II. Tit. 9. 13., **λευκὸν ἰδεῖν κόρακα** (a white crow to all appearance).

we abominate Phoenicians more than the Lesbians, and it seems to me the man does something of the same sort as the former who drinks menstrual blood (**μᾶλλον βδελλυττόμεθα τοὺς φοινικίζοντας τῶν λεσβιαζόντων, ᾧ [1] φαίνεταί μοι παραπλήσιόν τι πάσχειν ὁ καὶ καταμηνίου πίνων.**) *A sensible man will neither seek to collect experiences on the point, nor yet on a practice, which it is true involves less*, but still is sufficiently shameful, that of smearing a part of the body with excrement, because he has some hurt at that spot,—or with human seed. Xenocrates calls this latter commonly **γόνος** (seed, semen), and distinguishes with minute care between cases where simple seed rubbed in by itself is of benefit, and cases where the female has the same effect after combination with the male, as it is discharged from the woman's womb."

This explanation of Galen's to the effect that the **φοινικίζων** (one who phoenicizes) resembles the man who drinks menstrual blood, shows clearly that **φοινικίζειν** is *not*, as all the Lexicons give it, and *Forbiger* (loco citato) also assumes, identical with **λεσβιάζειν.** It is true *Forbiger* (p. 329. Note v.) gives the meaning *cunnilingere* as well, although the explanation is undoubtedly unsatisfactory which he offers *á propos* of an Epigram, [2]—one certainly apposite in this connection, to the effect that the reason

[1] Instead of ᾧ φαίνεται *Rost* has proposed to read ὧν φαίνεται. (*Forbiger*, on the Hermaphrod. of Panormita, p. 281. Note b.

[2] *Brunck*, Analecta Vol. III. p. 334.,

Δημῶναξ, μὴ πάντα κάτω βλέπε, μηδὲ χαρίζου τῇ γλώσσῃ· δεινὴν χοῖρος ἄκανθαν ἔχει. Καὶ συζῇς ἡμῖν. ἐν Φοινίκῃ δὲ καθεύδεις, κοὐκ ὢν ἐκ Σεμέλης μηροτραφὴς γέγονας.

(Demonax, be not for ever looking downwards, and be not complacent with your tongue; that organ — the *pudenda muliebria* — has a sharp thorn. And indeed you live with us, *but you sleep in Phoenicia*, and though no child of Semelé, are thigh-bred).

for this signification is, *quod cunnilingos a natando in mari quodam Phoenicei coloris* (*mari rubro*) *dixissent*, (that they had called them *cunnilingues* from their swimming as it were in a sea of Phoenician purple colour—a red sea); for the words in the Epigram, **ἐν φοινίκῃ δὲ καθεύδεις** (but you sleep in Phoenicia) cannot stand for anything else but simply **φοινικίζειν**, as indeed the passage from *Aloisia Sigaea*, which is quoted by Forbiger himself, proves conclusively [1]: *Cum vellet mediam lambere, se velle dicebat in Liguriam*, (When he wanted to lick my middle, he used to say he would fain *be into Liguria*—that is, would fain lick, *ligurire*). Accordingly just as **λεσβιάζειν** came into use as the distinctive name for the vice of the *fellator*, because it was practised to a distinctive degree in Lesbos, so too to be a *cunnilingue* was called **φοινικίζειν**,

[1] In particular it is the following Epigram in *Brunck's* Analecta that has given occasion to this explanation:

Ἀλφειοῦ στόμα φεῦγε· φιλεῖ κόλπους Ἀρεθούσης.
πρηνὴς ἐμπίπτων ἁλμυρὸν ἐς πέλαγος.

(Fly the Alpheus' mouth; he loves the bosom of Arethusa, *falling headlong into the salt sea*). *Forbiger* might have further cited the following passage from *Aristophanes*, Knights 1086, 87.,

ΑΛ. Καὶ γὰρ ἐμοὶ καὶ γῆς καὶ τῆς ἐρυθρᾶς γε θαλάσσης
χὤτι γ' ἐν Ἐκβατάνοις δικάσεις, λείχων ἐπίπαστα.

(Verily for me you shall be judge over earth and the Red Sea to boot and all the realm of Ecbatana, *licking up* comfit-cakes,—? pickles). Here **ἐπίπαστα** is, as probably also in v. 103., the Salgama (pickles in brine) of *Ausonius*, Epigr. 125.; which moreover affords at any rate a partial explanation of the passage in *Pollux*, Onomast. bk. VI. ch. 9. p. 61., bk. X. ch. 24. p. 96. Still, even if according to this *Phoenicia* were used in the sense of the genital organs of women at time of menstruation, it by no means follows that **φοινικίζειν** meant *only* to have dealings with women in menstruation, any more than it does that it is identical with **καταμηνίου πίνων** (drinking of menstrual blood), as it has been shown just above not to be. In fact *Galen* says explicitly: **φαίνεταί μοι παραπλήσιον**, (it appears to me to be something *similar!*)

because the habit was at home among the Phoenicians. Undoubtedly men's shamelessness was carried so far that they actually used women and girls at their period of menstruation for this purpose,—a fact of the highest interest for us, as we shall show directly. *Seneca* [1] expresses himself plainly enough on the subject: "Quid tu, cum Mamercum Scaurum consulem "faceres, ingnorabas, ancillarum suarum men-"struum ore illum hiante exceptare? num "quid enim ipse dissimulabat? num quid purus "videri volebat? (How came it you were ignorant, when making Mamercus Scaurus consul, *that he was in the habit of catching in his open mouth the menstrual discharge of his maidservants?* Did he make any concealment of it himself? did he pose as a pure-minded man? nay! not he). Again in another place [2]:

"Nuper Natalis tam improbae linguae quam im-"purae, in cuius ore feminae purgabantur. (Quite lately Natalis showed himself as malignant of tongue as he is unchaste, *into whose mouth women were used to purge themselves*).

Now if first of all we bear steadfastly in mind that this **φοινικίζειν** was a vice, which prevailed primarily and especially among the Phoenicians and was later on disseminated abroad by them, and then consider how the Greeks designated every vice, and particularly excesses in love, as **νόσος** (disease), in the same way precisely as the Romans used *morbus* (disease),—comp. § 17—we *must* see that **φοινικίζειν** is the same thing as **νόσος φοινικίη** (Phoenician disease), and shall be in a position to form an opinion on the Gloss [3] falsely ascribed to *Galen*, which reads: **φοινικίη νόσος· ἡ κατὰ Φοινίκην καὶ κατὰ τὰ ἄλλα ἀνατολικὰ μέρη πλεονάζουσα. δηλοῦσθαι δὲ κἀνταῦθα δοκεῖ ἡ ἐλεφαντιάσις.** (*Phoenician disease*: a disease prevalent in Phoenicia

[1] *Seneca*, De beneficiis bk. IV. ch. 31.

[2] *Seneca*, Epist. 87.

[3] *Galen*, Works. edit. Kühn, Vol. XIX. p. 153.

and about the Eastern parts. Elephantiasis *appears* to be signified by this).

Even granting the first part of this Gloss to have been really written by *Galen*, the last sentence at any rate is obviously an extraneous and later addition. This is at once indicated by the use of the word **δοκεῖ** (it appears), which comes in curiously, standing as it does next-door to the *definite* statement that this **νόσος** (disease) was common in Phoenicia; for surely anyone who knew this, must also have known what the disease was. Again if he had wished to describe it by some such phrase as the English "a sort of Elephantiasis", he could hardly have failed to express himself in a different way to what he has. But as a matter of fact, *Galen* knew perfectly well, as we have already seen, what **φοινικίζειν** was, and consequently what the **φοινικίη νόσος** (Phoenician disease) was, and it could not by any possibility have occurred to him to suppose it any form of Elephantiasis. Unfortunately *Prof. Naumann* [1] has allowed himself to be misled by this extraneous addition; he writes: "In the Work of a Pseudo-Galen is given a short explanation of the **φοινικίη νόσος** (Phoenician disease), or rather to speak strictly, the *conjecture* is made, [2] that this malady, a common one in Phoenicia and the East, may have been Elephantiasis. True indeed the word might *with equal likelihood* express a disease characterized by redness of the skin **φοινίκιος** s. **φοινίκεος** i. q. puniceus, purpureus, cruentus; **φοινιγμὸς** irritatio cutis per vesicantia—**φοινίκιος** or **φοινίκεος** =

[1] *Naumann*, Handb. der Klinik (Text-book of Clinical Medicine), Vol. 7. p. 88.

[2] The author at any rate is more cautious than *Sprengel*, who (*Th. Batemann*), Prakt. Darstellung der Hautkrankheiten (Practical Exposition of Diseases of the Skin), Halle 1815., p. 427. Note) writes: "Hippocrates appears to mention it (Elephantiasis) under the name **φοινικίη νόσος** (Phoenician disease), which *Galen* (Explan. voc. Hipp.) *distinctly and definitely* explains as Elephantiasis.

Phoenician purple, purple, blood-red; **φοινιγμὸς** = irritation of the skin by rubefacients). Or should we suppose *some leprous-venereal malady* endemic and aboriginal among the trading Phoenicians to be signified, which was called the *Morbus Phoeniceus* (Phoenician disease) in the same way as in more modern times people spoke of the *Morbus Gallicus* (French disease,—Syphilis)? In any case it is remarkable that *Themison* (who also noted incidentally that Satyriasis at times attacks a population epidemically,—speaks of the special frequency of Satyriasis in Crete (*Caelius Aurelianus*, Acut. Morb. bk. III. ch. 18). As is well known, Phoenician and Hellenic Colonies had converged here; and the island remained in uninterrupted and active commercial intercourse with the maritime cities of Phoenicia.

According to the general supposition the Gloss of the Pseudo-Galen has reference to a passage of *Hippocrates* occurring in the Second book of the Prorrhetica,[1] where we read as follows: "But **λειχῆνες**,—tetters, as also **λέπραι** and **λεῦκαι**,—scaly leprosies and white leprosies, where any of these occur in the young or mere children, or after appearing on a small scale shall then increase but slowly, in these cases it is not right to call the exanthema or eruption an apostasis, (transitional state), but a **νόσημα**,—condition of disease. On the other hand where any of these affections occurs on

[1] *Hippocrates*, edit. Kühn Vol. I. pp. 223, 233., *Λειχῆνες δὲ καὶ λέπραι καὶ λεῦκαι, οἷσι μεν νέοισιν ἢ παισὶν ἐοῦσιν ἐγένετό τι τούτων, ἢ κατὰ μικρὸν φανὲν αὔξεται ἐν πολλῷ χρόνῳ, τούτοισι μὲν οὐ χρὴ ἀπόστασιν νομίζειν τὸ ἐξάνθημα, ἀλλὰ νόσημα· οἷσι δὲ ἐγένετο τούτων τι πολύ τε καὶ ἐξαπίνης, τοῦτο ἂν εἴη ἀπόστησις· γίνονται δὲ λεῦκαι μὲν ἐκ τῶν θανατωδεστάτων νοσημάτων, οἷον καὶ ἡ νοῦσος ἡ φθινικὴ καλεομένη. αἱ δὲ λέπραὶ καὶ οἱ λειχῆνες ἐκ τῶν μελαγχολικῶν. ἰῆσθαι δὲ τουτέων εὐπετέστερά ἐστιν ὅσα νεωτάτοισί τε γίνεται καὶ νεώτατά ἐστι, καὶ τοῦ σώματος ἐν τοῖσι μαλθακωτάτοισι καὶ σαρκωδεστάτοισι φύεται.* (for translation see text above).

a large scale and suddenly, it would then be an apostasis. But whereas **λεῦκαι** arise out of *the most deadly diseases*, as e.g. the **νοῦσος ἡ φθινική,**— wasting disease, as it is called, **λέπραι** and **λειχῆνες** do so from the melancholic, or diseases proceeding from black bile. And of such the easier to cure are those that occur in the youngest patients and are of the latest origin, and arise in the softest and most fleshy parts of the body." *Foesius* observes on the passage: "Nemini autem dubium est, quin hac parte "mendosi sint codices omnes, cum **ἡ νοῦσος** "**ἡ φθινικὴ καλουμένη** scribitur. Nam **φοινικίη** "**νόσος** ex Galeni exegesi procul omni dubio repo- "nendum. (Now no one can doubt that *all the MSS. are deceptive* here, reading as they do **ἡ νοῦσος ἡ φθινίκη.** For **φοινικίη νόσος** must undoubtedly be restored from the Exegesis of Galen). *J. W. Wedel*[1] on the contrary writes: "Legunt quidam pro **φοινικίη** "—**φθινικὴ**, et vertunt tabem seu morbum tabidum, "sed contra fidem codicum correctiorum, quibus Galenus ipse assentitur, et rei ipsius, de qua textus agit, evidentiam. (Some read **φθινικὴ** for **φοινικίη,** and render it *wasting* or *wasting disease,—but against the authority of the better class of MSS.*, with which Galen himself agrees, and against the evidence of the context of the matter treated of). In the latter of these two statements Wedel, in spite of his mistaken view of the matter generally, is perfectly right; whether he is so in the former as well, we are not in a position to say, for alas! we lack the critical apparatus absolutely indispensable for

[1] *J. W. Wedel*, Progr. de Morbo phoeniceo Hippocratis, (Graduation Exercise on the Phœnician disease of Hippocrates), Jena 1702. 4to., reprinted in *E. G. Baldinger*, Selecta doctorum virorum opuscula in quibus Hippocrates explicatur, denuo edita, (Select Tracts of Learned Men dealing with the Interpretation of Hippocrates, — Second ed.), Göttingen 1782., pp. 215—222. The Author does not seem to be really self-consistent; he wavers between Elephantiasis and Purpura.

such a decision, not so much as the Edition of *Mackius* being on the shelves of our University Library.

In the first place we ought to make quite sure what Hippocrates understood under the name **λεῦκαι.** A disease of the Skin no doubt; but of what particular nature it was, would seem not to be so easy to determine. According to *Coac. praenotion.* (Vol. I. p. 321.) Hippocrates distinguished a **λεύκη συγγενής** and a **λεύκη μὴ συγγενής** (**λεύκη** inborn, and not inborn), the latter attacking individuals only after puberty. *Hesychius* says **λεύκη, ἄνθός τι τῶν περὶ τὸ σῶμα γινόμενον, ἄλφος δὲ λευκή τις ἐν τῷ σώματι.** (**λεύκη,**—white leprosy, an eruption coming out on the exterior parts of the body, but **ἄλφος,**—dull-white leprosy, a form of **λεύκη** *in* the body). *Galen, Definit. med.* (Vol. XIX. p. 140) **λευκή ἐστιν ἡ ἐπὶ λευκὸν χρῶμα τοῦ σώματος παρὰ φύσιν μεταβολή.** (**λεύκη** is the change to an unnatural white colour of the body). According to this it would appear to be merely superficial discolorations of the skin that writers understood by **λεῦκαι,**—a view that *Rayer,* [1] seems to coincide with. *Pollux* on the other hand offers an explanation as follows: **ἀλφὸς μέλας, ἐπιδρομὴ σκιώδης, ἐπιπόλαιος, εὐίατος, ἀλφὸς λευκὸς, λευκότης ἐπιτρέχουσα τῇ ἐπιδερματίδι, αὐχμηρὰ, δυσίατος· λεύκη, ὅταν ἐπιτείνῃ ἡ**

[1] *Rayer, Maladies de la peau.* Bruxelles 1836. p. 385. Et quoique les termes de la description du λεύκη se rapportent assez bien à la leucopathie partielle, la plupart des interprètes et des critiques, se fondant sur une passage d'Hippocrate (Prorrhet. lib. II.) ont pensé, que sous ce nom les anciens avoient indiqué une maladie grave, l'éléphantiasis anesthétique ou la lèpre des juifs. (*Rayer*, Diseases of the Skin. Brussels 1836., p. 385., And although the terms in which this λεύκη is described are pretty well consistent with the symptoms of partial leucopathy, still the majority of interpreters and critics, taking their stand on a passage of Hippocrates (Prorrhet. bk. II.) have held that under this name the Ancients indicated a serious disease, viz. anaesthetic elephantiasis or the leprosy of Jews).

λευκότης, καὶ φύσῃ τρίχωσιν λευκήν, εἰ δὲ κεντήσειας, ὕφαιμος, δυσίατος, ἔστιν ὅτε ὑπέρυθρος· ἐπανθεῖ δὲ αὐτὸ (?) **τοῖς χείλεσιν, οἷον ἁλὸς ἄχνη.** (Black **ἀλφὸς,** a dark-coloured spreading eruption, superficial and easily curable; white **ἀλφὸς,** a whiteness running over the epidermis (of the prepuce), dry harsh and difficult to cure; **λεύκη,** when the whiteness extends, and produces a growth of white hairs, and if you prick it, it is suffused with blood, difficult to cure, also sometimes reddish in hue. And the eruption comes out on the lips *like sea-foam*). Here **λεύκη** is evidently a much more deeply penetrating malady, as indeed it is described by *Celsus* [1] and *Galen.* [2] It corresponds with the white Leprosy of Moses. But the most curious thing is the statement appended to the effect that the affection broke out on the lips like sea-foam. This is certainly to be referred to some other form of **λεύκη,** unless indeed we are to take it in connection with the succeeding words in the text, **λειχὴν ἄγριος**

[1] *Celsus*, Bk. V. ch. 27. 19., λεύκη habet quiddam simile alpho, sed magis albida est et altius descendit: in eaque albi pili sunt, et lanugini similes. (λεύκη has some resemblance to alphus, but is more white in colour, and penetrates deeper; also in it there are white hairs of a woolly appearance). In these last words the interpreters have supposed themselves to find the ἁλὸς ἄχνη (sea-foam) of *Pollux*, Onom. IV. 193., expressed!

[2] *Galen*, Isag., edit. Kühn Vol. XIV. p. 758., — De symptomat. differ. Vol. VII. p. 63. — De symptomat. caus. bk. II. ibid. pp. 225 sqq., where the λεύκη is described as a consequence of *nutritio depravata* (morbid nutrition), whereby τὴν σάρκα γίνεσθαι φλεγματικωτέραν (the flesh becomes over phlegmatic). Comp. *Aetius*, Tetrab. IV. I. ch. 133. *Paulus Aegineta*, bk. IV. ch. 5. *Actuarius*, Meth. med. II. 11. VI. 8. *Oribasius*, De morb. curat. III. 58. *Scip. Gentilis*, Comment. in Apuleii apologiam, note 524. — *Suidas* s. v. λεύκη· παρὰ Ἡροδότῳ πάθος τι περὶ ὅλον τὸ σῶμα, (under word λεύκη: in Herodotus, a complaint affecting the whole surface of the body). In *Alexander*, Aphrodis. Problem. I. 146, λεῦκαι signify the white flecks on the finger-nails.

(malignant tetter), in which case, as we have seen with regard to Mentagra (Tetter of the chin), the remark is based on a perfectly sound observation; and besides, the **αὐτὸ** gives absolutely no sense. On the other hand if Pollux' datum in reference to the seat of **λεύκη** is correct, it must obviously afford much light for clearing up the meaning of the passage in Hippocrates, and in deference to it we shall be bound to read **φοινικίη** instead of **φθινικὴ**, [1]—an

[1] *Pollux*, Onomast IV. ch. 25. p. 187., mentions among forms of wasting-diseases **φθίνης νόσος**, for which some editors, and quite rightly, prefer to read **φθίνας νόσος** (wasting disease). *Suidas* also says **φθίνας ἡ νόσος**, but without giving any further explanation; on the contrary in *Hesychius* we find: s. v. **φθινά[ς] ἡ ἐρυσίβη, καὶ εἶδος ἐλαίας** (under word **φθινά**; the red blight, also a species of olive). But by **ἐρυσίβη** is signified *mildew, blight, smut on grain*, the same thing therefore as the Romans called *rubigo* or *robigo*, on which *Servius*, on Virg. Georg. I. 151., has the following observation: Robigo genus est vitii, quo culmi pereunt, quod a rusticanis calamitas dicitur. Hoc autem genus vitii ex nebula nasci solet, cum nigrescunt et consumuntur frumenta. Inde Robigus deus et sacra eius septimo Kalendas Maias Robigalia appellantur. Sed haec abusive robigo dicitur; nam proprie robigo est, ut Varro dicit, vitium obscoenae libidinis quod ulcus vocatur: id autem abundantia et superfluitate humoris solet nasci, quae Graece **σατυρίασις** dicitur. (*Robigo* is a sort of blight, that kills the corn-stalks, which is spoken of as a *disaster* by the peasants. Now this kind of blight commonly springs from a mist or exhalation, the crops blackening and being burnt up. Hence the god Robigus, and his feast-day on the seventh day before the Kalends of May (April 24.), known as the Robigalia. But this is called *robigo* only by a misnomer; for properly speaking *robigo* is, as Varro says, a vitiation due to abominable licentiousness, and is called an ulcer, and it commonly springs from that abundance and over-copiousness of the humour, which in Greek is called Satyriasis). These words are for our purpose of the highest importance, teaching us as they do, that *a distinctive form of ulceration, that the patient had brought on himself by sexual excesses, was not only familiar*

emendation that presents no difficulty, since *φθινικὴ* might very easily be read for *φοινικίη*, and indeed (as pointed out in the Note) was actually so read.

among the Romans but actually bore the *special* name of *robigo*. It must have displayed a distinctive redness, and have consumed the parts affected similarly to the smut or rust of grain, or the rust of iron. It is surely a sufficient indication to call the chancre-ulcer a blight, a burning: Comp. anthrax, carbo (malignant pustule, carbuncle). To this day in Germany it is vulgarly said of any one attacked by the primary forms of Venereal disease, "the man has burned himself". *Festus*, (edit. Dacier p. 451.) says: *Robum* rubro colore et quae rufo significare, at bovem quoque rustici appellant, manifestum est, unde et *materia quae plurimas venas eius coloris habet* dicta est rubor, (*Robus* clearly indicates things of a red or reddish colour,—now countrymen even speak of an ox as *robus*; hence *any substance having manifold veins of this colour* is called *rubor*). Now such is habitually the case with the penis attacked by phimosis or paraphimosis and under the morbid condition of constant erection (Satyriasis) superinduced by these. Again this shows us the reason why Priapus is so frequently called "*ruber* hortorum custos" (the *red* keeper of gardens), — *Priapeia* Praef. 5.; and why he is said, "*Ruber* sedere cum *rubente* fascino, (to sit, *red* with his *ruddy* verge), — *Horace*, Odes 84. Sat. I. 8. 5. Now as the blight in grain was regarded specially as a consequence of the dew (mil*dew*), and *ros* (dew) again is used in the sense of the male semen, as well as for the moisture secreted in the female vagina during coition, we might draw yet another analogy from this, and at the same time a proof of the *verecundia loquentium* (shamefacedness in speech), — p. 43., of the *old* Romans. Thus it would seem the Greeks too indicated by their *φθινὰς* the same thing as the Romans by *robigo*. That it was a human disease, is clearly enough shown by the passage from Pollux, and besides we can see it was so from another in *Plutarch* in his Life of Galba (ch. 21.), where he says: *Τιγελλῖνον μὲν οὐ πολὺν ἔτι βιώσεσθαι φάσκοντος· χρόνον, ὑπὸ φ θ ι ν ά δ ο ς ν ό σ ο υ δαπανώμενον*, (For he said that Tigellinus would not live much longer, being exhausted by a wasting disease), —a quotation proving at the same time the deadliness of the malady. Once more, *Hesychius* has for *φθινὰ* also *φοινία*, saying, *φ ο ι ν ί α*.

But one emendation leads on to another, and we shall find ourselves bound, on the analogy of the **θαυμαστὸν πάθος** (wonderful complaint) in Dio

ἐρυσίβη (φοινία: red blight, and as the adjective corresponding would necessarily be φοινικίος or φοινίκινος, it follows that φοινικίη νόσος and φθινικη νόσος, — φθινικὴ being the adjective from φθινὴ or φθινὰς, (which however would more strictly speaking be φθινακή), would mean exactly the same thing, viz. an "Ulcus rubrum et rodens ex coitu cum foeda muliere natum" (red eating ulcer, coming from coition with an unclean woman), the fatal event of which affection was a matter of common observation among the Ancients. Now if this interpretation is the right one in the passage of Hippocrates, it is clear that λεῦκαι were the consequences of this malady, and accordingly we should have a proof that in Antiquity, no less than in modern times, primary ulcers not only preceded secondary affections of the skin, but were actually *recognized as such*. However as the proofs for this *aperçu* are still too fragmentary on the side of the ancient Physicians, we must suspend our immediate judgement on the point, and content ourselves for the present with saying, that φοινικίη νοῦσος stood orginally in the text in the sense of *cunnilingere* (to be a *cunnilingue*), whereas a later inquirer put φθινικὴ into its place, inasmuch as in his time their meanings had become identical as that of a bodily ailment, and so *the consequence* of the vice instead of the vice itself found its way even into the text. For granted φθινὰς has the meaning of *robigo* (blight), there is no doubt this only came to be the case as late as in the time of the Alexandrine critics. Besides this, φοινικιστὴς is also found in the *Etymologicum Magnum* for *Cunnilingus*; we read: γλωττοκομεῖον, ἐν ᾧ οἱ αὐληταὶ ἀπετίθεσαν τάς γλώττας· εἴρηται δὲ καὶ τὸ γυναικεῖον αἰδοῖον ὑπὸ Εὐβούλου φοινικιστὴν σκώπτοντος· (γλωττοκομεῖον, tongue-hole, place in which fluteplayers insert their tongues; *the female privates* also called so by Eubulus, making a scoff at the φοινικιστὴς, — *cunnilingue*). The *Etymologicum Magnum* further has as synonyms for *cunnilingere*: γλωττοστροφεῖν, περιλαλεῖν καὶ στωμύλλεσθαι· γλωττοδεψεῖν, αἰσχρουργεῖν (*to ply the tongue*: to talk excessively, to babble; *to work or soften with the tongue*: to do obscenely), and for *cunnilingus*, γλώσσαργον, στόμαργον (*tongue-busy*: mouth-busy).

Chrysostom, to read here also **θαυμαστωτάτων νοσημάτων** (of the most wonderful diseases) for **θανατωδεστάτων ν.,** and translate accordingly: "but **λεῦκαι** arise out of the most terrible aberrations of the mind," such for instance as the vice of the *cunnilingue* is. If we examine further, we shall see it is not **λευκαὶ** but **λεῦκαι** that stands in the text, so it cannot be a question of a skin-affection of the leprosy type at all, for **λευκὸς** (white) rather implies transparent and shiny, and *Martial* (XI. 99.) in a passage to be discussed more fully later on, says:

> Non ulcus acre, pustulaeve lucentes,
> Nec triste mentum, sordidique lichenes,

(No biting ulcer, or *shiny pustules*, nor yet disfigured chin, and foul scabs). Accordingly we have here nothing whatever to do with the leprous-like **λευκή,** but only with *pustulae lucentes* (shiny pustules), which as we shall show presently were a consequence of the practices of the *cunnilingue*. We have the more right to assume this, as the old Physicians ascribe **λευκὴ** to the **φλέγμα** (phlegmatic humour),—an explanation all the more likely to have been given, as directly afterwards follow the words, **αἱ δὲ λέπραι καὶ οἱ λειχῆνες ἐκ τῶν μελαγχολικῶν** (but leprosies and tetters arise out of the melancholic diseases). True this is in contradiction with another passage of Hippocrates, [1] for in this we read: **λέπρη καὶ κνησμὸς καὶ ψώρη καὶ λειχῆνες καὶ ἀλφὸς καὶ ἀλώπεκες ὑπὸ φλέγματος γίνονται.** (*leprosy*, and itch, and scab, and *tetters*, and dull-white leprosy, and manges, arise from *phlegm*). This much at any rate appears to us to result, viz. that the whole passage under discussion cannot possibly be by Hippocrates, but much more probably is due to some author of the

[1] *Hippocrates*, **περὶ παθῶν**, edit. Kühn Vol. II. p. 409. It is true this Work is reckoned among the spurious ones, and *Galen* (Vol. XI. p. 63.) ascribes it to *Polybius*.

Alexandrine age, who enjoyed ample opportunities for studying the consequences of the unnatural excesses as so often observed since Pompey the Great's time.

To assume that Hippocrates was actually acquainted with these in any completeness would up to the present be premature; at any rate we are bound, so far as our study of his writings enables us to judge, to deny him any knowledge of the fact that sexual excesses were the cause of the different affections of the genital organs chronicled by him. Of course he may have supposed all this to be notorious and the knowledge of it common property, but a host of statements would be found to tell against any such supposition. Opportunities of making acquaintance with the vice of the *cunnilingue* could certainly not have been lacking, it being so familiar a thing in his time that *Aristophanes* [1] again and again derided it in his Comedies. Whatever conclusion we come to on this head, at least the passage of Hippocrates cannot justify anyone in maintaining

[1] *Aristophanes*, Acharnians 271.:

Πολλῷ γὰρ ἔσθ' ἥδιον, ὦ Φαλῆς Φαλῆς
κλέπτουσαν εὑρόνθ' ὡρικὴν ὑληφόρον,
τὴν Στρυμοδώρου Θρᾷτταν ἐκ τοῦ Φελλέως,
μέσην λαβόντ' ἄραντα, καταβαλόντα καταγιγαρτίσαι·

(For 'tis much pleasanter, Phales, Phales! when you have found a blooming woodcutter girl filching wood, say Strymodorus' Thracian maid from Phelleus, to take her round the middle and lift her up and throw her down and take the kernel right away),—where perhaps we should read *Στυμοδώρου* for *Στρυμοδώρου*. Knights 1284.,

Τὴν γὰρ αὑτοῦ γλῶτταν αἰσχραῖς ἡδοναῖς λυμαίνεται,
ἐν κασαυρίοισι λείχων τὸν ἀπόπτυστον δρόσον,
καὶ μολύνων τὴν ὑπήνην, καὶ κυκῶν τὰς ἐσχάρας.

(For he pollutes his own tongue with foul delights, in the stews licking up the abominable dew, defiling the hair on the upper lip, and tumbling the girls' *nymphae*). Peace 885.,

Τὸν ζωμὸν αὐτῆς προσπεσὼν ἐκλάψεται.

(Falling upon her he will suck up *her broth*).

that the **φοινικίη νοῦσος**,—(Phœnician disease) was true Elephantiasis, even if, as may be, the preliminary proposition that elephantiasis was a *consequence* of debauchery be made good,—a point to which we propose later on to return. On the subject of Satyriasis in Crete, we have already expressed our views.

Just as the Phoenicians carried the seed of the vice to Greece and other lands, so at a later period was it disseminated from Syria to Italy; and so *Ausonius* says (Epigr. 128.):

Eunus Syriscus inguinum liguritor,
Opicus [1] magister (sic eum ducet Phyllis)
Muliebre membrum quadriangulum cernit:
Triquetro coactu *Δ* literam ducit.
De valle femorum altrinsecus pares rugas,
Mediumque, fissi rima qua patet, callem
ψ dicit esse: nam trifissilis forma est.
Cui ipse linguam quum dedit suam, *Λ* est:
Veramque in illis esse *Φ* notam sentit.
Quid imperite, *P* putas ibi scriptum
Ubi locari *I* convenit longum?
Miselle doctor, *Ȣ* tibi sit obscoeno,
Tuumque nomen *Θ* sectilis signet.

(Eunus from Syria, glutton of the privy parts, Opican (clownish) master (Phyllis teaches him his letters) sees the woman's organ four-cornered: when compressed to a triangle he makes it out the letter *Δ*. From the valley between the thighs start two furrows, a pair one on either side, while between them is a line, where lies the opening, the crack of the fissure; this he declares is ψ; for 'tis three-pronged in outline. Then when he puts in his own tongue to it, lo! it is *Λ*; and he can feel there is a true *Φ* marked therein. What, dunce, think you a ***P*** is

[1] *Juvenal*, Satir. VI. 455.:

Nec curanda viris Opicae castigat amicae
Verba Soloecismum liceat fecisse marito.

(And rebukes the expressions of her clownish (Opican) friend, things not worth men's notice. Surely a husband should be allowed to make a solecism).

inscribed there, where a long *I* should by rights be placed? Miserable, contemptible scholar, may the 8 (a noose) reward your foulness, and the cleft Θ (letter of condemnation, being initial of **θάνατος**,—death) be set against your name!) The more detailed interpretation of these obscene hieroglyphics the reader may find in the commentators on the passage, as well as in *Forberg*, loco citato p. 335.

Diseases of the Cunnilingue.

§ 24.

Can anyone believe such a vice as this was practised without incurring punishment? Yet there prevails amongst the Physicians of Antiquity, even including Galen, who knew the facts, an unbroken silence. It is impossible to suppose that girls and women could have their genital organs purged in this mode altogether without evil results, more particularly as actual experience in more modern times has proved that as a consequence of the habit of *cunnilingere* inflammations of the external genitals have been set up in girls, as well as ulcerations in older women through the licking of these parts by dogs. Among Ancient writers we have found no vouchers for this; but on the other hand several such exist to show the mischief that results from the habit to the *cunnilingue* himself. Excluding from consideration the *pale complexion* [1]

[1] *Martial*, bk. I. Epigr. 78.,

Pulchre valet Charinus, et tamen pallet.
Parce bibit Charinus, et tamen pallet.
Bene concoquit Charinus, et tamen pallet.
Sole utitur Charinus, et tamen pallet.
Tingit cutem Charinus, et tamen pallet.
Cunnum Charinus lingit et tamen pallet.

(Charinus is in excellent health, and yet he is pale. Charinus drinks moderately, and yet he is pale. Charinus digests well, yet he is pale. Charinus takes the sun, yet he is pale. Charinus dyes his skin, yet he is pale. *Charinus licks a woman's organ, yet he is pale*).

and evil *smell from the mouth*, which were equally consequences of the other forms of vice already mentioned, we have *paralysis of the tongue* mentioned, at any rate in one passage [1]:

> Sidere percussa est subito tibi, Zoile, lingua,
> Dum lingis. Certe, Zoile, nunc futuis.

(Your tongue, Zoilus, has been stricken with a sudden doom, while in the act of licking. Why! surely, Zoilus, you copulate now). True this malady must be counted as one of very rare occurrence; but this is by no means the case with the ulcerations, which would seem not always to have confined their attacks to the tongue, but to have extended also, just as with the *fellator*, to the other parts of the mouth as well. This cannot but have had the effect of making it very difficult in diagnosis to distinguish between an affection of the sort due to *fellation* and one due to the vice of the *cunnilingue*.

Here again it is *Martial* to whom we are indebted for the proofs of our assertions. He leaves no room for doubt as to the way Manneius was punished for his debauchery in the following passage [2]:

> Lingua maritus, moechus ore Manneius,
> Summoenianis inquinatior buccis:
> Quem cum fenestra vidit a Suburrana
> Obscoena nudum lena, fornicem claudit,
> Mediumque mavult basiare, quam summum:
> Modo qui per omnes viscerum tubos ibat,
> Et voce certa consciaque dicebat:
> Puer, an puella matris esset in ventre;
> (Gaudete cunni, vestra namque res acta est!)
> Arrigere linguam non potest fututricem
> Nam, dum tumenti mersus haeret in vulva [3]

[1] *Martial*, bk. XI. Epigr. 86. As to this Zoilus see *Martial*, bk. XI. Epigr. 61.

[2] *Martial*, Bk.III.Epigr.61.

[3] *Greek Anthology* bk. II. Tit. 13. Note 19.,

> Τὴν φωνὴν ἐνοπήν σε λέγειν ἐδίδαξεν Ὅμηρος,
> Τὴν γλῶσσαν δ' ἐν ὀπῇ τίς σ' ἐδίδαξεν ἔχειν.

(Homer taught you to utter your voice and speak whole

Et vagientes intus audit infantes,
Partem gulosam solvit indecens morbus;
Nec purus esse nunc potest, nec impurus.

(*Manneius was a husband with his tongue, a fornicator with his mouth, a more polluted wretch than the big-cheeked wenches of the suburbs.* When a vile bawd saw him naked from a window in the Suburra, she shuts her brothel up, and had rather kiss his middle than his head. The man who but now could *penetrate every vessel of the inwards,* and say with assured voice and certain knowledge whether it were a boy or a girl in the mother's belly,—rejoice, rejoice, organs of women, for your business is done for you,—the same *cannot erect a fornicating tongue.* For at the very moment *he is plunged tight in the swollen vulva,* and hears the babes whimpering within, lo! *a shocking disease paralyses his greedy tongue. Now can he be neither clean, nor yet unclean*).

The Commentators, in particular *Farnabius,* refer the complaint spoken of in the passage just quoted to paralysis of the tongue. Farnabius says in fact: "Paralysisne **ἀπὸ τῆς ἀφέδρου καὶ τῶν ἐμμηνιῶν,** "quorum malefico humore marcescunt segetes, apes "moriuntur etc., Plin. c. 15 Lib. V., an sideratio?" (Is paralysis intended, *resulting from the menstruation and menstrual* discharges, the poisonous humour of which will wither up crops, kill bees, etc.—Pliny ch. 15. Bk. V., or a sudden stroke?) Even supposing us willing to admit the possibility of menstrual blood bringing on paralysis of the tongue, there can at any rate be no question of such a thing here, inasmuch as it was with a pregnant woman Manneius carried out his vicious practises, and women in pregnancy do not *usually* menstruate,—a fact about which the Philologist naturally enough was only imperfectly posted. Of course the possibility is always there,

words, but, pray! who taught you to have your tongue in a hole?) Here ὀπὴ (hole) obviously stands for the female organ,—a meaning omitted in the Lexicons.

although the Poet says nothing about it; and the expression *vulva tumens* (swollen organ) evidently stands here, as is clearly shown by what follows, for *uterus gravidus* (pregnant womb) [1]. The *solvere* (to loose, destroy) points in any case to a destruction, a dwindling, of the part, brought about by the *indecens morbus* (shocking disease),—which disease might very likely find its explanation in the *scelerata lues* (noxious contagion) mentioned on page 258 above. As a result of this, naturally enough not only did *arrigere* (to erect—the tongue) become impossible, but the *impurus (Cunnilingus)* (unclean cunnilingue) grew generally incapable of practising his vice. Nor yet was he *purus* (clean) [2] altogether, for was he not a *cunnilingue?*—and now he was even less *purus*, because he suffered from the *indecens morbus* (shocking disease), which even Farnabius has so far rightly understood, that he explains *nec purus* (nor yet clean) by *morbo illo contaminatus* (because contaminated by the said disease).

Rather more doubtful and difficult is the interpretation of the following passage of *Martial* [3], which would yet appear to be pertinent here:

[1] So too in the following Epigram of *Ausonius* (127.),

Eune, quod uxoris gravidae putria inguina lambis,
Festinas glossas non natis tradere natis.

(Eunus, you lick the flabby organs of your pregnant wife; is it you are in a hurry to give learned explanations to your babes unborn?) we should explain the *putria inguina* not so much as *rotten, ulcerous*, but rather as *laxata* or *laxa* (relaxed, flabby). Similarly *Horace*, Epod. VIII. 7., speaks of *mammae putres* (the flabby dugs) of an old woman.

[2] *Martial*, IX. 63.,

Ad coenam invitant omnes te, Phoebe, cinaedi:
Mentula quem pascit, non, puto, purus homo est.

(All the *cinaedi*, Phoebus, invite you to dinner: a man the penis feeds is not, I think, a *clean* man).

Petronius, Sat., Non taces, nocturne percussor, qui ne tum quidem, quum fortiter faceres, cum *pura muliere* pugnasti. (Silence, stabber by night, who not even when you were at your best, ever faced *a clean woman*).

[3] *Martial*, Bk. IV. Epigr. 43.

Non dixi, Coracine, te cinaedum;
Non sum tam temerarius, nec audax,
Nec mendacia qui loquar libenter.
Si dixi, Coracine, te cinaedum,
Iratam mihi Pontiae lagenam,
Iratum calicem mihi Metili.
I u r o p e r S y r i o s t i b i t u m o r e s,
I u r o p e r B e r e c y n t h i o s f u r o r e s.
Quod dixi tamen, hoc leve et pusillum est.
Quod notum est, quod et ipse non negabis:
D i x i t e, Coracine, c u n n i l i n g u m.

(I never called you a *cinaedus*, Coracinus; I am not so rash or so reckless, not being one to speak lies willingly. If I called you a *cinaedus*, Coracinus, may Pontia's jar be my enemy, and Metilius' poisoned cup. *I take oath by your Syrian tumours, by your Berecynthian frenzies.* What I *did* say is a trivial, an insignificant thing, a thing well known, that you will not yourself deny,—*I said*, Coracinus. *you were a cunnilingue*).

What were these *Syrii tumores* (Syrian tumours) that afflicted the *cunnilingue* Coracinus? *Beroaldus*, Annotat. ch. 25., understands them as "tumores et "vibices a cultris et flagris quibus sacerdotes Cybeles "(quam deam Syriam esse volunt) se sauciabant." (the swellings and weals from the knives and scourges with which the priests of Cybelé,—whom they claim to be the Syrian goddess—used to wound themselves). *Farnabius* on the contrary thinks only *Berecynthios furores* (Berecynthian frenzies) to be intended in this explanation, and makes the *tumores Syrii* mean "*ulcera et morbos quibus credebatur irata Isis inflare peierantes*," (ulcers and maladies with which the angry Isis was supposed to afflict false swearers), appealing to the passage of Persius [1], already brought forward a few pages back (p. 254.), which reads:

Hinc grandes Galli et cum sistro lusca sacerdos,
I n c u s s e r e D e o s i n f l a n t e s c o r p o r a, si non
Praedictum ter mane caput gustaveris alli.

[1] *Persius*, Satir. V. 186—188.

(Then the tall Galli, and the one-eyed priestess with her sacred rattle, instil terror of *the gods that make men's bodies swell*, unless three times at dawn you have eaten the prescribed head of garlic).

Whether this passage affords any direct proof would seem doubtful, inasmuch as the *inflare corpus* (to make the body swell) properly speaking only refers to the abdomen. To this also the eating of the allium (garlic), which no doubt first won its magic significance on account of its carminative properties, appears to point.

However another explanation is possible. Referring back to the passage of *Porphyrius* quoted above on p. 254., the *tumores* Coracinus had contracted in consequence of his general incontinence with women, which incontinence had at last brought him as a *senex?* (old man) to such a condition of weakness that nothing was left him but the vice of *cunnilingere* to satisfy his still unexhausted lubricity. A side light in this case may be thrown on the matter by Horace's description of the *Anus libidinosa* (The lecherous old woman) in Epodes VIII. 9. 19.:

Venter mollis et femur tumentibus
Exile suris additum. — Fascinum
Quod ut superbo provoces ab inguine
Ore allaborandum est tibi.

(Flabby belly and skinny thigh joined with swollen calves,—A tool, that requires you, in order to call it up from the supercilious groin, to work it with the mouth). *Casaubon* in his commentary on the passage of *Persius* is for connecting this, as well as the *Tumores Syrii*, with **ἕλκεα Συριακά** (Syrian sores), and—as quoted on p. 253 above—to regard them as a consequence of the wrath of the *Dea Syria* (Syrian goddess). No doubt as a matter of fact the *tumores* were a result of debauchery, one that was prevalent in Syria and was disseminated thence to Rome, for they attacked a *cunnilingue* no less than other debauchees; but this brings us no nearer to a knowledge of their nature. We should perhaps be inclined to regard them as swellings of the tonsils or of the lympathic glands of the throat. having the same significance as the inguinal buboes in affections of the genitals.

But what are the *Berecynthii furores* (Berecynthian frenzies)? Possibly nocturnal pains in the bones, that torment a patient to the pitch of frenzy? The mataphor, drawn from the nocturnal rites of Cybelė, must be admitted to be a happy one. Still, however acceptable conjectures of the sort may be to many, we cannot take them seriously. It appears to us most judicious to regard the *Syrii tumores* as being ulcerations that covered the body of Coracinus, and by their violent itching reduced him to a state of frenzy. Our view as stated is confirmed by Epigram 108. of *Ausonius:*

IN SCABIOSUM POLYGITONEM.

Thermarum in solio si quis Polygitona vidit
Ulcera membrorum scabie putrefacta foventem,
Praeposuit cunctis spectacula talia ludis.
Principio tremulis gannitibus aëra pulsat,
Verbaque lascivos meretricum imitantia coetus
Vibrat et obscoenae numeros pruriginis implet.
Brachia deinde rotat velut enthea daemone Maenas,
Pectus, crura, latus, ventrem. femora, inguina, suras,
Tergum, colla, humeros luteae Symplegadis antrum.
Tam diversa locis vaga carnificina pererrat,
Donec marcentem calidi fervore lavacri
Blandus letali solvat dulcedine morbus.
Desectos sic fama viros, ubi cassa libido
Femineos coetus et non sua bella lacessit,
Irrita vexato consumere gaudia lecto:
Titillata brevi quum iam sub fine voluptas
Fervet et ingesto peragit ludibria morsu.
Turpia non aliter Polygiton membra resolvit,
Et quia debentur suprema piacula vitae,
Ad Phlegethonteas sese iam praeparat undas.

(*To the scabby Polygiton.*—If any man caught sight of Polygiton on the seat of the Thermae bathing the sores on his limbs all rotten with scab, he preferred so entertaining a spectacle to all the games. First he beats the air with twittering, whining noises, and utters broken sounds in imitation of the wanton embraces of harlots, and completes the symphony of his foul-minded lechery. *Then he twirls his arms about like a Maenad under the god's afflatus;* breast, legs, flank, belly, thighs, *groin*, *calves*, back, neck, shoulders, cave of the bemired Symplegades,—i.e. hollow between buttocks,—in so many different places does the shooting torture fly, until he droops and faints in the warmth of the hot bath and the disease is soothed and gives a fatal respite. So it is said castrated eunuchs, when barren desire tries hard for embraces with women and for contests they cannot properly engage in, are consumed with empty transports on the tossed and tumbled bed,—till eventually their lust, tickled and tickled, flames high for a last moment, and completes the wanton act by applying the mouth and biting. So with Polygiton a final spasm relaxes his disfigured limbs, and the last sin-offerings of his life being due, thus makes himself ready for the waves of Phlegethon).

True the connexion with the vice of *cunnilingere* is apparently lost here, but this also may be preserved without any great straining of the words, as we shall see presently; and accordingly the *Tumores Syrii* can be quite well regarded as a consequence of the vice of the *cunnilingus*.

Mentagra (Tetter of the Chin).

§ 25.

Ever since the so-called first appearance of Venereal Disease, most of the advocates of the antiquity of the complaint have made a point of bringing in

Mentagra [1] within the purview of the quotations they adduce to prove their contention, although strictly speaking they were never likely to succeed in a direct demonstration that the disease was really and truly connected with sexual excesses. Accordingly, to the present day the majority of them see in it nothing more than a form of Leprosy, particularly as *Hensler* [2] and *Sprengel* were among those who decided in favour of its leprous character. Instead of giving a useless list of names of the different authors, who in former days declared for the one view or the other, we think it more expedient to quote first of all the capital authority, a passage in Pliny [3], setting this down as it stands so as to be able afterwards to form a correct appreciation of its bearing:

Cap. I. "Sensit et facies hominum novos omnique aevo priore incognitos, non Italiae modo, "verum etiam universae prope Europae morbos: "tunc quoque non tota Italia, nec per Illyricum

[1] *Wendelinus Hock de Brackenau* entitled his Treatise on the Venereal Disease: *Mentagra*, sive Tractatus de causis, praeseruatis, regimine et cura Morbi Gallici, vulgo Mala Francosz., etc., (Mentagra, or a Treatise on the Causes, Preventives, Treatment and Cure of the so called French Disease, etc.). Strasburg 1514. 4to. *Sartorius* Frid. praes. *Conrad. Johrenio*, Diss. de mentagra ad loc. Plinii Secundi hist. nat. lib. XXVI. cap. 1. (Dissertation on mentagra in connexion with the passage of Pliny Secundus' Hist. Naturalis bk. XXVI. ch. 1.). Frankfurt-on-Oder N. D. 49 pp. 4to. Gives a sort of exegesis of the passage, speaks in first place of new diseases in general, passes on to the Venereal Disease, the antiquity of which the author upholds, and finally discusses Mentagra, which he holds to be a leprous-syphilitic affection. The work is still quite worth reading, more especially as the author quotes some passages from the Chronicle of *Anhalt von Beckmann*, at that time still unprinted, and which we find mentioned hardly anywhere else.

[2] *Hensler*, „Vom abendländischen Aussatze im Mittelalter", (On Occidental Leprosy in the Middle Ages). Hamburg 1790. pp. 67, 206, 307.

[3] *Pliny*, Hist. Nat. Bk. XXVI. chs. 1, 2, 3.

"Galliasve aut Hispanias magnopere vagatos, aut "alibi, quam Romae circaque: sine dolore quidem "illos ac sine pernicie vitae: sed tanta foeditate, ut "quaecunque mors praeferenda esset.

Cap. II. "Gravissimum ex his lichenas appel- "lavere Graeco nomine: Latine, quoniam a "mento fere oriebatur, ioculari primum lasci- "via, (ut est procax natura multorum in alienis "miseriis) mox et usurpato vocabulo, mentagram: "occupantem in multis totos utique vultus, oculis "tantum immunibus, descendentem [1] vero et in colla "pectusque ac manus, foedo cutis furfure [2].

[1] *Galen*, De ccmp. med. secundum locos, edit. Kühn Vol. XII. p. 841. *προσχαριζόμενον τῇ ἐξωτάτῳ γραμμῇ τοῦ λειχῆνος μικρόν τι τῶν ἀπαθῶν σωμάτων.* (giving up to the external mark of the scab yet another small part of the bodies hitherto unaffected).

[2] *Galen*, (De comp. med. secundum locos bk. V., edit. Kühn Vol. XII. p. 830.) quotes from Criton the following description in further confirmation: *Πρός δὲ τοὺς ἐπὶ τῶν γενείων λειχῆνας πάθος ἀηδέστατον, καὶ γὰρ κνησμοὺς ἐπιφέρει καὶ περίστασιν τῶν πεπονθότων καὶ κίνδυνον οὐκ ὀλίγον, ἕρπει γὰρ ἔστιν ὅτε καθ' ὅλου τοῦ προσώπου, καὶ ὀφθαλμῶν ἅπτεται, καὶ σχεδὸν τῆς ἀνωτάτω δυσμορφίας ἐστὶν αἴτιον, καὶ διὰ τοῦτο χρηστέον ἂν εἴη ἐπιμελέστερον τῇ θεραπείᾳ, ἐφορῶντα τοὺς παροξυσμοὺς καὶ τὰ διαλείμματα καὶ συγκρίνοντα ἀπὸ τῶν κεχρονισμένων τὰ νεοσύστατα, ἐφ' ὧν ἁρμόσει χρῆσθαι τοῖς ξηραίνουσι φαρμάκοις· ὅταν δ' εἰς ψώραν ἢ λέπραν μεταπέσῃ πρὸς τοῖς ξηραίνουσι χρῆσθαι καὶ τοῖς ῥύπουσιν.* (But in the case of *lichenes*, scabs, on the chin the malady is most troublesome. Now it brings on itchings and a critical condition of the afflicted and no small danger; for it creeps sometimns over the whole face, *and attacks the eyes*, and generally is productive of the *most utter disfigurement.* Wherefore physicians should devote more than ordinary care to its treatment, watching *the crises of the malady*, *and the intervals, and judging from the symbtoms that have become chronic such as have but just broken out*, on the appearance of which it will be expedient to exhibit siccatlve medicines. On the other

Cap. III. "Non fuerat haec lues apud maiores "patresque nostros. Et primum Tiberii Claudi, "Caesaris principatu medio irrepsit in Italiam, "quodam Perusino equite Romano Quaestorio scriba, "quum in Asia apparuisset inde contagionem eius "importante. Nec sensere id malum feminae aut "servitia, plebesque humilis, aut media: sed proceres "veloci transitu osculi maxime: foediore multorum "qui perpeti medicinam toleraverant, citatrice, quam "morbo. Causticis [1] namque curabatur, ni usque in "ossa corpus exustum esset, rebellante taedio. Ad-"venerunt ex Aegypto, genitrice talium viti-"orum, medici, hanc solam operam afferentes, "magna sua praeda. Siquidem certum est, Manilium "Cornutum, e Praetoriis legatum Aquitanicae provin-"ciae, H.S. CC. elocasse in eo morbo curandum "sese."

(Ch. I. Moreover the human *face* experienced new diseases, and such as had been unknown in any former age not merely to Italy but to the whole of Europe very nearly, and these not widely diffused over Italy generally, or through Illyricum or the provinces of Gaul or of Spain, or indeed anywhere else but just in Rome and its neighbourhood. They were painless, it is true, and did not involve loss of life, but were of such a horrible nature that death in any form would have been preferable.

Ch. II. The most serious of these diseases they called *lichenes*,—scabs, a Greek name; in Latin, as the malady generally showed itself first on the chin, it was known as *mentagra*,—chin-bane, scab or tetter

hand when *it has resolved itself into the itch or leprosy*, exhibit cathartics in combination with the siccatives). The same is contributed also by *Aëtius*, Tetrab. II. serm. 4. ch. 16. Besides the discrepant statement to the effect that the eyes are attacked as well, the most noteworthy points are the crises and intervals Mentagra went through, and its passing over into Psora and Lepra (Itch and Leprosy).

[1] *Galen* and *Aëtius*, loco citato, give particulars of the composition of a number of these.

of the chin, at the first by may of jest and mockery—for it is the nature of the multitude to make merry at others' misfortunes,—but soon this became the recognized word. In many persons it covered absolutely the whole countenance, the eyes alone being left unaffected, with a horrible scurf of the skin, going down sometimes to the neck as well, and breast, and hands.

Ch. III. *This plague* had not existed among our ancestors or fathers. For the first time it crept into Italy in the middle of the reign of *Tiberius Claudius Caesar,* a certain Perusinius, a Roman knight and Quaestorian secretary, after a period of service in Asia, importing the contagion from there. But women did not suffer from the malady, or slaves, nor yet common folk of humble or middle-class station; but nobles, and this particularly by the rapid infection of an embrace. In many cases the scar, where patients had submitted to medical treatment, was more horrible than the disease itself. For indeed it was curable by caustics, except when the body had been consumed to the very bones, the slowness of the treatment defeating its own end. Physicians arrived from Egypt, *mother-land of such taints*, practising this cure exclusively, to their own great profit. If, that is, it is true that Manilius Cornutus, of the Praetorians and governor of the Province of Aquitania, offered 200,000 sesterces for his cure when attacked by this disease).

Here if ever, it particularly behoves us to begin with an elucidation of the meaning of the name given to the malady under discussion. *Gruner* [1] long ago called attention to the divergence of opinion as to the signification of **λειχῆνες** (scabs) among the writers of Antiquity, but without success in putting the actual facts in a clear light. We must try if we can be more fortunate. An old etymologist says: **λειχὴν παρὰ τὸ λείχω, καὶ γὰρ φάσιν ἐκ τοῦ**

[1] *Gruner*, Morborum antiquitates pp. 162—171.

λείχειν τὸ πάθος ἐπάιρεται [1], (**λειχὴν** comes from **λείχω,**—I lick, becanse they say the complaint is set up by licking). On this we may say.—there is no doubt **λειχῆνες** and **λιχῆνες** are derived from **λείχειν** or **λίχειν,** but the explanation *Kraus* gives of the reason in his Lexicon we cannot think conceivable, viz. "because Lichen, the same as a parasitic plant does, or a skin-disease in animals, always creeps round further and further (see *Herpes,*—creeping eruption), or *as it were licks its way*," for **λείχειν** is not so much *lambere,* **λάπτειν,**—to lick over, lick along, as *lingere, ligurire* [2],—to lick up, lick up greedily. At the same time it is true the word (*lambere*) was used by the Romans in a somewhat similar sense, so perhaps we ought not to refer to *lambit flamma* (a flame licks), but rather to Plautus' expression (*Pers. prolog. 5.*), "*quorum imagines lambunt hederae sequaces*" (whose images creeping ivy-tendrils lick, i.e. entwine). Most probably there are two different stems underlying the word. Of these one is **λέγειν,** —to lay, etc., hence **λέγνη,** the edging, the border, **λίγνυς,** soot (depositing itself on the edge), together with the bye-forms **λέχω, λίχω,** with which in fact **λιχὴν,** *moss* [3], so far as it forms on the edge, the surface, fringes it, would be connected. The other stem will be **λίγω,** or **λείγω** (comp. **λίβω** and **λείβω**), **λείχω** and **λειχην. λίγγω, λίζω,** to which would have to be referred also **λίγυς** and **λιγυρὸς,**—clear, shrill (ligurire, lingere,—to lick greedily, to lick), in

[1] *J. C. Dieterich*, Iatreum Hippocraticum, continens Narthecium medicinae veteris et novae (Hippocratic Remedies, containing a Treasury of Ancient and Modern Medicine), Ulm 1661. 4to., p. 692.

[2] Hence also *Diogenes Laertius*, VI. 2. 6., ἅλα λείχειν (to lick up salt).

[3] The explanation of *Galen*, De simpl. medicam. temperam. et facult. bk. VII. ch. 11. 6. (edit. Kühn, XII. p. 57.): λειχὴν ὠνομάσθαι δ' οὔπω δοκεῖ διὰ τὸ λειχῆνας θεραπεύειν (and it seems lichen,—moss, is so called because it cures lichenes,—scabs), is hardly likely to find any one else to subscribe to it.

all of which the underlying sense is of licking, and the noise connected with it.

It is plain that later on the derivatives of these stems suffered manifold variations and corruptions; but how much of all this is to be attributed to speakers and writers among the Greeks themselves, and how much to subsequent transcribers and editors of their work, it might be difficult to decide. But every day we have occasion to note a number of words, to which accident or other circumstances have given an ambiguous character. These, used quite unsuspectingly by the ignorant, make the better informed person blush, or else extort a smile from him that often enough causes the speaker no little embarrassment to know the reason. Undoubtedly it was the same with the Greeks and Romans, and so confusions between **λίχω** and **λείχω, λιχὴν** and **λειχὴν,** might have easily arisen, from which people were subsequently unable to extricate themselves. Originally perhaps **λείχω,** equally with *lingo* and *ligurio* (to lick), may have had the simple sense of licking, and only through later accretions to the meaning, have acquired an ambiguous character; soon however this got transferred to it to the exclusion of all others, and we find it used preferentially as the regular word for *cunnilingere.* The correctness of our conclusion would seem to follow above all from the passage of *Aristophanes* [1] given

[1] *Aristophanes,* Knights 1280—1283. In the Wasps, 1280—1283, *Aristophanes* says, speaking of the same Ariphrades:

Εἶτ' Ἀριφράδην πολύ τι θυμοσοφικώτατον,
ὃν τινά ποτ' ὤμοσε μαθόντα παρὰ μηδενὸς,
ἀλλ' ἀπὸ σοφῆς φύσεος αὐτόματον ἐκμαθεῖν
γλωττοποιεῖν εἰς τὰ πορνεῖ' εἰσιόνθ' ἑκάστοτε

(Then Ariphrades, much more ingenious-clever, who he swore without ever having learnt the trick from any, but all out of his own wisdom, discovered how to work the tongue, going into the brothels everywhere).

below, where it is the additional words that narrow down the meaning of **λείχω** (I lick), and definitely bring out the special signification. The words are said of Ariphrades, who reminds us of the ***ἀποφρὰς*** (unmentionable), the name Lucian appropriates to Timarchus:

Οὐδὲ παμπόνηρος, ἀλλὰ καὶ προσεξεύρηκέ τι·
τὴν γὰρ αὐτοῦ γλῶτταν αἰσχραῖς ἡδοναῖς μαίνεται,
ἐν κασαυρίοισι λείχων τὴν ἀπόπτυστον δρόσον,
καὶ μολύνων τὴν ὑπήνην, καὶ κυκῶν τὰς ἐσχάρας.

(Nor yet utterly villainous is he, but he has discovered yet another device; for he polluted his own tongue with foul delights, *in the stews licking up the abominable dew*, defiling the hair on the upper lip, and tumbling the girls' *nymphae*).

In the following Epigram [2] of an unknown author

Also Peace 883—885.:

TP. τίς; *OIK.* ὅστις; Ἀριφράδης,
ἄγειν παρ' αὐτὸν ἀντιβολῶν. *TP.* Ἀλλ', ὦ μέλε,
τὸν ζωμὸν αὐτῆς προσπεσὼν ἐκλάψεται.

(*Trygaeus.* Who? *Servant.* Who; why Ariphrades, begging to bring her to him *Trygaeus* But, dear man, he will fall on her, and lick up her broth).

[2] *Anthologia Graeca*, cum versione Latina *Hugonis Grotii*, edita ab H. de Bosch (*Greek Anthology*, with Latin version by *Hugo Grotius*, edit. H. de Bosch) Utrecht 1795. 4to., Vol. I. p. 38. bk. II. Tit. 5. Epigr. 9. *Brunck's* Analecta, Vol. III. p. 165. Epigr. 76. Here too should be quoted the following Epigram (*Brunck's* Analecta, Vol. II. p. 386. Anthology, bk. II. Tit. 5. Epgir. 8.) of *Ammianus*, which at the same time speaks for the general meaning of *licking:*

Οὐχ ὅτι τὸν κάλαμον λείχεις, διὰ τοῦτό σε μισῶ,
Ἀλλ' ὅτι τοῦτο ποιεῖς καὶ δίχα τοῦ καλάμου.

(Not because you lick the *reed*, not for this do I abominate you; but because you do so even without the reed). *Ausonius*, Epigr. 126., endeavours in another way, by initial letters, to indicate λείχει (he licks):

λείχω is found used absolutely, without any supplementary words:

> *Λαΐς*, "*Ερως*, et "*Ιτυς*, *Χείρων* et "*Ερως*, "*Ιτυς* alter
> Nomina si scribis, prima elementa adime:
> Ut facias verbum, quod tu facis, Eune magister:
> Dicere me Latium non decet opprobrium.

(*Λαΐς*, "*Ερως*, and "*Ιτυς*, *Χείρων* and "*Ερως*, "*Ιτυς* repeated,—if you write these names, then take off the first letters, you make a verb with them that means what you do, learned Eunus; it does not become me to name the abomination in Latian speech). At the same time we see from this that in the IVth. Century, where *Ausonius* lived at Bordeaux, the vice of the *cunnilingue* was still constantly practised and that not even in secret. Should the words of *Clement of Alexandria*, Paedagog. II. ch. 8. p. 178., also be brought into connection with this: *ἡ δὲ ἐπιτήδευσις τῆς εὐωδίας, δελεάρ ἐστι ῥαθυμίας, πόῤῥωθεν εἰς λίχνον ἐπιθυμίον ἐπισπωμένης*. (And the cultivation of sweet perfume is a bait of idleness, indirectly alluring to dainty voluptuousness)? The *male olere* (to have an evil smell) held good equally for the *cunnilingue*.

Diogenes Laertius, V. 65., quotes verses of *Crates*, where we read: *οὔτε λίχνος, πόρνης ἐπαγγελλόμενος παρῇσι* (nor dainty desire, proclaimed on the cheeks of a harlot); the same occur also in *Clement of Alexandria*, loco citato ch. 10. Finally yet another quotation, from *Martial* (XI. 59.), should come in here; he says to a pathic:

> At tibi nil faciam: sed lota mentula laeva
> *λειχάζειν* cupidae dicet avaritiae,

(But to *you* I will do no harm; nay! rather shall my member, when your left hand has done its work and been washed, say to your grasping avarice,—now lick, fellate, me). This passage has been misunderstood by most of the commentators, because they chose to read *lana* (woollen cloth) for *laeva* (the left hand), or else thought to find here a reference to manustupration (masturbation with the hand). But really it means nothing more than that the poet declares he will resort to *irrumation*, after his mentula (member) has been washed with the left hand, [the Latin cannot mean this; *lotā* is ablative case, and must be taken with *laevā*. *Transl.*], —a usage to which we shall come back again subsequently; but which is at once clearly authenticated by a fragment of *Lucilius*, where we read:

> Laeva lacrimas mutoni absterget amica.

(With the left hand his mistress wipes the tears from his penis).

Χεἰλων καὶ λειχων ἴσα γράμματα· ἐς τἰ δὲ τοῦτο;
Λείχει καὶ Χείλων, κἂν ἴσα, κἂν ἄνισα.

(**Χείλων,**—a proper name, also means *of the lips,*—and **λείχων,**—licking,—have the like letters; now what does this point to? Chilon licks lips, whether lips like his own, or whether unlike). In explanation of this Epigram *Forbiger* says (loco citato p. 326.): "Lusus in Chilonem cunnilingum. Hunc ait iure "quodam suo lingere, qui vel nomine iisdem literis "constante prae se fert lingentem et lingentem qui-"dem tum labra oris, ut labris ligentis simìlia, tum "cunni, ut dissimilia." (Pun on the name of Chilon, a *cunnilingue.* The poet says he (Chilon) licks by a sort of inherent right of his own, who even in his name, made up of the same letters, proclaims himself as licking, and licking now the lips of the mouth, which are like the lips of the licker, now those of the female organ, which are unlike). **Χεῖλος** was in fact used also of the lips of a woman's organ, the *nymphae;* the Scholiast on **τὰς ἐσχάρας** (the *nymphae*) in the passage from Aristophanes given a little above, interprets this word by **τὰ χείλη τῶν γυναικείων αἰδοίων** (the lips of the female privates). According to *Schneider* in his Lexicon **χείλων** (adj.) signifies *thick-lipped.* Perhaps it was this very Epigram that led *Lambert Bosius* to make the statement that **χείλων** arose by a mere transposition of the letters from **λείχον.**

Now if **λειχήν,**—for we consider it should be thus accented,—is derived from **λείχω** (I lick), we cannot but regard it as meaning: something *produced by licking, a complaint brought on by licking,* and particularly *by the licking of the cunnilingue!* Surely the Greeks could hardly have expressed themselves more clearly. Then the fact that the name came from the mouth of the common people is the very best reason for its not having been understood by the educated. Yet all the while an entirely similar form of expression has grown up in the mouth of the German common geople, the real meaning of which very few have fathomed, but which most certainly arose in the same way as the Greek λείχην. No doubt many of my readers have again and again heard it said of some one with an eruption round the mouth, that is, someone suffering from *Herpes labialis* (Creeping eruption of the lips): "Well! you *have* been licking!"—for which educated people substitute the obviously insufficient, "You *have* been picking!" Very commonly again one may hear: "You *have* been licking *greben*, or picking *greben*; and this word *greben* is understood as being identical with *grieben,—greaves* in English, i.e. the remnants of lard that has been cut up into pieces and fried, because the separate pustules of the *herpes labialis* resemble in appearance the *greaves*. So people sometimes also say still more explicitly, "You *have* been licking, or picking, *greaves;* and one of them has been left sticking to your mouth, to prove your greediness!"

This explanation may seem a very likely one to many; nevertheless we incline to believe the word to be of later origin, and to have arisen from ignorance of the actual facts. We consider it more probable that *greben* owes its origin to some corruption of language growing out of *gremium*, the bosom. We have been led to this conjecture by a statement of *Adelung's* in his Dictionary, Article "Grieben", where he says: "In middle-Latin *grieben*, (greaves), were called, in accordance with a common interchange of the letters b. and m. *gremium*",—though indeed we cannot regard the word as solely and entirely mediæval Latin, for it is found occurring as early as *Pliny* (Hist. Nat. XII. 19.) and *Columella* (Res Rust. XII. 19. 3.), and is evidently connected with *cremare* (to burn). So just as in this case *cremium* and *gremium* may have been used interchangeably, has *grebe* grown out of *greme* in German, and the latter come to be used as a synonym of *griebe*,—the latter words according to this having as little in common with one another as the former. However those better practised in the science of word formation must here decide!

Now as to the word *Mentagra* (Tetter, Scab). This was evidently a word first framed by the Romans, as is distinctly stated not alone by *Pliny*, but by *Galen* as well (De compos. medic. secundum locos Bk. V., edit. Kühn Vol. XII. p. 839.). The latter says: **'Εκδόριον λειχήνων· ταύτῃ Πάμφιλος χρησάμενος ἐπὶ 'Ρώμης πλεῖστον ἐπορίσατο ἐπικρατούσης ἐν τῇ πόλει τῆς μεντάγρας λεγομένης.** (Blister for Lichenes (Scabs); in this way Pamphilus in his practise at Rome made most headway against *the Mentagra as it was called, then prevalent in the city*). It is usually considered to be formed on the analogy of *Podagra*, *Chiragra* (gout of the feet, gout of the hands) etc. from *mentum*, the chin, and **ἄγρα,** the act of catching, seizing hold of,—so a disease that attacks the chin. But more probably all these words are compounded not with **ἄγρα** at all, but with **ἄλγος** (suffering). That it to say just as **ἀλγαλέος,** by Attic interchange of letters, becomes **ἀργαλέος** (grievous), **κεφαλαλγία** becomes **κεφαλαργία** (head-ache), and **ληθαλγία, ληθαργία** (drowsiness, lethargy), so from **ποδαλγία** we get **ποδαργία,** and then by metathesis **ποδάγρα** (gout). (Comp. *Doederlein* "Lateinische Synonyme und Etymologien",—Latin Synonyms and Etymologies, Pt. 4. p. 424.). The remark *Pliny* adds however "*ioculari primum lascivia*" (at first by way of jesting mockery) evidently points to some ambiguity underlying the word. But whether this consists in the recognition of the likeness in sound between *mentum*, the chin, and *menta*, or *mentula*, the virile member, or is to be looked for in the **ἄγρα,** it might be difficult to determine. Still it seems probable, but without wishing to entirely exclude the former hypothesis, that the latter is the case, as will appear directly.

Galen [1] distinguishes between **λειχὴν ἁπλοῦς** and **λειχὴν ἄγριος** (simple *lichen*, and malignant *lichen*) in his enumeration of Skin-diseases, and still more plainly in another place [2] he says: "**λειχὴν** is likewise a Skin-disease; there are two forms of it, **ὁ μὲν ἥμερος καὶ πρᾳότερος, ὁ δὲ ἄγριος καὶ χαλεπώτερος** (the one benignant and milder, the other malignant and more serious). But in both of them minute scales are detached from the skin, and the part of the skin underneath the scales is reddened and almost ulcerated. The affection arises from a salt phlegmatic humour (**φλέγματος ἁλμυροῦ**) and yellow gall, hence the scales fall from the skin as in glazed pottery-ware (? **ἐπὶ τῶν ἁλμῶν τῶν κεραμίων**). The affection is cured by internal phlegmagogues and external embrocations." We have already on p. 139. above, in the footnote on **ἄγριος** (wild, savage) and **χαλεπός** (hard, harsh), noted how these words are used with special reference to the vice of paederastia, but they are also applied generally to the vice, the different forms of which we have been examining here. This follows from *Plato* [3] and *Plutarch* [4], at any rate so far as **ἄγριος** is con-

[1] *Galen*, Isagoge ch. 18. (edit. Kühn Vol. XIV. 779).

[2] *Galen*, loco citato ch. 13. pp. 657, 758).

[3] *Plato*, Phaedo p. 81 A., οἱ ἀφικομένη ὑπάρχει αὐτῇ εὐδαίμονι εἶναι, πλάνης καὶ ἀγνοίας καὶ φόβων καὶ ἀγρίων ἐρώτων καὶ τῶν ἄλλων κακῶν τῶν ἀνθρωπείων ἀπηλλαγμένῃ. (So having come there, the soul is in a state of assured happiness being free of error and ignorance and fear, and *fierce passions* and the other ills of mankind).

[4] *Plutarch*, De solert. anim. p. 972 D., Ἔρωτες δὲ πολλῶν οἱ μὲν ἄγριοι καὶ περιμανεῖς γεγόνασιν, οἱ δὲ ἔχοντες οὐκ ἀπάνθρωπον ὡραϊσμόν. (But for the passions of many, some are naturally fierce and frantic, but there are others again that show no anti-social effeminacy). The *Etymologicum Magnum* says: ἄγριοι οἱ παιδεράσται, ἤτοι ὅτι ἄγριόν ἐστι τὸ πάθος ἡ παιδεραστία. (wild,—means the paederasts, that is, because the *passion of paederastia is a wild one*). Perhaps too the phrase of

cerned, which indeed we may conveniently render by *vicious*. The original meaning being overlooked, **λείχην** and **λιχὴν** had been taken as synonymous,—possibly the Latin *lichenos* first led to the mistake; then naturally enough an appropriate epithet was sought, to signify the *lichen* which was the result of licking in a vicious fashion. But this according to the already existing mode of speech could be nothing else than **ἄγριος** [1] again,—**λειχὴν ἄγριος**, with which **λειχὴν ἁπλοῦς**, *lichen insons*, (simple, innocent *lichen*) was naturally contrasted.

Yet while *Criton*, as cited in *Aëtius*. simply and quite correctly interpreted Mentagra by **ἄγριος λειχὴν** (fierce, malignant lichen), *Galen* appears to have been still ignorant of the special meaning. This is shown by the words **ἥμερος** and **πρᾳότερος** (gentle, benignant,—milder), which obviously are correct opposites of **ἄγριος** only *if* the latter is understood, as it is in *Celsus*, as equivalent to *ferus* (fierce, malignant), but in no way account for the **ἁπλοῦς** (simple, innocent), which Galen no doubt found already established as distinguishing epithet of **λιχὴν.** How little he fathomed the nature of the evil, is proved by his ætiology of it, which makes the complaint result from the **φλέγμα ἁλμυρὸν** (salt phlegmatic humour) and the **χολὴ ξανθὴ** (yellow gall). The unprofessional *Martial* had a better word to say on the subject when he wrote his *sordidique lichenes* (filthy, squalid-looking lichens). Similarly it would seem the *agra* in Mentagra should be taken as pointing to **ἄγριος** (fierce. malignant). Can it be perhaps that in this way the **μολύνων τὴν ὑπήνην** (polluting the hair on the upper lip) of *Aristophanes*,

Theocritus is referable to the same: **ἄγριον, ἄγριον ἕλκος ἔχει κατὰ μηρὸν Ἄδωνις** (a savage, savage wound has Adonis in the thigh).

[1] In *Hesychius* occurs also the form **ἀγριοψωρία** (malignant itch). Whether the latter is connected with our subject, technical investigations must inform us. The passing over of Mentagra into Psora (Itch) points that way.

the Latin *barbam inquinare* (to pollute the beard), have come to be used as synonyms for *cunnilingere?* *Martial* seems to imply it by his *triste mentum, mentum periculosum* (disfigured chin, perilous chin). Perhaps too the *Sycosis menti* (Sycosis,—fig-like eruption, of the chin) of *Celsus* and the later Greek medical writers should likewise be regarded as coming under this head. At a matter of fact, *Archigenes* says so in so many words, as cited in *Galen* (De comp. med. secundum locos, Bk. V. edit. Kühn Vol. XII. p. 847.), **ἐπὶ δὲ τῶν συκωδῶν τῶν ἐπὶ τοῦ γενείου, λεγομένων δὲ μενταγρῶν, ὑπὸ δέ τινων λειχήνων ἀγρίων, ποιεῖ κ. τ. λ.** (but in the case of the sycotic, or fig-like, eruptions on the chin, which are called mentagrae, and by others malignant lichens, he proceeds as follows, etc.), and calls the affection of the chin, as do other Physicians, generally **ἐξανθήματα ἐν τοῖς γενείοις** (efflorescences, eruptions on the chin),—p. 824.

If we have thus succeeded in establishing the meanings of *lichens* and *mentagra*, the rest of the passage of *Pliny* will admit of easy explanation. The disease in many cases it seems invaded the whole face, in the same way as the *atra lues* (black contagion) in the passages quoted above from *Martial* under *fellation.* Perhaps all of these,—indeed *Pliny* also says *lues*,—are to be referred, as is actually done bv *Farnabius* in his notes, to *mentagra*, seeing that the disease could perfectly well, though certainly much seldomer, arise equally from the practise of *fellation.* The *double entendre* between *mentum* (the chin) and *menta* or *mentula* (the virile member) would so acquire all the more point.

The expression *foedo cutis furfure* (with a horrible scurf of the skin) appears to have led a number of authors to believe that this was the capital characteristic of the complaint, and that the distinction between **λιχὴν** and **λείχην** was merely one of degree. This view was advocated in particular by

Willian [1], who ascribes it also to *Paulus Aegineta* [2] as well as to *Oribasius* [3] though both of these authors limit themselves to saying that the moderately siccative remedies are of no benefit in **λείχην ἄγριος** (malignant lichen), whereas the more violent ones aggravate it, and that for this reason it was called **ἄγριος.** Hence Willian's *Lichen agrius* (malignant lichen) has nothing in common with the *lichen* of the Greeks and Romans but the mere name, for it follows clearly from the words *foediore cicatrice* (with a more horrible scar) that occur a little further down in *Pliny*, that a process of skinning ever by ulceration was part of the disease, and did not owe its existence solely to the caustic remedies employed.

The *immunity of women* [4] equally admits of easy

[1] Willian, "Die Hautkrankheiten" (Skin-Diseases). transl. by F. Friese, Breslau 1794. 4to., Vol. 1. pp. 29 and 32.

[2] *Paulus Aegineta*, De re Med. bk. IV. ch. 3., *ἀγρίους δὲ καλοῦσι λειχῆνας τοὺς ὑπὸ τῶν μετρίως ξηραινόντων οὐδὲν ὀνιναμένους. ὑπὸ δὲ τῶν σφοδρῶς παροξύνοντας.* (now they call *malignant lichens* those which get no benefit from the milder siccatives, and are actually aggravated by the more violent).

[3] *Oribasius*, De morb. curat., edit. Eunap. bk. III. ch. 59., in Steph. collect. p. 637., Ergo quibus nihil affertur auxilii ab iis medicamentis quae mediocriter siccant et exacerbantur ab iis quae siccant vehementer, eas *λειχῆνας ἄγριους* vocant. (Accordingly such *lichens* as are in no way benefited by remedies that are moderate siccatives, and are aggravated by those that are violent ones, these they call *λειχῆνας ἀγρίους* (malignant lichens).

[4] *Jöhrens*, in his Dissertation already cited speaks thus on the subject (p. 47): "De feminis, cum suavia maritorum evitare nequiverint, quomodo ab ista infectione liberae evaserint, maius restat dubium: nos opinamur, cum viri barbam saepius radi soliti fuerint, ea propter patentibus a novacula poris virulentum illud fermentum aut incentivum toxicum facilis sese insinuare et characterem suum imprimere; imberbes contra feminas, glabritie cutis resistente porisque minus patulis, sospitari potuisse." (In the case of women, when they have been unable to avoid the caresses of husbands, it remains very doubtful how they have got off free from this infection.

explanation, for in the first place women were not likely to have readily conceived the idea of acting after the manner of a *cunnilingue* [1], and even if *fellation* is admitted to be an occasionally concurrent cause of *mentagra*, still it would seem, as already stated, to supervene much less often as a consequence of the latter vice; while in cases where it does, it is of a milder form and it is rather the internal parts of the mouth that are imperilled. Besides, it is to be remembered that women generally speaking suffer less frequently from pustulous disorders of the cutaneous glands affecting the face than men do, as is well seen at the present day with Acne. In the parts neighbouring on the genitals this is exactly reversed. Still this immunity of women must not be insisted on too far, as those persons of the female sex who used to practise *fellation*, the Summoenianae (women

Our own opinion is that as men have always been accustomed to have the beard shaved frequently, for this reason the pores being opened more widely by the action of the razor, that virulent ferment and active poison creeps in more easily and produces its characteristic effect. On the other hand women being beardless, the baldness of the skin offering an obstacle and the *pores being less open*, have been able to escape).

[1] However this did happen in isolated cases, as is shown by the the example of Philaenis, who indeed was a Tribad properly, in *Martial*, bk. VII. Epigr. 67.,

Post haec omnia cum libidinatur,
Non fellat, putat hoc parum virile.
Sed plane medias vorat puellas.
Di mentem tibi dent tuam, Philaeni,
Cunnum lingere quae putas virile.

(After all these indulgences when she still feels lustful, she does not *fellate*, this she deems unmanly; she just mouths girls' middles. The gods give you your desire, Philaenis, you who think it a *manly* vice to act the cunnilingue). Comp. bk. IV. Epigr. 41. But it was always a very exceptional thing to find this vice practised among women; in fact *Juvenal*, Sat. II. 47—49., denies it altogether:

Non erit ullum
Exemplum in nostro tam detestabile sexu,
Taedia non lambit Cluviam, nec Flora Catullam.

(No such detestable example is to be found in our sex,— Taedia does not lick Cluvia, nor Flora Catulla).

of the suburbs) lay too completely outside the range of *Pliny's* observation.

As to the *servi* (slaves) and *Plebs humilis* (Commons of humble station), these were surely unlikely, however little restraint they may have put on their sensual appetites, to have readily fallen into suchlike forms of vice,—forms which spring as a rule from the brain of unoccupied, rich idlers. We have only to appeal to modern experience to substantiate this. How many individuals of the lowest and middle classes have the records of forensic medicine to show as having been paederasts and so on? Wild aberrations in morals have at no period begun with the common man! So we see it was the Proceres (Nobles) who were in an especial degree attacked by the *mentagra.*

At the same time the most conspicuous cause of *mentagra*, the practice of *cunnilingere* was by no means the *only* way of getting it, for the malady, like *condylomata* on the genital organs, was evidently connected with a contagion,—a fact which is clearly enough brought out by the layman *Pliny*, whereas the Physicians say nothing about this. Accordingly the disorder was capable of being disseminated by *kissing* from one individual to another. But it was not the *velox transitus osculi* (swift transmission of a kiss) that was instrumental in spreading the disease, but rather the *basium* (wanton kiss),—which depended on some yet unidentified lascivious device [1], sucking, playing with

[1] It is a surprising circumstance that the words *basium*, *basiare*, *basiator* (kiss, to kiss, kisser) appear only to have come into use by the Romans from the time of Catullus onwards, and are found almost exclusively in Martial, Juvenal and the still later Petronius, so coinciding with a period in which dissoluteness of morals had reached the highest pitch among the Romans. Some would derive the word *basium* from *βάζω*, loqui, (to speak); so perhaps it may have been used in a similar way to *narrare* (to tell) in *Martial* (III. 84.) in the sense of *cunnilingere*. *Βάζω, βαίνω, βεινῶ* and *βινῶ* (to speak, to go, to have sexual intercourse) seem all to have one and the same stem. The second of the two Epigrams of *Martial* quoted in the text reminds us

the tongue or the like. Still we must remember that at the very time the *mentagra* was spreading with such terrible rapidity, a perfect *mania for kissing* had broken out at Rome. *Martial* describes this admirably in the two following Epigrams, which are of the very highest importance in connection with our subject:

Book XII. Epigram 59:

DE IMPORTUNIS BASIATORIBUS.

Tantum dat tibi Roma basiorum
Post annos modo quindecim reverso,
Quantum Lesbia non dedit Catullo.
Te vicinia tota, te pilosus
Hircoso premit osculo colonus.
Hinc instat tibi textor, inde fullo,
Hinc sutor modo pelle basiata,
Hinc menti dominus periculosi,
Hinc defioculusque et inde lippus,
Fellatorque recensque cunnilingus.
Iam tanti tibi non fuit redire.

(*Of pestilent Kissers:* Rome bestows more kisses on you, on your return to her after fifteen years' absence, than ever Lesbia gave Catullus. The whole neighbourhood kisses you, and the hirsute countryman presses you in his goaty embrace. One side the weaver is upon you, the other the fuller, here the cobbler who but now kissed his leather; here comes *the owner of a perilous chin*, here the one-eyed man and here the blear, and the *fellator*, and the *cunnilingue*

almost involuntarily of the first Tarsica of Chrysostom. Apparently *basium* and *basiare* always imply a *vicious kiss*, to *kiss viciously*, in a general way. Hence *Martial*, XI. 62., Mediumque mavult basiare quam summum, (And she had rather kiss his middle than his head). *Petronius*, Sat., Ultime cinaedus supervenit,—extortis nos clunibus cecidit, modo basiis olidissimis inquinavit. (Finally a *cinaedus* appeared,—he made at us with writhing buttocks, and anon befouled us with most evil-smelling kisses).

fresh from work. Now surely to return was not of such importance to you as all this.)

Book XI. Epigram 98:

AD BASSUM.

Effugere non est, Basse, basiatores.
Instant, morantur, persequuntur, occurrunt
Et hinc et illinc, usquequaque, quacunque.
Non ulcus acre pustulaeve lucentes,
Nec triste mentum sordidique lichenes,
Nec labra pingui delibuta ceroto,
Nec congelati gutta proderit nasi.
Et aestuantem basiant et algentem,
Et nuptiale basium reservantem.
Non te cucullis asseret caput tectum,
Lectica nec te tuta pelle veloque,
Nec vindicabit sella saepius clausa.
Rimas per omnes basiator intrabit.
Non consulatus ipse, non tribunatus,
Saevique fasces, nec superba clamosi
Lictoris abiget virga basiatorem.
Sedeas in alto tu licet tribunali,
Et e curuli iura gentibus reddas:
Ascendet illa basiator atque illa:
Febricitantem basiabit et flentem:
Dabit oscitanti basium natantique,
Dabit et cacanti. Remedium mali solum est
Facias amicum, basiare quem nolis.

(*To Bassus:* Escape the kissers, no! it is not to be done, Bassus. They set upon you, wait for you, pursue you, meet you, here, there, and everywhere, in every street, at every corner. *Neither acrid ulcer nor shiny pustules, neither disfigured chin* nor foul scabs, nor lips anointed with pink salve, nor the drop at the tip of a frozen nose will save you. They kiss a man sweating with heat and starving with cold, nay! even a man keeping his lips pure for the nuptial kiss. A head muffled in hoods will not exempt you, nor a litter guarded with rug and curtain, nor the sedan kept closed most of the time get you off.

The kisser will in by every chink. Not the very consulship, not the tribuneship, not the stern fasces and threatening rod of the shouting lictor will keep away the kisser. Though you sit exalted on the high tribunal, or give laws to the people from the curule seat, both to one and the other the kisser will climb up. He will kiss a man shaking with fever, and drivelling with cold. He will give a kiss to a man gaping, to a man swimming, even to a man shitting! The one and only cure for the plague is to make a real friend, whom you will not need to kiss).

Now we shall be in a position to explain to our satisfaction what *Martial* meant by *basia lasciva* (wanton kisses,—XI. 24.—*basia maligna* (pestilent kisses),—XII. 55.—and *Petronius* (ch. 23.) by his *conspuere aliquem basio immundissimo* (to beslobber anyone with a most filthy kiss); and we shall be in no way surprised at the fact that *mentagra* not only attacked the Roman nobles as a virtual epidemic, but that the *velox transitus osculi* (the swift transmission of a kiss) was alleged by Pliny as a reason of its communication.

Finally as to the historical factor in connection with *mentagra*,—it is implied in the account Pliny gives that it was *only at Rome* it was regarded as a new disease. It must have been already known to the Greeks, for they possessed the name *Lichen* for it. The Greek physicians, of whom several of the ones quoted by *Galen* lived some considerable time before Claudius, know nothing about the disease being a new one, while *Galen* himself says simply, **ἐπικρατούσης ἐν τῇ πόλει τῆς μεντάγρας λεγομένης,** (when the *mentagra* as it was called *was prevalent* in the city). *Plutarch* again, though he (Symposiaca bk. VIII. Quaest. 9.) wrote a special Chapter on new diseases, with particular reference to Elephantiasis, never mentions *mentagra* at all. He represents it as having been introduced into Rome from Asia, and it was from Egypt, the *Genetrix* *talium vitiorum* (Mother-land of suchlike abominations), the Physicians [1] were imported who understood how to cure the disorder. We have more than once noted that Asia was the breeding place of sexual excesses, and described how vice spread from thence over different countries and how as a result of these practices the affections of the parts naturally concerned that arose first in Asia subsequently passed on to these same countries. For Rome this was in an especial degree the case with Egypt, where the undermining of morality had gone farthest; *Martial* [2] spoke justly when he said "*Nequitias tellus scit dare nulla magis,*" (No other land knows better how to produce finished rascality). But the intercourse with Asia and Egypt arose mainly in the time of Pompey, and became from that period ever more active, while concurrently luxury was on the increase and the old Virtus (manly virtue) of the Romans disappearing more and more every day,—above all when Tiberius by his own example elevated every form of vice into a sort of fancy article demanded by fashion.

Not that the Emperor went unpunished, for he himself probably suffered from *mentagra*. *Julian* [3]

[1] *Galen*, loco citato, mentions in particular the physicians. *Crito* and *Pamphilus*, who lived in the reign of Domitian, and who accordingly were contemporaries of *Martial's*, as pre-eminently successful in the treatment of *mentagra*.

[2] Also *Hippocrates*, De aere aq. et loc. p. 549. Vol. I. ed. Kühn, says: ἀλλὰ τὴν ἡδονὴν κρατέειν, διότι πολύμορφα γίνεται τὰ ἐν τοῖς θηρίοις· περὶ μὲν οὖν Αἰγυπτίων καὶ Λιβύων οὕτως ἔχειν μοι δοκεῖ. (But that *love of pleasure* gained the mastery, inasmuch as the passions in beasts are of many forms; now with regard to the *Egyptians* and Libyans this seems to me to be the case).

[3] *Julian*, Caesares, in "Opera Omnia" Paris 1630. 4to., Pt. II. p. 9., Ἐπιστραφέντες δὲ πρὸς τὴν καθέδραν ὤφθησαν ὠτειλαὶ κατὰ τὸν νῶτον μυρίαι, καυτῆρες τινὲς καὶ ξέσματα, καὶ πληγαὶ χαλεπαὶ καὶ μώλωπες, ὑπὸ τῆς ἀκολασίας καὶ ὠμότητος, ψωραί τινες καὶ λειχῆνες, οἷον ἐγκεκαυμένοι. (for translation see text).

says of him, that when Romulus had invited to the feast of the Saturnalia all gods and Caesars, Tiberius appeared with the rest, "but when he turned round to take his seat, on his back could be seen in thousands scars, marks of burnings and scrapings, indurated weals and callosities, results of his excesses and wild lusts, cankers and scabs as it were burnt in". Nay! according to *Suetonius* [1] his face itself bore *crebri et subtiles tumores* (a multitude of minute swellings); and *Tacitus* [2] says of him: *Praegracilis et incurva proceritas, nudus capillo vertex, ulcerosa facies, ac plerumque medicaminibus interstincta,* (Tall and of a most graceful, albeit bowed, figure; the head bald, the face covered *with ulcers,* and generally patched with medical plasters). When *Galen* [3] mentions a **τροχίσκος πρὸς ἕρπητας ὁ Τιβηρίου Καίσαρος** (a lozenge for creeping eruptions, Tiberius Caesar's), this does not in any way necessarily imply that this was prescribed as a remedy against eruptive symptoms on the *face,* for Tiberius, as we see from the passage quoted from *Julian,* suffered from eruptions on all the other parts of his body. Even if an affection of the face was intended, the expression **ἕρπης** (creeping eruption), in view of the marked tendency of the disease to spread to neighbouring parts, was not at all an unnatural one to be used; and we may say, speaking generally, that the view which holds the Greeks to have indicated by the word **ἕρπης** any one definite and distinct form of eruption is entirely mistaken. *Bertrandi* [4] indeed endeavours to show that *mentagra* was a form of malignant tetter. That the application of plasters as a remedy in *mentagra* was frequently recommended and

[1] *Suetonius,* Vita Tiberii ch. 68.

[2] *Tacitus,* Annals bk. IV. ch. 57.

[3] *Galen,* De composit. medicament. secundum genera bk. V. ch. 12. edit. Kühn Vol. XIII. p. 836.

[4] *Bertrandi,* "Abh. von den Geschwüren (Treatise on Ulcers) from the Italian. Erfurt 1790. 8vo. § 200.

employed is shown both by *Galen* and *Aëtius* [1].

But in proportion as the exciting cause grew ever more and more common, the *cunnilingue* being now no longer contented with girls, but employing for the satisfaction of his shameful mania women and even pregnant women as well, and at last actually women during menstruation, the resulting consequences were bound to occur not only more frequently but also in a more dangerous form. At first it was merely single pustules, which appeared round the mouth and took possession of the chin, and which were confounded with *Sycosis menti* (Sycosis,—fig-like eruption of the chin), a complaint liable to arise from other causes as well and one long since familiar, without attracting particular attention as anything uncommon. Later on when neither morbid vaginal phlegm nor yet menstrual blood repelled the *cunnilingue* any longer, there was set up a diseased process in the cutaneous glands, the resulting secretion rapidly drying formed a white crust or scurf, and this was detached in flakes resembling bran. All this could not fail to arouse remark, and accordingly the Romans, little practised in medical diagnosis, saw in it a new disease, which in turn received a new name. Just as in more modern times the introduction of Venereal disease was attributed to a leprous Knight from the Holy Land, so now at Rome *Perusinus, eques Romanus, Quaestorius scriba* (Perusinus, a Roman knight, a secretary in the Quaestorian office) was held

[1] *Aëtius*, Tetrab. II. serm. 4. ch. 16., Quandoquidem vero plurimi sunt qui illitionum usum aversantur, malunt-que adhibere emplastra, utpote quae neque per sudores obtortos defluant, neque rarefacta etiam cutem circumtendant, annectam et horum aliquot apparatus. (However, inasmuch as there are many who are opposed to the use of salves, and prefer to apply plasters, on the ground that the latter are not liable to run through sweatings that are superinduced nor yet to liquify and spread on the skin, I will add some forms of these plasters).

responsible for bringing *mentagra* from Asia. As a matter of fact he probably got his *mentagra* in Asia in exactly the same manner in which it was acquired in Rome,—if indeed we are on general grounds to give any weight to this part of the story. At any rate modern times have given us many examples of how much credence mankind is ready to give to an account of the introduction of a disease by one definite individual. But the disease did not stop at the cutaneous glands, the hair-glands were also involved, the hair fell away, and ulcers formed, which spread around with destructive virulence, as was particularly the case in Martial's day. On the other hand it is true deep-seated ulceration never supervened, but the disease rather extended on the surface from the face onwards, spreading more or less over the whole of the rest of the body [1], and thus assumed the form of Psora (Itch) or Lepra (Leprosy),—a phænomenon we shall have to return to once more later, its right appreciation being of the

[1] *Plinius Valerianus*, De re medica bk. II. 56., Graeco nomine lichenes appellatur, quod vulgo mentagram appellant, et est vitium, quod per totam faciem solet serpere, oculis tantum immunibus; descendit vero in collum et pectus ac manus, foedat cutem; eosque, qui sic vexantur, osculari non convenit, quoniam contactus eorum perniciosus fore perhibetur. (In Greek nomenclature the name *lichenes* is given to what the common people call *mentagra*, and is a malady that as a rule creeps over the whole face, the eyes alone being unaffected. But it also goes down to the neck and breast and hands, disfiguring the skin. It is not right for those so afflicted to kiss, for their contact is said to be injurious.—*Marcellus Empiricus*, De med. liber ch. 19., Ad lichenem sive mentagram, quod vitium neglectum solet per totam faciem et per totum corpus serpere et plures homines inquinare. Nam Soranus medicus quondam ducentis hominibus hoc morbo laborantibus curandis in Aquitania se locavit. (For *lichen* or *mentagra*, a malady which if neglected will creep over the whole face and the whole body, and disfigures many men. Indeed Soranus a Physician at one time sold his professional services in Aquitania to two hundred patients suffering from this disease).

utmost importance for the History of Venereal Disease.

Now, since on the one hand every *cunnilingue* is not attacked by *mentagra*, while on the other sometimes ulcers of the inner portion of the mouth, sometimes *mentagra*, and the latter sometimes local, sometimes of wide extent, are noted, the following question calls for an answer. What circumstances conditioned these phænomena and, generally, the special frequency of *mentagra* in Italy? Leaving out of account a variety of other considerations, we are bound in this place to call in along with other factors of our explanation some special and particular influence of the *Genius epidemicus* (the aggregate of epidemical conditions at large), which just at that time favoured the rise of skin complaints. However slight the material Antiquity affords us on this point, and especially so far as concerns the time a little before and after Our Lord's birth, still we *do* find a datum for Italy at any rate which we certainly ought not to leave unutilized. This is the statement of *Pliny* (ch. 5. and Bk. XX. ch. 52.) to the effect that it was in the time of Pompey the Great, or according to *Plutarch* (loco citato) in that of Asclepiades, that *elephantiasis* first showed itself in Italy. It follows that at that period favourable external circumstances also were in existence in connection with the conditions of disease at large,—as indeed the ready extension of *mentagra* from the chin onwards to the rest of the body proves even more clearly.

But it must not for a moment be supposed that therefore *mentagra* was of *epidemic origin*. Without at all wishing to embark on the consideration of the ætiological factors of *elephantiasis*, we may just mention the fact that according to Pliny's account this disease too, equally with *mentagra*, would seem to have always begun with the *face* [1]. The conjecture

[1] *Marcellus Empiricus*, De medicam. liber ch. 19., Adversum Elephantiasin, quod malum plerumque a facie auspicatur, primumque oritur quasi lenticulis variis et inaequalibus, cute alba-

is all but unavoidable, that very possibly in either case it was the practices of the *cunnilingue* that supplied the exciting cause for the misfortune; and this would also probably explain how it was *elephantiasis* came to be connected in men's minds with the *Morbus phoeniceus* (Phoenician disease). Still, as already explained, this would only be equivalent to making it responsible in *individual* cases,—cases that tend inevitably to render the proper under-

alibi tenui, plerisque locis dura et quasi scabida et ad postremum sic increscit ut ossibus, caro adstricta, tumescentibus primum digitis atque articulis indurescat. Hic morbus peculiariter Aegyptiorum populis notus est nec solum in vulgus extremum, sed etiam reges ipsos frequenter irrepsit, unde adversus hoc malum solia ipsis in balneo repleta humano sanguine parabantur. Mustelae igitur exustae cinis et eiusdem belluae, id est elephantis sanguis immixtus et inlitus, huiusmodi corporibus medetur. (*Against elephantiasis, which malady is generally seen in the face, beginning first with a sort of scales of various shape and different size, the skin being white, in some parts thick, in others thin, in most places hard and with a sort of scab over it; eventually the malady increases to such a degree that the flesh is as it were drawn tight over the bones, the fingers and joints swelling first, and becomes indurated.* This disease was particularly familiar among the peoples of Egypt, and not merely did it affect the lowest vulgar, but even frequently crept in amongst kings themselves, whence it came that, to combat the evil, baths filled with human blood were prepared for them in the bath-house. The ashes therefore of a burned weasel and the blood of the corresponding beast, that is to say the elephant, were mixed together and used as an ointment in the remedial treatment of bodies so afflicted. — *Actuarius*, Meth. med. bk. VI. ch. 6. On diseases of the *Face*, reads: Ad affectus eminentes, *facieique pruritus ac principum elephantiae*, (For the principal affections, *itchings of the face and the beginnings of elephantiasis*). Again *Aretaeus*, De sign. chron. bk. II. ch. 13. edit. Kühn p. 179., says: τὰ πολλὰ μὲν ὅκως καὶ ἀπὸ σκοπιῆς τοῦ προσώπου ἀρχόμενον τηλεφανὲς πῦρ κακόν, (Most oftentimes resembling a far-seen bale-fire *beginning from the watch-tower, as it were, of the face*).

standing of the action of *elephantiasis*, as well as of its history, considerably more difficult. May it not also be to some extent the case that under the general name of *elephantiasis* forms of disease of very different sorts have been confounded? The views held by the Ancients on this and on the other skin diseases still remain in too much obscurity for anyone to be able to give a decisive judgement on the point. For the rest most probably the *atra lues* and *scelerata lues* (black contagion, abominable contagion), spoken of above, likewise come under the category of *mentagra*. This we have felt ourselves contrained to ascribe not solely to the practise of the vice of the *cunnilingue* as a cause, but to *fellation* also,—only that in the latter case, as we have pointed out, it is rather the inner, in the former rather the external parts, that became affected.

Morbus Campanus.

(Campanian Disease).

§ 26.

Several of the commentators on *Horace*, and particularly *Laevinus Torrentius* [1] have referred the much-discussed *Morbus Campanus* [2] to the head of *mentagra;*

[1] Commentar. in Horatium. Antwerp 1608. Vol. II. p. 469.

[2] *Zachar. Platner*, De Morbo Compano ad verba Horatii bk. I. Sat. V. v. LXII. prolusio (Dissertation on the Companian Disease as mentioned by Horace). Leipzig 1732. 4to., also reprinted in his Opuscula, Leipzig 1794. 4to. Vot. II. pp. 21—28. The author holds the disease to have been a sort of warts, having a resemblance with those observed in Syphilitic patients.—*Nebel*, E. L. W., De morbis veterum obscuris (On some Obscure Diseases

accordingly this will be no inappropriate place at any rate to mention it, though without aiming at a complete explanation. *Horace* represents two buffoons, *Messius* and *Sarmentus*, as rallying each other for the amusement of the company:

— — Messi clarum genus Osci,
Sarmenti domina extat, ab his maioribus orti
Ad pugnam venere. Prior Sarmentus: Equi te
Esse feri similem dico. Ridemus: et ipse
Messius: Accipio; caput et movet. O, tua cornu
Ni foret exsecto frons, inquit, quid faceres, cum
Sic mutilus miniteris? At illi foeda cicatrix
Setosam laevi frontem turpaverat oris.
Campanum in morbum, in faciem permulta iocatus
Pastorem saltaret uti Cyclopa, rogabat;
Nil illi larva aut tragicis opus esse cothurnis.
Multa Cicirrus ad haec.

(Messius was sprung of the renowned race of the Oscans, Sarmentus' mistress is yet living; from these ancestors derived, they came to the fray. First begins Sarmentus: "I declare you are just like an unbroken horse." At this sally we laugh, and Messius himself says: "I accept the likeness," and tosses his head. "Oh! if your horn had not been amputated from your brow," says he then, "what *would* you do, since you threaten us so fiercely, mutilated as you are?" Now an ugly scar disfigured the left side of his shaggy brow. After making a number of jibes at his *Campanian disease*, and his face, he asked him to dance the shepherd Cyclops; saying there needed no mask and tragic buskins. Many jests Cicirrus added as well).

Messius who is chiefly spoken of in the above passage, is in the first place represented as an Oscan by birth. Now the whole race of the Oscans was,

of the Ancients), Sect. I., Giessen 1794. 8vo. pp. 18—25. The author believes the Morbus Campanus to have been identical with Sycosis or θύμιον (large wart), but to have had no connection with the *Lues Venerea* (Venereal Contagion).

as *Festus* informs us, notorious for its unnatural excesses in matters of Love; we read in him, p. 191: "Obscum duas diversas et contrarias significationes "habet. Nam Cloatius putat eo vocabulo significari "sacrum, quo etiam leges sacrae Oscae dicuntur, et "in omnibus fere antiquis commentariis scribitur "Opicum pro Obsco, ut in Titini fabula quinta: "Qui Obsce et Volsce fabulantur, nam Latine nesciunt. "A quo etiam verba impudentia, et elata appellantur "obscena, quia frequentissimus fuit usus "Oscis libidinum spurcarum. (*Obscum* has two different and contrary meanings. For Cloatius considers *sacred* to be signified by the word, in which sense sacred laws are spoken of as leges Oscae (*Oscan* laws), and in almost all the old commentaries *Opicum* is written for *Obscum*, as in the fifth Fable of Titinius: "Who converse in *Obscan* and Volscian, because they know not how in Latin." Whence also indecent words, and swelling ones, are called *obscene, because the practice of unclean lusts was most frequent among the Oscans*[1].

Again on p. 194., "Oscos, quos dicimus, ait Verrius "Opscos ante dictos, teste Ennio, cum dicat: De "muris res gerit Opscus. Adiicit etiam, quod stupra "inconcessae libidinis obscena dicantur, "ab eius gentis consuetudine inducta. "Quod verum esse non satis adducor, cum apud "antiquos omnes fere obscena dicta sint, quae mali "ominis habebantur. (The *Oscans*, as we call them,

[1] Noteworthy is the explanation of *Isidore*, Etymol. bk. IV. ch. 9. 17., *Oscedo* est, qua infantum ora exulcerantur, dicta a languore oscitantium. (*Oscedo* is a complaint whereby children's mouths become ulcerated, so called from the languor of those gaping); the latter part is unintellible. Were these *oscitantes* (gapers) possibly *fellators? Lucian*, Pseudolog. ch. 27. says of Timarchus, *ἀναπετάσας τὸ στόμα, καὶ ὡς ἔνι πλατύτατον κεχηνὼς, ἠνείχου τυφλούμενος ὑπ' αὐτοῦ τὴν γνάθον.* (having spread open your mouth, and with a gape as wide as is possible to make, you were borne away, your jaw blocked by him).

Verrius says were formerly called *Opscans*, on the evidence of Ennius, for he says: "The Opscan directs his attack upon the walls." He adds further that *debaucheries of lawless love are called "obscene", as taking this name from the habits of the nation in question.* But I am not sufficiently convinced of the truth of this, inasmuch as in nearly all the ancient writers things are called *obscene* that were held to be of evil omen). However what the *spurca libido* (unclean lust) consisted in may be readily conjectured from the following explanations of *Festus: Oscines aves* Appius Claudius esse ait, quae *ore canentes* faciant auspicium, ut *corvus* [1], cornix, noctua, (Divinatory birds—*Oscines* aves—are, says Appius Claudius, such as give an augury by *singing with the mouth*, as *the raven*, the crow, the owl); if only we remember how the *fellator*, as was shown on a previous page, was nicknamed *corvus* (raven). Again in an Epigram of *Ausonius* already quoted a *cunnilingue* is called *Opicus magister;* so that we cannot doubt the question is here of that vice which is practised with the mouth.

In another Epigram of *Ausonius* quoted and explained above, where the different forms of the *obscoena Venus* (obscene Love) are specified, Crispa there mentioned practises,

Et quam Nolanis capitalis luxus inussit,

(That vice too which headlong wantonness branded on the men of Nola), and this *capitalis luxus* [2] of

[1] *Horace*, Odes III. 27. 11. *Ausonius*, Idyll. XI. 15.

[2] *Luxus* in the sense of sexual excess occurs not unfrequently in ancient writers, e.g. in *Tacitus*, Hist. IV. 14., *Suetonius*, Nero 29. *Capua luxurians* is well known from the history of Hannibal. It is worth noting that *Paracelsus* gives the name *luxus* to Venereal disease; he says, De causis et origine luis Gallicae, (Of the Causes and Origin of the French Contagion), bk. I. ch. 5.: Luxus autem nomen quod attinet, illud ab influentia, id est, efficiente causa desumptum esse intelligendum est. Est autem luxus irritatio quaedam ac titillatus spermatis, ad perficiendum actum venereum, a

the men of Nola, as the general sense of the whole passage clearly shows, is nothing else but *fellation.* But the town of Nola was in Campania, and the inhabitants of Campania again consisted for the most part of Oscans; so whatever is true of the latter, must needs also apply to the Campanians. The Nolans and Oscans or Opicans being *fellators* and *cunnilingues,* the Campanians must be so too; and as a matter of fact *Plautus* (Trinum. II. 4. 144.) tells us: *Campas genus multo Syrorum antidit patientia,* (The Campanian race far outdoes that of the Syrians in *passivity*).

Now Messius being represented as an Oscan, and this by way of mockery, as all expounders admit, the point of the jest must evidently refer to this *luxus capitalis,* and Messius accordingly be regarded as a *fellator.* Now let us look if this view finds any confirmation in what follows [2]. First of all Sarmentus says Messius is *equi feri similis* (like an unbroken horse). Wherein precisely the satire of this consists

morbis in corpore latentibus causata, itaque Veneris impressione a morbo in actu ipso facta, tum ex vulgari luxu fit luxus morbi seu morbidus. Proinde luxus hic non naturalis sed Satyricus dicendus erit. (But *luxus* the name that is applied to it, this name must be understood as being taken from the influencing circumstance or efficient cause. Now *luxus* is a certain irritation or tickling of the seed, leading to the performance of the Venereal act and caused by diseases latent in the body, and so a strong motion of love being made in consequence of the disease in the act itself, then from the common expression *luxus,* is formed *luxus* of the disease, or morbid *luxus.* It follows this *luxus* will have to be called not natural, but *Satyric luxus*).

[1] Possibly a *double entendre* lurks even in the *ad pugnam venere* (they came to the fight). *Festus,* under the word, says: Osculana pugna in proverbio, quo significabatur victos vincere, (An Osculan—otherwise Asculan,—fight a proberbial saying that signified the vanquished being victorious). The Roman general Laevinus was beaten by King Pyrrhus at Asculum, soon after at the same place the King was himself beaten by Sulpicius.

is indeed somewhat doubtful, the commentators maintaining an obstinate silence on the point; but there *must* be some allusion of some sort intended. We can scarcely suppose this to be to the *Hectoreus equus* (the Hectorean stallion) of Ovid [1] or the *equus supinus* (the stallion lying supine) of Horace,—Sat. II. 7. 50. [2]. The unbroken horse is noticeable as galloping with head down between the fore-feet, a position taken, as we have already pointed out, by the *cunnilingue*, but which in accordance with the passage of Lucian quoted above can equally well be that of the *fellator* [3]. Messius must have understood the allusion, for he says, "*Accipio*",—*caput et movet*, ("I accept",—and moves his head). Sarmentus takes the movement as a threat, for he in his turn understands the *equus ferus* (wild horse) in yet another sense as *aries* (a ram) [4], and adds:

[1] Ovid, De arte amandi bk. III. v. 778., Nunquam Thebais Hectoreo nupta resedit equo, (Never did his Theban bride—Andromaché,—sit on the Hectorean stallion). Comp. *Martial*, bk. XI. Epigr. 105.

[2] It is worthy of note that *Rhazes*, Elchavi seu Continens, Brescia 1486. fol., p. 276., mentions eertain ulcers on the verge, that come from *ascensio mulieris supra virum* (the woman getting on the man)!

[3] *Seneca*, Nat. Quaest. bk. I. ch. 16., also says of Hostius, who had contrived magnifying mirrors for his use, in order to see himself in all positions: Et quia non tam diligenter intueri poterat, *cum compressus erat et caput merserat, inguinibusque alienis obhaeserat*, opus sibi suum per imagines offerebat, (But as he could not so accurately see, when he was shut in and had plunged down his head, and was fast to another's private parts, under those circumstances he had his doings represented to him by pictures). —*Catullus*, LXXXIII. 7.,

Nam nihil est quidquam sceleris quo prodeat ultra,
Non si *demisso* se ipse voret *capite*.

(For there exists no further form of wickedness that he can resort to,—not even if he devour himself *with down-pressed head*). *Propertius*, bk. II. 15. 22., Mecum habuit positum lenta puella caput, (A limber girl held her head down-pressed along with me).

[4] Equum, qui nunc aries appellatur, in muralibus machinis, Epeum ad Troiam (sc. invenisse), (The horse, which

If only your horn had not been amputated! What should make you threaten to butt, *mutilus* (mutilated) [1] as you are?

Now in explanation of what it was led Sarmentus to indulge in this jest, Horace goes on to say that Messius carried on the left side of his brow a hideous scar. At this Sarmentus directs his wit, making allusion to the *Campanus morbus* (Campanian disease) and Messius' disfigured face, finishing up by asking the latter *pastorem saltaret uti Cyclopa* (to dance the shepherd Cyclops), adding that for this he would need neither mask nor tragic buskins. But the *Campanus morbus* [2] is indeed nothing else but the

now is called the ram, among engines for attacking walls, Epeus invented at Troy), says *Pliny*, Hist. Nat. bk. VII. ch. 57. (edit. Franz, Vol. III. p. 287.); similarly *Pausanias*, bk. I. ch. 23., *ἵππος δούρειος μηχάνημα εἰς διάλυσιν τοῦ τείχους* (a horse of wood an engine for the destruction of the wall). Further *ἵππος* (horse) is used as a nickname for a lewd man. The Scholiast on *Oribasius*, Collect. Med. bk. XXIV. ch. 8. in *A. Mai*, Auct. Class. e vatican. codd. edit. Vol. IV. p. 30. mentions *ἵππος πύργος* (horse tower), but in what sense we have not been able to decide.

[1] *Mutilus*, *κολοβὸς*, *κόλος*, the special expression for beasts that have lost one or both horns. Thus *mutilus aries* (a mutilated, hornless, ram) *Columella* de R.R. VII. 3., *capella mutila* (mutilated she-goat) VII. 6., *bos mutilus* (mutilated ox) *Varro*, De ling. Lat. VIII. ch. 26. (Heindorf).

[2] The Scholiast *Acro* even in his time says on this passage: Campanum in morbum. Aut oris foeditatem aut arrogantiam. Dicuntur enim Campani foedi osse, arrogantes. Sic foeda accipiamus. Aliter, Campani, qui et Osci dicebantur ore immundi. Unde etiam Oscenos dicimus. (As to the Campanian disease, this is either foulness of mouth, or arrogance. For the Campanians are said to be foul, arrogant. So let us take it as foul. In another sense, the Campanians, who were also called Oscans are filthy of mouth. For which reason we say *Osceni*—obscene). *Lambinus* expresses himself yet more distinctly: Campani, qui antea Osci dicebantur, habiti sunt ore impuro atque incesto; *τοῦτ᾽ ἔστι τῷ στόματι αἰσχροποιοῦντες καὶ λεσβιάζοντες*, morbum igitur animi intellige, ut Od. I. 37. (The Campanians, who were previ-

capitalis luxus (headlong wantonness) of the Nolans, the peculiar vice of the Oscans, *fellation* in fact, which Messius practised, and to which he owed his *foeda cicatrix* (hideous scar), his disfigured face; and on both these points Sarmentus proceeds to rally him at great length (*permulta iocatus*,—indulging in very many jests), without Horace however recording his wit any further. In the *pastorem Cyclopa saltare* (to dance the shepherd Cyclops) again is contained an allusion that has hitherto been quite misunderstood, one which *Lucian* in his Pseudologistae (ch. 27.) will best explain for us. He says to Timarchus: "But in Italy, great gods! you acquired the heroic nickname of **ὁ Κύκλωψ** (the Cyclops), because at one time you wanted to practise your vice in imitation of the old legend, as it is found in *Homer*, and actually, as you lay there drunk, held the **κισσύβιον** (wassail-bowl) in your hand like a wanton Polyphemus; and the young man hired for the purpose with outstretched *hasta* (spear), that was well sharpened, threw himself upon you like another Odysseus, to thrust out your eye [1].

Yet did he miss his aim, and the spear turned slantwise beside you;
So that its point sped past, the edge of your chin merely grazing.

ously called Oscans, were considered of impure and abominable mouth; that is to say as acting uncleanly with the mouth or *Lesbianizing;* understand therefore a mental disease, as in Od. I. 37.). The Latin *Morbus* is frequently so used.

[1] *Homer*, Iliad XI. 233.

(κἀκεῖνον)
Ἀτρείδης μὲν ἅμαρτε, παραὶ δὲ οἱ ἐτράπετ' ἔγχος·
αἰχμὴ δ' ἐξεσύθη παρὰ νείατον ἀνθερεῶνα.

(Now him Atreides missed, and his spear was turned aside past him, and the point sped rushing past the very edge of his chin). Similarly *Diogenes* according to Diogenes Laertius' (VI. 53.) report parodied the Homeric verse (Iliad X. 282): "No sleeper must drive a spear through your back," as he woke a handsome youth, who lay incautiously asleep.

Thus it is by no means unreasonable to speak of you as using "cold-mouthed phrases" (**Ψυχρολογεῖν**). But you, Cyclops, opening you mouth, and gaping as wide as mortal man can, had your cheeks plugged by him, or better you longed, as Charybdis with the ships was fain to swallow down helm and sail and all, you longed to absorb the whole **Οὖτις** (No-man)."

Finally the nickname Messius bears, *Cicirrus* or *Cicerrus*, would seem to embody a jesting allusion, as it was no doubt given him on account of his throaty, croaking voice. It signifies the same thing as **κερκίδες** (hawks) in Dio Chrysostom, and like that word is to be derived from **κέρχω** (to croak) [1].

The *Morbus Phoeniceus* (Phoenician disease) was not, as we have seen, elephantiasis at all, and neither was the *Morbus Campanus* (Campanian disease) mentagra. But just as elephantiasis might supervene as a consequence of *Morbus Phoeniceus*, so the *foeda cicatrix* (hideous scar), a mark left behind it by a previous malady, was a consequence of the *Morbus Campanus*. Now what was the nature of this malady that the mark it left behind showed as a *foeda cicatrix*, is precisely what we would wish to determine. The Commentators all take the *cornu exsectum* (a horn amputated) as giving the explanation, though this is by no means absolutely necessary according to the general drift of the passage as explained; and Sarmentus might perfectly well under these circumstances, arguing from the presence of a scar, assume or at any rate profess to assume as the cause from which this had originated, the previous existence of a horny excrescence, without the latter as an actual matter of fact having ever had any previous existence. To us at any rate the *cornu exsectum* appears to stand in only a remote connection with

[1] In *Festus*, under the word bigenera (hybrids), we read; *Cicursus* ex apro et scropha domestica, (*Cicursus* from the wildboar and the domestic sow). Comp. *Varro*, De. L. L. bk. VII. p. 368. edit. Sp.

the *foeda cicatrix*, which was no doubt later on made the subject of manifold further witticisms; only Horace has given us no more details about the matter, either because they had entirely escaped his memory, or possibly because he had not perfectly grasped the point of these jokes. Certainly the conspicuously placed *at* (but) seems to point to a distinction of what follows from what precedes—unless indeed it is so placed merely to mark the transition from the *oratio directa* to the *oratio indirecta*.

However, granted there actually was an excrescence previously existing, which had been removed by the knife, of what nature was the said excrescence? It is scarcely possible, with Heindorf, to suppose the Satyriasis of Aristotle [1] to be intended here; with much greater probability *Schneider* in his Greek Dictionary, under the word **διονυσιακὸς** (Dionysiac, connected with Dionysus) drew attention to the definition of *Galen* (edit. Kühn XIX. p. 443.): **διονυσίσκοι εἰσὶν ὀστώδεις ὑπεροχαὶ ἐγγὺς κροτάφων γιγνόμεναι. λέγονται δὲ κέρατα ἀπὸ τῶν κερασφορούντων ζώων κεκλημένα.** (**διονυσίσκοι** are bony excrescences growing near the temples, and they are called horns, so named from the animals that carry horns). A passage of *Heliodorus (Cocchi Ant., Graecorum chirurgici libri, e collect. Nicetae Florent.* 1754. fol., p. 125.) which *Oribasius, De fracturis*, has preserved, gives a slightly different account; it reads: **Ὀστώδης ἐπίφυσις ἐν παντὶ μὲν γίγνεται μέρει τοῦ σώματος, πλεοναζόντως δὲ ἐν**

[1] *Aristotle*, De Generatione Animalium, bk. IV. ch. 3., *Παραπλήσιον τούτῳ καὶ τὸ νόσημα τὸ καλούμενον σατυρίασις· καὶ γὰρ ἐν τούτῳ διὰ ῥεύματος ἢ πνεύματος ἀπέπτου πλῆθος εἰς τὰ μόρια τοῦ προσώπου παρεμπεσόντος ἄλλου ζώου καὶ σατύρου φαίνεται τὸ πρόσωπον.* (Akin to this also is the disease know as Satyriasis; for in this complaint, in consequence of the super-abundance of rheum or crude humour that has become segregated to the regions of the face, the latter seems that of a strange animal or a Satyr).

τῇ κεφαλῇ, μάλιστα δὲ πλησίον τῶν κροτάφων· Οταν δὲ δύο ἐπιφύσεις γένωνται πλησιάζουσαι τοῖς κροτάφοις, κέρατα ταῦτα τινες εἴωθασιν ὀνομάζειν, ἔνιοι δὲ διονυσιακοὺς τοὺς οὕτω πεπονθότας ἀνθρώπους προσηγόρευσαν. (Bony outgrowth may occur in every part of the body, but pre-eminently on the head, and particularly near the temples. But when there are two such growths in the neighbourhood of the temples, some are wont to call them *horns*, but others name the patients so afflicted **διονυσιακοὶ**). Then follows the description of the outgrowth, and the method of its removal by excision. On this passage *Cocchi* found an old marginal gloss from the hand of Nicotas (?), **κέρατα μὲν λέγεται ἀπὸ τῆς τῶν κεράτων ἐκφύσεως, τῶν γιγνομένων τοῖς ἀλόγοις ζώοις. Διονυσιακοὺς δὲ αὐτοὺς προσαγορεύουσιν, ἀπὸ τῆς πρὸς τὸν θεὸν ἐμφερείας ὡς αὐτός φησιν ἐν τοῖς χειρουργουμένοις,**—(they arc called horns from the growth of the horns that appear on the lower animals. And they name them **διονυσιακοὶ** from the likeness to the god Dionysus, as he says himself, in the carved figures),—which on the whole confirms the statement of Heliodorus, though he (Cocchi) prefers, following this indication, to emend the passage of Galen also so as to read, **διονυσιακοί, οἷς ὀστώδεις ὑπεροχαὶ ἔγγος κροτάφων γίγνονται,** (Dionysiaci, so they are called, i.e. those in whom bony excrescences grow near the temples). This much, that we should read **διονυσιακοὶ** for **διονυσίσκοι,** is evident, but whether the rest of the emendations are to be accepted may well be open to doubt, as the second clause of the sentence, "and they are called **κέρατα** (horns), so named from the animals that carry horns", obviously implies that the term **διονυσιακοὶ** is used in reference not to the individual, but to the outgrowth. Schneider indeed agrees with the emendation of Cocchi, but has in error put Sarmentus in the place of Messius.

Now supposing the latter has actually had an earlier bony outgrowth, it is not exactly evident why after its skilful removal a *foeda cicatrix* (hideous scar) should have remained,—if indeed we do not prefer to regard the *foedus* (hideous, foul) as perhaps pointing to the *cause* that had occasioned the outgrowth in question. In that case it would certainly be interesting to see thus referred to the vice of the *fellator* affections of the bones carrying the same meaning as our own tophi (concretions on the bone in gouty affections). But in all probability it was merely cutaneous tubercles that had been removed by surgical means, the actual cautery or the knife, and these, as is invariably their nature to do, had left behind an ugly scar. Thus Messius would seem to have resembled Calvus *tuberossimae frontis* (with brow most thickly covered with tubercles) in Petronius (ch. 15.) and the face represented on a gem, of which a delineation is said to be found in *Corius'* Museum Etruriae Plate II. fig. 3.,—a work we have been unable to procure. But enough of the Morbus Campanus [1]!

[1] Besides Acro, *Florus Christianus* also, in his notes on Aristophanes' Wasps v. 1337., referred the morbus Campanus to *fellation*, saying, Hac detestanda libidine iuxta Lesbios usi sunt etiam Campani sive Nolani, ut ex Ausonio et Horatio patet, quorum testimonia non arcessam, quia hoc occupatum ab eruditioribus. Hoc tantum dicam, aenigma illud, quod in Clodii Metelli uxorem iactum putant: In triclinio Coa, in cubiculo Nola, respicere ad hanc Lesbiam et Campanam foeditatem. (This hateful form of lust was practised by the *Campanians* or Nolans, as well as by the Lesbians, as is manifest from what Ausonius and Horace say,—whose evidence however I will not quote, this ground being already preoccupied by more learned writers. This much only will I add, viz. the riddle that was directed against the wife of Metellus Clodius: "On the banquet-couch a Coan, in the bed-chamber a Nolan," and which is thought to allude to this Lesbian and Campanian abomination). The riddle is found in *Quintilian*, Instit. Orat. VIII. 6.; but is differently explained by Forberg,

Sodomy, or Bestiality.

§ 27.

In the various forms of vice hitherto considered we have seen mankind approximating more and more closely to the animal and putting himself to a greater or less degree on the same footing; now we behold him in *Sodomy* [1] sinking finally far *below* the level of the animal, renouncing not merely the human but even the animal nature, in virtue of which he has been able so far to call himself at lowest a member of the species. So it is with complete justice that *Plutarch* [2] says: "At gallus si gallum conscendat "absente gallina, vivus comburitur, aruspice aliquo "pronuntiante grave atroxque id esse ostentum. Ita "ipsi homines hoc confessi sunt, castitate a brutis "se superari, eaque naturae vim non facere voluptatum "percipiendarum causa. Vestras libidines natura, "quamquam legis auxilio fulta, tamen intra suos non "potest coercere fines: quin eae instar fluvii exundan-"tes atrocem foeditatem, tumultum confusionemque "naturae gignant in re venerea. Nam et capras, "porcas, equas iniverunt viri, et feminae insano "mascularum bestiarum amore exarserunt. Ex huius-"modi enim coitibus vobis sunt Minotuari, Silvani "seu Aegipanes atque (ut mea fert sententia) etiam

loco citato p. 283. He says: *Coam* dici, quod voluerit in triclinio coire, *Nolam*, quod noluerit in cubiculo, (that she was called a *Coan*, because willing to have intercourse on the banquet-couch, a Nolan, because unwilling to do so in the bed-chamber), that is to say, Clodia would satisfy her lust only publicly, not in private.

[1] *Hier. Magius*, Bk. V. De sodomitica immanitate ad Leg. cum vir nubit. 31. C. ad leg. Jul. De adulter.— *Wolfart*, Diss. de sodomia vera et spuria in hermaphrod. Erfurt 1743.— *Bechmann*, De coitu damnato. Pt. II, ch. 1.—*Schurig*, Gynaecology, § 2. ch. 7.

[2] *Plutarch*, Bruta animalia ratione uti, (That brutes employ reason), ch. 15.

"Sphinges et Centauri nati [1]. Enimvero fame coactus "canis aut avis aliquando cadavere humano vescitur; "ad coitum nullus unquam est homo a bestia sol- "licitatus, bestias vero cum ad hanc, tum ad alias "voluptates vos vi trahitis ac contra jus usurpatis." (But if the cock tread the cock in the absence of the hen, he is burned alive, any augur pronouncing this to be a serious and sinister prodigy. Thus men have themselves admitted that they are surpassed by brutes in chastity, and that the latter do not do violence to nature with a view to the gratification of their desires. Whereas your lusts nature cannot, though seconded by the aid of law, restrain within their due bounds, or stay them from overflowing like a river in flood and producing horrid abominations, a wild cataclysm and confusion of nature in matters of love. For men have had intercourse with she-goats and sows and mares, while women have been inflamed with mad love of male beasts. Indeed it is from such unions that your Minotaurs have been engendered, and Silvani or Aegipans, and—as I suppose,—the Sphinxes too and Centaurs [1]. True under compulsion of hunger, dog and bird sometimes feed on a human corpse; but no man has ever been invited to coition by any beast, though you constrain beasts by force to this as well as to other shameful pleasures, and use them contrary to all right).

Like all other forms of vicious lust, Sodomy too was an outcome of Asiatic [2] and Egyptian luxury,

[1] Lucretius, De rerum natura, bk. V. 888.,

Ne forte ex homine et veterino semine equorum
Confieri credas Centauros posse, nec esse.

(Never suppose that the Centaurs *could* be framed from man and the bestial seed of horses, and *were* not so framed). *Clement of Alexandria*, Coh. p. 51. Aristonymus the Ephesian begat with a she-ass, Fulvius Stella with a mare, the former a girl, the latter a boy. *Plutarch*, Parall. ch. 26.

[2] Leviticus, Ch.XX, 15-19., "And if a man lie with a beast, he shall surely be put

and already in quite early times familiar in those regions,—in fact, as is the case with sexual excesses generally, this vice appears to have developed from the religious cult of the countries named. Among the Egyptians [2] at any rate we meet with Mendes, the sacred Goat or Pan, worshipped by means of Sodomy on the part of his female devotees, who were shut up along with him.

to death: and ye shall slay the beast. And if a woman approach unto any beast, and lie down thereto, thou shalt kill the woman, and the beast: they shall surely be put to death." Comp. *Philo*, De specialibus legibus,—Works, edit. Mangey, Vol. II. p. 307.

[2] *Plutarch*, Bruta animalia ratione uti, (That brutes employ Reason), ch. X., *ὁ Μενδήσιος ἐν Αἰγύπτῳ τράγος λέγεται πολλαῖς καὶ καλαῖς συνειργνυμένος γυναιξὶν οὐκ εἶναι μίγνυσθαι πρόθυμος; ἀλλὰ πρὸς τὰς αἶγας ἐπτόηται μᾶλλον.* (The Mendesian Goat in Egypt is said, though shut up with many beautiful women, not to be eager to have intercourse with them; but rather is he inflamed towards the she-goats). Yet this did sometimes happen; *Herodotus*, Hist. bk. II. ch. 46., *Καλεῖται δὲ ὅ τε τράγος καὶ ὁ Πὰν Αἰγυπτιστὶ Μένδης· ἐγένετο δ' ἐν τῷ νομῷ τούτῳ ἐπ' ἐμεῦ τοῦτο τὸ τέρας. γυναικὶ τράγος ἐμίσγετο ἀναφανδόν· τοῦτο ἐς ἐπίδεξιν ἀνθρώπων ἀπίκετο.* (Now the goat and Pan are called in Egyptian Mendes; and there occured in this district in my time the following marvel,—a he-goat had intercourse with a woman openly; and this came to be an example among men). Strabo. XVII. p. 802., *Μένδης, ὅπου τὸν Πᾶνα τιμῶσι, καὶ ζῶον τράγον· οἱ τράγοι ἐνταῦθα γυναιξὶ μίγνυνται.* (Mendes, where they honour Pan, and a live goat; the he-goats there have intercourse with women). In a fragment (from Pindar) there given, we read:

ἔσχατον Νείλου κέρας αἰγιβάται
ὅθι τράγοι γυναιξὶ μίγνυνται.

(The furthest mouth of the Nile, where bucking he-goats conjoin with women). The Museum Herculanense actually preserves representations of the thing on Monuments. *Plutarch*, De solertia animalium (Of the Intelligence of Animals), ch. 49., relates a similar case even with crocodiles, which was said to have happened at Antaeopolis.

Boettiger[1] goes so far as to conjecture that the tame snakes in the temple of Aesculapius, which were also kept in private houses[2] as a plaything of the women, were trained and employed by them for purposes of Sodomy. In confirmation a passage is brought forward in this connection by *Forberg*, loco citato, p. 368, from *Suetonius*[3], in which the mother of Augustus, Atia, is spoken of: "In Ascle-"piadis Mendetis **Θεολογουμένων** libris lego, Atiam "cum ad sollemne Apollinis sacrum media nocte "venisset, posita in templo lectica, dum ceterae "matronae dormirent, obdormisse; draconem repente "irrepsisse ad eam paulloque post egressum: illamque "expergefactam q u a s i a c o n c u b i t u m a r i t i "p u r i f i c a s s e s e et statim in corpore eius "exstitisse maculam, velut depicti draconis, nec "potuisse unquam eximi, adeo ut mox publicis balneis "perpetuo abstinuerit"[4]. (In the books of the

[1] *Boettiger*, "Sabina oder Morgenscenen in Putzzimmer einer Römerin, (Sabina, or Morning Scenes at the Toilette of a Roman Lady), Bk. II. p. 454.

[2] *Pliny*, Hist. Nat. Bk. XXXIX. ch. 4., Anguis Aesculapius Epidauro Romam advectus est, vulgoque pascitur et in domibus. (The snake of Aesculapius was introduced from Epidaurus to Rome, and is very commonly kept there, even in houses). *Martial*, bk. VII. Epigr. 86., Si gelidum collo nectit Gracilla draconem. (If Gracilla twines a clammy snake round her neck). Comp. *Lucian*, Alexander, Works, Vol. IV. p. 259. *Philostratus*, Heroic. Bk. VIII. ch. 1.

[3] Suetonius, Vita Augusti, ch. 94.

[4] This last statement acquires no little additional interest from the fact that according to more modern observations on the part of *J. Carver* (Voyage dans l'Amérique Sept., etc. trad. de l'Anglais,—Travels in North America, etc., transl. from the English, Yverdun 1784., pp. 355 sqq.) and Crêve-Cœur (Lettres du Cultivateur Américain,—Letters from an American Farmer, Vol. III. p. 48), the bite of the rattle-snake would appear to call up on the skin of the person bitten, each recurrent year, marks resembling the hue of the snake. Comp. *C. W. Stark*, "Allgem. Pathologie" (General Pathology), Leipzig 1838. p. 364. Perhaps too the expression **κίναδος** belongs in this connection, of

Theologoumena (sacred writings) of the Asclepiad Mendes I read how Atia, who had come to the wonted festival of Apollo at midnight, when her litter had been set down in the Temple, and the other matrons were sleeping, herself fell asleep; how a snake suddenly crept in to her,. and presently emerged again; and how on waking she *purified herself as after intercourse with her husband*, and immediately there appeared a mark on her body, representing the likeness of a snake, which could never be got rid of, so much so that soon she left off ever after frequenting the public baths).

However the Roman women seem to have especially made use of the ass [1] for the satisfaction of their *nymphomania*, an animal that was famed in Antiquity for its salaciousness.

That under such circumstances the women's genitals, and the men's no less, were exposed to many sorts of injury, may be readily supposed; though we have

which the Scholiast on Aristophanes, Clouds 447., says, εἶδός τι ϑηρίον. — κακοῦργος οὖν, φησὶν, ὡς ἀλώπηξ, τινὲς δὲ κίναδος ζῶον μικρὸν τὸ αἰδοῖον εἰςωϑοῦν καὶ ἐξωϑοῦν. (a kind of beast,—mischievous, they say, as a fox, but others say κίναδος means a little animal that *forces its way in and out of the privates*). Suidas brings forward the same statement, under the word κίναδος From the connection in which *Democritus* mentions it in Stobaeus' Sermon. 42., περὶ κιναδέων τε καὶ ἑρπετέων (Of κίναδοι and Creeping Things), *Schneider* in his Lexicon supposes it to signify *snakes* particularly. Again *Schmieder*, Arrian's Indica p. 50., interprets it by ὄφις (a snake). The close resemblance with κίναιδος (Cinaedus) is striking.

[1] *Juvenal*, Sat. VI. 332, 33.

> Hic si
> Quaeritur, et desunt homines: more nulla per ipsam,
> Quominus imposito clunem summittat asello.

(If he is sought in vain, and men are not to be found; *she* makes no delay, but straightway submits her rear to the *donkey* that is made to mount her). Comp. *Appuleius*, Metamorphos. Bk. X. 226. Pasiphaé's bull is familiar to all. Comp. Suetonius, Nero II. Martial, Spectac. VI.

sought in vain so far for any direct evidence of the fact. So we may perhaps be allowed to quote here an observation originating with *Abu Oseibah*, De vitis medicorum illustrium, (On the Lives of Famous Physicians), according to *Reiske*[1]. This properly speaking belongs to a later period chronologically, but it is pertinent in the present connection. Reiske says: "Caput XIII. habet observationem—2. de "ingenti penis inflammatione, quae nata "fuerat ex impuro cum bestia con-"cubitu, cum coruncula urethram obstruente, "sanata modo prorsum empirico atque crudeli. Im-"positum glabro lapidi penem medicus subito praeter "aegri expectationem, qua poterat vi percutiebat "manu in pugnum coacta, ut obturaculum et ulcus "dissiliret. Sapit hic casus luem veneream; "et posset inservire illis pro argumento, qui morbum "hunc etiam veteribus cognitum fuisse contendunt. "Cadit autem is casus circa annum Christi 940. (Chapter XIII contains the following observation,—2. Of an violent *inflammation of the penis, which had originated in unclean intercourse with a beast*, with a coruncle, or knot, contricting the urethra, cured in a manner to the last degree empirical and cruel. The penis being laid on a rough stone, the Physician suddenly when the patient was not expecting it, struck it as heavily as ever he could with his doubled fist, so that the stoppage and ulcer might burst. This case has a smack of the *Venereal disease* about it; and might serve as an argument for those who hold that this disease was known to the Ancients as well. But the case falls about the year of Our Lord 940.)

[1] *Jo. Jac. Reiske* and *Jo. Ern. Fabri*, Opuscula medica ex monumentis Arabum et Ebraeorum, (Minor Medical Treatises derived from the Monuments of the Arabs and Jews), Revised edition by *Ch. G. Gruner*, Halle 1776. 8vo., p. 61.

Climate.

§ 28.

Now that we have made ourselves acquainted with the various use to which the Ancients put the genital organs, we are confronted inevitably with the question,—how were the genitals themselves affected by it all? Impossible to suppose they can have preserved their integrity absolutely intact, while at the same time such parts as were substituted in use for the one or the other form of them, were exposed,—as is abundantly proved by the different diseases described, diseases affecting the *pathic*, the *fellator* and the *cunnilingue* respectively,—to manifold complaints, and very often had to pay severely for the misuse to which they were put. Granting that the unnatural use of the mouth and the rectum must necessarily have endangered those parts specifically more than the penis, an organ particularly adapted and intended for friction, still this will by no means imply the entire immunity of the latter from ill effects. Indeed the fact of such immunity is sufficiently disproved by the passages quoted specifically under paederastia, without taking into account at all the large number of actual maladies of the genitals that are mentioned by professional and non-professional writers of Antiquity. With some of these we have already made acquaintance,—maladies which no one would for a moment think of ascribing *exclusively* to the practice of the vice of paederastia.

Accordingly we must look for other factors, which being in part unconnected with the use of the genitals, are not like this to be regarded as an immediately efficient cause, but rather as predisposing circumstances, exercising from the first an independent influence on the normal condition of those organs. For mere use or misuse cannot possibly be taken as in itself a sufficient reason to account for disease, even though the Ancients may have looked upon complaints of the genitals partly as a direct consequence of *illicita Venus* (unlawful Love), or in other words as it were a result of the vengeance of outraged Nature. The genitals, like all organs of the human body, exhibit over and above their functional activity on behalf of the general organism and its reproduction, evidences also of an independent activity directed towards the maintenance of their own integrity and individual existence,—and these are bound to differ more or less according to difference of locality and difference of time, as indeed may be predicated of the organism as a whole, if we trust the indications it gives.

Now this differentiation according to locality is conditioned above all else by climate; hence the question we have now first of all to answer is this: *what influence did climate manifest in Ancient times on the activity of the genital organs in general and in particular?* and, *to what extent may a factor favourable to the rise of affections of the genitals be deduced from it?* True, direct information on the point has so far reached us only sparingly, still such as we have is enough to justify a general view on the whole question, especially if we reinforce it with the results of more recent observation,—always provided this be done with proper precaution, for we sometimes find the Ancients commending the climate of a particular country as being exceedingly healthy, whereas in more modern times exactly the opposite is noted. As the evidence extant and available extends only to Asia, and in particular Syria, Palestine and Asia Minor, to Egypt, Greece and Italy, there can for the present be no question except as to the climate of these countries.

Next as to *the influence of sexual activity in general, Hippocrates* [1] himself tells us, after discussing the climate of Asia: "But ἡδονὴ (pleasure) must necessarily predominate (among them), and this is why

[1] *Hippocrates*, De aere aq. et loc., edit. Kühn Vol. I. p. 549.

among animals so many varieties are found; and I suppose this to be equally true in the case of the Egyptians and Lydians also." Of course ἡδονή in this passage signifies concupiscence in particular;—no special proof is needed of this. As a matter of fact we observe at the present day how in hot climates, where the whole vegetative life presents a luxuriant character, and all Nature appears to feel the procreative impulse unceasingly, man too falls in with the universal stress and strain of each species to maintain its foothold. Yet as this must inevitably be done at the expense of the individual life, we see the effort very frequently resulting in the production of barren or sexless blossoms, and not fruit at all. The son of the South is like a tree growing in rich, rank soil; he ripens betimes to the sexual life, but equally early is constrained to abandon it again. The youthful imagination springs up in its fresh quick activity, while the body withers concurrently, and stung by lust,—lust that is yet further exaggerated by the misuse of *aphrodisiacs*, at last has nothing left but to drag out an invalid existence, finding a morbid gratification in the artificial ways and means whereby imagination, sickened and debauched by its own extravagances, seeks to supply from extraneous sources the failing titillation of desire the organ craves. No better confirmation of all this can be found than what is supplied already in our investigations as so far conducted.

We saw how in Asia lust and its abominable brood arose and extended thence over neighbouring lands, and how the rhythmic rites of the *Venus ebria* (drunken Venus) could indeed refine, but hardly increase their excesses. Babylon, Syria and Egypt were the nurseries of licentiousness, finding only at Rome a really self-taught and competent rival. The clear sky of Greece could cover only inhabitants of corresponding character in body and mind, and none but a Greek was capable of setting up the ideal, and verifying it in practice, of a fair soul in a fair body. Deep as the Greek may have sunk in degradation after the fall of national liberty and under foreign influence, and though unbridled lust may have often mastered individuals, it never dominated the nation as a whole, it was artificially brought into existence and was never dependent on climate. Even at Rome, colossal as was the scale on which vice manifested itself, it ever remained but a foreign importation, for which foreign wantons had first paved the way at a period when the climate of Asia exerted a more immediate influence there than that of Greece.

Like licentiousness in general, Polygamy also, in part owing its existence to it as it does, was a consequence of the Asiatic climate; but how far it may be fairly held to have influenced the rise of Venereal disease, we do not as yet venture to decide; we feel constrained to keep this point over for later investigations. The same applies to Polyandry,—in its strict sense, when we regard it as a form of marriage; though of course over and above this it comes into connection with vice, inasmuch as every prostitute lives in a state of Polyandry, as does every amateur of the sex in one of Polygamy. Under these circumstances affections of the genitals cannot but arise among persons otherwise healthy, as every Physician of large practice can verify by examples, and as experiments on animals have sufficiently demonstrated to be the case [1]. Nevertheless these hints, for we cannot and ought not to look upon them as anything more than hints, as any more complete discussion would carry us too far a-field for our present purpose,—may very well suffice to

[1] Comp. *Simon Zeller von Zellenberg*, Abhandl. über die ersten Erscheinungen venerischer Lokal-Krankheitsformen und deren Behandlung, (Treatise on the first Appearances of Local Forms of Venereal disease, and their Treatment), (One treatise under six heads), —Vienna 1820. large 8vo. pp. 11—18.

recall to the reader's memory the influence exerted by climate on the genital functions, especially as adequate proofs in confirmation of all this are comprised in our preceding Sections.

§ 29.

Far more important in view of our immediate object is the *influence exerted by Climate on the individual activity of the genital organs*, and here again we have in the first place to fix our eyes on Asia and Egypt. The burning rays of the sun to which these regions and their inhabitants are exposed, increase in a marked way the activity of the skin, and of course in the same proportion do the secretions from the mucous surfaces become less in quantity, but their product more highly charged in quality. Then, this being the case, a certain acridity or corroding quality of the secretion is readily set up, often making itself noticeable by a characteristic smell. This same influence must equally manifest itself in the mucous membrane of the inner parts of the genitals, and vaginal mucus accordingly acquire an acrid quality, if it is not removed pretty frequently from the surface of the membrane, and becoming as it were rancid, exert a corrosive effect on everything it comes in contact with [1].

[1] According to *Al. Donné*, Recherches microscopiques sur la nature des mucus et la matière des divers écoulements des organes genitourinaires chez l'homme et chez la femme, (Microscopic Researches into the Nature of the Mucous Secretions and the Constituents of the Various Discharges from the genito-urinary Organs in Male and Female), Paris 1837., the vaginal mucus disengaged under normal circumstances *always exhibits an acid reaction*.

[2] According to *J. P. Schotte*, Von einem ansteckenden, schwarzgallichten Faulfieber, welches im Jahr 1778 in Senegall herrschte, (Account of a Contagious, black biliary, putrid Fever, prevalent in Senegal in the Year 1778), from the English (Stendal) 1786. 8vo., p. 103., both men and women in Senegal get ulcers, quite without any

Now shortly before as well as shortly after the commencement of menstruation the secretion of mucus in the genitals is increased, and thus the menstrual blood, having in any case a tendency to decomposition, will mingle with this acrid, strong-smelling mucous discharge, and in this way assume a foul, acrid character itself[1]. This is the origin

syphilitic contagion, in the one sex on the *glans penis* or the under side of the prepuce, in the other on the inner side of the *labia*.

[1] *Virey*, De la Femme, 2nd. edition, Brussels 1826., p. 70., En effet, dans la chaleur, lorsque les excrétions de la peau, des glandes sébacées, des cryptes du vagin, augmentent en abondance et en fétidité, il n'est pas étonnant que le sang menstruel, pour peu qu'il séjourne en ces parties voisines de l'anus, qui sont dans un état d'orgasme, acquière bientôt de l'odeur. (Indeed in a hot climate, when the secretions from the skin, from the sebaceous glands, from the recesses of the vagina, increase in abundance and in foulness, it is not surprising that the menstrual blood, remaining for a time as it does in the regions contiguous to the anus, these regions being in a state of sur-excitation, quickly acquires an evil smell). So *Haller* too says (Elem. Physiolog. Vol. VII. pt. II. p. 146.), Ex Asia videtur opinio de menstrui sanguinis foetida et venenata natura ad nos pervenisse, et per medicos potissimum Arabes ad Europaeos transiisse. In calidissimis certe regionibus, si ad aestuosum aerem immundities accesserit, non repugnat, sanguinem in loco calente, in vicinia faecum alvinarum retentum, acrem fieri et foetire. . . . Lentorem aliquem possit mucus admistus addidisse. (*It is from Asia that the opinion as to the fetid and poisonous character of menstrual blood would seem to have come to us*, being transmitted mainly by the Arab physicians to those of Europe. No doubt in very hot climates, if dirty habits be added to the extreme heat of the atmosphere, there is nothing at all unlikely in the blood, retained as it is in a hot locality, in close proximity to the faeces in the bowels, growing sour and smelling foul.... *A certain viscous quality may very well have been added by the admixture of mucous discharge*). What has been observed as to the injuriousness of menstrual blood by our predecessors since *Pliny* (Hist. Nat. VII. 15. XIX. 10. XXVIII.

of the ill repute into which menstrual blood, and this especially in hot climates, has fallen from the earliest times onwards, for no doubt the virulent qualities alleged against it really belong to it solely and entirely as a result of the admixture with it of this vaginal mucus. Sea-water and fresh river-water are each of them separately innocuous for health, but mix them together so as to make brackish water, and the exhalations given off become highly detrimental!

A similar state of things exists also in connection with the male genital organs. The surface of the *glans penis*, where it lies contiguous to the external skin, exhibits along with the latter an increased secretion from the sebaceous follicles [1], the discharge from which, if it is allowed to remain any length

7.) may be found partially collected in *Schurig*, Parthenologia 227—240. Comp. *Frank de Frankenau*, Satyrae Medicae (Medical Satires), p. 89. Comp. pp. 54. sqq.—*Hensler*, Geschichte der Lustseuche, (History of Venereal Disease), Vol. I. pp. 204 sqq., where it is demonstrated that a great proportion of the Writers on Venereal disease at the beginning of the XVIth. Century attribute its rise to intercourse with women during menstruation.

[1] *Burdach*, Die Physiologie als Erfahrungswissenschaft, (Physiology as an Experimental Science), 2nd. edition, Vol. I. p. 196.—*Boerhaave*, Tract. de lue venerea, (Treatise on Venereal Contagion), Venice 1753., p. 6., says, In Asia ad partes genitales sub praeputio naturaliter sordes colliguntur, quae acres redditae generant multa mala, quae praecipue ad luem veneream accedere proxime videntur; non vere sunt lues venerea; imo nostri nautae hoc etiam experiuntur, dum in illis terris degunt, nam nisi quotidie praeputium eluerent aqua salsa et aceto, vel similibus remediis brevi eodem morbo laborarent. (In Asia filth of sorts naturally enough collects on the genital parts beneath the prepuce, and this turning sour originates many complaints, which seem above all others to approximate closely to the Venereal disease. This our sailors found out, when living in those regions; for if they did not daily thoroughly wash the prepuce with salt water and vinegar, or similar remedies, they would soon suffer from the disease in question).

of time between the prepuce and the *glans* [1], likewise acquires an acrid quality; then re-acting on these parts, sets up an inflammatory condition of the aforesaid sebaceous follicles. "In fact", says *Niebuhr* [2] the Medical Officer of the English at Haleb (Russel) ascertained that in hot countries more copious humours collect about the *glans penis* than in cold; and a friend of mine in India, who in that hot climate had employed only the ordinary European precautions to ensure cleanliness, got a sort of ulcers on the *glans*, an inconvenience he would have been much more likely to escape, had he been circumcised. Subsequently he always washed this part of his person very carefully, and from that time forth experienced no trace of a recurrence of the trouble. Washing the whole body and particularly the privates is an absolute necessity in hot countries; and it is perhaps for this reason that the religious founders of the Jews, the Mohammedans, the Fire-Worshippers, the Heathen in India, etc., have commanded the observation of this practice."

In close accord with this is the story *Flavius Josephus* [3] relates of *Apion* the Egyptian: "Wherefore

[1] *Thevenot*, Travels, Pt. I., p. 58., says, "The Arabs in fact have the prepuce so long that, if they did not have it circumcised. they would suffer much inconvenience from it; and little children are to be seen among them whose prepuce hangs down to a very considerable length;—not to mention that, supposing their foreskin uncircumcised, every time after passing water some drops would remain behind, rendering them unclean."

[2] *Niebuhr*, Beschreibung von Arabien, (Description of Arabia) Copenhagen 1772, 4to., p. 77.

[3] *Josephus*, Contra Apionem bk. II. ch. 13., ὅθεν εἰκότως μοι δοκεῖ τῆς εἰς τοὺς πατρίους αὐτοῦ νόμους βλασφημίας δοῦναι δίκην Ἀπίων τὴν πρέπουσαν· περιετμήθη γὰρ ἐξ ἀνάγκης, ἑλκώσεως αὐτῷ περὶ τὸ αἰδοῖον γενομένης· καὶ μηδὲν ὠφεληθεὶς ὑπὸ τῆς περιτομῆς ἀλλὰ σηπόμενος ἐν δειναῖς ὀδύναις ἀπέθανεν. (for translation see text). The expression περὶ τὸ αἰδοῖον (about the privates)

it appears to me Apion deservedly paid a fitting penalty for his scorn of ancestral customs; for only when forced by necessity was he circumcised, ulceration having been set up about his privates (his *glans penis*); and as a matter of fact the circumcision proved vain, for gangrene supervened, and he died in terrible pain." Again the passage just quoted will also afford a clear understanding of the following from *Philo*[1]:

"Therefore were it more becoming, quitting childish and frivolous mockery altogether, intelligently and earnestly to investigate the causes in which this custom (Circumcision) originated, rather than to accuse whole nations of folly in a spirit of mere prejudice. It certainly does not seem probable to an intelligent enquirer, approaching the question in this mood, that so many thousands of folk in every age should have been circumcised without a sufficient cause, submitting to great pain merely to mutilate their own and their children's bodies. On the other hand there are many inducements to adopt outright and follow up the custom of our forefathers; and in an especial degree the four following. First, *the prevention of a virulent disease and one very difficult to cure.* This is known as *Anthrax*,—a denomination derived, as I suppose, from the ardent (fierce)

is evidently to be understood here as meaning the *glans penis*, or at any rate the prepuce. This is implied by the general sense of the whole passage.

[1] *Philo*, De circumcisione, Works edit. Th. Mangey Vol. II. p. 211. "Εν μὲν, χαλεπῆς νόσου καὶ δυσιάτου πάθους ἀπαλλαγὴν, ἣν ἄνθρακα καλοῦσιν, ἀπὸ τοῦ καίειν ἐντυφόμενον, ὡς οἶμαι, ταύτης τῆς προσηγορίας τυχόντος, ἥτις οὐ κολώτερον τοῖς τὰς ἀκροποσθίας ἔχουσιν ἐγγίνετο· Δεύτερον, τὴν δὲ ὅλου τοῦ σώματος καθαρότητα πρὸς τὸ ἁρμόττειν τάξει ἱερωμένῃ. Παρ' ὃ καὶ ξυρῶντο τὰ σώματα προςυπερβάλλοντες οἱ ἐν Αἰγύπτῳ τῶν ἱερέων. ὑποσυλλέγετο γὰρ καὶ ὑποστέλλει καὶ θριξὶ καὶ ποσθίαις ἔνια τῶν ὀφειλόντων καθαίρεσθαι. (for translation see text above).

burning (ἀπὸ τοῦ καίειν ἐντυφόμενον) that accompanies it, and *readily arises in such as have the foreskin intact.* Secondly, to secure that purity of the whole person obligatory upon the Priestly caste. Whence it comes that the Priests in Egypt also scrupulously shave the whole body; for there is something collects and is deposited underneath the hair as well as under the foreskin, that must be removed."

From a comparison of these two passages from Niebuhr and from Philo respectively it may be gathered that the *anthrax* disease above mentioned did not in any way owe its rise to a *specifically* syphilitic origin, as has been now and again assumed by different enquirers. What we really learn from them is to recognize the liability of the sebaceous follicles of the *glans penis* to lapse into a condition of ulceration. True this tendency can be minimised to some extent by circumcision, as well as by unremitting care to secure cleanliness; yet it can never be completely removed, conditioned as it really is by climatic influences that do not admit of elimination. When once the corroding vaginal mucus of the woman, particularly in combination with the menstrual blood with its readiness to undergo putrefaction [1] re-acting on the mucous membrane,

[1] That is to say so far as it is suffered to remain for any length of time in the vagina and comes more or less in contact with the atmospheric air; for in the case of healthy menstrual blood no injurious combination is set up at all or any foul acridity developed, as *John Stedman* (Physiolog. Versuche und Beobachtungen,—Physiological Investigations and Observations, transl. from the English, Leipzig 1778. 8vo., pp. 50—54.) long ago maintained. It is more probable however that any slight putrefactive action occurring is in each case due not so much to this as to the *acid quality* of the menstrual blood, which in conjunction with the acid vaginal mucus undergoes a kind of acetous fermentation in the vagina, the product of which has thus a corrosive effect. *Retzius* indeed has lately not only found menstrual blood to possess an exceedingly acid reaction, but even proved that

has set up sores and ulcers, then follows as a necessary consequence a still more dangerous mixture of matter and mucus. Next when under these conditions the man's *glans*, possessing as it does an equally great liability in its cutaneous glands to be attacked by ulceration, enters in coition a vagina in this state, it cannot occasion much surprise if blennorhoea of the urethra or ulceration of the *glans penis* supervene [1], especially if we consider the fact that

it contains free phosphoric and lactic acids. Comp. Arsberättelse om Svenska Läkare Sällskapets Arbeten, 1835., pp. 19—21. Froriep's Notiz, Vol. 49., p. 237.

[1] Hence too *Hugo Grotius* writes (Commentar. ad Mosis lib. III. — Commentary on Book of Leviticus, ch. 15.): Sciendum est autem in Syria et locis vicinis non minus **τὴν γονόῤῥοιαν** quam **τὰ ἐμμήνια** habere aliquid contagione nocens, (But it is to be observed that in Syria and the neighbouring regions **ἡ γονοῤῥοία** (discharge from the genitals) no less than **τὰ ἐμμήνια** (menstrual discharge) contains a principle contagiously injurious). Even *Astruc*, the eager advocate of the American origin of Venereal disease, says (Vol. I. p. 92.): Sane constat in hac nostra Europa, quae magis temperata est, si cum menstruatis res habeatur, balanum et praeputium leviore phlogosi aut superficiariis pustulis, quae tamen brevi cessant, plerumque affici. Quanto graviora ergo iis impendere credendum est, quos in calidiore et aestuante climate misceri cum foeminis non pudet, dum illis menses actu fluunt natura acerrimi et quasi virosi. Ideo forsan factum est, ut medici Arabes, qui regiones calidiores incolebant, quam Graeci et Latini, et primi et saepe disseruerint de pustulis et ulceribus virgae, oriundis ex coitu cum foeda muliere, hoc est (?), cum muliere menstruata. (It is an undoubted fact that in this Europe of ours, though enjoying a more temperate climate, if intercourse is had with women during menstruation, the *glans penis* and prepuce are *generally* attacked by some little inflammation or by superficial pustules, which however soon disappear. What much more serious consequences then must we suppose threaten those who in a warmer climate, one steaming with heat, are not ashamed to make coition with women, whilst their *menses* are actually flowing, these being from the nature of the case exceedingly acrid and almost poisonous. Perhaps this is why the Arab physicians, who lived in warmer

the act of coition sets the organs concerned in enhanced activity, making them more susceptible than ever to external injurious irritations. This is yet more likely to be the case, as concurrently a large amount of secretion is yielded by the morbidly affected mucous surface of the vagina, and very possibly this secretion undergoes under the influence of nervous excitation (as the saliva does under the influence of anger) some vital-chemical, contagious alteration of composition. Again supposing the woman to be at the time of coition actually in menstruation, a period when her genital organs are *ipso facto* roused to a condition of exaggerated activity, the disturbance must be yet greater, and the mischief resulting even more manifest.

This will in part account for the fact that ulcers on the genitals, brought about by coition, are so ready in Asia to assume a putrid character, and show that the Ancients had good reason to designate them by the name **ἄνθραξ** (anthrax, malignant pustule). For that **ἄνθραξ** was actually a consequence of coition we may see from a passage, already cited by Hensler and Simon, from Bishop *Palladius* [1], who

countries than the Greek and Latin practitioners, first and most often treated of pustules and ulcers of the verge, arising from coition with an unclean woman, that is to say (?) with a woman during menstruation). Comp. *Fr. Eagle* and *Judd* in Behrend's Syphilologie, Vol. I. 117 and 285.

[1] *Palladius*, Lausiaca historia, ch. 39. in Magna Bibliotheca Patrum (Great Library of the Fathers), Vol. XIII., Paris 1644. fol., p. 950.: *Οὕτως δὲ γαστριμαργῶν καὶ οἰνοφλυγῶν ἐνέπεσεν καὶ εἰς τὸν βόρβυρον τῆς γυναικείης* *ἐπιθυμίας· καὶ ὡς ἐσκέπτετο ἁμαρτῆσαι μιμάδι τινὶ προσομιλῶν συνεχῶς τὰ πρὸς τὸ ἕλκος ἑαυτοῦ διελέγετο· τούτων οὕτως ὑπ' αὐτοῦ διαπραττομένων γέγονεν αὐτῷ κατά τινα οἰκονομίαν ἄνθραξ κατὰ τῆς βαλάνου· καὶ ἐπὶ τοσοῦτον ἐνόσησεν ἑξαμηνιαῖον χρόνον, ὡς κατασαπῆναι αὐτοῦ τὰ μορία καὶ αὐτομάτως ἀποπεσεῖν· ὕστερον δὲ ὑγιάνας καὶ ἐπανελθὼν ἄνευ τούτων τῶν μελῶν, καὶ εἰς φρόνημα θεϊκὸν ἐλθὼν*

καὶ εἰς μνήμην τῆς οὐρανίου πολιτείας, καὶ ἐξομολογησάμενος πάντα τὰ συμβεβηκότα αὐτῷ τοῖς ἁγίοις πατράσιν, ἐνεργῆσαι μὴ φθάσας ἐκοιμήθη μετὰ ὀλίγας ἡμέρας. (for translation see text above). For κατά τινα οἰκονομίαν (by a certain providence) we ought probably to read κατὰ θινὰν or θείαν οἰκονομίαν, a collocation of words constantly found in Palladius, and occuring in this very chapter a few lines before, in the sense of "by Divine providence". On the other hand the words τὰ πρὸς τὸ ἕλκος ἑαυτοῦ διελέγετο are to us absolutely unintelligible. *Helvetius* translates the passage: Incidit in coenum femineae cupiditatis et cum peccare constituisset cum quadam mima assidue colloquutus, *ulcus suum aperuit*, (He fell into the mire of lust after women, and having set his mind on sinning, constantly conversing with a certain actress, *he opened his sore*. Indeed the γυναικείη ἐπιθυμία (womanly lust) itself is ambiguous, as strictly speaking it points to something unmanly, and if we compare with it the γυναικεία νοῦσος (womanly disease) of Dio Chrysostom (p. 209.), our thoughts cannot but turn to the vice of the pathic,—which however Hero could not very well practise with an actress, and to which he could hardly owe an *anthrax* on the *glans penis*. But ch. 35. shows us plainly enough that *Palladius* in using the phrase means lust, indulgence with women, accomplishing coition. It is related in that chapter of the Abbot Elias, how he had founded a nunnery, and was thereupon assailed by violent desire to abuse the nuns; wherefore he prayed, ἀπόκτεινόν με, ἵνα μὴ ἴδω αὐτὰς θλιβομένας. ἢ τὸ πάθος μου λάβε, ἵνα αὐτῶν φροντίζω κατὰ λόγον. (Kill me, that I may not see them troubled, or else take away my *passion*, that I may look upon them with reason and moderation). Thereafter he fell asleep and dreamed the angels had castrated him, and on waking found indeed that he still possessed his genitals, but he declared, ὅτι οὐκέτι ἀνέβη εἰς τὴν καρδίαν μου πάθος γυναικὸς ἐπιθυμίας. (there no more entered into my heart the passion of *lust after* women). But now what does τὰ πρὸς τὸ ἕλκος mean? Guided by the general sense, we might take it as meaning the genital organs, though we have searched in vain for analogous passages. But in that case it could be made to apply only to the female genitals or to the rectum, because these only exhibit a breach of continuity (ἕλκος,—a wound); or else we should have to suppose the seed to be looked upon in a sort of way as matter discharged, and the

relates of a certain Hero, how the Demon led him

male genitals, which secrete it, therefore called ἕλκος (a wound), for otherwise the ἑαυτοῦ (his own) cannot be got in. No less uncertain is the meaning of διελέγετο; "to converse" cannot possibly be taken as the sense here. *Suidas* and *Hesychius* explain διαλέγεσθαι by συνουσιάζειν (to associate with). *Pollux*, Onomast. V. 93. περὶ μίξεως ζώων (On the intercourse of Animals) says, διαλεχθῆναι. — οὐδ' ἡ διάλεξις, ἀλλὰ διειλέχθην αὐτῇ καὶ διειλεγμένος εἰμὶ ὡς Ὑπερίδης. II. 125. Ὑπερίδης δὲ διειλεγμένος, ἐπ' ἀφροδισίων. Ἀριστοφάνης δὲ διαλέξασθαι ἔφη. (διελεχθῆναι, — not ordinary conversation, but it means "I had converse with her", or "I am conversant", as says Hyperides, II. 125. Now Hyperides says "conversant with", speaking of love intercourse; and Aristophanes "to have converse with"). Comp. Küster and Brunck on Aristophanes' Plut. 1083. Moeris p. 131. Abresch, lect. Aristaenet. p. 50. But the meaning of accomplishing coition is implied already in προςομιλῶν (associating with), so that διαλέγεσθαι must here indicate some other more special circumstance. The Scholiast of Aristophanes on Lys. 720 interprets διαλέγουσιν by διορύττουσιν (bore through), penetrate); accordingly we must take διαλέγεσθαι as deponent, in which case we should have to read. τὰ πρὸς τὸ ἕλκος αὐτῆς διελέγετο (he penetrated *her* private parts), and make the τὰ πρὸς ἕλκος refer to the actress and her hymen (or fibula?), just as in the passage cited from Josephus on p. 315. the expression περὶ τὸ αἰδοῖον (about the privates) signifies the foreskin. If we would keep ἑαυτοῦ (his own), then we must take διαλέγομαι in the sense of καθαίρειν (to purify) (Hesychius says διαλέγειν, ἀνακαθαίρειν, — to purify), and put in an οὐκ (not),—i.e. he did not purify his genitals. If we keep to the meaning of separation, division, we might understand the sentence as saying that Hero tore apart his foreskin; though really ἕλκος could scarcely be applied with any propriety to the male genitals at all. For its being used of the female genitals on the other hand a good analogy is offered by ἐσχάρα (a scab), which occurs in Aristophanes, Knights 1296. and often elsewhere. Eustathius, on Odyss. p. 1823., says: δῆλον δ' ὅτι ἐσχάραν καὶ τὸ γυναικεῖον ἐκάλουν μόριον. (Now it is evident they used to call the female part ἐσχάρα). However in this case the learned reader must be left to decide for himself.

to Alexandria, how he there visited theatres and horse-races, and roamed round the taverns. "And thus, being by this time a glutton and a drunkard, he *fell moreover into the mire of lust after women;* and being now set upon sinning, *he lived with a certain actress*, (and had carnal intercourse with her?). *Then when he had done all this, by a (Divine) providence he got an "anthrax" on the glans penis; and was so sick for six months that his (private) parts rotted away and dropped off of themselves.* But subsequently recovering and getting off with the loss of these members, coming to a knowledge of God and a remembrance of the heavenly kingdom, and after confessing all that had befallen him, he fell asleep a few days afterwards, without having had the time to manifest works (of repentance)." In spite of the difficulties some of the expressions in the text exhibit, the main fact is perfectly plain, and admits of no doubt whatever, viz. that Hero had brought the **ἄνθραξ** on himself by carnal intercourse with an actress, and the moral reflections Palladius tags on to it cannot invalidate the fact. The objections *Astruc* raises against the conclusiveness of the passage have already been refuted by *Hensler* (Geschichte der Lustseuche,—History of Venereal Disease, I. pp. 317 sqq.), who while citing as parallel instances the passages adduced by *Becket* from the early XVth Century, very justly remarks: "What proof *would* they have, if this is not conclusive?"

Did the female genitals perhaps receive the names **ἐσχάρα** (scab) and **ἄνθραξ** (malignant pustule), *because* they very often made men a present of these things?!

In any case it is an interesting fact that to this day in India *anthrax* and chancrous ulcers are looked upon as akin, and both according to *Sir William Jones* (Asiatic Researches Vol. II.) are known by the name Nar Farsi or Ateshi Farsi (*Ignis Persicus*—Persian Fire) to the Cabirajas or Indian physicians. Now if we think of the great care taken by the Jews to ensure the multiplication of their race, the readiness with which various forms of ulceration pass over into mortification in hot localities,—as is shown by the examples of Apion and Hero,—and consequently the serious liability of the organs of generation to be destroyed, it will occasion less surprise when we read among the laws of *Moses* [1] the following injunction: "And if a man shall lie with a woman having her sickness, and shall uncover her nackedness; he hath discovered her fountain, and she hath uncovered the fountain of her blood; and both of them shall be cut off from among their people." Surely great and serious resulting injuries must in no inconsiderable number of instances have been before his eyes for a Lawgiver to feel himself constrained to assign the death penalty to the act of coition with women during menstruation,—and this in spite of the fact that he had already in a general way declared the woman at this time, as well as everything she touched, to be unclean. Again on the other hand coition with women in this condition must with the Jews have been amongst things practised with more than ordinary

[1] *Leviticus* ch. 20. v. 18. It is true *Maimonides* according to *Selden*, Uxor Hebraica (The Jewish Wife), Frankfurt 1673. 4to., p. 133., says: At vero si esset mensibus immunda, tametsi deducta fuerit, etiam et coitus sit secutus, nuptiae non perficiebantur. (But indeed if she were unclean with menstruation, though she had been led forth to a husband's house, *even if coition had followed*, the marriage was not proceeded with)—but in that case of course it happened unwittingly; though no doubt it may very well on the other hand have been done not unfrequently wittingly. *Festus* explains the Latin word *imbubinare* by "menstruo mulierum sanguine inquinare" to pollute with the menstrual blood of women), which might almost justify us in conjecturing, that *buboes* had been observed to originate from intercourse with women during menstruation. *Hippocrates*, De natura pueri (On the Bodily Constitution of the Boy), edit. Kühn Vol. I. p. 390., derives affections of the sort in women from arrested menstruation.

frequency, if only such an extreme punishment availed to check it; and so we cannot really be surprised to find that the Holy Books of that Nation perhaps earlier than the writings of any other People were acquainted only too well with diseases of the genital organs acquired by coition. The particular disease that broke out in consequence of the worship of Baal-Peor has been discussed above in §§ 8 and 9; while the fact that the Mosaic books contain the first traces of a knowledge of *Gonorrhoea* has long been regarded as proved beyond a doubt [1].

[1] *Leviticus* Ch. 15. Want of space forbids our giving this Chapter here; but anyone who will read it through carefully, must easily see that in it the question is merely of a morbid discharge from the genitals (basar), the duration of which was uncertain. For this reason those affected continued still unclean for nine days after the cessation of the flux, whereas the man who had encountered ordinary pollution (verse 16.) was unclean only till the evening. The Septuagint translators render the flux by ῥύσις (flowing, flux), the person affected by the flux γονοῤῥυής (having a flux from the genitals), while they say of ordinary pollution, ὡς ἐὰν ἐξέλθῃ ἐξ αὐτοῦ κοίτη σπέρματος ("if any man's *seed* of copulation go out of him"). *Astruc* and others wished to refer the flux from the genitals to Lepra (Leprosy), but in that case the Leprosy must needs have been previously noticeable in the person affected by the flux, and the flux therefore been really a symptom. Thus it would have demanded no further special ordinance for purification, as that commanded for Leprosy would have been used for it. Again the same would also have occurred, had the flux been noticed as *first* symptom of the Leprosy, for then the Priest was bound to have confined the person so affected and put him under observation, to see whether the other symptoms of Leprosy would show themselves as well. But of this there is nothing whatever to be found in the writings attributed to Moses, who clearly distinguishes between the flux and Leprosy, as also does the Author of II Samuel III. 29. Speaking generally, no other Author ever mentions the flux as a constant or frequent symptom of Leprosy, while *Schilling* even denies its occurrence altogether. Comp. *Hensler*, Vom abendl. Aussatze (On Oriental Leprosy), pp. 130, 396.

If the Climate already exerted such an influence on the aboriginal inhabitants, how much greater must this have been where foreigners were concerned, on whom all endemic excitants of disease in a country notoriously work with augmented virulence. In Antiquity this fact must have been even more conspicuously true, inasmuch as at that period the Nations still remained much more unmixed than they subsequently became. It is a thing which always hitherto, speaking generally, has been far too little taken account of by Pathologists, but which is surely of vast importance in connection with the rise and spread of Venereal disease,—without its being in any way implied that we must necessarily therefore adopt the theory of its American origin [1]. If

[1] *Astruc*, De morbis venereis (Of Venereal diseases), p. 93., Quid igitur mirum varia, heterogenea, acria multorum virorum semina (et smegmata we may add) una confusa, cum acerrimo et virulento menstruo sanguine mixta, intra uterum aestuantem et olidum spurcissimarum mulierum coercita, mora, heterogeneitate, calore loci brevi computruisse ac prima morbi venerei semina constituisse, quae in alios, si qui forsan continentiores erant, contagione dimanavere? . . . Cum ergo in omnibus terrae locis, ubi lues venerea antiquitus endemia fuisse videtur, eundem aeris fervorem cum pari incolarum impudicitia coniunctum fuisse manifestum sit, haud inanis inde locus est colligendi morbum natura eundem, quo regiones longissime dissitae et inter quas nulla fuit commercii communio, simili modo infestabantur, a simili causarum earundem concursu, in quo tantum convenirent, generatum olim fuisse et generari etiamnum, si indigenae iisdem moribus vivant. (What is there surprising then in the fact that the various, heterogeneous, acrid seminal fluids of a number of different men (and unguents as well, we may add), all confounded together and mixed with the exceedingly acrid and virulent menstrual blood, confined within the steaming hot and fetid womb of the dirtiest of women, by long continuance in one place, by heterogeneity of components, by the heat of the locality, should very soon have grown putrid, and so laid the first seeds of Venereal disease,—which then passed on by contagion to other men, men that were very possibly

we are not much mistaken, this factor was operative also in the case of the Plague of Baal-Peor. Now what holds good for the Jews, must equally hold good for the other peoples of Asia and of Egypt, and even in an enhanced degree, since these, as we have seen above, gave way to vicious indulgence to a yet more excessive degree.

Nevertheless, then as now distinctions no doubt existed, and probably in Antiquity as at the present day there were districts, whose physical conditions of climate might be regarded as actually forming a counteracting factor, and where in spite of excesses the genital organs seldom became diseased. The evidence for this must be given by later investigations, for we must of necessity first possess a geographical Nosology of Venereal disease at the present day, if we are ever to succeed in finding and utilizing the materials for the same in Antiquity. What has been so far collected by the meritorious *Schnurrer* in his Geographical Nosology is too incomplete to justify us at present in drawing any certain conclusions, more particularly as the greatest part of the material contributed by him is drawn from the communications of non-medical enquirers.

The climate of *Greece* neither exercised any pre-

more self-restrained? ... So, inasmnch as in all parts of the world, *wherever Venereal disease appears to have been endemic in Antiquity*, it is plain the same heat of the atmosphere was united with a similar immorality on the part of the inhabitants, there is therefore sufficient ground for concluding that the disease, identical in its nature and one whereby regions far removed from one another and between which existed no commercial intercourse were attacked in a like way, was originally produced by a like conjunction of identical causes, a conjunction wherein these only agreed, —and *is still so produced*, supposing the inhabitants to still live after the same fashion). *Wizmann* (loco citato p. 32.) moreover is of opinion that Venereal disease under the conditions just named originates in Turkey to this day *in its true form*. A similar view is shared by *Eagle* and *Judd* (loco citato p. 306.).

eminently stimulating effect on the sexual activity of the genitals, nor yet did it afford a ground for the enhancement of their individual activity. Thus enjoying as it did in consequence of that happy combination of its seasons justly celebrated by ancient Writers [1] the advantages, without the disadvantages, of the Tropics, and its inhabitants possessing all functions in a more vigorous proportion, the climate could not possibly have been directly favourable to the rise of affections of the genitals; and for this reason made unnecessary all precautionary measures aimed at them, such as were required in Asia. *Italy* exhibits but little analogy with the Greek climate; still it cannot certainly without considerable qualification be reckoned among factors favourable to maladies of the genital organs. From this we may at any rate partly explain why the physicians of Greece and Rome give so little satisfactory information on the diseases in question, though indeed, as we shall see presently, in this case other and quite distinct factors were at work.

§ 30.

We have now seen that Climate is *ipso facto* an important factor favourable to the rise of affections of the genital organs. How much *more* powerful an influence must it exert on such affections when

[1] *Herodotus*, bk. III. ch. 106., ἡ Ἑλλὰς τὰς ὥρας πολλόν τι κάλλιστα κεκραμένας ἔλαχε. (Hellas possesses seasons in many respects most admirably combined). Comp. *Dahlmann*, Herodotus pp. 90. sqq. *Plato* again praises the εὐκρασία τῶν ὡρῶν (happy mingling of the seasons) of Hellas in more than one passage; e.g. Timaeus 24, C., Critias III E., Epinom. 987 D.; and *Aristophanes* in a fragment of his Horae preserved by Athenaeus, Deipnos. IX. p. 372. says of Attica:

ὥστ' οὐκέτ' οὐδεὶς οἶδ'
ὁπηνίκ' ἐστὶ τοὐνιαυτοῦ.

(So never yet has any man been able to tell precisely in what part of the year he is).

already in existence. Thus the question, *what influence did Climate manifest in Antiquity on the character and course of affections of the genitals*, is one of the utmost moment in connection with a History of Venereal disease,—the more so as on a correct answer being given to it depends the correctness of our views as to the form taken in such cases by the morbid process in Ancient times. True such a question presupposes the existence of these affections, and ought therefore, strictly speaking, only to be raised after the conclusion of our present investigations. However we think enough evidence has already been adduced in the preceding pages to remove all possible doubt from the mind of an attentive reader as to such being the case. Besides, this appears to us the more convenient course,—to survey in its entirety the influence exerted by Climate, rather than to take up our investigation of the subject afresh in different places, and thus to a greater or less extent mangle the discussion of it.

Preponderance of the vegetative principle combined with a certain slackness of tissue is the character of all organisms coming under the influence of the climate of Southern lands. In these countries an extra-ordinary stimulus acts on the mucous membrane of the genitals, and the character described will find its expression here also. Reaction will proceed not so much from the arterial side, or show itself under the guise of sthenic inflammation, but rather take the form merely of intensified secretion. What this increased secretion aims at is the removal of the abnormal stimulus, and the flow of mucus so originating manifests itself as simple, so to speak merely catarrhal, blennorrhoea. This, where the atmosphere is not impregnated with moist vapours, readily disappears, if only somewhat greater care is bestowed on the maintenance of cleanliness,—and all the more so, as re-absorption, which in hot climates acts vigorously on all the mucous membranes generally, very soon gets the upper hand again in the case of that of the genital organs, seconded as it is by the activity of the external skin. The latter is always in a condition of enhanced action at the same time, while the extent of its surface of course markedly exceeds that of the mucous membrane of the genitals. On the other hand where the atmosphere is especially moist, the activity of the skin, as well as the process of re-absorption internally, appears to be less; and so under these circumstances the mucous flow will assume more of a chronic character, but at the same time to an even greater degree be free from inflammatory reaction.

All the more recent observations agree in one thing, viz. that in Southern countries the gonorrhoeal forms predominate, and speaking generally, almost always run a mild course that hardly calls for medical interference. There is no doubt Climatic conditions in Antiquity differed but little from those of to-day; so that we may safely assume that equally in Ancient times blennorrhoea showed the same general characteristics, a fact which existing traditions moreover prove beyond question. The frequency of blennorrhoea of the genital organs in Antiquity is shown at once by the just quoted passage from the Mosaic Books, while its mildness of character may be gathered amongst other things from the remedies employed by the old Physicians, who almost without exception followed the principle laid down by *Celsus* (VI. 18.), to treat gonorrhoea *levibus medicamentis* (with gentle remedial measures), if they were called upon to apply treatment at all. At least this is true of acute blennorrhoea; the chronic form of the complaint, with which alone as a general rule they had to do, of course required astringents. No doubt each failure of arterial reaction afforded yet another reason for the belief on the part of the Ancients that gonorrhoea was a result of weakness of the seed-secreting vessels, and their idea that the discharge was merely badly prepared semen. Supposing, as must have happened, that marks of increased activity appeared, these proceeded not so much from the circulatory system at all as from the nerves, and *Galen* [1] was correct in referring Priapism under these conditions to spasmodic convulsion.

So much for mucous discharge. It was the same also with the various forms of ulceration of the genitals. The conditions to be enumerated presently in the next Section were already present to counteract their rise in any considerable proportion. Further, if they did appear in the high lands of Asia and in Upper Egypt more frequently than did blennorhoea,—this much is shown plainly at any rate by present-day experience,—still they lasted but a short time, as the preponderant activity of vegetative growth, seconded by extraneous assistance, soon mastered the disease, and quickly restored again the loss of tissue. The course of events was otherwise indeed on lower levels, as in Syria and Lower Egypt, districts which besides their high temperature also showed a considerable degree of moisture in the atmosphere and soil. Here accordingly the different forms of ulceration, unless careful precautions were taken, assumed a malignant character, and readily passed over into gangrene (*ἄνθραξ*), as we saw a little above happened in the cases of Apion and Hero. By this means it is true every specific characteristic of the morbid alteration was annihilated; *but* this only made the risk to the individual so much the greater, the patient being at best only too apt to lose the organ attacked

[1] *Galen*, De symptomat. causis bk. III. ch. 11., edit. Kühn Vol. VII. p. 267., *καὶ μὴν αἱ γονόῤῥοιαι, χωρὶς μὲν τοῦ συντείνεσθαι τὸ αἰδοῖον, ἀῤῥωσίᾳ τῆς καθεκτικῆς δυνάμεως τῆς ἐν τοῖς σπερματικοῖς ἀγγείοις· ἐντεινομένου δέ πως, οἷον σπασμῷ τινι παραπλήσιον πασχόντων ἐπιτελοῦνται.* (Moreover gonorrhoeas, except in the case of the member being in a state of tension, arise from weakness of the retentive capacity tn the spermatic vessels; but when there is tension of any sort, they are subject to a kind of spasm resembling that of convulsive patients).

Again, though sometimes the part escaped destruction by gangrene, even then its cure was often difficult owing to the fact that, where the malady had been neglected, worms made their appearance in the ulcers[1], and set up so profuse and so far

[1] *Larrey*, "Relation historique et chirurgicale de l'expédition de l'armée d'Orient, en Egypt et en Syrie," (Historical and Surgical Account of the Expedition of the Army of the East, in Egypt and Syria), Paris 1803. p. 116., Pendant le travail de la suppuration, les blessés furent seulement incommodés des vers ou larves de la mouche bleue, commune en Syrie. L'incubation des oeufs que cette mouche deposait sans cesse dans les plaies ou dans les appareils, étoit favorisée par la chaleur de la saison, l'humidité de l'atmosphère et la qualité de la toile à pansement (elle étoit de coton) la seule qu'on ait pu se procurer dans cette contrée. La présence de ces vers dans les plaies paraissait en accélérer la suppuration, causait des demangeaisons incommodes aux blessés et nous forçait de les panser trois ou quatre fois le jour. Ces insectes, formés en quelques heures, se développaient avec une telle rapidité, que du jour au lendemain, ils étaient de la grosseur d'un tuyau de plume de poulet. On faisait à chaque pansement des lotions d'une forte décoction de rhue et de petite sauge, qui suffisaient pour les détruire; mais ils se reproduisaient bientot après par le défaut des moyens propres à écarter l'approche des mouches et à prévenir l'incubation de leurs oeufs. (During the action of suppuration, the only inconvenience the wounded met with was from the worms or larvae of the blue fly, common in Syria. The hatching of the eggs, which this fly was continually depositing in the wounds or their dressings, was favoured by the heat of the season, the moisture of the atmosphere, and the nature of the material used for bandages. This was cotton, the only material for the purpose that could be procured in that country. The presence of these worms in the wounds appeared to accelerate their suppuration, caused the wounded men to suffer from troublesome itchings and forced us to renew the dressings three or four times a day. These insects, formed in a few hours, developed with such extraordinary rapidity, that from one day to the next, they reached the size of a fowl's quill. At each dressing lotions were applied of a strong decoction of rue and dwarf sage, which was effectual in destroying them; but they reappeared again very

spreading a suppuration that the patient eventually succumbed to it. Of this we have an example in the Emperor Galerius Maximianus, mentioned by *Eusebius*[1], and to which allusion is made as early

soon afterwards owing to the want of proper means for preventing the approach of the flies and hindering the hatching of their eggs). Compare what Larrey (p. 278.) says as to the climate of Syria.

[1] *Eusebius*, Histor. Eccles. bk. VIII. 14., *τί δεῖ τὰς ἐμπαθεῖς ἀνδρὸς αἰσχρουργίας μνημονεύειν; ἢ τῶν πρὸς αὐτοῦ μεμοιχευμένων ἀπαριθμεῖσθαι τὴν πληθύν; οὐκ ἦν γέ τοι πόλιν αὐτὸν παρελθεῖν, μὴ οὐχὶ ἐκ παντὸς φθορὰς γυναικῶν παρθένων τε ἁρπαγὰς εἰργασμένον.* — cap. 16. *μέτεισι γοῦν αὐτὸν θεήλατος κόλασις· ἐξ αὐτῆς αὐτοῦ καταρξαμένη σαρκὸς, καὶ μέχρι τῆς ψυχῆς παρελθοῦσα. ἀθρόα μὲν γὰρ περὶ τὰ μέσα τῶν ἀποῤῥήτων τοῦ σώματος ἀπόστασις γίγνεται αὐτῷ· εἶθ' ἕλκος ἐν βάθει συριγγῶδες καὶ τούτων ἀνιάτος νομὴ κατὰ τῶν ἐνδοτάτω σπλάγχνων· ἀφ' ὧν ἄλεκτόν τι πλῆθος σκωλήκων βρύειν, θανατώδη τε ὀδμὴν ἀποπνέειν, τοῦ παντὸς ὄγκου τῶν σωμάτων ἐκ πολυτροφίας αὐτῷ καὶ πρὸς τῆς νόσου εἰς ὑπερβολὴν πλήθους πιμελῆς μεταβεβληκότος· ἣν τότε κατασεπεῖσαν, ἀφόρητον καὶ φρικτοτάτην τοῖς πλησιάζουσι παρέχειν τὴν θέαν, ἰατρῶν δ' οὖν οἱ μὲν, οὐδ' ὅλως ὑπομεῖναι τὴν τοῦ δυσώδους ὑπερβάλλουσαν ἀτοπίαν οἷοί τε, κατεσφάττοντο. οἱ δὲ διῳδηκότος τοῦ παντὸς ὄγκου καὶ εἰς ἀνέλπιστον σωτηρίας ἀποπεπτωκότος μηδὲν ἐπικουρεῖν δυνάμενοι, ἀνηλεῶς ἐκτείνοντο.* (What need to recall the passions and abominations of the man? or to count the multitude of debaucheries done by him? Nay, he could not pass through a city without leaving behind him everywhere ruin of women and rape of virgins.—ch. 16. Yet heaven-sent punishment overtakes him, commencing with his very flesh and going on to assail the life. For an incessant suppurative inflammation attacks him in the region of the private parts of the body; then later on a wound penetrating deep in like a fistula and an incurable eating sore affecting these inmost intestines. Then from these an indescribable number of worms bred, and a corpse-like smell was given off, the whole bulk of the bodily parts having through high living and under the influence of the disease changed into an exaggerated superfluity of fat. Then this rotting away, displayed an intolerable and an appalling

as in the Book of Ecclesiasticus (XIX. 2, 3.), when the Author, Jesus the son of Sirach, says: "Wine and women will make men of understanding to fall away: and he that cleaveth to harlots will become impudent. *Moths (otherwise* [1]*—Rottenness and worms)* shall have him to heritage, and a bold man shall be taken away." The use of knife and actual cautery must naturally have played an important part under these circumstances in the treatment adopted; but these the patient often dreaded more than the malady itself, and chose suicide rather than submit to them, like the "Municeps" whose story Pliny tells in the passage quoted in a previous chapter. But now supposing suchlike ulcers to be

spectacle to his attendants; while among his physicians, some finding themselves utterly unable to endure the exceeding horribleness of the stench, put an end to their lives; while others, the whole bulk having gone to complete rottenness, and the patient in a condition that admitted no hope of recovery, being unable to afford any help, were cruelly put to death). This passage occurs as well, word for word, in *Nicephorus*, Histor. Eccles. VII. 22. Aur. Victor. Epit. ch. 40., Galerius Maximianus *consumptis genitalibus* defecit, (Galerius Maximianus died, *the genital organs being destroyed*).—*Zosimus*, Hist. II. 11. speaks merely of **τραῦμα δυσίατον** (a wound difficult to cure), and *Paulus Diaconus*, Hist. miscell. XI. 5., says: putrefacto introrsum pectore, et vitalibus dissolutis, cum ultra horrorem humanae miseriae etiam vermes eructaret, medicique iam ultra foetorem non ferentes, crebro iussu eius occiderentur etc. (the bosom having putrefied within, and the vitals rotted away, when exceeding the climax of human horror and suffering he began to bring up worms, and his physicians unable to bear the excessive foulness of the stench, were being executed at his frequent order, etc). The same fate happened to *Herod*, of whom *Josephus*, Antiq. XVII. 6. says: **τοῦ αἰδοίου σῆψις σκώληκας ἐμποιοῦσα** (mortification of the genitals producing worms). Comp. *Bochart*, Hierozoicon, edit. Rosenmüller vol. III. p. 520.

[1] This reading is clearly preferable. The Septuagint translators render it **σήπη καὶ σκώληκες κληρονομήσουσιν αὐτὸν**, (Rottenness and worms shall be his heritage), where however it must be admitted **σῆτες** (moths) is also retained by the Editors.

situated in the mouth of a *fellator* or *cunnilingue*, then their course must have been all the more rapid, and the danger involved all the greater, if the patient lived in such a climate as described; and it was in this way the **Αἰγύπτια καὶ Συριακὰ** and **Βουβαστικὰ ἕλκεα** (Egyptian and Syrian sores, Bubastic sores) mentioned above acquired their evil repute. Still in the majority of cases these climatic influences could be counteracted by appropriate medical aid and dietetic measures, or at any rate their effect considerably reduced. Hence it was that cases of the sort only very rarely appeared in Antiquity, and for this very reason were noted by the Historians, when they did occur.

The human organism possessed in Southern lands yet another way of combating the enemy's attacks, one which would seem to have escaped the notice of the Physicians of Antiquity, and which, though recognized in modern times, has yet never been at all adequately appreciated and utilized in the history of Venereal disease, viz. *the reaction exhibited by the skin in diseases of the genital organs in hot climates.* So long as authorities thought of the external skin as merely compacted of separate and distinct layers of tissue, there could not really be any question of an accurate knowledge of its functions whether under healthy or under morbid conditions. The investigations of *Breschet* and *Roussel de Vauzène* [1] as confirmed and reinforced by *Gurlt* [2], have now

[1] "Nouvelles recherches sur la structure de la peau", (Recent Investigations as to the Structure of the Skin), with 3 Plates. Paris 1835. 221 pp. 8vo.

[2] "Vergleichende Untersuchungen über die Haut des Menschen und der Haussäugethiere, besonders in Beziehung auf die Absonderungsorgane des Hauttalgs und des Schweisses, (Comparative Investigations as to the Skin in Man and the Domestic Mammals, with particular reference to the Organs of Secretion of the Sebaceous Humour and the Sweat), in *Muller's* Archiv. für Physiologie Jahrg. 1835., pp. 399—418. With copperplates, a comparison of which will very much facilitate the proper understanding of what follows.

taught us to understand that the skin, over and above these layers, possesses as a matter of fact,—a fact formerly only conjectured,—special organs belonging to the same class as the glands, to wit the skin, hair and sweat glands. These share amongst them the function hitherto ascribed to the skin generally, and especially bring into correlation the sympathies of the different parts, so much so that they may be said to be almost the sole and only seat of the manifold forms of skin-diseases. All this we endeavoured first to demonstrate in the series of Articles on Skin-diseases in "*Blasius'* Handwörterbuch der Chirurgie und Augenheilkunde" (Manual of Surgery and Ophthalmology), and so pave the way for a compendious Survey of our knowledge of the Skin-diseases up to the present time.

Now while the sweat-glands stand in a special çonnection of sympathy and antagonism with the lungs, the same correlation exists in a peculiar degree between the glands of the mucous membrane of the intestinal canal and of the genital organs on the one hand and the cutaneous glands on the other which secrete the *sebum* or sebaceous humour. It would take us too far a-field, if we undertook in this place to enter upon a detailed explanation of this circumstance, which however is still in sore need of further clearing up. We shall content ourselves with recalling the fact that Onanists (Masturbators) not only often betray themselves by having a nose with a shiny, tallowy looking surface that comes from excessive secretion of *sebum*, but also not less frequently by their face being covered with *acne* pustulus. One more fact we must mention is that the outbreak of *acne* very often with girls heralds the approach of each period of menstruation, and accompanies it [1]. These are signs clearly pointing

[1] Already we find *Lorry*, "Abh. von den Krankheiten der Haut," (Treatise on Diseases of the Skin), Vol. I. p. 50., saying: "There is found to exist moreover a certain sympathy between the generative parts of men and women

to the conclusion that stimulations of the genitals are reflected back on the glands of the skin, for *acne* is nothing else but an affection of these glands, as we have demonstrated in the Work just mentioned.

But indeed there are proofs of this antagonism still nearer to hand. How frequently have our physicians observed an eruption [1] resembling *roseola* or *urticaria* in character, at the—very often sudden—appearance of which the gonorrhoeal symptoms have much decreased in severity or disappeared altogether! These skin affections have been ascribed to the balsam of Copaiva or the Cubebs pepper administered in these cases, which are supposed to have stimulated the intestinal mucous membrane and so sympathetically excited the skin. This may very possibly sometimes be the case; but it could not but occur much more frequently, if the remedial agents mentioned are to bear the sole and entire blame. No doubt in some patients a particular idiosyncrasy may have

and the skin, which under the violent stimulus of sexual coition swells; but after it is over, sweat comes out on it, and *sometimes little heat-pimples appear*. p. 83., Now at puberty, a period when all the glands are opened, there is brought to the organs of transpiration a great quantity of a subtle and fluid material, there arises a peculiar smell, and if this matter has accumulated, it clogs the minute vessels, the humour contained in these becomes thick by retardation and solidification,—the result being a pimply eruption on the skin. This much is certain, that if both sexes are fully developed, and live chaste, an extensive series of mutually connected pustules may arise, *just as if they were produced by the swelling of the glands in the skin.* The pustules are ranged in the same order as that in which the glands lie; exactly as if they were the meeting-place of the humours that would seem to have been dispersed in the skin." Comp. *Haller*, Elem. physiolog. Vol. VII. bk. XXVIII. sect. 3. § 4.

[1] More precise information on this, as well as on several other opinions expressed in the course of these Inquiries as to the pathology of Venereal disease, the reader will find placed at his disposal in our forthcoming Work, "Introduction to a Scientific Knowledge of the Venereal Disease."

given rise to sympathetic action stimulative of the intestinal canal, but in the majority the reaction of the mucous membrane of the genitals on the cutaneous glands has undoubtedly been a chief contributory factor under epidemic influences, while the drugs exhibited have played only a subordinate part in producing the result. There are cases where the gonorrhœa has been treated simply and solely by mere antiphlogistic methods, and yet such an eruption has been observed.

But it is not in gonorrhœa only that these phænomena appear; they have been noted as well in chancre, being then ascribed to the sublimate of mercury and looked upon as affording a criterion that the drug had exercised its full effect on the original complaint. In most cases this was without doubt a mistake, for Biett, Rayer and other authorities have noted the most widely divergent forms of skin-disease to appear concurrently with the existence of chancre, and in consequence have come to regard them as primitive symptoms. In fact cases have actually been observed, where these were the sole primary symptoms of contagion after indulgence in unclean coition. At the same time it is only fair to say that this has been doubted in many quarters, observers trying to explain the fact of the absence of other symptoms by saying the ulcers, which are frequently very minute, may have been overlooked. At least experience has sufficiently taught us this much, that the so-called secondary symptoms, and therefore the skin-affections as well, appear the more readily in proportion as the ulcers of the genitals are smaller and more superficial; and we ourselves believe that never without local reaction on the genital organs from coition do so-called secondary appearances arise,—only it is not invariably ulcers that are to looked for.

Now when even in our temperate climate the cutaneous glands play a not unimportant part in the morbid processes of Venereal disease, how much more must this be the case in Asia and Egypt, where the activity of the skin generally and that of the cutaneous glands in particular is even under normal conditions far more conspicuously energetic, as may be seen from the constant oily state of the skin, more particularly in Negroes. This oily grease on the skin is in fact nothing more nor less than the product of the action of the cutaneous glands. These glands are peculiarly apt to become morbidly affected in travellers visiting the South during their acclimatisation; though natives too are yearly attacked in the Summer months by complaints of the skin-glands [1]. The fact has long been recognized [2] that

[1] Comp. *Hillary*, "Beobachtungen über die Veränderungen Luft und die damit verbundenen epidemischen Krankheiten auf der Insel Barbados," (Observations on Changes of Atmosphere and the Epidemic Sicknesses connected with them in the Island of Barbadoes), transl. from the English by J. Ch. G. Ackermann. Leipzig 1776. 8vo., pp. 3 sqq.

[2] *Alex. Traj. Petronius*, De morbo Gallico, (On the French Disease—Syphilis), bk. II. chs. 24., and 26 (Aphrodisiacus pp. 1225, 1226.) in his time says: Et in regione calida, quoniam secundum naturae suae impetum ad cutem fertur, minus saevire, in frigida vero, quoniam contra suam naturam ad interna migrare cogitur, magis. — Neque nos non lateat, in ambiente (ut dicunt) calido, quoniam ad cutim attractio fit, morbum hunc et secundum naturae suae impetum creari, et simul ad exteriora prorumpere solere. In frigido autem, quia intro repellitur contra suae naturae motum retroverti et solidas corporis partes saepius depasci. Frequentius etiam in regione calida quam frigida apparere; hic enim circumfusus aer, ne morbus ad cutim extendatur, prohibet (nam intro pellit), illic vero et ad cutim trahit et eandem retinet. (Moreover in a hot region, inasmuch as in accordance with the impulse of its nature it is carried to the skin, it is there less virulent; whereas in a cold one, as it is compelled against its nature to travel to the inward parts, it is more so.—Again we should not let this escape our notice, that in a hot environment (as they say), inasmuch as an attraction takes place towards the skin, this disease also according to the impulse of its nature is there brought into being, and is wont to

in Southern countries not only the greater number of skin-diseases, but even Venereal disease itself in an especial degree, appear as an exanthema of the skin, and for this reason it there displays far less destructive effects; but as a rule enquirers have contented themselves with the general habit, without (as pointed out before) adequately turning the fact to advantage in connection with the History and Theory of Venereal disease.

This preponderating bias towards the external skin

break out towards the external parts. On the other hand in a cold one, because it is drawn within, it is turned back contary to the motion of its nature, and more often feeds upon the solid parts of the body. Again it appears more frequently in a hot region than in a cold one; for in the latter case the surrounding air (driving it within as it does) hinders the disease from extending to the skin, whereas in the former it draws it to the skin and keeps it there). But specially pertinent in this connection is p. 1211. — *Puydebat*, "Über den Einfluss des Climas auf den Menschen," (Of the Influence of Climate on Man), in the "Bulletin méd. de Bordeaux, 1836. May 21. (Froriep Notiz. 1836. Vol. 49. p. 179.) writes: Die immer geöffneten Hautporen hauchen in den heissen Ländern einen reichlichen, mehr oder weniger stark riechenden Schweiss aus. Die Hautdrüsen sondern eine ölige Flüssigkeit in Menge ab, welche die Haut schlüpfrig macht und derselben jenes bei den Negern so auffallende Ansehn giebt. Dieser Zustand der Haut macht sie zu Exanthemen, z. B. Masern, Blattern, Syphilis, Lepra, Elephantiasis geneigt. (The ever open skin-pores expire in hot countries a rich and more or less strongly smelling sweat. The cutaneous glands secrete an oily fluid in quantities, which makes the skin slippery and gives it that appearance so striking in Negroes. This state of the skin makes it liable to exanthematic effections, e.g. Measles, Small-pox, Syphilis, Leprosy, Elephantiasis). — In cold countries the transpiration of the skin is very weak; in consequence the internal secretions are increased in quantity, while in hot countries they are lessened from a directly opposite cause." Comp. *J. von Röser*, "Ueber einige Krankheiten des Orients," (On some Diseases of the East). Augsburg 1837., pp. 67—71., to whose statements we shall have to return on several future occasions.

must obviously manifest itself equally in other diseases of the mucous membranes, and so too in those of the genital organs. Reabsorption in particular, acting with increased vigour on the mucous surfaces, will prove its beneficial presence also in the diseases affecting them. The foreign matter that comes in contact with these surfaces is assimilated to a less degree by the mucous glands and by those of the *glans penis*, and no time is allowed it to exert a destructive influence on the small surface receiving it; on the other hand it is quickly thrown back on the much more extensive surface of the external skin, and there dealt with by the cutaneous glands with their powerful secretive and assimilatory action, being either assimilated or expelled externally.

In particular localities this quickly happens without any striking symptoms being locally perceptible in the skin, as e.g. in Numidia, Libya [1] and the Northern part of Peru [2], where the disease is said to cure itself without extraneous medical aid, and among the inhabitants generally to be practically

[1] *Joannes Leo*, "Descriptio Africae", (Description of Africa), Leyden 1632. 12mo., p. 86., Paucis admodum toto Atlante, tota Numidia totaque Libya hoc notum est contagium. Quodsi quisquam fuerit qui se eo infectum sentiat, mox in Numidiam aut in Nigritarum regionem proficiscitur, cuius tanta est aeris temperies, ut optimae sanitati restitutus inde in patriam redeat: quod quidem multis accidisse ipse meis vidi oculis, qui nullo adhibito neque pharmaco neque medico, praeter saluberrimum iam dictum aërem, revaluerant. (To very few persons indeed in the whole of the Atlas, the whole of Numidia and of Libya, is this contagion known. But if there should be any man who feels himself attacked by it, he presently journeys into Numidia or the district of the Nigritae, where the nature of the air is such that he returns home again restored to excellent good health. This I have seen happen to many with my own eyes, who without help of druggist or doctor recovered by the exceeding salubrity of the air as aforesaid). Comp. *Scaliger*, Exercitat. CLXXX. ch. 18. — *Petronius*, loco citato p. 1213.

[2] *Schnurrer*, "Geographische Nosologie," (Geographical Nosology, — Distribution of Diseases), p. 454.

non-existent (?). Though this is not the case in other countries, still the cutaneous glands become involved in the morbid process of the disease, and secrete with augmented copiousness, and the secretion being simultaneously altered in character, it fails to be driven out externally, inasmuch as external elimination is at once stopped owing to the fact that the cutaneous glands, like the uterus in pregnancy, close their orifice, so as to be enabled to carry out their function in their recesses. For this reason the glands swell, and manifest themselves in the form of *papillae* or tubercles (very often as little bladders, or blebs), changing later either into pustules, if the morbid products are eventually expelled [1], or else gradually

[1] *Brown, W. G.* "Reisen in Afrika, Egypten und Syrien." (Travels in Africa, Egypt and Syria), transl. from the English by C. Sprengel. Weimar 1800. 8vo., p. 389., tells us of a marine at Kahira, who had become infected, how the man, having in the mean time taken no means whatever to combat the disease and without giving up either the use of brandy or the practice of copulation, two months later got a violent itching eruption over his whole body, and particularly on the head and over the glands of the neck. This he treated by sprinkling over it a sort of red earth, whereupon it dried up and disappeared, so that four weeks later he found himself completely cured and his skin as clean and smooth as before. *Schnurrer*, loco citato p. 453., also gives the story, but with sundry inaccuracies. Similar observations were made by *Th. Clarke* at the Cape of Good Hope, London Med. Gazette 1833. *Behrend*, Syphilidologie Vol. I. pp. 241 sqq. The Minorite *Conti* declared in opposition to *Norberg* (Biörnstähl's Briefe, 6 vol. p. 410.): "Christian no less than Mussulman in the East is strictly forbidden to cohabit with a woman before the eighth day after her purification. If it *is* done within that period, the man's body is poisoned: he experiences swelling, ulcers, sores, itch and pains in the limbs, and shows all the symptoms of leprosy. At this time the female does not become pregnant, because the blood is unclean, but if conception does occur, the child also gets a bad itch, and generally is affected like his parents." *Fr. Eagle* (Lancet July 1836., Note 671.). *Behrend's* Syphilidologie, Vol. I. p. 118., relates a number

disappear, if the process of assimilation and reabsorption has been sufficiently vigorous. Supposing damp, cold or other unfavourable influences to be at work, suppuration may very well supervene, or degenerative processes commence, and so on, and *the disease pass over into leprosy and elephantiasis.* This is above all the case in Egypt, where from the first, chancres on the genitals would seem to possess a marked tendency towards scurfy and scabby formations [1].

If these are the facts at the present day,—and no one doubts they are,—there only remains the question: were they so in Ancient times as well? Here we come face to face with the difficult problem as to the relation of leprosy with Venereal disease,—a problem which for Centuries has been the subject of dispute, and in spite of the very careful enquiries of a Hensler and of other investigators, cannot by any means be regarded as solved. Our own investigations on the Leprosy of the Ancients are as yet too incomplete, and the nature of the subject demands such far-reaching inquisition into the most widely different individual phænomena, that we are compelled, in order to economise our space, to renounce all idea of submitting the subject to any more detailed examination in the present Work. Besides, in our Second Part we shall be coming back to it again, when we have under investigation the question as to whether or no the Venereal disease of the XVth Century was developed from leprosy.

of cases that occurred in London where after intercourse with women during menstruation both gonorrhœa and chancre supervened.

[1] *Von Roeser*, loco citato p. 69. *Sonnerat*, "Reise nach Ostindien", (Journey to the East Indies), I. 94, 99. *Schnurrer*, Geogr. Nosologie p. 409. Note, says: "In Hindostan in particular experience has shown that a badly treated syphilis changes into leprosy." That this is not a thing of such extreme rarity in Europe either, we shall prove more fully in another place. Meantime compare what *Hensler*, "Vom Abendländischen Aussatze", (On Oriental Leprosy), pp. 228 sqq., says on the subject.

For our present purpose the following statement must suffice: The Climate of Asia and Egypt was in Antiquity, as mentioned already, undoubtedly but little different from what it is to-day, and the influence it exerted therefore must have shared in this resemblance [1].

As to *mentagra*, we have already proved a little above that it was a consequence of the vice of the *cunnilingue*, and as according to Pliny's report the latter claimed Egypt for its fatherland, obviously the climate of that country must have been in part responsible for its origination. Now affections of the genital organs being found in Antiquity as the result of sexual intercourse, it follows that in this direction also Climate must have exerted its influence, and that in the very same way as we have just above seen it do,—in other words manifold affections of the skin must have originated in consequence of irritation and other morbid effects on the genital organs. True the Ancient physicians say not a word of this; but then they derive the greater proportion of the skin-diseases, which they mass all together in the most admired confusion, from internal mischief of various sorts, and regard them all as *apostases* (suppurative inflammations carrying off the effect of fevers, etc.),—at any rate a proof they were not entirely unacquainted with the antagonistic relations existing between the skin and other organs.

[1] *Galen*, Ad Glaucon. de meth. med. II., edit. Kühn Vol. XI. p. 142., says: κατὰ γοῦν τὴν Ἀλεξάνδρειαν ἐλεφαντιῶσι πάμπολλοι διά τε τὴν δίαιταν καὶ τὴν θερμότητα τοῦ χωρίου· — ἅτε δὲ θερμοῦ τοῦ περιέχοντος ὄντος καὶ ἡ ῥοπὴ τῆς φορᾶς αὐτῶν πρὸς τὸ θέρμα γίνεται· (At any rate in the neighbourhood of Alexandria very many persons suffer from elephantiasis as well through their mode of life as owing to *the heat of the locality*;—for indeed as a result of the excessive heat of the climate, the tendency of their constitution is also towards heat). In Germany and Mysia he asserts the disease is seldom observed, and in Scythia almost never.

So far as the genitals are concerned, they seem to have adequately realized only the *consensus* between the uterus and the skin [1], whereas in male subjects they appear to have put down most of the effects observed to the liver. But on these points we shall have something further to say later on. Still the assertion to the effect that Eunuchs are not attacked by *calvities* (baldness) (*Hippocrates*, I. 400; *Galen*, XVIII. A. 40., also p. 42., where mention is made of the excesses *in Baccho et Venere*—in Wine and Love—peculiarly prevalent at his epoch), which was a frequent consequence of vice in Antiquity [2], points to the *consensus* between genitals and skin having been already noted. Even more is the fact, vouched for by *Archigenes* [3], that

[1] Phlyctaenae (blisters) in erysipelas of the uterus are mentioned by Hippocrates, De ant. mulierum, edit. Kühn II. p. 541. *Galen*, edit. Kühn Vol. XVII. A. p. 358., *ἴσθι γὰρ ὅτι τὰ ἐξανθήματα ἐν ταῖς τῆς μήτρας διαθέσεσιν εἰς τὸ δέρμα ἐκραγέντα σημαίνουσιν ὅτι ἡ φλεγμονὴ ἡ ἐρυσίπελας ἐκ τοῦ ἀποζέοντος καὶ λεπτοῦ αἵματος ἐν ταῖς μήτραις ἐγγίνεται, ὡς ἐν τῷ περὶ γυναικείης φύσεως γέγραπται.* (Be assured that those eruptions that break out on the skin in certain morbid conditions of the womb signify that the inflammation or erysipelas proceeds from the deficiency and poorness of the blood in the womb, as is stated in my Work, On the Female Constitution).

[2] *Aristotle*, Problem IV. 18.

[3] *Aëtius*, Tetrab, IV. serm. 1. ch. 122., Novimus quosdam audaciores qui sibi ipsis testes ferro resecarunt; castratis enim non in peius malum ipsum procedet. Neque enim temere reperias, inquit Archigenes, ullum aliquem castratum elephantiasi laborantem, neque item facile mulierem. Quare etiam quidam ex confidentioribus medicis manum admoverunt, et quotquot sane ex eis ex sectione periculum evaserunt, per consequentis curationis usum perfecte ab hac maligna affectione liberati sunt. (We know of some bolder spirits who have amputated their own testicles with the knife; for after castration the actual evil will not then proceed to any worse length. For, says Archigenes, you will not readily find any single case of a castatred man suffering from elephantiasis, nor will you easily discover a woman at all affected by this disease. Wherefore, in fact, some of the more daring practitioners

castration was recommended by some Physicians as a cure for elephantiasis, such as to arouse the suspicion that the physicians of Antiquity knew perfectly well what influence affections of the genital organs exerted on diseases of the skin. This is made all the more likely by Archigenes (ch. 120.) not only speaking of the disease as being contagious, but also describing the skin-affection as secondary in character. He further declares its cause to be unknown, puts on record the extreme lubricity of the patients (Satyriasis pp. 74, 133, 269.), and even says in so many words that such as were castrated did not contract elephantiasis!

We have seen how *mentagra* attacked the *cunni-*

have operated, and there is no doubt that such of their patients as escaped the dangerous effects of the operation, have been through the employment of subsequent precautions completely freed from this malignant complaint). Comp. *Hensler*, "Vom Aussatz", (On Leprosy), p. 401. With regard to *the immunity of women*, an assertion likewise made in connection with *mentagra* (p. 288), *von Roeser* writes (loco citato p. 67.) referring to Venereal disease: "Above all it is now the case in Greece and Turkey that the practising physician,—and I have been assured of the fact by many persons,—exceedingly seldom meets with syphilitic female patients in his practice; that yet notwithstanding this none of *the sequelæ and different forms of subsequent mischief* that are usually found resulting from the disease when every kind of medical aid is neglected, are seen in patients of that sex."—P. 71., "Only poison would seem, as a result of the secretive process exerted by the affected parts of the skin and the mucous membrane, which is much more powerful in women than in men, to be more readily eliminated from the body than is the case with men, so much so indeed that it is an almost unheard of thing in Egypt to find a female patient under medical treatment." — still this does not justify the conclusion that women *never* suffered from Venereal disease, as even von Roeser himself admits. Again Larrey, loco citato p. 253., actually found himself constrained in view of the wide dissemination of the disease among the French soldiers, to establish a special hospital for infected women, in order to check the spread of the complaint."

lingue, and afterwards passed over into *psora;* in just the same way might elephantiasis,—a complaint indeed which the Gloss of the Pseudo-Galen actually puts in connection with the Morbus Phoeniceus (Phoenician Disease),—be brought on by indulgence in coition. This is in no way contradicted by the preference the disease exhibits for first making its appearance in the face, inasmuch as the cutaneous glands of the face are in a relation of special sympathy with the genital organs. That leprosy too no less than elephantiasis was communicated and contracted by coition is shown by a host of examples given in the Mediæval Historians [1]; in fact, a large number of Physicians held Venereal disease to be a species of leprosy or elephantiasis, while some made it actually originate in the act of coition with leprous persons; yet for all that we do not, according to *Hensler*, ("Vom Aussatz",—On Leprosy, p. 396.), find it anywhere recorded that the genital organs were first affected,—apart that is from what *Astruc* has brought forward on purpose to suppoıt his own view. As everybody knows, *he* refers all local evils existing prior to the end of the XVth Century to Leprosy.

But what would follow supposing traces *were* actually to be found proving that what was known in Asia as leprosy did as a matter of fact first show itself in the genitals? Before we enter upon the closer examination of reasons for this supposition, we must quote a passage from the Work of *Von Roeser* already several times mentioned, a passage equally important for the pathology of Venereal disease as for its History. *Von Roeser*, (p. 68.) writes thus: "Primary syphilis manifests itself *in Egypt in the very rarest cases on the prepuce or glans of the verge;* the chancres are more commonly found on the outer skin of the penis nearer the *mons Veneris*,

[1] Comp. *Foot*, "Abh. über die Lustseuche" (Treatise on Venereal Disease), transl. from the English by *H. Ch. Reich*, Vol. I. p. 62.

or actually on this in the hairy parts which among Egyptians and Arabs are generally kept shaved, *or else on the scrotum*. *Pruner*[1] told me that the occurrence of a chancre on the prepuce, which indeed is absent in Mohammedans owing to circumcision, or on the *glans penis* is in the ratio of 1 : 3 to chancres on the last mentioned parts, hence in that country Astruc's opinion that syphilitic ulcers hardly ever formed on the exterior of the verge, is strongly contradicted,—as is no less true amongst ourselves. That circumcision is not the sole cause of this phænomenon is manifest from the fact that in Smyrna and Constantinople I saw plenty of chancres on the *glans*, as well as amongst Jews at home, though I am not going to deny that circumcision may have some share in causing the rarity of the appearance of a chancre on the *glans*,—but this does not in any way explain the frequency of their appearance on the scrotum and the *mons Veneris*. A tendency to take the exanthematic type, a tendency which makes itself known also by the fact of *many chancres* commonly appearing at once and *showing in a marked degree a preference for scurfy and scabby forms*, might very possibly afford a better explanation of the phænomenon in question."

Now as to the supposition just expressed, this is based on a repeated examination of a passage of the very utmost importance in the history of leprosy, viz. Ch. XIII. of Leviticus—a chapter which has exercised Theologians no less than Physicians for Centuries, but without our being enabled to regard the investigations it has given rise to as in any way concluded. However it is no intention of ours to provide in this place a commentary on this Chapter, more particularly as we do not possess the philological acquirements necessary for a critical appreciation of the results so far obtained. Neither, speaking in general terms, has anything like

[1] Surgeon in Chief of the Esbekieh Hospital at Cairo.

sufficient progress in the study of original sources for the history of leprosy as yet been made to enable an adequate judgement to be formed; we much prefer to limit our efforts at present to contributing sundry observations, which stand in close connection with our immediate object, and at the same time may afford readers, whether scientific or philological authorities, an opportunity of favouring us with their judgement as specialists.

The correct understanding of the whole passage appears to us to depend in the first place on the success of the endeavour to find a certain and definite explanation of the expression בְּעוֹר בְּשָׂרוֹ (b'ôr b'sarô, —"skin of the flesh" in English Authorized Version). Luther rendered this by: *on the skin of his flesh;* the Septuagint translators give it as **ἐν δέρματι χρωτὸς αὐτοῦ** (in the skin of the surface); while *de Wette* (whose Translation of the passage generally we hereby ask the reader to consult, space not allowing us to quote the whole Chapter) translates it *on the skin of his body*, and understands by the expression every part of the external skin.

Supposing this translation the correct one, it will be a hard matter to explain how it was the hair should simultaneously have turned *white*, a circumstance which strangely enough caused even Hensler no surprise. Rosenmüller in his Scholia on the passage says: *Schilling (De lepra p. 7) observat, in lepra alba pilos albescere*, (*Schilling*, On Leprosy p. 7. notes that in white leprosy the hair grows white); but it is only the *partes pilosae aut capillatae* (hairy parts, parts covered with long hair) that are here intended, and these are to be understood as including merely the head, eye-brows, chin, armpits and pubic region. Obviously the hair on other parts of the body cannot be taken here into consideration, as it is specifically almost colourless, and though it is true it may have had a stronger coloration in many Jews, surely they did not *all* belong to the race of Esau. Again all writers on leprosy, when this mischief affecting the hair is in question, speak solely of the hair of the parts named [1]. So when *Haly Abbas* in a passage quoted by Hensler (*Excerpta* p. 9.), in which he is treating of *Allopitia* and *Tyria* (forms of leprosy), says, *Nonnunquam totius accidit pilis corporis* (Sometimes this happens to all the hair of the body), this also is to be understood merely of the parts above named. Indeed *Hensler* himself (Vom Aussatz,—On Leprosy, p. 304.) assumes this when, after speaking of the hair of the head and beard, he goes on: "But this mischief may also attack other hairy parts of the body. *Haly Abbas* says, (*Excerpta* p. 9.) At times this affects also the hair of the whole body. True the passage of *Hippocrates*, in view of the erroneous punctuation, seems to belong more properly to what follows, still even by itself it would be probable enough, as *the preliminary symptoms are found particularly in the arm-pit and the groin*, and might of course extend their ravages there, just as much as on the head." However should anyone wish to understand here *all* the hairy parts of the body mentioned, and suppose the Author to be speaking in the first instance in a general sense, then

[1] The passage of *Aretaeus* (Morb. chron. bk. II. ch. 13. edit Kühn p. 180.) can hardly be cited as evidence on the other side in this case, as the question there discussed is elephantiasis, not the leprosy of the Jews at all. Any how we read there: *τρίχες ἐν μὲν τῷ παντὶ προτεθνήσκουσι, χερσὶ μηροῖσι κνήμῃσι, αὖθις ἥβῃ, γενείοισι ἀραιαὶ, ψεδναὶ δὲ καὶ ἐπὶ τῇ κεφαλῇ κόμαι· τὸ δὲ μᾶλλον πρόωροι, πολιοὶ καὶ φαλάκρωσις ἀθρόη· οὐκ εἰς μακρὸν δὲ ἥβη καὶ ἐπιμίμνοιεν παυραὶ τρίχες, ἀπρεπέστεραὶ τῶν ἀποιχομένων.* (Hair dies first in every part, on hands, thighs, shins; again on pubes and cheeks it becomes thin, and scanty also on the head. The locks are prematurely white, and baldness becomes general; nor is it long before pubes and cheeks are bare, and if a few scanty hairs should remain, they are uncomely as compared with those that have disappeared). Nor would it be any fairer to cite the fact that Albinos are covered over the whole body with a fine, white, woolly hair.

what follows will not agree, for the hair of the head and beard was *not* changed into *white*, but into *yellow* (עָחֹב), as V. 30 states. There are left therefore only the eye-brows, arm-pits and the pubic region, to which the transformation to white can apply.

Granting these considerations to be correct, it is impossible to understand the *b'ôr b'sarô* as signifying the whole exterior surface of the skin; it must imply a local limitation. But the limited area intended can be nothing but *the genitals*, and this agrees best at once with the facts and with the usages of Biblical phraseology. In more than one passage, in fact, of the Old Testament *basar*, like *σάρξ* (flesh) in the New, has the meaning of "sexual parts"; and even in English the word *flesh*, particularly in ecclesiastical language, is consecrated by custom in this sense. So Luther was perfectly justified in the passage under discussion in translating as he did: *on the skin of his flesh*, that is to say, of his genitals. The particular combination of *b'ôr b'sarô* we have not it is true been able to find used generally in the books of the Old Testament, but we must not therefore conclude absolutely that it is unique and peculiar to this XIIIth. Chapter; though indeed, if such *were* the case, it would merely be an additional confirmation of the explanation we have given.

So far as the matter of fact goes, such an assumption offers no difficulties,—indeed it actually removes several, as e.g. that connected with the coloration of the skin, and not only proves that already at that date pustules on the genitals had been observed that were free from any suspicion of malignant character, but further that along with a suspicious pustule or similar symptom (scurf, ulcer) there went a simultaneous general affection of the skin as a whole, which was held to be diagnostic for the local malady, and accordingly proclaimed even the suspected leper free from taint after his recovery from it. For evidently we must take verses 12 and 13 as indicating this, where it is stated in so many words: "And if the leprosy break out (פָּרַח,—blossom) abroad in the skin, and the leprosy cover all the skin of him that hath the plague from his head even to his feet, as far as appeareth to the priest; then the priest shall look: and behold, if the leprosy have covered all his flesh, he shall pronounce him clean that hath the plague; it is all turned white: he is clean." (English Revised Version). The last words have been wrongly referred by some Interpreters to the "Bohak" (bright spot), which is mentioned in verse 39., but really nothing more than this is intended:—after the eruption is dried up, and the skin has returned to its natural white colour, then the hitherto sick man is to be declared clean [1].

This diagnostic eruption again points to another fact, viz. that the leprosy must have had its seat in a part of the body, the cutaneous glands of which stand in a relation of lively sympathy with those of the skin generally, and this according to modern experience can only be the cutaneous glands of the genital organs. Sometimes inoculation with cow-pox lymph brings out a general eruption of the whole skin, but this circumstance cannot well be made pertinent here, as really and truly the lymph is a resultant product of a feverish affection, and therefore its innate tendency is towards a reproduction of

[1] Already *J. D. Michaelis*, "Fragen an eine Gesellschaft gelehrter Männer, die auf Befehl Ihro Majestät des Königs von Dänemark nach Arabien reisen," (Questions addressed to a Society of Learned Men, travelling at the Command of HM. the King of Denmark to Arabia), Frankfurt-on-the-Main 1762., p. 23., says in the 11th. question on Leprosy under head No. 8.: "Does it possess a natural diagnostic mark in this, if it breaks out everywhere at once, and covers the whole body? From Leviticus XIII. 12—13. we might seem to be almost justified in concluding this to be so. But I am in doubt how in that case this passage is to be interpreted in accordance with the history of the disease." Comp. p. 335. Note 1.

itself under circumstances of feverish stimulation, and to set the whole organism, and consequently the whole cutaneous glandular system, in a state of enhanced activity. How the diagnostic eruption comes about may be gathered from the statement of the case given just above; while the passage quoted from *von Roeser's* Work will explain the rest. Still for the present this much may suffice to put the expert reader in a position to test our conjecture,—for indeed so far it makes no profession to be more than a conjecture. Supposing it found tenable, then the further consequences that cannot but grow from it for the elucidation of the Chapter in discussion may be readily developed. On the other hand, if it is devoid of justification, it would be quite useless further to elaborate a hypothesis, plunging a subject obscure enough without this in even deeper darkness. Further than this we only need to mention that *Hensler* and others hold *mentagra* to be indicated in the bald chin and scurfy (scall) chin of Leviticus (XIII. 29 sqq.), which if they are right would merely be another point in favour of our view.

Finally there can hardly be any need for us to observe that we have no idea of holding leprosy in general to be a consequence of excesses; on the contrary we believe, to return to the problem we started with at the beginning of this Section, that we are bound to agree to the opinion first explicitly laid down by *Becket* [1], viz. *that under the widely comprehensive notion of Leprosy were included other forms of skin-diseases owing their existence to some previous affection of the genital organs*,—in precisely the same way as this happened in the Middle Ages, and as may be the case occasionally even at the present day.

[1] Philosoph. Transactions Vol. XXXI. *Foot*, Treatise on Venereal Disease, Vol. I. pp. 25 sqq.

§ 31.

What precise influence Climate exerted on the form taken and course run by affections of the genital organs *in Greece and Italy*, can be only approximately laid down, as the information supplied by Physicians, though ample in quantity, mostly leaves the point indefinite as to where the observations were made, whether in Asia Minor and Egypt (Alexandria), or in Greece and Italy. The last named country indeed was, as is well known, almost entirely devoid of independent native medical Writers.

The mild, genial sky of Greece and Italy impressed on all forms of disease, including diseases of the genitals, a mild character. There, on the confines of East and West, we find, it is true, the same natural tendencies prevailing as in Asia, but always on a less exaggerated scale. *Von Roeser* (loco citato p. 70.) says: "In conclusion we should note further that in Egypt gonorrhœa is a complaint of very rare occurrence, in Greece and Turkey a very common one. That the exanthematic character taken by syphilis is not (?) responsible for the fact of its not manifesting itself as gonorrhoea is confirmed by the circumstance that it occurs much more frequently in Greece than amongst ourselves, whereas syphilis in that country has (though not in an identical form) the exanthematic type to an even greater degree than in our own." *D. Hennen*[1] found Venereal disease rare in Cephalonia, but on the contrary gonorrhœa quite common.

No doubt the tendency to determine towards the skin is clearly noticeable in Greece as well, but not to such an extent as to outweigh the local affection. The latter accordingly takes a more independent

[1] *D. Hennen*, Sketches of the Medical Topography of the Mediterranean. London 1830.

form than is the case in Asia, and for this reason, though making its appearance more frequently, neither follows so rapid a course nor shows so destructive a character,—if only the organism is seconded to some extent in the efforts to combat the malady. This is shown by the statements *Galen* has left as to gonorrhœa and ulcers occurring in connection with bubonic swellings,—a matter we shall have occasion to speak of later. While in Asia the skin affection is manifested by the formation of pustules and scurf, in Greece and neighbouring countries of the South it rather takes the shape of *papillae* and small blisters or blebs, and only in obstinate cases breaks out in tubercles. Hence *lepra*, *psora*, *lichen*, and *elephantiasis* are the forms under which we must look for it in the medical Writers of Antiquity, who however say nothing as to the origin of these diseases, or else, as we have seen before, refer them all to deficiency of the moist humours [1].

We have never yet succeeded, though we have before now expended much time on the effort, in getting a clear grasp of the ideas the Ancient physicians intended to express by the different designations they gave to the various skin-diseases. So we are constrained to postpone deeper investigation of the question to a subsequent occasion, or wait to see whether meantime some other enquirer, better

[1] *Galen*, De febr. diff., bk. I., edit. Kühn Vol. VII. 284 sqq., *δριμὺ δ' ἀποῤῥοῖ καὶ δακνῶδες περίττωμα τοῖς ἤτοι κακοχυμοτέροις, ἢ ἐδέσματα μοχθηρὰ προσφερομένοις τοιαῦτα γοῦν ἐδέσματα καὶ νῦν ἀναγκασθέντες ἐσθίειν πολλοὶ διὰ λιμὸν οἱ μὲν ἀπέθανον ἀπὸ σηπεδονωδῶν τε καὶ λοιμωδῶν πυρετῶν, οἱ δὲ ἐξανθήμασιν ἑάλωσαν ψωρώδεσι τε καὶ λεπρώδεσιν.* (But there discharges an acrid and biting excretion, and this in patients already only too much afflicted with evil humours, or else food becomes noxious to them, though normally able to tolerate such food; and now being forced to eat, many died in consequence of the plague, some from putrefying and pestilential fevers, while others again *were attacked by exanthematic eruptions of the psora and lepra types*).

equipped for the work, may not throw light on the chaos. Only so far as *Scabies* (Scab) is concerned, it would seem allowable to assume allusions to be intended to vicious living as a cause of the malady. It cannot be without a reason that for centuries this one above all other skin diseases seems to have fallen under special disrepute; and the term to have been used by poets, by *Martial*[1] for example, to indicate that sensual indulgence had been at work. In fact, several of the earliest Writers on Venereal disease hold it to be a sort of *scabies*, and even at a later period there is for long frequent mention made of *Venereal scars or scabs*. Possibly also in Greece lepra (leprosy) was looked upon as a form of skin-disease that was come by in no reputable way, and commonly regarded as an inheritance of the debauchees[2], just as we saw to be the case with *mentagra* at Rome.

[1] Martial, Bk. VI. Epigr. 37.,

O quanta scabie miser laborat!
Culum non habet, est tamen cinadus.

(How sad a scurvy (*scabies*) does the wretch groan under! Bottom all gone; and yet he is a cinaedus!)
Bk. XI. Epigr. 8.,

Penelopae licet esse tibi sub principe Nerva
Sed prohibet scabies ingeniumque vetus.

(You may be a Penelope under Nerva as Emperor; only that *scurvy* hinders you and inveterate viciousness). The *mala scabies* (horrid scurvy) from *Horace*, Ars Poet, 453., is familiar; as well as the statement of *Justin* (Hist. XXXVI. 2.) to the effect that the Jews were driven out of Egypt on account of Scabies and Vitiligo (Tetter), that the Egyptians might not be infected by them. Comp. *Michaelis*, "Mosaisches Recht", (Mosaic Law) IV. 209. The infectious nature of psora is declared also by *Aristotle*, Problem. VII. 8. *Galen*, De puls. diff., IV. 1. The transition of *mentagra* into *psora* has been already mentioned.

[2] *Aristophanes*, Birds 151. makes Euelpides say: *βδελλύττομαι τὸν Λέπρεον ἀπὸ Μελανθίου* (I detest the "Leprean" of Melanthius), on which the Scholiast remarks: *Μελάνθιος ὁ τραγικός· κωμωδεῖται γὰρ εἰς μαλακίαν καὶ ὀψοφαγιάν. Πλάτων δὲ αὐτὸν ἐν Σκύθαις ὡς λάλον σκώπτει· εἶχε δὲ Μελάνθιος λέπραν.* (Melanthius the

Affections of the external skin consequent upon complaints of the genital organs being thus no less common in Ancient times than they are to-day, it follows that in inverse proportion forms of ulceration of the palate and nose, as well as complaints affecting the bones, must have fallen into the background and have been of more rare occurrence, just as is observed to be the case in the present day [1]. So, to combine all the varying forms under one generalisation, we may say that this represents a type of disease of an exceedingly mild and favourable character, particularly if attention is directed only to the external symptoms, as indeed was habitually done by the old pathologists. For even the skin-affection itself presents so little that is characteristic, or at any rate shows itself

Tragedian; for he is derided on account of his luxurious living and gluttony. But Plato laughs at him in the "Scythians" as a *garrulous* person; now Melanthius had *leprosy*). The same thing is mentioned in the "Peace", 803., with the addition, *καὶ πολὺ μᾶλλον ἐν Κόλαξιν Εὔπολις ὡς κίναιδον αὐτὸν διαβάλλει καὶ κόλακα· ἀλλὰ καὶ ὡς λευκὰς ἔχοντα καὶ λεπράς.* (and still more severely does Eupolis in his "Flatterers" ridicule him as being *pathic* and a flatterer; moreover as having whites,—white leprosies,—and leprosies). Here we would particularly call attention to the *λευκαί* (white leprosies), which we have already noted as a consequence of the habits of the *cunnilingue;* and with this the *λάλον* (garrulous, talkative) of the Comic poet Plato agrées very well, for *Hesychius* explains *γλωσσοστροφεῖν* (to ply the tongue) by *περιλαλεῖν* and *στωμύλλεσθαι* (*to be very talkative, to babble*). Thus *lepra* would seem to be attached as penaltyto the vice of the pathic, Elephantiasis is stated to be infectious by *Aretaeus*, Morb. chron., II. 12. and *Paulus Aegineta*, IV. 1.; however, present day experience tells us nothing of this, and the later Greek physicians refer it again to deficient gall (Marx, Orig. contag., p. 78.); what was the meaning of its great contagiousness in earlier times?

[1] *Von Roeser*, loco citato p. 69. Inflammation of the throat, or ulcerations of the throat, are very rare; still rarer are diseases of the bones, and then only taking the form of swellings of the periosteum.

under such varying shapes, that even at the present day its diagnosis is extremely difficult, being very often based solely and entirely on the admission of the patient, whether voluntary or forced from him, of having suffered from gonorrhœa or chancre. But if the so-called secondary symptoms are more or less completely absent, or lack distinctness, what is there then left beyond the primary affections of the genitals and their succedanea? Full and sufficient descriptions of these are not lacking; we have already quoted numerous examples, and we shall find others yet clearer and more precise later on.

Before quitting the subject of the influence exerted by Climate, we are bound to return once more to the question, *in what relation did contagion*, if contagion there was, *stand to this climatic influence?* The existence of contagion in the case of gonorrhœa is certified by the passage of *Galen* already quoted by Naumann, which we propose later on to give in full, besides being implied long before by the law of purification of the Mosaic Books. So far as ulcerous formations, condylomata and skin-affections such as *mentagra* etc., are concerned, proof is supplied by the facts we have previously given. According to more modern experience all forms of contagion exhibit in Southern countries a more fugitive type than elsewhere and spread with proportionately greater readiness. Whereas in such as are naturally fugitive, the intensity may for that very reason be less injurious, fixed and stable forms of contagion on the contrary must obviously lose in strength, at any rate so far as their local effects go. They will be the less able to make good a lodgement in the organism, from the fact that, stimulating the latter as they do to a general activity, they are the more readily resisted and prevented by this very state of enhanced activity. For just as, speaking generally, chronic complaints, uncomplicated by fever, can only be removed by artificially setting up a feverish condition, that is to say by calling on the organism as a whole to share in the local manifestations of disease. Precisely the same is true of local affections set up by any fixed and stable contagion, and so the removal of the actual contagion can only be successfully brought about either by direct decomposition and destruction of the affected tissue or by metamorphosis into a fugitive form.

Now inasmuch as the contagion was rapidly thrown off from the point of first infection upon the cutaneous glands,—and this happened the more readily, the more fugitive its character was,—the affections there set up by it standing in such clear relation as they did with the primary sumptoms, were necessarily bound also to exhibit a greater or less degree of the contagious character, as indeed is observed according to *Jos. Frank*, *Biett* and other authorities even in Europe to the present day. In Greece, where the transformation was less often to pustular and scurfy forms, more frequently merely to papillae or at worst little bladder-like risings, or blebs (Phlyctaenae), while at the same time the energy of the skin was not so pronounced, the interval between the appearance of the primary and secondary symptoms was greater, and the contagiousness of the skin-affections undoubtedly less prominent, it cost the organism in that climate much more strenuous effort to set in action the elimination of the disease by the skin. Consequently the nervous system as well was injuriously affected by sympathy to a greater extent, while the exanthematic forms showed themselves in more obvious conjunction with itch *(psora !)*. This was partially the case in Italy too, though here the climate approximated more nearly to that of Lower Egypt, leading to a more frequent appearance of pustulous forms, as shown by the prevalence in that country of *mentagra*.

But just as climatic influence relaxed the intensity of contagion, and diminished concurrently the malignancy of disease-types, local as well as general, so on the contrary, in those cases where other influences tended to counteract its effect, while the organism was not strong enough to overmaster the assaults of the enemy by general or local activity, it sought to guard against the contagion rising to a higher degree of independence; it set up mortification of the ulcers, by which means the contagion itself was directly destroyed. From all this it may be concluded, that although climate must evidently be acknowledged to be an important factor favourable to the rise of affections of the genital organs in Antiquity as much as at the present day, yet on the other hand it tended by its own action to combat the mischief it had originated; and so, at any rate so far as the development of the morbid process is concerned, is to be regarded to an almost equal degree as a counteracting influence at the same time.

§ 32.

The experience of all ages has conclusively proved that a large proportion of such morbid phænomena as occur in consequence of local climatic conditions are capable equally of being produced sooner or later in countries and neighbourhoods the climate of which is entirely different by help of the *genius epidemicus;* and that the readiness with which they are so produced varies in direct ratio with the degree in which the climate is associated with and seconds the favourable factors. It is indeed extremely difficult, in view of the low level of development to which the science of Epidemics, in general no less than in particular, has as yet attained, to show this as applicable in any given case, more especially if it is a question of the epidemic condition of some disease of which the pathological relations themselves are far from being as yet adequately known. Still this must not prevent us from making at any rate an attempt at investigation of the question, how much or how little effort has been manifested by such influence in the course of years.

But the influence of the genius epidemicus on diseases in general is a twofold one. *Either* it supplies the capital, most essential external circumstances conditioning the production of a disaese, in fact is related to it as cause to effect. In virtue of it the disease is an *epidemic* disease, coming into existence for the first time concurrently with the development of the genius epidemicus, disappearing again with the cessation of its prevalence, and once again springing up if and when the genius epidemicus makes a second re-appearance. *Or else* the most essential external conditioning circumstances are specifically independent of the genius epidemicus; while the latter takes merely a remote share in the way of favouring or counteracting the production of the disease, manifesting its influence rather in modifying the form and direction of such morbid reactions as have arisen in the organism without its intervention at all,—in other words *the disease is subject to epidemic influence.*

Unfortunately hitherto these two kinds of influence exerted by the genius epidemicus have been only too often confounded, and no adequate distinction drawn between epidemic diseases on the one hand and diseases subject to epidemic influence on the other. This has been especially so with regard to Venereal disease, the epidemic character of which curiously enough enquirers have felt bound to vindicate, es well at the beginning of the XVth. Century as here and there even at the present day. The baselessness of such an opinion is so perfectly obvious to anyone who weighs the matter with any care, that we really do not think it necessary to devote more pains now to proving the point, particularly as we propose to treat it more fully in another place. On the other hand Venereal disease *is* subject to epidemic influence, in fact it is so perhaps to a greater extent than many other forms of sickness, as will be clearly shown in the course of our historical investigations. Accordingly the only question still wanting an answer is, how far such influence may have been effectual in Antiquity. This question of course presupposes the existence already of a number of diseases appearing in consequence of Venereal excesses; still we possess sufficient proof, as previously stated in the course of our enquiries into the influence of climate, to justify a provisional assumption of their existence for our immediate purpose. For openly admitting as we do our ignorance in relation to the influence of the genius epidemicus on sexual activity generally and on the individual activity of the genital organs in particular, and noting the problem to be one that can only be solved in the future, there is nothing else left us to investigate here but this, viz. *the influence of the genius epidemicus in reference to the forms taken and course followed by diseases occurring in consequence of Veneteal excesses.*

It may be collected from later experience and observation that there are three clearly marked forms of the genius epidemicus or *epidemic condition*, that exercise a preponderating influence on affections of the genitals and Venereal disease, and condition the frequency of the occurrence of one or the other type of these, viz. *catarrhal*, conditioning blennorrhœal affections. the *exanthematic*, conditioning complaints of the cutaneous glands, and the *typhoïdal*, conditioning various forms of chancre and their malignancy.

With regard to the influence of the *genius epidemicus catarrhalis* and *exanthematicus*, it would seem to be difficult to arrive at any definite conclusion as to what precisely this was in Asia and the South of Europe, since the Climate was *ipso facto*, as already shown, pre-eminently favourable to blennorrhœal and cutaneous affections; nevertheless the rise and spread of mentagra as well as of elephantiasis in the time of Pompey the Great does afford some indication at any rate so far as Italy is concerned. No doubt the Hippocratic writers several times mention the prevalence of skin affections at particular periods; but the expressions they employ are too general to make it possible for us to take these into special consideration in this place. However there is one passage we must make an exception of,—a passage of the greatest importance for our purpose, even though in all probability it refers to the commencement of a combined erysipelas-typhoïdal condition, to which we shall have occasion to return again later. In it Hippocrates relates how after a dry Summer with Southerly winds and frequent rain there followed a mild, wet Winter, next cold and even snow-storms succeeded in the Spring with much rain, and finally a very hot Summer again. In the Spring began inflammatory fevers and erysipelas, and [1] "in many cases aphthae and ulcerations formed in the mouth, many rheums occurred in the genitals taking the form of ulcers and abcesses on the external and internal surface of the sexual parts; also eye troubles, with discharge, obstinate, persistent and painful; also growths, which are called **σῦκα** (figs) on the inner and outer surface of the eye-lids, causing many to lose their sight; besides they frequently occurred on other parts liable to ulceration and particularly on the genital organs." In this passage the expressions **ἑλκώματα, φύματα, ἔξωθεν ἔσωθεν τὰ περὶ βουβῶνας** (ulcers and abcesses on the external and internal surface of the sexual parts) is as a rule misunderstood by the annotators. But

[1] *Hippocrates*, Epidem. Bk. III., edit. Kühn Vol. III. p. 486., *στόματα πολλοῖσιν ἀφθώδεα, ἑλκώδεα· ῥεύματα περὶ τὰ αἰδοιᾶ πολλά· ἑλκώματα, φύματα, ἔξωθεν ἔσωθεν τὰ περὶ βουβῶνας, ὀφθαλμίαι ὑγραὶ, μακραὶ χρόνιαι μετὰ πόνων· ἐπιφύσεις βλεφάρων ἔξωθεν ἔσωθεν, πολλῶν φθείροντες τὰς ὄψιας, ἃ σῦκα ἐπονομάζουσιν· ἐφύετο δὲ καὶ ἐπὶ τῶν ἄλλων ἑλκέων πολλὰ καὶ αἰδοίοισιν.* (for translation see text above).

really **ἔξωθεν** (on the outside) evidently refers to **ἑλκώματα** (ulcers), while **ἔσωθεν** (on the inside) goes with **φύματα** (abcesses), and signifies a swelling and inflammation of a mucous gland resulting in suppuration, as may be seen from the next quoted Aphorism [1]. "Such patients as have **φύματα** (abcesses) in the urethra find relief, so soon as these have suppurated and broken." That this relief (**λύσις**) consisted in the cessation of pain and of the retention of urine may be gathered not only from Galen's commentary on the first passage, and from the **λύεται ὁ πόνος** (the suffering is relieved) in the

[1] *Hippocrates*, Bk. IV. Aphor. 82., edit. Kühn Vol. III. p. 735., *ὁκόσοισιν ἐν τῇ οὐρήθρῃ φύματα φύεται, τουτέοισι διαπυήσαντος καὶ ἐκραγέντος λύσις*. (for translation see text above). The same Aphorism is repeated again Bk. VII. Aphor. 57. p. 763., *ὁκόσοισιν ἐν τῇ οὐρήθρῃ φύματα γίνονται, τουτέοισι διαπυήσαντος καὶ ἐκραγέντος λύεται ὁ πόνος*. (Patients having abcesses in the urethra, *find relief from the suffering*, so soon as these have suppurated and broken).—*Celsus*, bk. II. ch. 8. translates this by: Quibus in fistula urinae minuti abscessus, quos *φύματα* Graeci vocant, esse coeperunt, iis ubi pus ea parte profluxit, sanitas redditur. (Patients in whom small abcesses have been set up in the urinary canal, which the Greeks call *φύματα*, recover when once matter has flowed out at the spot).—*Galen*, in his Explanation of the first Aphorism of Hippocrates (edit. Kühn Vol. XVII. B. p. 778.) says: *πρόχειρον γὰρ παντὶ γνῶναι τῶν ἐν τῷ πόρῳ τῷ οὐρητικῷ τῷ κατὰ τὸ αἰδοῖον, τοῦτο γὰρ οὐρήθραν καλοῦσι· συνισταμένων φυμάτων τὴν λύσιν γίγνεσθαι ῥαγέντων· ἐνδέχεται γὰρ ἰσχουρίαν δή τινα γενέσθαι καὶ διὰ τὸ τοιοῦτον φῦμα καὶ μέντοι καὶ ὡς τὸ φῦμα τοῦτο ῥαγὲν ἰάσεται τὴν ἰσχουρίαν εὔδηλον*. (For it is within the knowledge of every observer that in the case of abcesses that have been set up in the urinary canal in the region of the privates,—called the urethra,—relief is afforded when once these have burst. For it is likely some retention of urine occurs on account of such abcess, and so the fact of this abcess having burst will obviously remedy the retention). Comp. *Galen*, De loc. affect. Bk. I. ch. 1., bk. VI. ch. 6. *Paulus Aegineta* bk. IV. ch. 22.

repetition of the same Aphorism, but Hippocrates actually says so distinctly in a third passage [1].

Supposing the view, still generally held even in the last Century, that regards gonorrhœa as a result of an ulcer in the urethra, to have been already adopted in Hippocrates' time,—and inasmuch as the expression **γονοῤῥοία,** so far as we know, never occurs in his writings, the assumption would not only not be absurd, but such a view would really be preferable to that which makes out the discharge to be badly made semen,—we shall find in this passage an expression of the fact of the more common occurrence of gonorrhœa, the most troublesome symptom of which, viz. the pain suffered during micturition (**πόνος, δυσουρία, ἰσχουρία,** suffering, difficulty in micturition, retention of urine), disappears, as is well known, concurrently with the commencement of the discharge (**πύου ῥαγέντος, φυμάτων ῥαγέντων,**—when the pus has broken out, when the abcess has broken), or if it does not entirely disappear, is at any rate sensibly diminished. But it is not really needful to accept this as having been the ruling opinion; the facts may very well be accounted for by supposing that in virtue of the *epidemic condition* a strongly marked tendency was set up on the part of the glandular organs to inflammatory and suppurative action, by which not merely the glands of the external skin (**ἑλκώματα ἔξωθεν,**—ulcerations on the outside, Moses' שְׂאֵת, שְׁחִין), but also those of the mucous membrane of the urethra (**φύματα ἔσωθεν,**—abcesses on the inside) were affected,

[1] *Hippocrates*, Coact. praenot., edit. Kühn Vol. I. p. 312., *οἶσι δὲ φῦμα περὶ τὴν κύστιν ἐστὶ τὸ παρέχον τὴν δυσουρίην, παντοίως σχηματισθέντες ὀχλέονται· λύσις δὲ τούτου γίνεται πύου ῥαγέντος.* (Patients having an abcess in the region of the bladder that causes difficulty of micturition, find themselves troubled and effected in all sorts of ways; *but relief from this is experienced, when once the matter has broken out*).

exactly as is observed at the present day, especially in the chronic forms of gonorrhœa.

The gonorrhœa then in this case would seem to have been of a more malignant type and to have been combined with ulceration. This best agrees with the general delineation of the *epidemic condition* as a whole, the exanthematic character of which declared itself in the fig-like growths or tumours,—the **σῦκα αἰδοίοισιν** (figs on the genitals). *Grimm* (Vol. I. p. 490.) already remarks on this passage of Hippocrates: "One might be tempted in this case to regard the ulcerations of the genital parts and their consequences, the fig-like tumours, as being the first signs of disease due to incontinence. Indeed what was there to hinder an evil of the sort in those times and under a warm climate from signalizing itself,—then subsequently so far losing its malignant character that its nature was completely misunderstood? Something of the same kind actually happens under our own eyes in connection with this very disease."

§ 33.

Still more important were the effects of these meteorological conditions on ulcers of the genitals *already in existence*. We read (loco citato p. 482.): "Even before the beginning of Spring, concurrently with the commencement of the cold time, erysipelas made frequent appearances sometimes with, sometimes without, visible cause; it showed itself highly malignant in type, and carried off many. Many again suffered from painful affections of the pharynx (anginae,—sore throats), loss of voice (affections of the windpipe), inflammatory fevers with delirium, aphthae in the mouth, **φύματα** (abscesses) in the genital organs, ophthalmias, **ἄνθρακες** (malignant pustules), etc.—Also many got erysipelas from external causes, at such spots as these had happened to affect them, even after the smallest injuries [1], and in all parts of the body. Above all sexagenarians suffered in this way in the head, if they were treated in the smallest degree carelessly. Even under careful and scientific treatment wide-spread phlegmonous affections frequently occurred, while the erysipelas spread to a serious extent and with great rapidity in all directions. In most of the patients so affected the metamorphosis that succeeded was to ulcerations, whilst *muscles, sinews and bones fell away to a serious degree.* But the morbid product that collected did not resemble ordinary matter (pus), but was a sort of putrid *sanies*, occurring equally in combination and by itself [2]. Such as were attacked in the head, became bald over the whole head and chin, the bones were laid bare and fell away, and such ῥεύματα (morbid discharges) as described occurred frequently, whether with or without fever. Symptoms of the kind however were more terrifying than really destructive [3],

[1] *Hippocrates*, De aere aquis et locis, edit. Kühn Vol. I. p. 526., κῆν μὲν τὸ θέρος αὐχμηρὸν γένηται, θᾶσσον παύονται αἱ νοῦσοι· ἢν δὲ ἔπομβρον, πολυχρόνιοι γίνονται καὶ φαγεδαίνας κοινῶς ἐγγίνεσθαι ἀπὸ πάσης προφάσιος, ἢν ἕλκος ἐγγένηται. (And if the Summer is a dry one, the diseases will cease more speedily: if on the other hand it is rainy, they become chronic, and such that cancerous sores are set up on any pretext, if an injury of any sort occur).

[2] *Galen*, in his Commentary on this passage (Vol. XVII. A. p. 671) says in this connection: διεσήπετο δ' ὑπὸ τῶν μοχθηρῶν χυμῶν ὑγρῶν τὰ στερεά· ποικίλον δ' εἶναι τὸ ῥεῦμα διὰ τὴν τῶν σηπομένων διαφθορὰν εὔλογον· ὑπὸ γὰρ κοινῆς αἰτίας τῆς σηπεδόνος ἕκαστον τῶν σηπομένων ἴδιον εἶδος ἴσχει τῆς διαφθορᾶς. (But under influence of the morbid moist juices the solid parts rotted away; so it is only reasonable to expect the discharge to be complex, resulting from the destruction of the parts rotted away; for although proceeding from one common cause, that of decomposition, each of the rotting parts has its own particular form of decomposition).

[3] *Galen*, in his Commentary loco citato p. 672., adds: φοβερωτέραν εἶχε φαντασίαν ἐν τοῖς περὶ κεφαλὴν μορίοις, διὰ τὸ κἂν βραχὺ τὴν παρὰ φύσιν ἐνταῦθα παραλαχ-

for among patients in whom these (*ῥεύματα*) came to maturity and resulted in suppuration, the majority were saved; on the contary many died among those in whom the phlegmonous affections and the erysipelas disappeared, without undergoing any such metamorphosis into other forms of disease. Moreover the same thing happened to those in whose case (the morbid product) attacked some other part of the body. For with many of them the whole upper and fore arm fell away; while in some patients the disease attacked the ribs, the sole difference being

θείη, πλέον γίνεσθαι τὸ αἶσχος ἢ κατὰ τὰ ἄλλα μόρια μεγάλην ἐκτροπὴν εἰς τὸ παρὰ φύσιν ἔχοντα. μηροῦ μὲν γὰρ τὸ βραχίονος ἢ κνήμης ἢ πήχεως ἀποῤῥυὲν δέρμα μικροτέραν ἔχει φαντασίαν, εἰ δὲ τῆς κεφαλῆς συναποπέσοιεν αἱ τρίχες τῷ δέρματι καὶ πολὺ μᾶλλον ἡ τοῦ γενείου σὺν αὐταῖς, ἡ μὲν φαντασία τοῦ πάθους γίνεται μεγάλη, ὁ κίνδυνος δ' ἧττον ἢ εἰ περὶ αἰδοῖα συμβαιή τὸ τοιοῦτον πάθος ἢ λάρυγγα καὶ θώρακα καὶ τι τῶν κυρίων· οὐ μόνον δὲ τά περὶ τὴν κεφαλὴν οὕτως γινόμενα φοβερὰ μᾶλλον ἦν ἢ κακίω, ἀλλὰ καὶ καθ' ὁτιοῦν ἄλλο μέρος οὕτως ἐκπίπτοντα· κακίω γὰρ ἦν ἐφ' ὧν ἀπέστησεν εἰς τὸ βάθος ὁ τὸ ἐρυσίπελας ἐργαζόμενος χυμὸς κ. τ. λ. (It offered a more terrifying appearance where the parts about the head were affected, because even if only a small deviation occur there from what is normal, the feeling of disgust experienced is greater than in connection with other parts of the body, even when showing a great divergence towards what is abnormal. For the fact of the skin of the thigh being perished, or even when showing of the upper arm, or of the leg, or fore-arm, affords a less formidable appearance, but if the hair fall from the head and the skin along with it, and still more if that of the cheeks and chin go with it, the appearance of injury is very great; but the danger is all the while really less than if the like were to happen to the private parts or larynx and thorax or any of the vital parts. And not only are such things when they happen to the head more terrifying than actually dangerous, but also when it so falls out with regard to any other part; for much more dangerous is the case of those in whom the humour that sets up erysipelas has penetrated deeply in, etc.).

whether some destruction was wrought on their anterior or posterior aspect; in others again the whole thigh or the lower leg or the whole foot was laid bare. *But the most dangerous of all was, when this or the like happened in the neighbourhood of the private parts or to the private parts themselves,* and the mischief manifested itself in the form of ulcers, and as the result of external causes. In many patients suchlike symptoms occurred during, before, as well as after the fever"[1].

Galen, who has left us a Commentary on this passage (Vol. XVII. A.) mentions in the first place that aphthae, **φύματα** (abscesses) of the genitals, etc. specifically possessed (p. 661.) nothing of **κακοηθεία** (malignity), but only when as in this case they occurred in conjunction with a putrid general condition. "The putrid character easily arises even without a pestilential general condition, if the parts are attacked by phlegmonous affections or erysipelas, and spreads likewise over the neighbouring parts lying uppermost; hence it is we are compelled after cutting away the decayed tissues to cauterize the place. It is no wonder then, when such a condition has arisen that upper and fore-arm, thigh and lower leg, ribs and head are attacked, if the private parts suffer above all others.—So far the author has discussed those affections of a kind akin to erysipelas which associate themselves with ulcerations or other comparatively

[1] Hippocrates, loco citato p. 284., *πολλοῖσι μὲν γὰρ βραχίων καὶ πῆχυς ὅλος [ὅλως] περιεῤῥύη· οἷσι δ' ἐπὶ τὰ πλευρὰ ταῦτα ἐκακοῦτο ἢ τῶν ἔμπροσθέν τι ἢ τῶν ὄπισθεν· οἷσι δὲ ὅλος ὁ μηρὸς ἢ τὰ περικνήμια ἐψιλοῦτο καὶ ποὺς ὅλος· ἦν δὲ πάντων χαλεπώτατον τῶν τοιούτων, ὅτε περὶ ἥβην καὶ αἰδοῖα γενοίατο, καὶ τὰ μὲν περὶ ἕλκεα καὶ μετὰ προφάσιος τοιαῦτα· πολλοῖσι δὲ ἐν πυρετοῖσι καὶ πρὸ πυρετοῦ καὶ ἐπί πυρετοῖσι ξυνέπιπτεν.* (for translation see text above). For *ἢ τὰ περικνήμια ἐψιλοῦτο* should evidently be read more correctly with *Galen*, De temperam. bk. I., edit. Kühn Vol. I. p. 532. *ἢ τὰ περὶ τὴν κνήμην ἀπεψιλοῦτο.*

insignificant external cause; in what follows he speaks of such attacks as occurred without any such occasioning cause" [1].

Now if we examine these statements, so far as they are of immediate interest in view of our object, we may unhesitatingly conclude from them, that in Hippocrates' time a large number of patients suffered from ulcers of the genitals. These it seems under the influence of the prevailing typhoïdal conditions were assailed by inflammation of an erysipelas-like type, rapidly passing over into humid gangrene, which latter destroyed the parts attacked, readily extended its ravages, and eventually killed the patient. This is an observation which *Galen* likewise had frequent occasion to make (so probably under the head of Influence of the Climate of Asia, pp. 318, 326, 329.), without any exactly definite typhoïdal conditions having been prevalent [2], and even saw himself under these circumstances very generally constrained, in order to put a stop to the spread of the mortification, *to amputate the gangrenous tissue, and afterwards cauterize the wound.* What was the origin of these ulcers of the genitals

[1] *Galen*, Vol. XVII. A. p. 674., *Καὶ χωρὶς λοιμώδους καταστάσεως, ὅταν ἐν τούτοις τοῖς χωρίοις ἤτοι φλεγμονή τις ἢ ἐρυσίπελας γένηται, ῥᾷστά τε σήπεται καὶ συμπαθείας ἐργάζεται τῶν ὑπερκειμένων μορίων· διὸ καὶ πολλάκις ἀναγκαζόμεθα μετὰ τὸ περικόψαι τὰ σεσηπότα τὴν χώραν ἐκκαίειν· οὐδὲν οὖν θαυμαστὸν, τοιαύτης καταστάσεως γινομένης ὡς καὶ βραχίονα καὶ μηρὸν καὶ κνήμην, πλευράν τε καὶ κεφαλὴν διασήπειν, ἐπὶ πλεῖστον ἥκειν κακώσεως τὰ περὶ αἰδοῖα ... Ἄχρι τοῦ νῦν ὁ λόγος αὐτῷ γέγονε περὶ τῶν ἐρυσιπελάτων, ὅσα δ' ἕλκωσιν ἤ τι μικρὸν οὕτως ἄλλο τῶν ἔξωθεν αἰτίων συνέστη· ἐφεξῆς δὲ περὶ τῶν ἄνευ τοιαύτης αἰτίας γενομένων ποιήσεται τὸν λόγον.* (for translation see text above).

[2]. Hippocrates moreover, Aphorism. Vol. I. p. 724., says: *τοῦ δὲ θέρεος ... καὶ σηπεδόνες αἰδοίων καὶ ἵδρωα.* (And in the Summer.... occur also *putrefactions of the privates* and transpirations).

is indeed not stated; but it is certain they were not invariably conditioned by the prevailing *genius epidemicus*. Besides, since Hippocrates several times mentions them without giving the cause that produced them, it is a more likely conjecture to suppose that this cause was one universally familiar (it consisted in an act of unclean intercourse with women), than to assume it to have been *absolutely unknown* to physicians generally [1].

Again the result of this investigation is of still more especial interest in so far as it enables us to

[1] Very possibly in many cases these affections of the extremities and genital organs owed their existence to *anthrax* or *carbuncle;* for not only does *Hippocrates* (p. 487.) say that ἄνθρακες πολλοὶ κατὰ θέρος καὶ ἄλλα ἃ σήψ καλέεται (many cases of malignant pustule in Summer-time, as well as other complaints known under the general name of putrefaction) appeared under these meteorological conditions, but *Galen* likewise (Method. med. bk. XIV., edit. Kühn Vol. X. p. 980.) observed an *anthrax* epidemic in Asia, that itself began with numerous *phlyctaenae* (blisterous swellings) resembling millet seeds; these subsequently broke and gave rise to an ἕλκος ἐσχαρῶδες (scabby sore). Indeed the destruction of the skin took place even without the previous occurrence of *phlyctaenae*. πολλάκις δὲ οὐ μία φλύκταινα γεννᾶται κνησαμένων, ἀλλὰ πολλαὶ μικραὶ καθάπερ τινὲς κέγχροι καταπυκνοῦσαι τὸ μέρος ὧν ἐκρηγνυμένων ὁμοίως ἐσχαρῶδες ἕλκος γεννᾶται· κατὰ δὲ τοὺς ἐπιδημήσαντας ἄνθρακας ἐν Ἀσίᾳ καὶ χωρὶς φλυκταινῶν ἐνίοις εὐθέως ἀπεδάρη τὸ δέρμα. (And often *not one phlyctaena* is originated on patients scratching themselves, but *many* minute ones like millet seeds, closely covering the affected part; and when these have broken, a kind of scabby sore is produced. And in cases of *anthrax* (malignant pustule), which was at one time epidemic in Asia, in some patients even without there having been previous *phlyctaenae*, the skin was immediately destroyed).—Comp. *Galen*, De tumor. praeternat. Vol. VII. p. 719. Further, this information is in any case of importance for the more correct appreciation of the facts as to the Plague of Athens.

properly appreciate Thucydides' notice of the so-called *Plague of Athens.* This has been discussed

[1] *Thucydides*, Peloponnesian War, bk. II. ch. 49., *Διεξῄει γὰρ διὰ παντὸς τοῦ σώματος ἄνωθεν ἀρξάμενον τὸ ἐν τῇ κεφαλῇ πρῶτον ἱδρυθὲν κακόν· καὶ εἴ τις ἐκ τῶν μεγίστων περιγένοιτο, τῶν γε ἀκρωτηρίων ἀντίληψις αὐτὸν ἐπεσήμαινε· κατέσκηπτε γὰρ ἐς αἰδοῖα καὶ ἐς ἄκρας χεῖρας καὶ πόδας· καὶ πολλοὶ στερισκόμενοι τούτων διέφευγον·* (for translation see text above). In this passage it is usual to read *ἀντίληψις αὐτοῦ ἐπεσήμαινε*, supplying *κακοῦ* from the previous clause to go with *αὐτοῦ*,—(the seizure of the disease itself on the extremities manifested itself); but even supposing the double genitive with *ἀντίληψις* defensible, the construction is still very awkward, and is made still more so by the fact that in taking it this way we are compelled to translate *ἐπεσήμαινε* by "manifested itself" (mali vis, apprehendens extremas corporis partes se prodebat, manifestam faciebat, —the strength of the disease declared itself, made itself manifest, in seizing the extermities of the body,—is Wittenbach's interpretation, Select. Hist. p. 367.), without by so doing obtaining any clear meaning of the sentence. On the other hand this is got directly we read with *Reiske* (Annotations p. 21. in his "Thucydides Reden, übersetzt von Reiske, nebst lateinischen Anmerkungen über dessen gesammtes Werk,—Speeches in Thucydides translated into German by Reiske, together with Latin Notes on his "Histories" generally, Leipzig 1761. 8vo.) *ἀντίληψις αὐτὸν ἐπεσήμαινε*, — a seizure put its mark on him. But whether *αὐτοῦ* is read or *αὐτὸν*, in any case it will be impossible to take the sentence as *Kraus*, p. 54., has done, when he says: "The pustulons suppurative eruption begins with the head and spreads little by little over the entire body even to the hands and feet. The fact that Thucydides had the eruption especially in his mind when he speaks of the gradual spread of the evil throughout the whole body is shown by the expressions chosen by him "'The disease goes through the entire body and *marks* (*ἐπεσήμαινε*) hands and feet.'" Now by what other of the symptoms mentioned would the affection of the hands and feet have been likely to make itself evident except by the eruption?" There must surely be few readers of Thucydides capable of putting so radically false an interpretation on the Historian's words.

by very many writers, and has given occassion to the most widely different explanations. He relates as follows: "For the disease which at first had its stronghold in the head, beginning from above downwards traversed by degrees the whole body; and even supposing a patient to have escaped the worst, yet a seizure of the extremities put its mark upon him. For it attacked the genitals and the extremities of the hands and feet; and many escaped death, but with the loss of these parts." Even more clearly does the poet *Lucretius* [1] paint the disease, when he says:

> Profluvium porro qui tetri sanguinis acre
> Exierat; tamen in nervos huic morbus et artus
> Ibat et in partes genitales corporis ipsas,
> Et graviter partim metuentes limina leti
> Vivebant ferro privati virili.

(Then too if any one had escaped the acrid discharge of noisome blood, the disease would yet pass into his sinews and joints and onward even *into the sexual organs of the body;* and some from excessive dread of the gates of death *would live bereaved of these parts by the knife.* Munro's translation).

Though we really are concerned only with the last words of Thucydides, so far as they relate to the genitals, yet what precedes has given occasion to such extraordinary interpretations that we feel bound to devote some attention to this as well. The whole passage proved itself an especial *stone of stumbling* to those writers who endeavoured to identify the Athenian plague with *scarlet-fever,* as *Malfatti* did, or with *small-pox,* like *Scuderi* and *Kraus.* In fact this is why the last named says as he does [2]: "The loss of the private parts and the extremities **στεϱισκόμενοι τούτων,**—being deprived

[1] *Lucretius,* De rerum natura bk. VI. 1205 sqq.

[2] *Kraus,* "Ueber das Alter der Menschenpocken," — (On the Antiquity of Small-pox), Hanover 1825., pp. 54 sqq.

of these, with the lose of these) would certainly seem to point merely to the loss of the *free use* of these parts, in consequence of ulcerations, swellings of the joints, lesions and contractions, for the entire members are not likely to have been destroyed by mortification or amputated by the surgeon? Indeed it is only in deference to the verses of Lucretius that the latter opinion has become the one generally held; but even Ancient commentators [1] have felt that the Roman poet may very possibly have mistaken Thucydides' meaning. Moreover I feel myself disposed to agree with them particularly on this ground, that the mortification of the whole of any of the greater limbs, though it *has* been observed in pestilential fevers, in *Typhus contagiosus putridus* (putrid infectious Typhus) amongst others, yet makes a comparatively rare symptom of the disease, and at the same time so dangerous a one that it can hardly be, as Thucydides alleges it was, that many (πολλοὶ) after such a serious affection escaped death, while on the contrary some (εἰσὶ δ' οἳ) only did so with the loss of the eyes." Any one who will compare the just quoted passages of Hippocrates and Galen with the account of Thucydides, will want no further proof that an a matter of fact mortification of the extremities did supervene, an occurence that even in later times [2] is not of the

[1] *Paulinus Fabius*, Praelectiones Marciae, etc. 352 (but he *defends* his accuracy, as do Lambinus and Mercurialis),— *Scuderi* Pt. I. p. 126. To these we may add *Petr. Victorius*, Variar. lect. bk. XXXV. ch. 8.

[2] As in the Antonine Plague in the year 235 A. D., — *Galen*, De usu part. III. ch. 5., De prob. pravisque alimentor. succ. ch. 1., edit. Kühn Vol. VI. p. 749.; *Cyprian*, Works, Venice 1728. fol., p. 465.)— Further note *Hecquet*, "Obs. sur la chute des os du pied dans une femme attaquée d'une fièvre maligne," (Observations on the Falling in of the Bones of the Foot in the case of a Woman attacked by a Malignant Fever), in Memoires de Paris 1746. Histor. p. 40.— *J. C. Brebis*, De sphacelo totius fere faciei post superatam febrem malignam oborto, (On the Mortification of almost the

extreme rarity that *Kraus* and others believe. Again the fact that *many* of those attacked escaped with their lives is the less surprising when one remembers that Thucydides is not speaking of entire arms and feet as having fallen off, but only of **ἄκρας χεῖρας καὶ πόδας,** that is to say, fingers and toes. However supposing any one to prefer not to supply **ἄκρων** with **τούτων,** but take it as used in its full extent, maintaining that hands and feet as well as genitals were entirely destroyed, even this would not belong to the category of *extremely rare* phænomena, for Hippocrates actually saw the extremities entirely fall off in similar circumstances, while if only the **ῥεύματα** (morbid discharges) came duly to maturity and matteration supervened, the major part (**οἱ πλεῖστοι τούτων ἐσώζοντο,**—the majority of these were saved) escaped with their life.

Finally the passage of Thucydides gives no sort of evidence to prove that the **ἀκρωτηρίων ἀντίληψις** (seizure of extremities) occured solely in those attacked by the fever as metastasis and so on. For the first sentence quoted, to the effect that the disease traversed the whole body, evidently refers back to the preceding clause **ἐπικατιόντος τοῦ νοσήματος ἐς τὴν κοιλίαν** (when the disease descends into the abdomen), and for this reason is

whole Face supervening after Recovery from a Malignant Fever), in Act. Acad. N. C. Vol. IV. p. 206. —*Percival* (Samml. auserles. Abh. Vol. XV. p. 335.) observed during an epidemic of putrid fever at Manchester many patients with violent erysipelas on the face and head; and in the Typhus epidemics of 1806—1813, *von Hildebrand* ("Ueber den ansteckenden Typhus," — On infectious Typhus), 2nd. edition, Vienna 1814., p. 200.) and *Horn* ("Erfahrungen über die Heilung des ansteckenden Nerven- und Lazarethfiebers," (Experiences in the Cure of infections Nervous and Hospital Fevers), 2nd. edition, Berlin 1814., pp. 49, 71.) saw violent inflammations of an erysipelas character set up in the nose, elbows, fingers and particularly the toes of their patients, which rapidly passed over into mortification.

connected with it by the conjunction **γὰρ**—"for". The succeeding words **καὶ εἴ τις ἐκ τῶν μεγίστων περιγένοιτο** (and even supposing a patient to have escaped the worst) may very well be taken in this way; **μεγίστων** (the greatest, worst things) is made not a Neuter absolute, like **τὰ ἔσχατα** (last extremities) and such like phrases in other places, but **κακῶν** (evils) is supplied to go with it, and the whole translated: "even supposing a patient escaped the greatest evils", that is to say if he were not attacked by the **λοῖμος** (Plague) in the forms of head and abdominal affections, "yet it marked him", that is it made its existence manifest by gangrene of the extremities supervening [1]. This Thucydides, a layman writing on a medical subject, supposes to be a mere manifestation of the **λοῖμος** (Plague), while Hippocrates regarded it as the proof of the erysipelas-putrid condition, which caused the already previously existing ulcers etc. to assume this character.

We have already mentioned the fact that at Athens ulcers of the feet were of frequent occurrence; and these must, no less than the ulcers of the genitals previously existing in any case, have necessarily been likewise assailed by the general unhealthy condition of things, and when this happened, have passed over into gangrene. Thucydides in fact says expressly at the beginning of his delineation of the disease (ch. 49.): **τὸ μὲν γὰρ ἔτος, ὡς ὡμολογεῖτο, ἐκ πάντων μάλιστα δὴ ἐκεῖνο ἄνοσον ἐς τὰς ἄλλας ἀσθενείας ἐτύγχανεν ὄν. εἰ δέ τις καὶ προέκαμνέ τι, ἐς τοῦτο πάντα ἀπεκρίθη.** (For indeed that year, as was universally admitted, chanced to be of all years one especially free from other diseases in general; and indeed if any

[1] A further, question arises whether we should not read, instead of *κατέσκηπτε γὰρ καὶ ἐς τὰ αἰδοῖα* (for it attacked the genitals also), *κατέσκηπτε γὰρ κακὸν ἐς τὰ αἰδοῖα* (for mischief, evil, attacked the genitals).

one suffered previously from any complaint, *all ended in this*, the plague." We have seen how Hippocrates observed the prevalence of ulcers of the genitals at the period of the special meteorological conditions he drew attention to, and without doubt in the same way such existed at Athens as well, and were subsequently dominated by the prevailing erysipelas-typhoïdal conditions. This was manifested in one of two ways; either the ulcers became gangrenous, or the patient was attacked by typhus, precisely as is noted to be the case at the present day [1]. But under either eventuality the existing contagion was annihilated, in the one case by the general feverish reaction of the organism [2]. But in those cases where neither fever nor mortification supervened, the contagion undoubtedly assumed a more strongly effective character, was more readily infectious, set up more deeply penetraiting ulcerations,

[1] *Joseph Franc*, Prax. med. univ. praecept. Pt. I. Vol. III. sect. 2., Typhus, ch. 2. § 4. Note 11. Observation 108., says: "Nothwithstanding the fact that in the General Hospital of Vienna Venereal patients were separated from others, yet it often happened at the time I was Physician in Chief there, that patients suffering from concealed Venereal disease or paying patients were admitted into the common Wards. Now if one or the other got typhus, or if such a patient was already lying there, or was brought there, *the Venereal cases without exception took the typhus*, and particularly so during the mercurial treatment."

[2] *Schönlein*, "Vorlesungen", (Prelections), Vol. II. p. 48., "The syphilitic exanthema either remains stationary when typhus arises, or disappears instantly and for ever — or the part affected with syphilis becomes gangrenous." "*Neumann*, "Specielle Pathologie und Therapie", (Special Pathology and Therapeutics), Vol. II. p. 107., "Violent, severe typhoïdal fevers cure syphilis completely; its symptoms disappear with the commencement of the illness and never return. —Again after Petechial fever I have in most cases observed that the syphilis troubles that disappeared at its commencement never came back again." *Historical* vouchers will be afforded in plenty by our later investigations.

and the tendency towards the skin being the predominating one, exanthematic eruptions with an inclination to ulcerative forms (ἐκθύματα μεγάλα, ἕρπητες πολλοῖσιν μεγάλοι,—great pustules, extensive creeping eruptions in many cases) were observed by Hippocrates to be set up in Summer, (loco citato p. 487.). All these are factors of the highest importance for the history of Venereal disease, as it is only by them that we shall be enabled to solve the great riddle of the origin of Venereal disease in the XVth. Century,—a riddle to which the answer would long ago have been found, if only enquirers had not been in the habit almost down to our own days of persistently looking upon Venereal disaese as an isolated phænomenon.

True it is impossible from the passage of Thucydides to decide with any certainty whether the extremities, hands, feet and genitals, fell off of their own accord or were removed by the knife; but our own opinion is that both was the case, for of course there were Physicians at Athens, and until they had learned their powerlessness against the prevailing sickness, they no doubt employed the remedial means at their disposal, and these consisted according to Hippocrates solelv and simply in the use of scalpel and cauterizing iron, all other measures having proved unavailing. That these were equally resorted to in ulcerations of the genitals we see from the passage of Galen quoted above, and the Poem of the Priapeia, p. 74, confirms the same in the most convincing way.

Enough has been alleged to prove how far the view expressed in many different forms, to the effect that, in the Athenian Plague as well as in the meteorological conditions and their results as laid down by Hippocrates, it is a question of Venereal disease, is justified by facts, and to show that even in Antiquity materials are to be found to demonstrate conclusively that the *genius epidemicus* exercised a not unimportant influence on the rise, form and course of the ulcerations of the genital organs. In what way this influence acted on the complaints consequent on paederastia and the vices of the *cunnilingue* and the *fellator* and affecting the posterior and mouth, we cannot at any rate at the moment demonstrate historically, but it seems only probable that previously existing ulcerations in the mouth and throat must under an erysipelas-typhoïdal general condition have proved themselves in the highest degree dangerous to the sufferers.

SECOND SECTION.

Influences which served to hinder to a greater or less degree the inception of Diseases consequent upon the Use or Misuse of the Genital Organs.

§ 34.

It has been fully proved in the course of our previous investigations that Asia and Egypt must be regarded as the two focus-points of exaggerated sensual licence, the conditions of climate being most favourable in those regions for the generation of affections consequent upon sexual excesses. So it may be fairly concluded without further proof that in the same parts of the world attention was early devoted to the problem how to render such influences,—no mere passing ones, be it observed, but continuously operative,—as little harmful as possible. Now in what way could this end be more adequately attained than by *cleanliness* carried out to the highest possible degree? As a matter of history, the merest superficial acquaintance with the customs and usages of Antiquity clearly shows that equally in Asia and in Egypt concern for bodily cleanliness had occupied the particular attention of both political and sacerdotal Legislators from the most remote period. More than this, it had come to be looked upon by the people as so entirely necessary, as to be all but inextricably blended with their very life and being. Any idea of vexatious compulsion entirely disappeared, and the laws and ordinances directed to this object are in force to this day as fully as they were thousands of years ago.

Inhabitants of the temperate zone who visited these lands were bound to think,—unless they gave more careful consideration to the subject than most were likely to do,—such almost universal and such scrupulous care for cleanliness exaggerated; and so we find, e.g. the Greek writers, who cite many of the usages of this description, invariably referring to them merely as a sort of curiosity. In later times, e.g. in *St. Athanasius*, [1] they are even condemned as being prompted by the Devil, in order to diminish the amount of time to be devoted to pious exercises. It may well be that in course of time a too scrupulously precise dependance on ancestral custom had brought many of these usages into ridicule, especially when they were practised in countries where in some cases the reasons for their observance altogether cease to be operative. Yet anyone who considers with due care the conditions under which they were originally introduced, will find himself constrained to admit that the Lawgiver was only obeying a behest of necessity.

If the different customs and usages of the Ancients in connection with their careful attention to cleanliness are examined more minutely, they are found to be divisible into two classes, according as (1.) their object was to prevent uncleanliness, or (2.) to banish it, when once admitted. All measures connected with sanitary police supervision, the enforcement of which in modern civilized States leads to such endless difficulties, were almost entirely in the hands of the Priests, to whom the People were accustomed to accord an unquestioning obedience. It was an easy matter therefore to prevent any

[1] Works, Vol. I. p. 765. Epistola ad Amunem, monachum. (Letter to Amunis, a monk).

injurious contamination from extending over a wide area; it sufficed simply to declare unclean whatever might prove injurious to health to eusure its being avoided in practice,—and in the majority of instances with the most scrupulous care. This is a factor in the problem that appears never to have been properly appreciated by our Historical Pathologists; otherwise they must long ago have abandoned many prejudices regarding the knowledge possessed by the Ancients as to contagious matter. For how *could* practical observations be collected on infection and the liability to infection, when every possible chance of infection was carefully and generally avoided? Most of the Peoples of Antiquity considered contact with a dead body a pollution, more than this, they thought even the neighbourhood of a corpse to have the same effect. They hung up notices to warn the passers-by, and placed vessels of water (**ἀδάνιον, ὄστρακον, γάστρα**—water-stoup, earthen vessel, water-pot) before the house where a dead man lay, that those who came in and out might be able to purify themselves again on the spot [1]. Of couse all did not go so far as the Persians, who declared every sick person unclean. Still it is a fact, and this most certainly not merely among the Jews, that all the various infectious skin-diseases that were massed together under the name of Leprosy [2], and

[1] *Euripides*, Alcestis 98.,

πυλῶν πάροιθεν δ' οὐχ ὁρῶ
πηγαῖον ὡς νομίζεται
χέρνιβ' ἐπὶ φθιτῶν πύλαις,
χαίτα τ' οὔτις ἐπὶ προθύροις
τομαῖος, ἃ δὴ νεκύων
πένθει πιτνεῖ.

(Before the doors I see no lustral water from the fountain, as is wont at the doors of the departed, and in the forecourt is no shorn hair, which is ever cut in mourning for the dead.) Comp. *Kirchmann*, De funeribus Rom. (On Roman Funerals) bk. I. last ch., bk. II, ch. 15. *Lomeier*, De veterum gentil. lustrationibus (On Public Purifications among the Ancients), ch. 16. *Casaubon*, On the "Characters" of Theophrastus, ch. 16.

[2] It may be mentioned by way of supplement thatLeprosy among the Ancients was pretty nearly universally regarded as a punishment from the gods.

also Gonorrhœa (Clap), made the sufferer, and also everything he touched, unclean, and caused them to be set apart where no one should come in contact with them; and this continued so long as the sickness lasted.

Now does it really need any further proof that these diseases developed a perfectly well-known form of contagious matter: or is an arbitary and imaginary theory to be adopted by preference, to the effect that injunctions of the sort owed their existence merely to the caprice of the Legislator, and were not based on any actual experience of real detriment resulting from their neglect in favour of others? At any rate it is certain that, where these laws were in force and where each individual followed them out exactly, a disease that is communicable only by close contact could not possibly be disseminated over any wide area. This could not take place under such circumstances, even though it had been engendered in its original form and continued prevalent for a long period of time.

However it was not only the sick that were avoided, but all possible causes as well that might lead to the disease. It was not only the effort required and the pain, but most likely the possibility also of injury resulting, that made the weakly Asiatic forgo the *Jus primae noctis* (Right of the first night), and declare unclean the supposed [1] injurious

Even the Greeks held this view, as comes out clearly from *Aeschylus*, Choeph. II. 2. This fact points to various conclusions as to liability to infection in Leprosy and the obscurity in which the causes of the disease are involved.

[1] In accordance with the explanations given on a previous page it might be thought quite conceivable that so long as the hymen was intact, a part of the mucous discharge of the vagina and of the menstrual blood was retained, and acquired a certain degree of malignity. This acting on points of the penis where the surface had been accidentally broken in the act of defloration, or even on the mucous membrane of the urethra, might exert an injurious influence.

effects of the vaginal blood that flowed on the rupture of the hymen, as well as the act of defloration itself. Pollution was guarded against in this case, as it was by the regulation banishing women during the time of menstruation from the neighbourhood of men, a regulation that had the binding force of law amongst almost all the Nations of Antiquity. The same held good for the time of purification of women who had been lying-in, [1] a condition which was supposed in some unexplained way to be able to exert a possibly injurious influence on the genital organs of the husband.

Depilation.

§ 35.

In spite of all this it might yet happen that contact with a sick person could not be avoided, and all possible causes of the diseases in question escaped. Attention therefore was naturally directed to the effort to make the admission of the contagion and of matters having deleterious effects as difficult as might be. There were two means for attaining this end held to be especially effective,—depilation and circumcision.

The hair as is well known is particularly apt to attract and retain all kinds of moisture; and it will of course do this in the case of the genital secretions, whether healthy or morbid, if they come in contact with it. These secretions will the more readily exert an injurious effect, as each hair is accompanied by at least two cutaneous glands, possessing an excretory duct or pore, and in those

[1] *Euripides*, Iphigeneia in Tauris 380. *Porphyrius*, bk. II. περὶ Ἀποχῆς (On Abstinence). *Dio Chrysostom*, Homily XIII, on Epist. to Ephesians.— *Theophrastus*, Charact. ch. 16.— *Th. Bartholinus*, Antiq. veteris puerperii synopsis (Synopsis of Antiquities of Childbirth in Old Times). Copenhagen 1646. 8vo.

parts of the body where a thicker and stronger growth of hair is found, develop a considerably increased degree of activity,—an increased activity which they exhibit in any case in hot countries. "Hence too the Priests in Egypt shave the body carefully; for there is something collects under the hair, that must be removed," *Philo* says in a passage cited above, and a fragment of *Theopompus* preserved by *Athenaeus* [1] also tells us, that

[1] Deipnosoph. bk. XII. p. 518., *Πάντες δὲ οἱ πρὸς ἑσπέραν οἰκοῦντες βάρβαροι πιττοῦνται καὶ ξυροῦνται τὰ σώματα· καὶ παρά γε τοῖς Τυῤῥηνοῖς ἐργαστήρια κατεσκεύασται πολλὰ, καὶ τεχνῖται τούτου τοῦ πράγματός εἰσιν, ὥσπερ παρ' ἡμῖν οἱ κουρεῖς· παρ' οὓς ὅταν εἰσέλθωσι, παρέχουσιν ἑαυτοὺς πάντα τρόπον, οὐδὲν αἰσχυνόμενοι τοὺς ὁρῶντας, οὐ δὲ τοὺς παριόντας· χρῶνται δὲ τούτῳ τῷ νόμῳ πολλοὶ καὶ τῶν Ἑλλήνων καὶ τῶν τὴν Ἰταλίαν οἰκούντων, μαθόντες παρὰ Σαμνιτῶν καὶ Μεσαπίων.* (Now all the Barbarians that dwell towards the West, use pitch as a depilatory, and shave their bodies. Indeed amongst the Tyrrhenians establishments are fitted up in numbers for this purpose, and there are artistes who practise this profession, like barbers among ourselves. And when men go into their shops, they expose themselves in every part, feeling no shame of spectators nor of passers-by. And this custom is followed also by many of the Greeks and of the inhabitants of Italy, who have learned it from Samnites and Messapians). The depilation of men and boys was attended to by women (*Martial*, XI. 79.) at the period of the highest degree of dissoluteness; in fact there was a special guild of snch women, known as *ustriculae*. *Tertullian*, De pallio ch. 4. In the same way men performed this service for women, as e.g. *Domitian*, according to *Suetonius*, ch. 22., Erat fama, quasi concubinas ipse develleret (Rumour went, to the effect that the Emperor used to "pluck" his mistresses with his own hand,) — and *Heliogabalus* according to *Lampridius*, ch. 31., In balneis semper cum mulieribus fuit, ita ut eas ipse psilothro curaret, ipse quoque barbam psilothro accurans, quodque pudendum dictu est, eodem quo mulieres accurabantur, et eadem hora. Rasit et virilia subactoribus suis ad novaculam manu sua, qua postea barbam fecit. (At the baths he was always with the women, going so far as to apply the "psilothrum"

this habit existed also among the Greeks, as well as among different peoples of Italy.

In later times however the habit gradually disappeared in these countries; and is only found again at the period of greatest luxury, when the Pathics endeavoured by the removal of hair from all parts of the body, except the head, to assimilate their outward appearance to the feminine type [1]. Especially were they bound to rid the posteriors [2] of hair, as one penetrating into the anus during unnatural connexion might easily cause small cuts at the orifice, and produce chafings of the penis. For the same reason paederasts, as indeed was the case with all amateurs of Love, invariably took care to remove all hair from the genitals [3], to avoid endangering

(a depilatory) in their treatment himself, finishing off his own beard also with "psilothrum", and using, disgusting to relate, the same as the women were being treated with, and at one and the same time. Moreover he shaved his debauchees' (pathics) privates to the navel with his own hand, and then shaved his own beard).

[1] They used to remove the hair on the *face* (*Martial*, III. 74.), from the *nose* (Ovid, Art. Amand. I. 520.) on the arches of the *eyebrows* (Cicero, Orat. pro Roscio), from the armpits (*Juvenal*, XIV. 194., *Seneca*, Epist. 115.), on the *arms* (*Martial*, III. 63.), the *hands* (*Martial*, V. 41.), on the *legs* (*Juvenal*, IX. 12.) As to the beard, that has already been spoken of.

[2] *Martial*, II. 62., Cui praestas culum, quem, Labiene, pilas. (To whom you give your fundament, Labienus, that you strip of hair).

[3] *Martial*, II. 62.,

Quod pectus, quod crura tibi, quod brachia vellis,
Quod cincta est brevibus mentula tonsa pilis,
Haec praestas, Labiene, tuae, quis nescit? amicae.

(You pluck your chest, your legs, your arms, your *shaven member* is surrounded by short hair,—all these pains you offer, everyone knows it, to your mistress.) Bk. IX. 28.,

Cum depilatos, Chreste coleos portes,
Et vulturino mentulam parem collo,
Et prostitutis laevius caput culis,
Nec vivat ullus in tuo pilus crure
Purgentque crebrae cana labra volsellae etc.

(For you have *your testicles freed from hair*, Chrestus, and *your member like a*

the posterior and the private parts of their mistresses. Even more than men, did *women* seek to remove the hair from their private parts, as they do to this day in the East. This appears never to have been the case among the Jews; but in Asia and in Egypt the custom was observed by all classes of the people, and probably from those lands first spread into Greece and Italy. It seems to have been adopted very generally by Greek women;[1] but it was *especially* hetaerae and "filles de joie"[2] who practised local as well as general depilation. A similar state

vulture's neck, and your head smoother than those posteriors that you prostitute. Not a hair lives on your leg, and frequent application of the tweezers keeps clean your shaven lips, etc.) Comp. Bk. IX. 48. 58. *Suetonius*, Otho 12. *Persius*, IV. 37. *Ausonius*, 131.

[1] *Aristophanes*, Lysistrat. 151.,

Εἰ γὰρ καθήμεθ' ἔνδον ἐντετριμμέναι
κἂν τοῖς χιτωνίοισι τοῖς ἀμοργίνοις
γυμναὶ παρίοιμεν, δέλτα παρατετιλμέναι,
στύοιντ' ἂν ἄνδρες κἀπιθυμοῖεν πλεκοῦν.

(For if we sat withindoors anointed with unguents, and if we appeared lightly, clad in robes of Amorgian flax, *our bellies plucked clear of hair*, the men would all have erections, and would be fain to lie with us.) For the same reason Mnesilochus was freed of hair on the genitals and in all other parts of the body, so as not to be recognised in the assemblage of women.

[2] Aristophanes, Eccl. 718., says of prostitutes:

καὶ τάς γε δούλας οὐχὶ δεῖ κοσμουμένας
τὴν τῶν ἐλευθέρων ὑφαρπάζειν Κύπριν,
ἀλλὰ παρὰ τοῖς δούλοισι κοιμᾶσθαι μόνον
κατωνάκῃ τὸν χοῖρον ἀποτετιλμένας.

(And the slave-women ought not to bedizen themselves and snatch away the love that is free-women's by rights; but should lie with slaves only, their pudenda plucked clean to please the wearer of the smock.) Frogs 515., *Ξ. πῶς λέγεις; ὀρχηστρίδες; Θ. ἡβυλλιῶσαι κἄρτι παρατετιλμέναι* (Xanthius. What say you? dancing-girls? Therap. Yes! young wenches, just *plucked clean*). Comp. Lysistrat. 88.

of things must have existed at Rome [1], where older women resorted to the removal of hair from the genitals as a means of concealing their age [2]. In

[1] *Martial*, bk. XII. Epigr. 32.,

Nec plena turpi matris olla resina
Summoenianae qua pilantur uxores.

(Nor yet your mother's jars full of foul resin, wherewith the suburban dames free themselves of hair.)

[2] Martial, bk. X. Epigr. 90.,

Quid vellis vetulum, Ligella, cunnum?
Quid busti cineres tui lacessis?
Tales munditiae decent puellas.
Erras, si tibi cunnus hic videtur,
Ad quem mentula pertinere desit.

(Why pluck you bare, Ligella, *your old organ?* why vex you the ashes of your tomb? Such *nice allurements* are for girls. You are mistaken if you think yours is of a sort that a man's member should be fain to belong to it.) This passage, together with those quoted a little above from Aristophanes and Theopompus, will explain sufficiently what *Horace* (Sat. I. 2. v. 36.) meant by his "mirator *cunni* Cupiennius *albi*," (Cupiennius admirer of a *white organ*), for the *albus* (white) here evidently stands for *rasus*, *depilatus*, *nudus*, (shaven, freed from hair, bare); as in *Juvenal*, Sat. I. 111., Nuper in hanc urbem *pedibus* qui venerat *albis*, (Who but now had arrived in this city with white, i. e. bare, feet.) The commentators have hitherto always explained it by *matrona stola alba*, seu *candida*, *vestita*, (a matron clad in a white, or glistening-white, robe), because, as *Heindorf* puts it, no other interpretation is to hand. But really there are several possible explanations on similar lines. It might be for "*canus* cunnus", (hoary, aged; organ) (*Martial*, bk. XI. 38., bk. II. 34.), though again the meaning of *depilatus* (free of hair), in another sense, might equally well be at the bottom of this, as is the case with *cana labra* (hoary, white, lips)—IX. 28. Or *albus* (white) may be taken as synonymous with *increta*, *cerussata* (whitened with chalk, painted with ceruse), to which *Martial* supplies the explanation, when he says (III. 42.),

Lomento rugas uteri quod condere tentas,
Polla, tibi ventrem, non mihi labra linis;

(When you endeavour to hide the wrinkles on your stomach with powder, 'tis your own belly, Polla, not my lips, you smear with the stuff), — as also bk. IX. 3., Illa *siligineis* pinguescit adultera *cunnis*, (It —i. e. your penis—in adulterous loves, grows fat on women's

any case whether in Greece or in Italy the purpose and special object of depilation seems to have been soon lost sight of, and the practice to have been still to some extent kept up merely as a matter of fashion. Nevertheless it is a fact that the habit has continued even down to modern times in these

organs powdered with fine wheaten flour); [but another way of taking the line is: She, i. e. your mistress,—adulterous dame, grows fat on wheaten cakes—cakes baked in the shape of *cunni.*] The *Lomentum*, which is not derived from *lavimentum* or *lavamentum* (something to wash with), as Scheller, following Voss, makes it to be, but from the Greek λείωμα faba communita (*ground* beans), was bean-meal (*Vegetius*, De re veterin. V. 62., says: in subtilissimo lomento, hoc est farina fabacea, (in the finest *lomentum*, that is bean-flour.); and at the present day the Japanese, it seems, according to *Thunberg*, use a kind of bean-meal instead of soap. Roman ladies were most careful to maintain the *aequor ventris* (smoothness of the belly)—*Aulus Gellius*, Noctes Att. I. 2.); whence *Martial*, (III. 72.) says, addressing Laufella, who refuses to bathe with him:

Aut tibi pannosae pendent a pectore mammae
Aut sulcos uteri prodere nuda times.

(Either your breasts hang flabby from your bosom, or you fear, if you strip, to betray the furrows on your belly.) To obviate wrinkles on the face, they sprinkled their faces with chalk; and so *Petronius*, (Satyr. ch. 23.) says: et inter rugas malarum tantum erat cretae, ut putares detectum parietem nimbo laborare, (and amidst the wrinkles of the cheeks was so much chalk, that you would think a partition-wall had been stripped and was wrapped in a cloud of dust); and we read in *Lucian's* poem (Greek Anthology, Bk. II. tit: 9.) μὴ τοίνυν τὸ πρόσωπον ἅπαν ψιμύθῳ κατάπλαττε. (Now don't besmear all your face with ceruse). However if *cunnus must* be taken as equivalent to *femina* (a woman), it would be on all fours with *albus amicus* (white, white-faced, friend) in *Martial* (bk. X. 12.), which *Farnabius* explains by σκιατρόφος (reared in the shade, delicate), answering more or less to our "*Wheyface*". As any rate *any* of these interpretations are for certain nearer the truth than the *stola alba* (clad in *a white robe*) one.

countries, and is actually followed there to some extent on the ground of cleanliness [1].

Depilation is completed by the *polishing* of the skin with punice, etc., a treatment that made it very much less liable to take up dirt of all kinds. This and the *anointing* of the body, that commonly followed it, as it did the bath (see later), guarded against the introduction of foreign matter into the tissues to an important extent, yet without interfering with transpiration, which in southern countries takes place more by the cutaneous glands than by the sweat-pores. This fact goes some way to explain how it was that the contagious plagues of Antiquity, generally of a transient character, never properly speaking acquired any wide extension, unless they were carried along with the *Genius epidemicus* at the same time; and that even the latter, as is the case at the present day, could seldom master and reverse

[1] Italae nonnullae se depiles tangere amant circa partes hymenaeo sacras, *veritae foetationem morpionum* (Some Italian women like to feel the skin bare of hair round those parts that are sacred to marriage, *fearing the foul breeding of lice*), writes *Rolfink*, "Ordo et methodus generationi dicat. partium cognoscendi fabricam, (Orderly and Systematic Knowledge of the Structure of the Parts devoted to Procreation). Jena 1664. 4to., p. 185. This may have been one motive among the Ancients also for the removal of the hair, for Aristotle in his time (Hist. Anim. bk. V. ch. 25.) is acquainted with felt-lice (crabs), and calls them *φθεῖρες ἄγριοι* (wild lice), without however mentioning what part of the person they infest. His words are: *ἔστι δὲ γένος φθειρῶν, οἳ καλοῦνται ἄγριοι, καὶ σκληρότεροι τῶν ἐν τοῖς πολλοῖς γιγνομένων· εἰσὶ δὲ οὗτοι καὶ δυσαφαίρετοι ἀπὸ τοῦ σώματος.* (There is another kind of lice, *called wild lice*, and more troublesome than the common sort. It is most difficult to rid the body of these). *Celsus*, De re medica bk. VI. chs. 6. and 15., mentions them as occurring in the eye-lashes: Genus quoque vitii est, qui inter pilos palpebrarum pediculi nascuntur. *φθειρίασιν* Graeci nominant. (There is another kind of taint, lice that breed among the hair of the eyelids; it is called in Greek *φθειρίασις*—lousiness.)

endemic predispositions. This last consideration merits the particular attention of the Historical Pathologist, as giving him a partial indication why Antiquity comes so far behind later times in regard to startling epidemics, at the same time teaching him to regard Asia as the home of Endemic, Europe of Epidemic Diseases. This ought to safeguard him against many over-hasty conclusions in his views of the progressive developement and evolution of disease in general. At the same time it will undoubtedly destroy not a few agreeable dreams, where he has allowed imagination to outrun reality.

Circumcision [1].

§ 36.

Herodotus himself represents circumcision as a very ancient usage even in his time, as to which it is a moot point whether the Egyptians or Ethiopians first

[1] *Lockervitzens, Christ.* Disp. II on Circumcision, Witepsk 1679. 4to.--*Antonius*, Dissertation on the Circumcision of the Gentiles, Leipzig 1682. 4to. — *Grapius*, Did Abraham borrow Circumcision from the Egyptians? Rostock 1699. 4to. Jena 1722. 4to.—*Vogel*, Graduation Exercise on Questions as to the Advantages of the Medical Employment of Circumcision, Göttingen 1763. 4to.—*Hofmann*, On Circumcision as deserving of the name of an Old Testament Sacrament. Altorf 1770. 4to.—*Ackermann, J. Ch. G.*, "Aufsätze über die Beschneidung" (Essays on Circumcision) in *Weise's* "Materialien fur Gottesgelahrtheit und Religion," (Materials for Theological and Religious Study), 1 vol. Gera 1784. 8vo., pp. 50 sqq. comp. *Blumenbach's* Med. Biblioth. Vol. I. p. 482. —*Meiners*, Christ., De circumcisionis origine et causis, (On the Origin and Reasons of Corcumcision), in Commentat. Societ. Göttingen Vol. XIV. pp. 207 sqq.—*Borhek*, "Is Circumcision Hebraic by First Origin? and What prompted Abraham to its Introduction? A Historico-exegetical Enquiry," Duisburg and Lemgo 1793. 8vo.—*Bauer, F. W.* "Description of the Religious Constitution of the Ancient Jews. Leipzig 1805. large 8vo. Vol. I. pp. 76 sqq. —*Cohen, Moses*, Dissertation

practised it. From the Egyptians it would seem to have passed on to the Phoenicians and Syrians in Palestine, from the Colchians to the Syrians living on the banks of the river Thermodon and Parthenius and to the Macronians [1]. To the present day we find Circumcision practised, as all the world knows, among the Mohammedans, Persians and Jews, among the Kaffirs on the South-East Coast of Africa, the Abyssinian Christians [2], the inhabitants of the Pacific Islands [3], as well on the mainland of America,—and this not merely among the coast dwellers, but also in several inland district of South America [4].

on Circumcision, regarded under its Religious, Hygienic and Pathological Aspects". Paris 1816. 4to.—*Brück, A. Th.* "A Word on the Advantages of Circumcision," in Rust's Magaz. Vol. VII. 1820. pp. 222—28.—*Hofmann, A. G.* in Ersch and Gruber's "Encyclopaedie", *Circumcision*, Vol. IX, (1822) pp. 265—70. —*Autenrieth, J. H.*, "Treatise on the Origen of Circumcision among savage and semi-savage Peoples, with reference to the Circumcision of the Israelites; together with a Critique by C. Chr. von Flatt." Tübingen 1829, large 8vo.

[1] *Herodotus*, Hist. Bk. II. ch. 104. *Origen*, Bk. V. ch. 41. Works edit. De la Rue, Vol. I. p. 609 D. — *Cyril*, Contra Julian. Bk. X. edit. Spanhem. p. 354. B.—*Diodorus Siculus*, Bk. I. ch. 28. *Strabo*, Geograph. Bk, XVII. ch. 2. 5. edit. Siebenkess. In *Sanchuniathon* (Fragments edit. Orelli, p. 36.) Circumcision is actually referred back to Cronos.

[2] *Ludolf*, Histor. Aethiop. Bk. III. ch. 1. pp. 30 sqq. *Paulus*, "Sammlg. morgenländischer Reisebechreibg." (Collection of Descriptions of Eastern Travel), Pt. III. p. 83.

[3] Forster's "Beobachtungen," (Observations), p. 842.—Cook's Last Voyage, Vol. I. p. 387., Vol. II. pp. 161, 233.

[4] *J. Gumilla*, "Histoire de l'Oronoque," (Hist. of Oronoko), Avignon 1708. Vol. I. p. 183. *Veigl* in *Murr's* "Sammlung der Reisen einiger Missionare," (Collection of Travels of Various Missionaries), p. 67. — *de Pauw*, "Reflections sur les Américains," (Reflections on the Natives of America), Vol. II. p. 148. *Spizelius, Theoph.*, Elevatio revelationis Montezinianae de repertis in America tribubus Israeliticis, (Confutation of the Montezinian revelation as to the Finding of the lost Tribes of Israel in America. Bâle 1661. 8vo. *Burdach*, Physiology. Vol. III. p. 386.

Without in this place going into the different reasons that have been alleged to account for the original introduction of Circumcision, especially among the Jews, we may yet say, looking back to our previous exposition in § 29., that we hold ourselves bound to see in Circumcision originally a religious-hygienic measure, intended to guard a part of the body already in the earliest times held in such high honour among the Egyptians, Indians etc. as was the penis, against any probable chance of defilement by uncleanliness (sebaceous smegma on the *glans penis*); for it was found that the uncurtailed prepuce made the maintenance of a clean *glans penis* much more difficult, favouring as it did the collection of the smegma resulting from the sebaceous secretions, and thus gave occasion for the formation of pustules and ulcers and the like inconveniences. These were referred not to the natural cause, but rather looked upon as a deserved punishment due to the anger of the offended deity to whom the penis was sacred, the deity being himself defiled and made unclean by the uncleanliness of the organ. To escape such anger men were ready enough to remove a part, the direct utility of which was as little obvious at the first glance as that of the hair that grew in its neighbourhood,—a proceeding they were the more willing to agree to, as the mischief the uncurtailed prepuce occasioned was often enough manifested.

At first only the Priests, who of course were at the same time the Physicians of primitive Peoples, were allowed to undertake the performance of this operation; subsequently it devolved upon the people generally as well, either by direct command or because they were now convinced of the utility of circumcision. This utility however must have grown less and less frequently visible in proportion as fewer uncircumcised individuals were left in evidence; and so in the same degree the hygienic motive fell more and more into the background. Thus only the religious was left, and this was now taken as the sole reason and sufficient explanation of the universal custom. Circumcision accordingly came to be a symbol signifying adoption among such as were initiated into the Egyptian Mysteries, and similarly adoption among the initiated of the Lord, adoption into the peculiar People of God. It is in this fashion the various discordant views as to the origin of circumcision, all of which proceeded in the first instance from a more or less one-sided point of view, may most satisfactorily be brought into agreement. True the motive for the operation was supplied by a pathological factor, but one which owed its force to a religious idea, and thus at first the knife was regarded not so much from the *physician's* point of view as from the *religious* side.

But again later, when religious ideas of the sort were more and more disappearing before a cool examination of actual nature, when the tale of diseases originating in the anger of a deity was growing every day fewer, belief became impossible in the religious meaning of circumcision, or indeed such belief was deliberately rejected, now that a clear and natural explanation of the rite was to be found. The religious motive in turn made way for the medical-hygienic, as in *Philo* in the passage quoted above, and even Our Lord seems to have held no other view of the rite, when he says [1]: "If a man received circumcision on the sabbath, that the law of Moses may not be broken; are ye wroth with me, because I *made a man every whit whole* on the sabbath?" *De Wette* in his Translation adds: "that is to say, not simply, as in circumcision, in one member, but in the whole body." In fact the question is here of the healing of the man "which had been thirty and eight years in his infirmity" (Ch. V.), whom Christ had made whole at the Pool

[1] Gospel of St. John, Ch. VII. v. 23., *Εἰ περιτομὴν λαμβάνει ἄνθρωπος ἐν σαββάτῳ, ἵνα μὴ λυθῇ ὁ νόμος Μωσέως, ἐμοὶ χολᾶτε ὅτι ὅλον ἄνθρωπον ὑγιῆ ἐποίησα ἐν σαββάτω.* (for translation see text above).

of Bethesda on the Sabbath, for which reason the Jews wished to put him to death. The sick man was afflicted in his whole body, i. e. in every limb, for without help he could not leave his bed and go down into the Pool. Thus Christ we see contrasts the healing of all the members with circumcision, making it plain that in his view the latter makes whole morely a single member, the penis, or at least puts it in such a condition that it cannot become sick ὑγιῆ ἐποίησα,—I made whole); accordingly the rite possessed for him only a purely medico-hygienic aim.

As to the introduction of Circumcision among the Jews, this may very likely, as we have already pointed, have taken place in the following mode: Evidently the Jews when in Egypt were not yet circumcised, as the speech of the lord Joshua clearly implies, "This day have I taken the reproach of Egypt from off you;" for in the eyes of the Egyptians the uncircumcised condition of the Jews was a reproach, just as in later times "Uncircumcised" was the strongest word of abuse with the Jews themselves. [1] Moses brought up by the Egyptian Priests, initiated into their secret wisdom, must necessarily have been circumcised, and so have known the hygienic as well as religious point of view. Convinced of its expediency, he determined to introduce it among the Jews, in order to make

[1] I Samuel, Ch. XVII. v. 14. It is true we find even in Genesis the covenant with Jehovah celebrated by Abraham by means of circumcision; but it was in later times only in each case that this custom was referred back to him as being racial father of the Nation. For the same reason in the case of Joshua the matter is so represented as if the Jews had been already circumcised at their expulsion from Egypt. If this had really and truly been the case, it is impossible to see why circumcision was not carried out on those born on the march to Canaan. They were perfectly able to keep other laws, and they could have observed this too, if it had been given them at the time!

them by outward sign in some sort a holy and pure priestly Nation.[1] For this reason we find the command to circumcise on the eighth day after birth specified among the *Laws of Purification*,[2] yet without any further supplemental addition,—which would certainly not have been omitted, if it had at that time been regarded as a symbolic sign of covenant. Circumcision did not yet possess its purely symbolic meaning; and so it is not yet included among the laws given at Sinai, where the blood of the Burnt Offerings seals the covenant with God.

But subsequently when the Jews at Shittim gave themselves to the licentious worship of Baal Peor, not merely the expediency stood out in glaring conspicuousness, but the positive necessity of observing the laws of purity in general, including that of circumcision in particular. Thus the long conceived idea of Moses came to maturity, to enjoin upon the People the rite of circumcision as special symbol of unity with Jehovah; though he could not hope to bring about its universal adoption by adults, until these were on the point of actually setting foot on the Promised Land. This could only be after the death of Moses; consequently it was Joshua at Arolath who first circumcised all those who had been born in the Wilderness. Now all the sufferings of the march were forgotten, the land flowing with milk and honey, that was to content all their highest wishes, lay before their eyes, and so they were willing enough to consent to purchase its everlasting possession at the cost of what is certainly a painful, but at the same time on the whole only a trifling, operation. But then when every male was circumcised, there was no longer any evidence, as explained above, to convince people of the necessity of the observance, and thus for the future Circumcision appeared in the guise of a *purely* religious

[1] Leviticus, Ch. XIX. v. 6.
[2] Leviticus, Ch. XII. v. 3.

symbol, as the sacramental outward and visible sign of adoption into sonship with Jehovah,—a point of view subsequently consistently kept to throughout the Old Testament.

Finally with regard to the notion, expressed in many different forms, that Circumcision was originally introduced on behalf of increased fruitfulness on the part of the Sons of Abraham, [1]—an idea found as early an in the pages of *Philo Judaeus*, it would appear not to be so much the greater length of the foreskin that came into question, but rather the same general reasons that ensured a condition of cleanliness in the procreative organs; for the alleged interruption of the ejaculation of the semen owing to the excessive length of the foreskin can after all only occur, if the latter is at the same time unduly contracted at its orifice in such a way that during the act of coition it cannot be drawn back over the *glans*. Supposing, as we have seen to be the case, complaints affecting the *glans penis* when covered with the normal prepuce to be readily set up through climatic influences, the free use of the organ of procreation must of course in this way have been interfered with, or even in extreme cases, completely prevented. But inasmuch as the Jew, in this resembling most of the Nations of Antiquity, made a numerous posterity his highest glory, [2] and as this could only be obtained on the condition of

[1] *J. G. Hofmann*, De causa foecunditatis gentis circumcisae in circumcisione quaerenda, (On the Reason for the Fertility of the Circumcised Race to be sought in the fact of their Circumcision), Leipzig 1739. 4to.—*S. B. Wolfsheimer*, De causis fecunditatis Hebraeorum nonnullis sacr. cod. praeceptibus nitentibus, (On the Causes of the Fertility of the Jews as dependent upon certain Precepts of the Sacred Volumes), Halle 1742. — *Bauer*, loco citato Vol. I. p. 63.

[2] The Talmud says: Quicunque Israelita liberis operam non dat, est velut *homicida*. (An Israelite, whoever he be, that fails to give heed to the procreation of children, is a kind of *murderer*). *Selden*, Uxor. Hebraic. Bk. I. ch. 9.

a healthy procreative member, every endeavour must obviously have been made to remove anything likely to be prejudicial to the part so profoundly reverenced, anything capable of disturbing, or even altogether frustraning, the due performance of its functions.

But just as this removal of a part of the prepuce, and the consequent increased possibilities of cleanliness of the *glans*, more or less counteracted the injurious effects of Climate tending to set up diseases of the *glans penis* in general, it must have equally exercised as against possible affections of this part resulting from coition a certain prophylactic influence,—though undoubtedly this was not *so* great as it has been in some quarters represented to be, as we intend to explain more fully elsewhere. Hence to some extent, but only to a limited extent, can the practice of circumcision be regarded as a proof of the existence of Venereal disease in Antiquity; but at the same time to refer it to this as *sole* motive, as *Stoll* [1] does, in quite inadmissible.

[1] *Stoll*, Praelectiones in diversos morbos chronicos, (Lectures on certain Chronic Diseases), Vol. I. p. 96, writes as follows: Antiquissimum cum Henslero pronuntiavi, atque inter Aegyptios, Judaeos, Graecos dein et Romanos perfrequentem ut quasdam harum gentium consuetudines, mores, leges ac statuta forte inde possis repertere.... Sic praeceptum circumcisionis, antiquissima plane consuetudo, idcirco fortassis instituta fuerat, atque tanquam ritus sacer, tanquam praeceptum quoddam, de quo dispensari nemo queat, introducebatur, quod circumcisus videatur difficilius morbum urethrae contrahere, rariusque ablato scilicet praeputio, intra quod virus haeret, rodit, cancros facit, quod et ipsum efficitur pessime in phymosi, paraphymosi. Glans ipsa in homine minus facile virus resorbere videtur, occallescens nempe... Nota viriginitatis sedulo examinata est in neonuptis puellis; custodia foeminarum per totum orientem; adulterii crimen, maxime foeminarum, morte expiatum videntur docere, scivisse antiquitatem remotissimam, morbum quendam gravem, immundum volgi-

What has here been said of *the Circumcision of men*, holds good also in the main of *that of maids and women.* This consists in the removal of the *praeputium clitoridis;* but neither the amputation of the Clitoris itself in so-called *Tribads* must be confounded with it, nor yet the operation on the exaggerated nymphae or inner *labia*, of women. The Arabs, among whom this practice,—female circumcision,—is especially rife at the present day as it was of old, [1] call the part that is subjected to circumcision نوى (*nava*), the circumcision itself بظر (*baltar*) or خفض (*chaphad*), and what is cut away in circumcision بظر (*bätr*). Usually the circumcision of maids

vaga Venere dari et communicari. (With *Hensler* I pronounce it—Venereal disease—to be of most ancient origin, and to have been of such frequency among the Egyptians, Jews, as well as the Greeks and Romans, that it may well *be possible to discover in it the cause of sundry habits, customs, laws and enactments of these Peoples* . . . For instance the precept of circumcision, evidently an extremely ancient custom, was very possibly first instituted for this reason, and was introduced in the guise of a sacred rite, a ceremonial precept from which there can be no dispensation, because the circumcised man would seem less readily to contract disease of the urethra, and in cases where the prepuce has been removed, inside which the poison remains adherent and corrodes, less frequently suffers from chancres, an effect that follows in its worst form in phymosis and paraphymosis. The *glans penis* itself in a man thus treated seems to absorb the poison less easily, being in fact grown partially callous . . . The fact that the sign of virginity was scrupously examined in newly married virgins, the careful guard kept over women throughout the East, the penalty of death attached to the crime of adultery, especially in women, *all seem to show that the remotest Antiquity was aware of some serious, foul disease being given and communicated by indiscriminate Love.*

[1] *Strabo*, Geograph. Bk. XVII. ch. 11. § 5.—*Reland*, De religione Muhamedan., (On the Mohammedan Religion), p. 75. *Niebuhr*, Description of Arabia, p. 70.

is first performed on the completion of the tenth year by women who make it their special business and who are known as مبقّرة (*mobatterat*). These women perambulate the streets and openly call out, "Any maids to circumcise?"[1] Besides the Arabs, Circumcision of maids is to be found among the Copts or modern Egyptians,[2] the Ethiopians,[3] in some districts of Persia,[4] among the Negroes in Bambuk[5] and the Panos in the province of Maynas in South America, the latter actually restricting the practice to the women.[6]

Baths and Bathing.

§ 37.

In spite of all precautions adopted it was impossible to keep away everything unclean from the body, while this latter by its own excrements was con-

[1] *Seezen*, in a letter to von Hammer on the Mines of the East. Vol. I. p. 65.

[2] *Paulus*, "Sammlung morgenländ. Reisebeschreibg.," (Collection of Descriptions of Eastern Travel), Vol. III. p. 83. — *Olivier's* "Reise in Aegypten, Syrien, etc.," (Travels in Egypt, Syria, etc.), p. 413. — *Seezen*, loco citato p. 65. Perhaps even the ancient Egyptians circumcised maids in their time. *Ambrosius*, Abraham Bk. II. ch. 11., in Works Vol. I. p. 347., Paris edition of 1686. *Galen*, De usu partium Bk. XV.

[3] *Ludolf*, History of the Ethiopians Bk. III. ch. 1.

[4] *Chardin*, Voyages en Perse, (Travels in Persia), Vol. X. p. 76., Amsterdam edition.

[5] *Mungo Park*, Travels p. 180.—Voyage au pays de Bambouc, (Journey to the Land of Bambuk), p. 48.

[6] *Veigl's* "Gründliche Nachrichten von der Landschaft Maynas in Südamerika,"(Trustworthy Account of the Province of Maynas in South America), in *Murr's* "Sammlung der Reisen einiger Missionarien von der Gesellschaft Jesu," (Collection of the Travels of various Missionaries of the Society of Jesus), Nüremberg 1785., p. 67.

stantly making itself more or less unclean; [1] hence

[1] *Plutarch*, On Isis and Osiris ch. 94. Hence we commonly find among the Ancients the custom, merely after the evacuation of urine and fæces, of cleansing the parts concerned. Accordingly *Josephus*, De Bello Judaic. Bk. II. ch. 8., says: *καίπερ δὲ φυσικῆς οὔσης τῆς τῶν σωματικῶν λυμάτων ἐκκρίσεως ἀπολούεσθαι μετ᾽ αὐτὴν, καθάπερ μεμιασμένοις, ἔθιζον.* (And even though the evacuation of the bodily defilements was in the course of nature, they were accustomed to wash themselves after it, as in the case of men polluted). The Romans used for the purpose a sponge fastened to the end of a stick, as we see from *Seneca*, Letter 70, where he says: Lignum, quod ad emendanda obscoena adhaerente spongia positum est, totum in gulam sparsit, (The stick that is placed with a sponge fixed to it for cleansing filth, this he shook right in his mouth). Slaves took stones, bulbs, etc. for the purpose. *Aristophanes*, Plut. IV. 1. After making water it was usual to wash the hands. *Petronius*, Satyr. 27. Exonerata ille vesica, aquam poposcit ad manus. (After relieving his bladder, he asked for water for his hands). This care for cleanliness roused, as mentioned before, the utmost anger on the part of Saint Athanasius; but it is to this day the custom among the Turks, for it is enjoined by the Koran (Sure IV. 42.), even adding that only one hand ought to be used (*Niebuhr*, Description of Arabia, p. 78.), namely the *left*. The same hand was used also by the Romans, as well as perhaps by all ancient Peoples. Hence *Martial* says, bk. XI. 59., sed lota mentula laeva .... (but my member, when my left hand has been washed ....). With the left hand, amica manus (the *mistress* hand), masturbation was performed, *Martial*, IX. 42. XI. 74.; it served to cover the genitals, *Lucian*, Amor. 13., hence according to *Ovid*, Ars amandi, Bk. II. 613.

Ipsa Venus pubem quoties velamina ponit,
Protegitur laeva semireducta manu

(Venus herself, as oft as she lays aside her garments, half withdrawn covers herself with her left hand), and Priapus is represented in Art holding the penis with the left hand, Priapeia 24. 34. If we are not mistaken, this was also the case with Horus among the Egyptians. What has just been said explains at the same time the reason why the left hand has from of old been held in disrepute, an idea still preserved in the expression, to marry, to be married, *with the left hand.*

it was only natural that from the most primitive times men's attention was directed towards means of removing the uncleanliness so contracted. But the defilement was never more than an external one; it concerned merely the skin and the orifices of the mucous membrane, while the matter requiring removal was of a sort soluble in water, and thus water was always the chief and foremost means employed to secure cleanliness. Doctrines of Cosmogony further confirmed the practice; these made water the origin of all things, a direct effluence of the deity and therefore itself divine,—a means not only of purification, but of sanctification as well.

Θάλασσα κλύζει πάντα τἀνθρώπων κακά,

(The sea washes away all evils of mankind) was the refrain, one that resounts to this day in our ears from the East; so that we cannot wonder that baths and bathing formed a capital factor both in the public and private life of the Ancients. Whatever view might be taken of sexual intercourse, all agreed in this, that a certain defilement was connected with it, which (as follows indeed from our exposition on earlier pages) might easily become injurious to the organs brought into activity, and could only be obviated by dint of *baths* and a system of *bathing*.[1]

[1] *Friedr. Hoffmann*, Diss. med. 3., asserit luem Veneream Constantinopolidos non grassari, quod feminae munditiei apprime studiosae post opus aquam sumant et locos diligenter colluant (asserts that Venereal disease is not prevalent at Constantinople, because the women being extremely careful of cleanliness take water after their work and scrupulously wash the parts), says *Astruc*, I. p. 108. This is further confirmed by *Oppenheim*, "Ueber den Zustand der Heilkunde etc. in der Türkei, (On the Condition of Medical Science etc. in Turkey), Hamburg 1838., p. 81., who writes: "Without the great cleanliness of the Turks, who after any single occasion of coition not only practise washing, but wherever at all possible, go to the bath as well, the disease (Venereal) would undoubtedly be still more widely spread."

Thus we read in *Herodotus*:[1] "But as often as a *Babylonian* has had intercourse with his wife, he sits down beside a lighted censer, and his wife does the same on the opposite side; then when morning has come, both *bathe* themselves, for they will touch no vessel until they have washed. The same practice is followed by the *Arabians* too." Whether bathing after *each* act of coition was a national custom of the *Egyptians*, we have been unable to discover, but *Clement of Alexandria*[2] states that they were forbidden, as was almost everywhere the case in Antiquity, to enter the temple without having washed or bathed themselves after sexual intercourse; while the Priests were bound to bathe after every nocturnal pollution.[3] This was equally an ordinance of the *Jews*, who at the same time were rendered by such pollutiou unclean till the evening. The last named People were also obliged to wash after every act of coition; at any rate *Josephus*[4] and *Philo*[5]

[1] Herodotus, Histor. Bk. I. ch. 198., *Ὀσάκις δ᾽ ἂν μιχθῇ γυναικὶ τῇ ἑωυτοῦ ἀνὴρ Βαβυλώνιος περὶ θυμίημα καταγιζόμενον ἵζει· ἑτέρωθι δὲ ἡ γυνὴ τὠυτὸ τοῦτο ποιέει· ὄρθρου δὲ γενομένου λοῦνται καὶ ἀμφότεροι· ἄγγεος γὰρ οὐδενὸς ἅψονται πρὶν ἂν λούσωνται· ταὐτὰ δὲ ταῦτα καὶ Ἀράβιοι ποιεῦσι.* (for translation see text above).

[2] *Eusebius*, Praeparat. evangel. p. 475. C., *Μηδὲ εἰς ἱερὰ εἰσιέναι ἀπὸ γυναικῶν ἀλούτοις ἐνομοθέτησαν.* (And they enjoined that men should not enter into temples unwashod after women).

[3] *Chaeremon* in *Porphyry*, *περὶ ἀποχ.* bk. IV. §. 7, The expression *pollutiones* (pollutions) for nocturnal ejaculation of seed shows the Romans also saw a defilement in this. Comp. *Heinsius* on Ovid's Art of Love, bk. III. 96.

[4] Josephus, Contra Apionem, bk. II. p. 1381., *καὶ μετὰ τὴν νομιμὸν συνουσίαν ἄνδρος καὶ γυναικὸς ἀπολούσασθαι κελεύει ὁ νόμος· ψυχῆς τε καὶ σώματος ἐγγίνεται μολυσμός.* (Even *after the lawful intercourse* of man and wife *the Law orders* men to wash: a defilement both of soul and body ensues).

[5] *Philo Judaeus*, De special. legg., *τοσαύτην δ᾽ ἔχει πρόνοιαν ὁ νόμος τοῦ μηδ᾽ ἐπὶ γάμοις νεωτερίζεσθαι, ὥστε*

declare it to have been so, for in the Old Testament it is nowhere enjoined. As is generally known, this custom has been kept up in the East down to the present day, eveu among the Christian populations,—affording a concurrent testimony to the necessity for its observance in these countries.

Whether the *Greeks* deliberately and with intention made use of baths and bathing immediately after sexual intercourse, it is difficult to ascertain quite for certain; but it seems probable, as not only does Mythology more than once [1] make express mention of the bath after coition, but the phrase **ὅσιος ἀπ' εὐνᾶς ὤν** (being holy, purified, after the couch) points to the same conclusion. Moreover there is a passage in *Lucian*, [2]—though it is quite true he

καὶ τοὺς συνιόντας εἰς ὁμιλίαν ἄνδρας καὶ γυναῖκας κατὰ τοὺς ἐπὶ γάμοις θεσμοὺς, ὅταν εὐνῆς ἀπαλλάττωντο, οὐ πρότερον ἐᾷ τινος ψαύειν ἢ λουτροῖς καὶ περιῤῥαντηρίοις χρῆσθαι. (But the Law takes such precautions that nothing strange and unlawful be done in marriage, that it suffers not even such as come together in intercourse, men and women united according to the laws of marriage, when they quit the bed, to touch anything before they have *employed baths and sprinklings*). The same Writer, De mercede meretricis non accepienda in sacrar., (Of Harlots' Hire not meet to be Taken in the Holy Place), Works edit. Mangey Vol. II. p. 265.), moreover states that in his time the public women made frequent use of warm baths.

[1] *Europa* bathed in Crete after coition with Zeus (Antigonus Carystius, Hist. mirab. 179.), Venus after the first embraces of Vulcan (Athenaeus, Deipnos. XV. p. 681.), Ceres after lying with Neptune (Pausanias, Arcad. p. 256.).

[2] In Amor. 42. Lucian says of the women (Hetaerae), *νύκτας ἐπὶ τούτοις διηγούμεναι, καὶ τοὺς ἑτερόχρωτας ὕπνους καὶ θηλύττητος εὐνὴν γέμουσαν· ἀφ' ἧς ἀναστὰς ἕκαστος εὐθὺ λουτροῦ χρεῖός ἐστι.* (passing their nights in this way, enjoying indiscrimate sleep and a couch teeming with wantonness; from the which each man when he has risen, straightway is in need of bathing). *Hesiod*, Works and Days 731., writes,

often describes Roman customs,—that might be thought to prove the same.

Clearer indications are forthcoming in the case of the *Romans*, who not only must not undertake any sacred function or enter a Temple, if they had failed to bathe after carrying out coition, [1] but were also bound generally after every act of cohabitation to wash the parts brought into use. At any rate this holds good of the women, and so applies to the Roman matron (comp. the passage of *Suetonius* quoted

μηδ' αἰδοῖα γονῇ πεπαλαγ-
μένος ἔνδοθι οἴκου
ἑστίῃ ἐμπελαδὸν παραφαινέ-
μεν, ἀλλ' ἀλέασθαι.

(Nor yet when done with generation, within the house hard by the hearth expose the privates, but retire aside).

[1] *Persius*, Sat. II. 15.,

Haec sancte ut poscas, Tiberino in gurgite mergis
Mane caput bis terque et noctem flumine purgas.

(That you may make this request free from taint, you plunge your head in Tiber's flood twice and three times at dawn, and *purge away your night in the stream*). *Gregory the Great*, Answers to ten Questions of Augustine, first English Bishop: Vir cum propria uxore dormiens, intrare ecclesiam, non debet, sed neque lotus intrare statim debet ... Et quamvis de hac re diversae hominum nationes diversa sentiant, atque custodire videantur, Romanorum tamen semper atque ab antiquioribus usus fuit, post ad mixtionem propriae coniugis et lavacrii purificationem ab ingressu ecclesiae paullatim reverenter abstinere. (A man sleeping with his own wife, ought not to enter a church, and not even when washed ought he to enter immediately after .... And although on this matter different nations of mankind hold different opinions and appear to keep different customs, yet the Romans' practice always and from the most ancient times has ever been, that subsequently to intercourse with his lawful wife and the purification of the bath a man reverently abstain for a while from entering a church). For the same reason *Tibullus* says, Carmina bk. II. 1.,

Vos quoque abesse procul jubeo discedite ab aris,
Queis tulit hesterna gaudia nocte, Venus.

(You too I bid stand afar off, depart ye from the altars, to whom yesternight Venus brought her joys). Comp. *Ovid*, Amor., bk. III. eleg. 6.

in § 27 as to Atia, the mother of Augustus, as well as in an even greater degree to the amica (mistress) or courtesan. The regular name for this was *aquam sūmere* (to take water).[1] Indeed there were actually special attendants *aquarioli* (water-boys),[1] whose business it

[1] *Ovid*, Amor., bk. III. eleg. 7. 84.

Neve suae possent intactam scire ministrae,
Dedecus hoc sumta dissimulavit aqua.

(And that her handmaids might not know her untouched, she dissembled this disgrace by *taking water*).
Ovid, Ars Amandi, bk. III. 619.,

Scilicet obstabit custos ne scribere possis,
Sumendae detur cum tibi tempus aquae.

(Of course your guard will put obstacles in the way to hinder your writing, though time be given you for *taking water*).
Martial, bk. VII. Epigr. 34.,

Ecquid femineos sequeris matrona recessus?
Secretusque tua, cunne, lavaris aqua?

(What! do you a matron penetrate into women's secret haunts? and by stealth are you washed, O female organ, in the water that appertains to you? *Petronius*, Sat. 94., Itaque extra cellam processit, tanquam *aquam peteret*. (And so she came forward outside her chamber, and if she *were going for water*. — *Cicero*, Orat. pro Caelio, ch. 14. represents his grandfather Appius Claudius Caecus, who (442 A.U.C.) had constructed the Appian Way, say to his depraved granddaughter: Ideo aquam adduxi ut ea tu inceste uterere? (Was it for this I brought the water to Rome, that you might use it for abominable purposes? Comp. Casaubon on Cicero, Letters to Atticus, bk. I. Letter 16. For the same reason women and girls who only rarely participated in sexual intercourse were called *siccae* (dry) (*Plautus*, Miles Glor. III. 1. 192. *Martial*, XI. Epigr. 82. *Petronius*, Sat. 37.), in contrast to the *uda puella* (wet girl) *Juvenal*, Sat. X. 321. *Martial*, XI. 17.), who was obliged to wash herself frequently. So too *illota* or *illauta* virgo (unwashed maid) stands for *intacta* virgo (untouched maid), as in *Plautus*, Poenul. I. sc. 2. 22. Nam quae lavata est, nisi perculta est, meo quidem animo, quasi *illauta* est. (For she who is washed, unless she is bedecked as well, in my opinion, is as good as *unwashed*). In fact the whole of this scene is important for our subject.

[2] *Festus*, p. 19. under word *Aquarioli:* Aquarioli dicebantur mulierum impudicarum sordidi asseclae. (Aquarioli, or

water-boys, a name given to the shameless attendants of immodest women). — *Tertullian*, Apologet. ch. 43. They were also known as *baccariones* from baccarium, a word which *Isidor* explains by aquarium (a water vessel). An old Gloss says: baccario **πορνοδιάκονος**, meritricibus aquam infundens (baccario, a prostitutes' attendant, one who pours water for whores); another: aquarioli, **βαλλάδες, βαλλὰς**, from **βάλλων ὕδωϱ**, ab aqua jaciunda (water-boys, or throwers, from throwing water). These aquarioli at the same time carried on the business of procurers; so *Juvenal* says, Sat. VI. 331., veniet conductus aquarius. (Some water-carrier will come, hired for the purpose). Comp. *Lipsius*, Antiq. lect. I. 12. Hence also the word *aquaculare* was used meaning lenocinari (to be a pandar); see *Turnebus*, Adversar. XIV. 12. XXVIII. 5. Besides this they held themselves, especially in the public baths, at the disposal of lustful women, very often earning in this way the Bath farthing they had to pay. Probably Dasius in *Martial*, bk. II. Epigr. 52., was such an Aquariolus.

Novit loturas Dasius numerare, poposcit
Mammosam Spatalen pro tribus, illa dedit.

(Dasius knew well how to count the women going to bathe; he asked big-bosomed Spatalé the price for three, and she gave it). Hence the *quadrantaria permutatio* (farthing barter) in Cicero, Orat pro Caelio ch. 26. Comp. *Juvenal*, Sat. VI. 428.,

Callidus et cristae digitos impressit aliptes,
Ac summum dominae femur exclamare coegit.

(The artful masseur too pressed his fingers on the clytoris, and made the upper part of his mistress' thigh resound under his hands). From the passage of *Martial* it follows that *Busch*, "Handbuch der Erfindungen," (Manual of Inventions), vol. II. p. 8., is mistaken in saying: *Women* and persons not yet adult had the bath *gratis;* in fact in the passage from Juvenal, Sat. II. 152., quoted by him, it is a question of boys only. For the rest, the Aquarioli recall the **λουτϱοφόϱοι** (water-bearers) of the Greeks; these were boys, whose duty it was to fetch the water for the Bride's bath before marriage. *Pollux*, Onomast. III. 43. *Harpocration*, under the word, p. 49. *Meursius*, Ceramicus ch. 14. p. 40. *Böttiger*, "Vasen gemälde (Vase-painting), I. p. 143. Again the **παϱανύμφοι** (groomsmen), who anointed the bride, and as a rule were from 17 to 19 years old, may be mentioned here by way of illustration. Hancarville, Antiquités Vol. I. plate 45. Vol. III. plate 43. Vol. IV. plate 69.

was not merely to fetch water for this purpose, but also in particular to bathe and cleanse the "filles de joie" after sexual intercourse. For this reason *Lampridius* says of the Emperor Commodus (ch. 2), *aquam gessit, ut lenonum ministeriis probrosis natum magis, quam in loco crederes, ad quem fortuna pervexit* (he fetched water, so that you would more readily suppose him born to perform the shameful offices of pandars than in the station whereto fortune raised him). Such cleanliness was especially obligatory on those who had to do with the preparation of food and drink, such as bakers, cooks and butlers; [1] and if we do not find it directly enjoined among many ancient Peoples, the only reason of this is that they were already accustomed to wash and bathe every morning [2] immediately on leaving their bed.

[1] *Columella*, De re rust. bk. XII. ch. 4., His autem omnibus placuit, eum, qui rerum harum officium susceperit, castum esse continentemque oportere, quoniam totum in eo sit, ne contractentur pocula vel cibi, nisi aut ab impubi aut certe abstinentissimo rebus venereis. Quibus si fuerit operatus vel vir vel femina, debere eos flumine aut perenni aqua, priusquam penora contingant, ablui. (But all were agreed upon this, that he who should undertake the performance of these duties ought to be chaste and continent, since all depends on his care that drink and food be not defiled, unless indeed they are prepared by one still immature or at any rate one extremely self-restrained in the matter of love. But if it has been indulged in by man or woman, they ought to be cleansed in the river or in flowing water, before they touch the victuals). From what precedes the words quoted, it may be conjectured that this custom prevailed also among the Carthaginians and Greeks.

[2] *Propertius*, bk. III. eleg. 9., At primum pura somnum tibi discute limpha. (But first shake off your sleep with pure water). *Apuleius*, Metamorphos. bk. II., Confestim discussa pigra quiete, alacer exsurgo meque purificandi studio, marino lavacro trado. (Soon as ever dull sleep is shaken off, at once I briskly rise, and with the desire of purification, I give myself to the bath of sea water.) *Tacitus*, Germania ch. 22., Statim e somno, quem plerumque in diem extrahunt, lavantur, sae-

In the same way as after natural coition the parts brought into use were bathed and washed, this was also done after *unnatural*, and so we read in the Collection of Priapeia (Carm. 40.):

Falce minax et parte tui maiore, Priape,
Ad fontem, quaeso, dic mihi qua sit iter?
Vade per has vites, quarum si carpseris uvas
Quas aliter sumas, hospes, habebis aquas —

(Standing in threatening attitude with my bristling pruning-knife and your better part, Priapus, I enquire: "Pri'thee tell me, which is my way to the fountain?" "Go through yonder vines, but if you dare to pluck the grapes, you will find, stranger, *water you must take* elsewhere). Clearly this is to be taken as meaning paederastia or irrumation looked upon as punishments inflicted for the theft contemplated; and shows us at the same time it was not without a "double entendre" that Priapus was set up as a direction-post to fountains, a point that *Lomeier* [1] has already brought out with perfect correctness. Again the *fellator* after his work used to cleanse the mouth with water, as we learn from several passages in *Martial;* thus amongst other places we read in one, of Lesbia, [2]

pius calida, ut apud quos plurimum hiems occupat. (Immediately on rising from sleep, which as a rule they prolong into the day-time, they wash, generally in warm water, as one would expect among men whose winter lasts most of the year).

[1] *Lomeier*, De lustrationibus veterum gentium, (Of the Lustrations of Ancient Peoples), ch. XVI. p. 167., Et Priapus iter ad fontem monstrare dicebatur, quod qui quaeve viros experirentur lotione opus haberent; (Moreover Priapus was said to point the way to the fountain, because such men, or women as had intercourse, were in need of washing); in confirmation of which he then alleges the passage quoted in the text.

[2] *Martial*, Bk. II. Epigr. 50. Comp. bk. II. 70., bk. III. 69. 81. *Petronius*, Sat. 67., Aquam in os non coniiciet. (He will not throw water into his mouth).

Quod fellas et aquam potes, nil Lesbia peccas,
Qua tibi parte opus est, Lesbia, sumis aquam.

(You *fellate* and then drink water; you do no wrong in this, Lesbia; where lies your work, there Lesbia you *take water*).

If we further add to this scrupulous cleanliness the quiet life led by the women of Antiquity, who spent most of their time, as women still do in the East, reclining, it is evident that in spite of the predisposing influence of Climate, injurious secretions from the vagina and uterus, or indeed ulcerations of these parts, must—speaking generally, and in proportion—have occurred but rarely. Moreover such maladies of the sort as were contractod were quickly got rid of again spontaneously, for very often even at the present day rest and cleanliness suffice by themselves for the removal of primary affections of the genitals. On the other hand it cannot be denied that a careless non-observance of these primeval laws of cleanliness must have then avenged itself all the more severely on the offending individual, and given occasion for the setting up of incurable diseases.

But great as the counteracting effect of the frequent use of baths in Antiquity was on the rise of diseases in general, and of those resulting from sexual excesses in particular, none the less in other ways did these same baths, directly or indirectly, *give occasion for their rise and spread.* As to their *direct* effect in this direction,—we certainly find but scanty evidence of any in the authorities, and even such as *are* forthcoming may very possibly be referred to the head of general want of cleanliness [1]. Still in view of the fact that at the present day the cellar baths of the Jews contribute to some degree to the spread of disease, and especially of skin-disease of different

[1] E. g. the Epigram of *Martial* (VI. 81.) on Charidemus, who accordidg to VI, 56. was a *fellator.*

types, as did baths generally in the Middle Ages, the conjecture is surely justified that similar results followed in Antiquity, especially at Rome under the Emperors.

Indirectly maladies consequent upon sexual excesses were helped on by the mere fact that the ancient Baths afforded manifold opportunities for such excesses. The bath-attendants, or *aquarioli* (water-boys), who fetched the water for bathing, not only carried on vicious practices with the women frequenting the place themselves, but also made a business of procuration, as already pointed out just above, p. 214. The lascivious Roman Ladies took their own slaves with them to the Baths, that they might attend upon their mistresses.[1] At first the same bathing Establishments were used equally by both sexes, but not at the same time; and according to *Dio Cassius*,[2] *Agrippa* would appear to have first, 721 A. U. C., established the public Baths at Rome for men and women, from which place later on Baths open to both sexes were introduced into Greece, as *Plutarch*[3]

[1] *Martial*, bk. VII. Epigr. 34. 35.,

Inguina succinctus nigra tibi servus aluta
Stat, quoties calidis tota foveris aquis.

(A slave girt about the loins with a pouch of black leather stands by you, as oft as you are washed all over with warm water). *Claudian*, I. 106.,

Pectebat dominae crines et saepe lavanti
Nudus in argento lympham portabat alumnae.

(He was wont to comb his mistress' hair, and oft when she bathed, naked, he would bring water for his lady in a silver ewer).

[2] *Dio Cassius*, Histor. bk. XLIX. ch. 43., *τά τε βαλανεῖα προῖκα δι' ἔτους καὶ ἀνδράσι καὶ γυναιξὶ λούεσθαι παρέσχε.* (And he opened the Baths gratuitously throughout the summer both to men and women). Comp. *Pliny.* Hist. nat. bk. XXVI. ch. 24. 9. Dio Cassios. LIV. 29.

[3] *Plutarch*, Cato Major ch. 39., *συλλούσασθαι δὲ μηδέποτε· καὶ τούτου κοινὸν ἔθος ἔοικε Ῥωμαίων εἶναι. καὶ γὰρ πενθεροῖς γάμβροι ἐφυλάττοντο συλλούεσθαι, δυσωπούμενοι τὴν ἀποκάλυψιν καὶ γύμνωσιν· εἶτα*

states. The Greeks called these Establishments **ἀνδρόγυνα λοῦτρα** (men-women, male-female, baths), and used to set up an image of Hermaphroditus in front of them.[1] In the Imperial period, when all shame was laid aside and Heliogabalus himself *in balneis semper cum mulieribus fuit* (always visited the Baths in company of the women) (*Lampridius* ch. 2), the use of the Baths both by men and women, and this at the same time, had become an established custom, as may be seen from several passages of *Martial*;[2] and it was in vain the Em-

μέντοι παρ' Ἑλλήνων τὸ γυμνοῦσθαι μαθόντες αὐτοὶ πάλιν τοῦ καὶ μετὰ γυναικῶν τοῦτο πράσσειν ἀναπεπλήκασι τοὺς Ἑλλήνας. (And never bathed together; indeed the common habit of doing so appears to be of Roman origin. For at first sons-in-law used to guard against bathing with fathers-in-law, feeling shame at such exposure and stripping naked. Later on however having learned the habit of stripping naked from the Greeks, they again in their turn have taught the Greeks that of doing so along with women). The *balnea virilia* (men's baths) are mentioned in *Aulus Gellius*, Noct. Att. X. 3., where he shows that they were also used by women.

[1] Catalect. Graecor. Poetarum,

ἀνδράσιν Ἑρμῆς εἰμί· γυναιξὶ δὲ Κύπρις ὁρῶμαι·
ἀμφοτέρων δὲ φέρω συμβολά μοι τοκέων
Τοὔνεκεν οὐκ ἀλόγως με τὸν Ἑρμαφρόδιτον ἔθεντο
ἀνδρογύνοις λουτροῖς παῖδα τὸν ἀμφίβολον.

(To men I am Hermes; for women I am looked upon as Cypris; and I bear the tokens of both my parents. Therefore not without good reason have they set me up, the Hermaphrodite, the boy of double nature, before male-female baths).

[2] *Martial*, Bk. VI. 34. bk. III. 51. bk. II. 76. As early as *Ovid*, Art of Love, bk. III. 639., we read:

Quum custode foris tunicam servante puellae
Celent furtivos balnea tuta iocos,

(When the doorkeeper at the entrance keeps the girl's garments, and the discreet baths cover surreptitious amusements); also in *Quintilian*, Institut. bk. V. ch. 9., nam si est signum adulterae lavari cum viris, etc. (if indeed it is a mark of a lewd woman to bathe with men).

perors *Hadrian*, [1] *Marcus Antoninus* [2] and *Alexander Severus* [3] endeavoured to restrain the abuse by enactments. These were just as unavailing as were the invectives of the Fathers of the Church. [4]

[1] *Spartian*, Life of Hadrian ch. 18., Lavacre pro sexibus separavit. (He assigned separate baths for the two sexes). Dio Cass. LXIX. ch. 8.

[2] *Julius Capitolinus*, Life of Marcus Antoninus ch. 23„ Lavacra mixta submovit, mores matronarum composuit diffluentes et iuvenum nobilium. (He abolished the mixed Baths, and restrained the loose habits of the Roman ladies and of the young nobles).

[3] *Lampridius*, Life of Alexander Severus ch. 24., Balnea mixta Romae exhiberi prohibuit, quod quidem iam ante prohibitum Heliogabalus fieri permiserat. (He forbad the opening of mixed Baths at Rome, a practice which, though previously prohibited, Heligabalus had allowed to be followed).

[4] *Clement of Alexandria*, Paedagog. bk. III. ch. 5., says of women: *καὶ δὴ τοῖς μὲν ἀνδράσι τοῖς σφῶν οὐκ ἂν ἀποδύσαιντο, προσποίητον αἰσχύνης ἀξιοπιστίαν μνώμεναι· ἔξεστι δὲ τοῖς βουλομένοις τῶν ἄλλων οἴκοι τὰς κατακλείστους, γυμνὰς ἐν τοῖς βαλανείοις θεάσασθαι· ἐνταῦθα γὰρ ἀποδύσασθαι τοῖς θεαταῖς, ὥσπερ καπήλοις σωμάτων, οὐκ αἰσχύνονται· ἀλλ' ὁ μὲν Ἡσίοδος* (Oper. et Dies lib. II. 371). *Μηδὲ γυναικείῳ λυτρῷ χρόα φαιδρύνεσθαι, παραινεῖ· κοινὰ δὲ ἀνέῳκται ἀνδράσιν ὁμοῦ καὶ γυναιξὶ τὰ βαλανεῖα· κἀντεῦθεν ἐπὶ ἀκρασίαν ἀποδύονται· ἐκ τοῦ γὰρ εἰσορᾶν, γίνεται ἀνθρώποις ἐρᾶν· ὥσπερ ἀποκλυζομένης τῆς αἰδοῦς αὐτοῖς κατὰ τὰ λουτρά· αἱ δὲ μὴ εἰς τοσοῦτον ἀπερυθριῶσαι, τοὺς μὲν ὀθνείους ἀποκλείουσιν, ἰδίοις δὲ οἰκέταις συλλούονται, καὶ δούλοις ἀποδύονται γυμναί, καὶ ἀνατρίβονται ὑπ' αὐτῶν, ἐξουσίαν δοῦσαι τῷ κατεπτηχότι τῆς ἐπιθυμίας, τὸ ἀδεὲς τῆς ψηλαφήσεως· οἱ γὰρ παρεισαγόμενοι παρὰ τὰ λουτρὰ ταῖς δεσποίναις γυμναῖς, μελέτην ἴσχουσιν ἀποδύσασθαι πρὸς τόλμαν ἐπιθυμίας ἔθει πονηρῷ παραγράφοντες τὸν φόβον.* (And of a truth they would not strip before their own husbands, feigning a pretended plausibility of mock-modesty; but for other men, whosoever will, may readily see the women that are so close shut up at home, naked at the Baths. For there they are nowise ashamed to strip before the spectators, looking on like dealers in human flesh; whereas Hesiod (Works and Days, bk.

The Bathing Apartments, from which antique Roman modesty had excluded almost every glimmer of external light, were now patent to the eyes of the passer-by. Fitted up with every device of the most refined luxury, [1] they were transformed into

II. 371.) advises "But do not, for the earning of a woman's price, let her wash her skin bright and clean." Now the Baths are open for men and women alike. And hence their stripping leads to incontinence; for from seeing, men come to desire, as though their modesty were washed away in the Baths. Other women that have not attained such effrontery, shut out strangers indeed, but wash along with their own house-slaves, and are stripped naked before their servants and are rubbed by them, giving opportunity to the man a-tremble with longing, the free right to handle without fear; for the men that are admitted into the Baths with their naked mistresses take care to strip in such a way as to correspond to the daring audacity of their longing, putting down fear to the count of evil habit). — *Cyprian*, De Virginum habitu: Quid vero, quae promiscuas balneas adeunt, quae oculis ad libidinem curiosis, pudori ac pudicitae dicata corpora prostituunt, quae cum viros ac a viris nudae vident turpiter ac videntur, nonne ipsae illecebram vitiis praestant. (But in truth, those women that frequent indiscrimate Baths, that expose to prying and lustful eyes their bodies that should be dedicate to modest shamefacedness, that along with men see what is disgraceful to see and in nakedness are seen by men, do not such women offer an enticement to sinfulness?) Comp. *Mercurialis*, De arte Gymnast. bk. I. ch. 10.—It is true we read in *Julius Caesar*, De bello Gallico bk. VI. ch. 21., of the ancient Germans: Intra annum vero vicessimum feminae notitiam habuisse, in turpissimis habent rebus; cuius rei nulla est occultatio, quod et *promiscue in fluminibus perluuntur*, (But to have known a woman under the twentieth year is held by them most disgraceful; and there is no concealment of it, as *they bathe indiscriminately in the rivers*); but here the antecedent clause bars any suspicion of sexual excesses having been invited by the practice.

[1] *Seneca*, Epist. 86. says, speaking of the bath of Scipio: Balneolum angustum, tenebricosum ex consuetudine antiqua; non videbatur maioribus nostris caldum nisi obscurum. (A little narrow bath-chamber, dim and gloomy after the antique fashion; our fathers could not

regular brothels; [1] and accordingly were not allowed to open their doors earlier than one hour before the ordinary establishments of this nature.

believe a bath warm unless it was dark too). — Next he describes explicitly the luxury of the Roman Baths, and then goes on, — In hoc balneo Scipionis minimae sunt rimae magis quam fenestrae, muro lapideo exsectae, ut sine iniuria munimenti lumen admitterent. At nunc blattaria vocant balnea, si qua non ita aptata sunt, ut totius diei solem fenestris amplissimis recipiant; nisi et lavantur et colorantur; nisi ex solio agros et maria prospiciant . . . Imo si scias, non quotidie lavabatur. Nam ut aiunt, qui priscos mores urbis tradiderunt, brachia et crura quotidie abluebant, quae scilicet sordes opere collegerant: ceterum toti nundinis lavabantur. Hoc loco dicet aliquis, liquet mihi immundissimos fuisse. Quid putas illos oluisse? militiam, laborem, virum. Postquam munda balnea inventa sunt, spurciores sunt. (In this bath of Scipio there are tiny chinks rather than windows, cut through the stone wall, so as to admit light without detriment to the shelter afforded. But nowadays men call them *Baths for night-moths*, any that are not disposed in such a way as to let the sunlight enter all day long by immense windows; if they are not washed and sun-burned at once; if they cannot look out on fields and sea from the pavement . . . If you must know the truth, he did not bathe every day. For we are told by those who have handed down accounts of the primitive manners of the City, our ancestors would wash daily arms and legs, for these had grown soiled with the dust of toil: but they washed all over only on market-days. Hearing this, it will be said, "It appears to me they must have very filthy people." Well! what think you it was they smelt of? Of fighting, and honest work, and manly vigour. Sweet, clean Baths have been introduced; but the population is only more foul). Comp. *Plutarch*, Quaest. convival. VIII. 9. *Sidonius Apollinaris* bk. II. Epist. 11. *Pliny*, Hist. nat. XXX. 54.

[1] *Ammianus Marcellinus*, XXVIII., Tales, ubi comitantibus singulos quadraginta ministris, tholos introierint balnearum, ubi sunt, minaciter clamantes, si apparuisse subito ignotam compererint meretricem, aut oppidanae quondam prostibulum plebis, vel meritorii corporis veterem lupam, certatim concurrunt, palpantesque ad venam deformitate magna blanditarum ita extollunt, ut Semiramin. (Such men, when with forty servants attending each master they

The same opportunities which the Baths gave for vice with women, they afforded no less for vice between men,—for paederastia. There it was that amateurs looked about for *bene vasatos* and **καλλιπύγους**, (men with fine instruments, men with handsome buttocks), and this among the Greeks as well as among the Romans, [1] though the latter in this as in other things beat the record of all other nations.

have entered the rotundas of the Baths, where they remain with loud threatening shouts, if they should note an unknown courtesan to have put in an appearance, or some prostitute once popular with the common herd, or some old harlot who has sold her person for years, they strive who shall be first on the spot, and wheedling her to the top of her bent, with mighty exaggeration of flattery, praise her beauty as though she were a Semiramis). *Lampridius*, Life of Heliogabalus ch. 26., Omnes de circo, de theatro, de stadio, de omnibus locis et *balneis*, meretrices collegit in aedes publicam. (All the prostitutes from circus, from theatre, from race-course, from all places and from *the Baths*, he brought together into public establishments). Comp. *Suetonius*, Caligula ch. 37.

[1] Martial, bk. I. Epigr. 24.,

Invitae nullum, nisi cum quo, Cotta, lavaris,
Et dant convivam balnea sola tibi.
Mirabar, quare nunquam me, Cotta, vocasses.
Iam scio, me nudum displicuisse tibi.

(You invite no man, Cotta, but your bathing companion; the Baths only supply a guest for you. I used to wonder, why you had never asked me; now I know that you did not like the look of me when naked). Comp. *Martial*, Bk. I. 97. bk. VII. 33. bk. IX. 34. *Juvenal*, Sat. VI. 373.

THIRD SECTION.

Relation of the Physician to Diseases consequent upon the Use or Misuse of the Genital Organs.

§ 38.

In the preceding Sections we have become acquainted with the various influences capable of favouring or counteracting the rise of diseases consequent upon the use or misuse of the genitals in Antiquity. At the same time we have shown how a multitude of affections of the most different kinds attacked, as a result of the unnatural gratification of sexual desire, those parts which under these circumstances had to undertake the rôle of the genital organs of the one or the other sex. Thirdly we have brought forward in the course of the enquiry at any rate some examples, proving beyond a doubt that the sexual parts themselves too under favourable external conditions sometimes became diseased as the consequence of indulgence in sexual intercourse. Still these results were for the most part based on the evidence of non-medical Writers, for of set purpose we abstained as much as possible from calling the professional Writers into Court on these points, so as to be able to treat in their proper mutual connexion whatever statements these latter have left us as to the maladies in question. This course appeared to us all the more necessary, as it is precisely the medical evidence which the opponents of the existence of Venereal disease in Antiquity believe themselves able to utilize in justification of their opinions.

But before we proceed to the detailed examination of the actual statements, it would seem expedient to get an answer to the following question: *whether indeed the Physicians of Antiquity generally were in a position to acquire an adequate knowledge. of the bodily consequences of vicious living?* In fact on the correct answer to this question obviously depends the correct appreciation of the medical Writings as sources for the History of Venereal disease. Only under the condition that this question may be answered in the affirmative, can the evidence supplied by the Physicians be regarded as satisfactory for their own period. That it cannot of course be so for all periods, has been pointed out already in our examination of the authorities for Antiquity generally. Indeed for long periods of time Physicians had no special *locus standi*, inasmuch as each individual in the case of the most usual maladies endeavoured to help himself, and if the family recipes left him stranded, then betook himself with prayers for assistance to the Gods and their intermediaries on earth, the Priests. This still continued, even after the Physicians had won their recognition as a special profession, and we find accordingly throughout Antiquity popular, sacerdotal, and professional or *medical* medicine, if we may be allowed the expression, continuing to exist simultaneously side by side, and not a trace anywhere of the ridiculous limitation according to which no man has a right to be well without the help of a doctor.

Now having made it clear by what we have said, that in order to gain knowledge of a disease in Antiquity it is by no means enough to go to the Physicians only, even when such existed, that the latter should never be regarded as sole possessors of whatever was known from the point of view of pathology and therapeutics, we are bound to apply the same rule in the case of diseases consequent upon vicious habits. Of this the foregoing Sections contain amply sufficient proofs. It has there been shown how the genital organs were under the protection of special deities. Diseases affecting them were ascribed to the vengeance of the said deities, as at Athens to Dionysus, at Lampsacus to Priapus. To them sufferers had recourse to win by their prayers the removal of the divine anger, as well as its consequences; and all this happened not only in times when Physicians did not as yet exist, but no less when they did and in defiance of them, as the poems of the Priapeia sufficiently prove.[1] How long these ideas lived on is shown by the pictures *Philo* (p. 315) and *Palladius* (p. 318) draw of their times, while the XVth. and XVIth. Centuries reproduced the same scenes.

The most obvious reason for this no doubt was the *enigma presented by the origin* of diseases of the genitals, particularly for any one unacquainted with the existence of contagions and their modes of activity. The man who with a healthy penis had accomplished coition, observed some days afterwards, though without resenting the fact, a mucous discharge to have been set up, or an ulcer, pustule, or what not, to have appeared. The cause of these affections he sought for in vain, for of course the mere act o coition was the very last thing he was likely to regard as such. Rather accustomed, wherever the cause of any phænomenon was unknown to him, to ascribe it to the intervention of the deity, he saw in his complaint likewise the **Θεῖον** (divine) as eventual cause. Naturally therefore it was divine

[1] It must be left to future investigation to decide, whether the great number of *phalli* found in so many places where Temples formerly existed, is not in part to be explained by supposing these figures to have formed thank-offerings for the happy recovery of the corresponding parts from sickness.

assistance, and not human, that would avail to relieve him of his pain. Long after this time moreover, when men had ceased to refer all diseases to the vengeance of the gods, and now discovered natural causes for maladies of the genitals, as for other diseases, anything rather than just the act of coition was looked upon as cause of the observed effects, as indeed is the case to this day among the Turks, [1] and as the earliest Writers on Venereal disease abundantly show to have been so in their time. That the Physicians were no exceptions to this rule, we shall show on a later page.

A much more weighty reason however why the patient attacked by some affection of the genitals turned not to men (Physicians) for help, but to the Gods, and the Priests who represented them, was the feeling of *shame*. Since first Adam and Eve had recourse to the fig-leaf, it has ever been a habit among all peoples of the ancient as of the modern

[1] *Oppenheim*, Ueber den Zustand der Heilkunde in der Türkei, (On the Condition of of Medical Knowledge in Turkey), p. 81., "Without the very great cleanliness of the Turks, who after every occasion of sexual intercourse not only wash carefully, but also wherever it is possible go to the bath likewise, the disease would undoubtedly be yet more widely spread than it is... Yet the Turk will never admit, or rather he simply cannot bring himself to conceive, that he has contracted an infection through unclean cohabitation, but will be found always to give some other cause as occasioning his sickness. In fact the language itself shows this; the Turkish expression for gonorrhœa is "*Belzouk*", literally: chill of the back (from *bel*, back and *zouk*, cold), and chill or overheating will always be represented as having brought it on. — Moreover *Zeller von Zellenberg*, Abh. über die ersten Erscheinungen venerischer Lokal-Krankheitsformen und deren Behandlung, (Dissertation on the earliest Appearances of Forms of Local Venereal Disease, and their Treatment), Vienna 1810., p. 7., is of the opinion, that the reason of the imperfect knowledge possessed by the Ancients of gonorrhœa, chancre and buboes is to be found in this delayed appearance of the symptoms of disease after coition.

world to withdraw the procreative parts from the view of others by covering them. But above all did the Ancients regard the exposure of these parts [1]

[1] We see this in the clearest possible way from the passage of *Herodotus*, bk. I. ch. 9, 10., where Candaules wishes to induce Gyges to see his wife naked, in order to convince him of her beauty, but the latter objects: *ἅμα δὲ κιθῶνι ἐκδυομένῳ συνεκδύεται καὶ τὴν αἰδῶ γυνή· πάλαι δὲ τὰ καλὰ ἀνθρώποισι ἐξεύρηται, ἐκ τῶν μανθάνειν δεῖ·* (but when she strips off her tunic, a woman strips off therewith her modesty likewise; now mankind have long ago ascertained what is honourable, and from this we must learn how to act). Then Herodotus adds to this further (ch. 10.), *παρὰ γὰρ τοῖσι Λυδοῖσι, σχεδὸν δὲ παρὰ τοῖσι ἄλλοισι βαρβάροισι, καὶ ἄνδρα ὀφθῆναι γυμνὸν, ἐς αἰσχύνην μεγάλην φέρει·* (for among the Lydians, as indeed among pretty nearly all Barbarians, for a person to be seen naked is counted for the greatest disgrace). Comp. *Plutarch*, De audiend. rat. p. 37. *Diogenes Laertius*, VIII. 43. *Plato*, Politics V. 6. p. 457. A., V. 3. p. 452., *Οὐ πολὺς χρόνος, ἐξ οὗ τοῖς Ἕλλησιν ἐδόκει αἰσχρὰ εἶναι καὶ γέλοια, ἅπερ νῦν τοῖς πολλοῖς τῶν βαρβάρων, γυμνοὺς ἄνδρας ὁρᾶσθαι.* (It is no long time since it appeared to the Greeks, as it does still to most of the Barbarian peoples, shameful and ridiculous for men to be seen naked). In reference to the genital organs *Hesiod* says (Works and Days 733.):

μηδ' αἰδοῖα γονῇ πεπαλαγμένος ἔνδοθι οἴκου
ἑστίῃ ἐμπελαδὸν παραφαινέμεν, ἀλλ' ἀλέασθαι·

(Nor yet when done with generation, within the house hard by the hearth expose the privates, but retire aside). St. Augustine, De civit. dei bk. XIV., Omnes gentes adeo tenent in usu pudenda velare, ut quidam barbari illas corporis partes nec in balneis undas habeant. (All nations in fact make it a habit to cover the privates, so much so that some Barbarians do not expose the parts of the body naked even in the Baths). *St. Ambrose*, Offic. I. 18., Licet plerique se et in lavacro, quantum possunt, tegant, ut vel illic, ubi nudum totum est corpus, huius modi intecta portio sit. (Most men may also cover themselves, as much as they can, even in the Bath, so that even there, where the whole body is naked, a part may so be hidden). *Arnobius*, bk. V., Propudiosa corporum monstratur obscoenitas, obiectanturque partes illae, quas

one of the severest trials to which modesty could be exposed; and rightly enough therefore designate them by the name of *pudenda*, *αιδοῖα*, *the parts of shame.* Neither the wide extension of Phallic worship, nor yet the compulsory exposure of the Ephebi [1] and the naked exercises of maidens and youths at Sparta [2],

pudor communis abscondere, quas naturalis verecundiae lex iubet, quas inter aures castas sine venia nefas est ac sine honoribus apellare praefatis. (The foulest abomination of men's bodies is exhibited, and those parts exposed, which common modesty, the natural law of shamefacedness, bids us conceal, which among ears polite it is forbidden to name without asking pardon and making a preface of apologies). —bk. III., Insignire his partibus, quas enumerare, quas persequi probus audeat nemo, nec sine summae foeditatis horrore mentis imaginatione concipere. (To parade those parts, which no honourable man dare name or describe, nor even without a shudder at such a height of foulness conceive a mental picture of). Comp. p. 42. and *Oppenheim*, loco citato p. 128., who undoubtedly ranks the importance of the vice of paederastia too high, when he finds in it the main reason for the feeling of shame prevalent among the Turks.

[1] *Aristophanes*, Wasps 578., *πάιδων τοίνυν δοκιμαζομένων αἰδοῖα πάρεστι θεᾶσθαι.* (Yet when boys are under test, men may see their privates). Comp. *Athenaeus*, Deipnos, bk. XII. p. 550. Petit, Ad legg. Attic. p. 227. At Rome likewise in cases of marriage disputes the men were obliged to offer their genital organs for examination (*Quintilian*, Declam. 279.), a Law which was only revoked by Justinian. Comp. *Gundlingiana* No. 23. pp. 342 sqq. We learn from *Plato*, Theaetet. 151., *ποίαν χρὴ ποίῳ ἀνδρὶ συνοῦσαν ὡς ἀρίστους παῖδας τικτειν*, (what sort of maid must mate with what sort of man to produce as fine children as may be), that the marriageable girls were examined by the midwives,—a proceedure that Plato wished to see universally introduced in his ideal State (De legg. bk. XII.). But against this *Theodoretus*, Contra Graecos bk. IX., declaims vigorously.

[2] In any case it is an error to suppose that by this it is implied that the maidens and young men were absolutely naked. They were merely *μονόπεπλοι* (single-frocked), clothed in a single short frock, slit up at the hips, for which reason they were also known by the

can fairly be cited in this connexion as proofs to the contrary.

In our own day the most accomplished voluptuaries are in no wise shocked at undertaking in secret the most shameful doings, but yet when it comes to showing the Physician the diseased instruments of their bestial lusts, often put this off so long as to run great risks of entirely losing the signs of their manhood; and without a doubt it was the same at the period when habitual depravity had reached its culminating point of enormity. Even Priapus himself asks (Carm. 3):

Nec mihi sit crimen, quod mentula semper operta est.

(Nor let it be laid as a crime against me, that my member is ever covered up.) If with this is compared

name φαινομηρίδες (showing the thighs) (*Pollux*, Onomastic. VII. 55.), a costume which was pretty much the general Doric one; thus *Moeris* says δωριάζειν τὸ παραγυμνοῦσθαι τινα μέρη, (to follow Dorian fashions, to expose certain parts). Comp. *Meursius*, Laconic. bk. I. end. *K. O. Müller*, The Dorians, IInd. Part pp. 263, 265. *Josephus*, De special legg., Works, Vol. II. p. 328. The meaning of γυμνὸς is nothing more than "lightly clad", in mere underclothing, without outer cloak. So *Eubulus*, (Athenaeus bk. XIII. p. 568.) says, speaking of the brothel-girls, γυμνάς—ἐν λεπτονήτοις ὑμέσιν ἑστωτας (standing "naked"—in light-spun garments). *Aelian*, Var. hist. XIII. 37., ἐν χιτωνίσκῳ γυμνὸς, ("naked" in a tunic). Similarly *nudus* (naked) in Latin, as *Cuper* (Observat. bk. I. ch. 7.) long ago pointed out, often has no other meaning, but merely stands for *tunicatus* (clad in the tunic), in tunic only, without cloak or toga. We see this very clearly in *Petronius*, Satir. 55., Aequum est induere nuptam ventum textilem,—Palam prostare nudam in nebula linea. ('Tis right a bride should put on woven wind,—that she should stand openly for sale, "naked" in a linen cloud!) In precisely the same way the Jews use their word עָרֹם (arôm), Isaiah Ch. XX. 2., Job Ch. XXIV. 7. 10. I Samuel ch. XIX. 24., and the Arabs مسلوخ (mesluch).

the poem from the Priapeia quoted on p. 74 of Vol. I., no one can fall to agree with us when we say that the field of observation open to Physicians in Antiquity with regard to diseases of the genitals can never have been at all extended. Even the Priests, at any rate in later times, were only resorted to in the more serious instances; but even so their journals of cases, supposing them ever to have kept such, would have been a far better source of information than those of the Physicians. We find a confirmation of this in the Mosaic Books of the Law, which contain the earliest and clearest delineations we possess of affections of the genital organs both in men and women.

But if men were so reluctant, how much more so must women have been, who were universally held to have committed a crime if they had given any part of their body to the eyes of a stranger. Just as the assistance of the Physician was disdained in childbirth, and to account for the fact the fable of Agnodicé invented, in the same way in complaints of the genitals women hesitated to submit themselves to the inquisition of the Physician. But seeing the female sexual organs are pre-eminently the home and breeding place of Venereal disease, this closed what was precisely the most direct way to a correct understanding of maladies of the genitals. The ancient Physicians, like our own forefathers, could at best make leucorrhœa the universal scape-goat; and accordingly even *Galen*, as we shall find presently, laid no stress on the circumstance, and drew no inference from it, that wherever men were attacked by gonorrhœa, the women with whom they had had coition likewise suffered from the complaint.

Further, to this general sense of shame was added a certain timidity before the professional status of real Physicians as a class, as well as the pretty universally prevalent idea of the *ignominiousness of a sickness brought on by a person's own fault*, at any rate among the educated part of the population.

This comes out in the following passage of *Plato*,[1] where he says: "Does it appear to you disgraceful to stand in need of medical help, when it is not wounds at all or such sicknesses as depend on the

[1] *Plato*, Republic, bk. II. p. 405. The Speech of *Lysias* 'Τπὲρ Φαυλίου contains a passage, preserved for us by *Athenaeus*, bk. XII. p. 552., in which these principles are expressed in Court, to induce the Judges to condemn the dissolute Cinesias: ***τοῦτον δὲ τὸν ὑπὸ πλείστων γινωσκόμενον οἱ θεοὶ οὕτως διέθεσαν, ὥστε τοὺς ἐχθροὺς αὐτοῦ βούλεσθαι ζῆν μᾶλλον ἢ τεθνάναι, παράδειγμα τοῖς ἄλλοις, ἵν' ἴδωσιν ὅτι τοῖς λίαν ὑβριστικῶς πρὸς τὰ θεῖα διακειμένοις, οὐκ εἰς τοὺς παῖδας ἀποτίθενται τὰς τιμωρίας, ἀλλ' αὐτοὺς κακῶς ἀπολύουσι, μείζους καὶ χαλεπωτέρας, καὶ τὰς νόσους, ἢ τοῖς ἄλλοις ἀνθρώποις, προσβάλλοντες· τὸ μὲν γὰρ ἀποθανεῖν ἢ καμεῖν νομίμως κοινὸν ἅπασιν ὑμῖν ἐστίν· τὸ δ' οὕτως ἔχοντα τοσοῦτον χρόνον διατελεῖν, καὶ καθ' ἑκάστην ἡμέραν ἀποθνήσκοντα μὴ δύνασθαι τελευτῆσαι τὸν βίον, τούτοις μόνοις, προσήκει τοῖς τὰ τοιαῦτα, ἅπερ οὗτος, ἐξημαρτηκόσιν.*** (But this man, who is known to most of you, the gods have brought to such a pass that his enemies may well wish him to live rather than die, to be an example to other men, showing them that where men's conduct is too violently overbearing towards the gods, these do not inflict punishments on their children, but pay them out in person with misfortunes, bringing down on them calamities and diseases greater and more severe than fall to the lot of others. For death and sickness are admittedly common to all of you; but to continue so long in such a condition, and dying every day, yet not be able to have done with his life, this is the fate only of men who have committed such evil deeds as he has). Again, the Taxili, an Indian people, regarded any bodily sickness as disgraceful, and on its appearance gave themselves to the fire; ***αἴσχιστον δ' αὐτοῖς νομίζεσθαι νόσον σωματικήν· τὸν δ' ὑπονοήσαντα καθ' αὑτοῦ τοῦτο ἐξάγειν ἑαυτὸν διὰ πυρὸς νήσαντα πυράν,*** (But they hold a bodily disease to be most disgraceful; and the man who has formed a suspicion of the existence of such in himself, goes through the fire, after making a funeral pyre) says *Strabo*, Geograph. bk. XV. p. 716. 65. We should compare with this the suicide of Festus spoken of above and of the "Municeps" *Pliny* tells of.

seasons that have befallen, but when a man through indolence and a way of life such as we have noted (i.e. a very luxurious one), is filled full of fluxes and accumulations of wind like a sea, giving occasion to the noble sons of Asclepius to designate these complaints by the names of superfetations and catarrhs?" This was more than a mere expression of individual opinion; there is no doubt affections of the genital organs, more especially if their relation to sexual intercourse was known, belonged to the class of diseases held to be most disgraceful, [1] and the Poet is justified in saying:

> Diis me legitimis nimisque magnis
> Ut Phoebo puta, filioque Phoebi
> Curatum dare mentulam verebar.

(To the lawful gods, deities too exalted for me, such for instance as Phoebus, and Phoebus' son, I feared to entrust my member for cure.) Thus it was not to the "noble sons of Asclepius", in other words the Physicians, who treated freemen only, that patients resorted for help, but to the gods, or else to the medical underlings (**ὑπηρέται τῶν ἰατρῶν**,—subordinate assistants of the physicians), to the slave-doctors and quacks, who plied their trade in the doctor's shops,—establishments where, as we have seen above, paederasts and pathics foregathered. Exactly the same state of things prevailed down to the middle of the last Century; and to this day a majority of such sufferers rarely as a matter of fact come under any other hands.

The knowledge and observations of these Cullers of simples and Compounders of balsams, if indeed as a rule they really possessed the former, or knew how

[1] *Aretaeus*, De caus. et sign. chron. morb. (On the Causes and Symptoms of Chronic Diseases), bk. II. ch. 5., says indeed explicitly of gonorrhœa: *ἀνώλεθρον μὲν ἡ γονόῤῥοια, ἀτερπὲς δὲ καὶ ἀηδὲς μέσφι ἀκοῆς*, (Gonorrhœa is not indeed a dangerous complaint, but it is one that is hateful and abominable of repute).

to make the latter, necessarily perished on their decease, or at best were passed on by tradition to their successors in the doctor's shops, without professional Physicians or medical Science being one whit advantaged. To such men it was a matter of perfect indifference what was the origin of the disease for which they sold their powders and decoctions, for as *Plato* (De legg. IV. 720) says, they paid no attention to the existing conditions of disease, and did not care to give a thought to any such thing. But at any rate,—and this was the chief point,—the patient was spared a humiliating confession, and was glad enough to buy the privilege even at the cost of possible ruin to his health. We must further remember that the "filles de joie" in Greece and at Rome were mostly slave-women, who from the very fact of their status could make no claim to treatment by free-born physicians, and that during the flourishing period of Greek medicine under the Hippocratic school it was chiefly persons of the lowest station or else sailors and foreign traders and the like who sought enjoyment in the arms of prostitutes. Such men by their constant change of abode made all continued observation a simple impossibility, so that the very imperfect knowledge possessed by the scientifically trained Physicians with regard to diseases of the genitals and their consequences need occasion little surprise.

It is true of course that at the period of universal degradation of morals Physicians must have found no lack of opportunities for observation; but the great majority of them were incapable of utilizing these, actually blocked the way of set purpose, as we shall see presently, that led in the direction of more accurate investigation, or else troubled their heads little about the cultivation of Science or the systematic record of observations. The latter, if they had published them, whether in writing or orally, could only have been detrimental, particularly in the case of physicians of the character of Charidemus' medical attendant,[1] to their own interests. In fact they were bound to call all their subtlety into play for the express purpose of concealing the true cause of diseases of this type, a circumstance which no doubt we have to thank for a large number of the extravagant and often more than ludicrous statements regarding the origin of Venereal disease in the XVth. and XVIth. Centuries.

But as a matter of fact the public itself was no less careful to guard the secret, as we gather from *Martial*,[2] as well as from the fact that *Galen* felt himself constrained even in his day to compose a special Treatise on dissimulated diseases. This sort of intentional deception on the part of patients was

[1] *Martial*, bk. VI. Epigr. 31.,

Uxorem, Charideme, tuam scis ipse sinisque
A medico futui. Vis sine febre mori!

(Your wife, Charidemus, you know *to be entered by the doctor* of your own knowledge, and suffer it. You are fain to die without a fever!) Similar instances occurred equally in the time of Hippocrates, as we gather from the oath, in which stands the clause: *εἰς οἰκίας δὲ ὁκοσας ἂν ἐσίω, ἐσελεύσομαι ἐπ' ὠφελείῃ καμνόντων, ἐκτὸς ἐὼν πάσης ἀδικίης ἑκουσίης καὶ φθορίης τῆς τε ἄλλης, καὶ ἀφροδισίων ἔργων, ἐπὶ τε γυναικείων σωμάτων καὶ ἀνθρώπων ἐλευθέρων τε καὶ δούλων.* (Also into whatsoever houses I enter, I will go in there for the succour of sick persons, devoid of all voluntary offence and all evil-doing, and above all of all amorous practices, whether on the persons of women or free men or slaves). At the same time we learn from this document, that even then paederastia was widespread enough already, and that physicians were actually not ashamed to abuse their patients in this, as in other vicious ways! Undoubtedly it is from no other reason that the Turk at this very moment will rather expire than allow a clyster to be administered to him.

[2] *Martial*, bk. II. Epigr. 40.,

Omnes Tongilium medici iussere lavari,
O stulti! febrem creditis esse? gula est.

(All the doctors ordered Tongilius to bathe; fools! think you it is a fever? it is gluttony that is the matter). Comp. bk. XI. Epigr. 87.

so much the easier, as Physicians in those times, as said above, in virtue of their pathological views,—some of which indeed may very well have originated in this way,—were little accessible to the truth. For these reasons they deserved, at any rate to some degree, the satiric lash of Martial; and were very generally ridiculed by the more discerning of the laity. This comes out in the importaut words of *Appuleius* (Metamorph. X. 211.) as follows: "Crederes "et illam fluctuare tantum vaporibus febrium: nisi "quod et flebat: Heu medicorum ignavae "mentes! Quid venae pulsus, quid caloris imtem-"perantia, quid fatigatus anhelitus et utrimque secus "iactatae crebriter laterum mutuae vicissitudines? "Dii boni! Quam facilis, licet non "artifici medico, cuivis tamen docto "venereae cupidinis comprehensio, "cum videas aliquem sine corporis calore flagrantem." (Could you imagine her so tempest-tossed by the vapours of mere fever,—not to mention that she kept forever crying: "*Oh! the sorry wits of doctors!*" What means the throbbing vein, the excessive temperature, the labouring breath, and the hurried interchange of heaving flank, panting now on one side now on the other? *Great heavens! how easy the diagnosis, not of course for a medical expert, but for any one learned in the symptoms of love*, when you see a person burning, yet without bodily fever-heat).

But does all this justify us in casting a stone at our medical colleagues of Ancient times? For the last three hundred years we imagine ourselves clearly acquainted with Venereal disease and all its forms; yet how many a bubo has been mistaken for a strangulated hernia, anal callosity, or the like, how many a case of vaginal gonorrhœa for simple *fluor albus* (white discharge, leucorrhœa), how many a condyloma on the posteriors for hæmorrhoidal swellings, and accordingly not treated as the physician in *Juvenal, medico ridente* (the physician grinning the while), treated them,—that is duly cut away or ligatured?

Lastly to all these reasons was added further the *mildness and absence of danger characterizing the disease* itself, at any rate in the majority of instances,—as proved in our earlier investigations. To our own day genuine amateurs of Love, thanks to those who supply "advice, direction and information" on these subjects, endeavour as a rule, at any rate in the earlier stages, to cure without assistance the wounds received in the fight. This was equally so in Antiquity, as the following significant passage of *Galen* [1] shows: "This is pretty well all I have to say at present as to ephemeral fevers. For *patients who have contracted fever consequent upon a bubo, do not consult*

[1] *Galen*, Method, medendi, bk. VIII. ch. 6., edit. Kühn Vol. X. p. 580., *σχεδὸν εἴρηταί μοι πάντα περὶ τῶν ἐφημέρων πυρετῶν· οἱ γὰρ ἐπὶ βουβῶσι πυρέξαντες οὐδὲ πυνθάνονται τῶν ἰατρῶν ὅ τι χρὴ ποιεῖν· ἀλλὰ τοῦθ' ἕλκους ἐφ' ᾧπερ ἂν ὁ βουβὼν αὐτοῖς εἴη γεγεννημένος, αὐτοῦ τε τοῦ βουβῶνος προνοησάμενοι, λούονται κατὰ τὴν παρακμὴν τοῦ γενομένου κ. τ. λ.* (for translation sec text above). The *Diatriton* mentioned in the next sentence was the fast till the third day, which was generally prescribed by *Thessalus* and the *methodic* school. For this reason it was called *διάτριτον θεσσαλείον* (Thessalus' *diatriton*), and the physicians who held to it *διατριτάριοι ἰατροὶ* (doctors of the *diatriton*), as we gather from the subsequent statement of *Galen*. Of the ephemera in case of buboes *Galen* also speaks, ad Glauconem meth. med. bk. I. ch. 2., edit. Kühn Vol. XI. p. 6., *καὶ οἱ ἐπὶ βουβῶσι δὲ πυρετοὶ τούτου τοῦ γένους εἰσὶ, πλὴν εἰ μὴ χωρὶς ἕλκους φανεροῦ γένοιντο*, (Moreover the fevers that follow on buboes are of this kind, the exception being if they have not been without open ulceration). *Celsus* moreover, De re med. bk. VI. ch., 18., says à propos of diseases of the genitals, that he means to undertake their description, quia in vulgus eorum curatio praecipue cognoscenda est, quae invitissimus quisque alteri ostendit, (because a general acquaintance is particularly desirable with the means of curing such complaints as every man is most reluctant to make known to another).

physicians as to what they must do; but after first treating the ulcer which occasioned the bubo and then the bubo itself, bathe after the abatement of the severity of the attack. After that if any one says a word as to the "diatriton" (fast till the third day), all laugh and declare him a precisian: I suppose because they are of the opinion that nothing must be resigned to nature that is not invariably there."

We know quite well that the Ancients called all glandular swellings buboes, and that they were perfectly well acquainted [1] with those glandular swellings in the arm-pits and the groin which follow upon ulcers of the fingers and toes; but this in no way justifies us in referring the above passage, which is certainly written in a general sense, *solely* to suchlike buboes and not equally to those in the soft tissues; more particularly as *Galen,* in the place where he is dealing expressly with the treatment of buboes and the phlegmonous affections preceding them and occasioning ulcers (loco citato p. 881), explicitly mentions phlegmonous symptoms as **κατὰ αἰδοῖον** (affecting the privates) and **γυναικὶ κατὰ μήτραν ἢ αἰδοῖον** (in women affecting womb and privates),—loco citato p. 893. Hence we think ourselves jus-

[1] *Galen,* Meth. med., bk. XIII. ch. 5. p. 881., *οὕτως οὖν καὶ δἰ ἕλκος ἐν δακτύλῳ γινόμενον ἤτοι ποδὸς ἢ χειρὸς οἱ κατὰ τὸν βουβῶνα καὶ τὴν μασχάλην ἀδένες ἐξαίρονταί τε καὶ φλεγμαίνουσι, τοῦ καταῤῥέοντος ἐπ᾽ ἄκρον τὸν κῶλον αἵματος ἀπολαβόντες πρῶτοι· καὶ κατὰ τράχηλον δὲ και παρ᾽ ὦτα πολλάκις ἐξήρθησαν ἀδένες, ἑλκῶν γενομένων ἤτοι κατὰ τὴν κεφαλὴν ἢ τὸν τράχηλον ἤ τι τῶν πλησίων μορίων· ὀνομάζουσι δὲ τοὺς οὕτως ἐξαρθέντας ἀδένας βουβῶνας.* (Thus then in consequence of an ulcer that has formed in a finger or toe the glands of the groin and the arm-pit become swollen and inflamed, having been the first to receive back the blood that flows down to the extremity of the limb. Moreover on the neck and about the ears glands are frequently swollen, when ulcers have been set up in the head or neck or any of the neighbouring parts. And glands swollen up in this way are known as buboes).

tified in drawing attention to the passage as containiug an indication of the reason why ulcers of the genital organs pursued a milder course and admitted of an easier cure in Antiquity, because the *ephemera* evidently facilitated the assimilation and eliminatian of the contagion, this taking place either at the point primarily attacked, or else occurring because it (the ephemeral fever) led to an enhanced activity of the cutaneous glands by provoking an exanthematous eruption.

§ 39.

But for no small part of this reluctance on the part of patients the Physicians were themselves to blame. We have no wish in this place to enlarge upon the possibility of professional indiscretion in their case, though long ago the Hippocratic masters saw themselves constrained to guard their scholars against it. [1] Of far greater weight was the nature of the *treatment*, especially that applied to ulcers of all kinds, which was excellently adapted to fill sufferers with fear and trembling. Already *Hippocrates* [2] taught that ulcers with callous margins must be cauterized or else cut away with the knife. *Galen* [3] declares himself even more plainly in the same sense: "But if the margins of the ulcer merely are discoloured and callous, they must be removed right to where the healthy flesh begins. Supposing this condition to have extended more widely, then the question

[1] Hippocratic Oath, in *Hippocrates*, Vol. I. p. 2., *ἃ δ᾽ ἂν ἐν θεραπείῃ ἤ ἴδω ἢ ἀκούσω, ἢ καὶ ἄνευ θεραπείης, κατὰ βίον ἀνθράπων, ἃ μὴ χρή ποτε ἐκκαλέεσθαι ἔξω, σιγήσομαι, ἄῤῥητα ἡγεύμενος εἶναι τὰ τοιαῦτα.* (and whatsoever I may see or hear in my practice, or even apart from practice, connected with men's life, what ought not in any case to be revealed, this I will say nought of, holding such secrets inviolable).

[2] *Hippocrates*, De locis in homine, edit. Kühn Vol. II. p. 139.

[3] *Galen*, Method. medendi bk. IV. ch. 2., edit. Kühn Vol. X. p. 238.

arises,—whether we ought to cut away all the diseased tissue, or prefer a more tedious method of cure. It is natural and necessary in this case to consult the inclination of the patient; for whereas some prefer to avoid the knife and submit to a more tedious treatment, others on the contrary are ready for anything, so long as they get cured." The same procedure was adopted with ulcers of the genitals, especially gangrenous ulcers, as is proved at once by the passage already quoted on p. 176 of Vol. II above.

The Asiatic, for whom the genital organs were an object of veneration, was no doubt horrified, as the Turk is to this day, [1] at the idea of any such operation on himself; while the licentious Roman, who must have dreaded its very probable result in the entire loss of the further use and enjoyment of the parts in question, [2] sought any other means for choice, preferred to have recourse to Priapus or even resorted to suicide, like the *Municeps* of

[1] *Oppenheim*, loco citato p. 123. The Eastern Christian woman in question actually assured Niebuhr herself that she would never agree to the knife being applied to her husband's genitals, and yet in this case it was merely a question of dividing an over short *frenulum*. *Michaelis*, "Mosaisches Recht", (Mosaic Law), Vol. IV. p. 3.

[2] Examples of such are at any rate plentiful in *Martial*, e.g. bk. XI. Epigr. 75.,

Curandum penem commisit Bacchara Graecus
Rivali medico: Bacchara Gallus erit.

(Bacchara entrusted the cure of his member to a rival doctor: Bacchara was a Greek, he will now be a Gaul,—"Gallus", castrated Priest of Cybelé).

bk. II. Epigr. 46.,

Quae tibi non stabat, praecisa est mentula, Glypte.
Demens, cum ferro quid tibi? Gallus eras.

(Your member, Glyptus, that you could never get to stand erect, has been cut. Fool,—why! what had you to do with the knife? You were a "Gallus" already).

bk. III. Epigr. 81.,

Abscissa est quare Samia tibi mentula testa,
Si tibi tam gratus, Baetice, cunnus erat?

(Why has your member been cut with a Samian potsherd, if the female organ, Baeticus, was so dear to you)?

Pliny mentioned on p. 257, before he trusted himself to the physicians who ever since the Carnifex (Butcher) Archagathus had appeared at Rome, strove to rival one another in infatuation for cautery and amputation. In any case it was only the direst necessity[1] that drove the sufferer under such circumstances to the physician; while the latter had really and truly no reason for enquiring into the origin of the evil, as very often absolutely no alternative was left him but to grasp the knife or cauterizing iron. In this way medical procedure could not but have fallen into disrepute, while physicians were in most instances necessarily deprived of all opportunity of systematic observation.

Whether there were other factors as well to induce the old Physicians to apply the ordinary treatment of ulcers in general to those of the genital organs, we cannot indeed as yet for the time being determine. Certainly the conjecture is an obvious one that they may well have had an inkling of the specific nature of such ulcers, and that it was not merely the local mischief they sought to put a stop to by early application of cautery and knife. However it is only further and more careful investigations that must be allowed to decide the point,—the more so, as the

[1] *Scribonius Largus*, De compos. medicam. edit. Bernhold, Strasburg 1786., p. 2., writes in his Introduction to the Callistus: Siquidem verum est, antiquos herbis ac radicibus eorum corporis vitia curasse: quia etiam tunc genus mortalium i n t e r i n i t i a n o n f a c i l e s e f e r r o c o m m i t t e b a t. Quod etiam nunc plerique faciunt, ne dicam omnes; et, nisi magna compulsi necessitate speque ipsius salutis, non patiunter sibi fieri, quae sane vix sunt toleranda. (If in fact it is true that the Ancients cured the diseases of their bodies by means of herbs and roots: for even then the race of mortals *at the beginning did not readily entrust its cure to the knife.* And this is what even now the most part do; and, unless constrained by a sore need and by the hope of actual recovery, do not suffer operations to be performed on them, which in very deed are hardly to be endured).

general *views as to the formation of ulcers* held by the Ancients seem in many respects to tell against it. Thus *Galen*[1] says: "The mode in which these (ulcers involving destruction of substance) are set up however is twofold; they arise either by removal of surrounding tissue (**ἐκ περιαιρέσεως**) or by eating away (**ἐξ ἀναβρώσεως**). How the former acts is well known. As to the eating away, if it proceed from the inward parts of the organism, it is an outcome of the evil humours; but if it arise from outside, then it is a result of the physician's remedial measures or of fire." From this we gather that all ulcers of the genitals, as well as others, which did not result from the action either of remedial measures or of fire, were held as being necessarily an outcome of the evil humours of the body. Further, that this view was not in any way peculiar to the time of Galen, but was a direct and necessary consequence of the further development of the pathology of "humours," follows from the circumstance that we find the same opinion expressed by *Hippocrates.*[2] Again *Plato* shared the latter author's general doctrine of *apostasis* (suppurative inflammation taking off evil humours) in his "Timaeus", where he derives from the white phlegm, striking outwards to the skin, cutaneous eruptions, rashes and the like maladies, from the acrid, salty phlegm on the other hand the fluxes of all types, bearing different names according to the different parts of the body affected.

If we do not choose to infer from this the proof of a then occurring, genuine and consistent genesis of the affections peculiar to the genitals, we are bound at any rate to admit that such a view must

[1] *Galen*, Method. medendi bk. IV. ch. 1., edit. Kühn Vol. X. p. 233.

[2] *Hippocrates*, Coact. praenot., edit. Kühn Vol. I. p. 343., *τὰ ἑρπηστικὰ ὑπεράνω βουβῶνος πρὸς κενεῶνα καὶ ἥβην γινόμενα, σημαίνει κοιλίην πονηρευομένην*. (Spreading eruptions that appear above the groin towards the flank and pubes point to an evil condition of stomach).

necessarily have debarred all thought of any *specific* character as belonging to ulcers of these organs,—the more so as to this very day we look in vain for any clear conception of really characteristic symptoms marking out Venereal ulcers in particular. Further, the knowledge that ulcers of the genitals were contracted through sexual intercourse, lacked entirely, so far as the ancient Physicians were concerned, the necessary confirmation and authority to induce them to make a special and distinctive class of morbid process to include them, because as a rule they paid no sort of attention to the occasioning cause, unless in virtue of its being still present and active, or else by the necessity for its elimination, it could afford some indication for therapeutic purposes. *Galen* brings this out best and most clearly in the following passage:[1] "Moreover it will be a fitting occasion now to make it clear that not one of the causes directly occasioning the diathesis, or particular condition of body, will give any indication as to treatment; guiding signs for the purpose must rather be gathered from the complaint itself. What is to be done in any individual case depends on the immediate purpose and the nature of the part attacked, on the predominant temperament and the like facts. For to put it shortly, *in no case can an indication as to what is beneficial be taken from any one of the factors that are no longer existent*,—i.e. in actual operation. But as it often happens that in order to diagnose some affection that cannot be recognized either by help of ratiocination or by the senses, we are obliged to inquire into the cause that occasioned it, laymen conclude the guiding signs for remedial treatment to be taken from the same source. But this is by no means so. This may be plainly seen in those instances where the diathesis is quite well known in all its details; for whether it be *ecchymosis or ulcer-*

[1] *Galen*, Method. medendi bk. IV. ch. 3., edit. Kühn Vol. X. pp. 243 sqq.

ation or erysipelas or putrescent ulcer (σηπεδὼν) *or phlegmonous affection in any organ, it is perfectly useless to trace out the cause that occasioned it* (αἴτιον ποίησαν), *if this latter is now no longer active.* On the other hand for any affection, a clear insight into which is lacking, a knowledge of the occasioning cause is useful."

This principle was equally applied to affections of the genitals, the antecedent act of coition being regarded as affording absolutely no help in diagnosis, as we see from the passage of *Galen* to be next discussed. In this passage the declaration of a gonorrhœal patient to the effect that the women with whom he had connection suffered no less than himself from the malady, was entirely without influence on our athor in the way of inducing him to assume and lay down a *specific* type of gonorrhœa. Under these circumstances it is really a matter for no surprise [1] that the old Physicians in discussing affections of the genitals never allege sexual intercourse as an occasioning factor amongst others; and the conclusion drawn that such affections in Antiquity were not contracted by coition, *because* the ancient Writers do not definitely and in every single instance assign this as a cause, evidences really and truly merely the absence of any accurate study of their works and the knowledge of their views that is acquired as a result of such study. It is abundantly clear however that the neglect of the etiological factors referred to led eventually to their being completely overlooked; and it is no less obvious

[1] Hence *Hensler* is quite right in saying as he does (History of Venereal Disease Vol. I. p. 298.): "It is extraordinary that a precision should have been demanded on the part of the Ancients, which they could not possibly possess, such indeed as cannot be expected in any disease during its childhood. As to requiring them to have announced the cause of the evil with certainty and clearness, this is always only the result of time and reiterated experience."

that this must needs have been a source of manifold mistakes, which degraded the physician in the eyes of the non-professional laity, very often made him ridiculous by reason of this ignorance, and brought down, as we have seen, many a cut of the satirist's whip on his devoted shoulders. But how many of our colleagues are there not at the present day whom Venereal disease involves in the same doubts and difficulties?

However it may perhaps be suggested that, although the ancient Physicians did not feel themselves obliged to make any mention of sexual intercourse as cause of affections of the genitals, they cannot for all that have failed to notice the phænomena of infection. To say nothing of the fact that in no small proportion of instances affections of the genitals under the favouring conditions previously described did not as a matter of fact arise through infection, but actually in a sense spontaneously, [1] and further that to this day we possess absolutely no criterion to distinguish such diseases arising in this way,—for it is only superficial and indolent observers that deny the possibility of such origination altogether,—apart from all this, the view which the Ancients took as a whole of the general question of infection was one in the highest degree inadequate. For this state of things,

[1] *Galen*, De locis affect. bk. VI. ch. 5., edit. Kühn Vol. VIII. p. 422., *φαινομένου δὲ σαφῶς, ἰσχυροτάτην ἔχειν τὴν δύναμιν ἐνίας τῶν οὐσιῶν, ὑπόλοιπον ἂν εἴη ζητεῖν, εἰ διαφθορά τις ἐν τοῖς ζώοις δύναται γενέσθαι τηλικαύτη τὸ μέγεθος, ὡς ἰῷ θηρίου παραπλησίαν ἔχειν ποιότητά τε καὶ δύναμιν.* (But it being plainly evident that there are some creatures have the power developed in the highest degree, it would be superfluous to enquire whether there can exist in animals a destructive force so great in amount as to possess a quality and power similar to poison in snakes). In fact he answers this question in the affirmative so far as regards semen and menstrual blood, appealing to the poisonous quality of the spittle of dogs in rabies.

as *Heyne* long ago pointed out, the **τὸ θεῖον** (the divine element), or in other words the prevalent opinion that infectious diseases were an infliction of the offended deity, is mainly responsible. In these very diseases of the genitals, we have in fact seen how they were ascribed to the wrath of Dionysus and Priapus; and how long such ideas lasted, and how intimately they were interwoven with the life of the people, may be gauged by the circumstance that even the Christian Fathers themselves took every pains and used every effort to maintain them.

Now is it really in any way reasonable to expect the physicians of those times to have so completely extricated themselves from the predominant range of ideas? and have we any right to abuse them for their beliefs at the present moment, when in our own day there are to be found not a few physicians who deny absolutely the contagiousness of Venereal disease under its different forms? All the old practitioners could do was to draw attention to the fact that underlying the **τὸ θεῖον** there lurked some natural cause, and this view Hippocrates did actually maintain in his writings. As to the indicative signs of this cause perceptible by the senses, as to the

[1] *Heyne*, De febribus epidemicis Romae falso in pestium censum relatis Progr., (On certain Epidemic Fevers at Rome incorrectly referred to the Category of Plagues,—a Graduation Exercise), Göttingen 1782., p. 4. (Works vol. III.), Hoc enim erat illud, quod antiquitatem omnino ab subtiliore naturae adeoque et morborum cognitione revocavit et retraxit, quod ea, quae ad interiorem eius notitiam spectabant, inprimisque quae ab solenni rerum cursu recedebant, ad religiones metumque deorum referebantur. (For indeed this was the cause which withdrew and kept back Antiquity generally from a more precise acquaintance with nature and so with diseases, viz. that everything which regarded the more intimate knowledge of it, and above all everything that was somewhat out of the common course of things, became a matter of religious scruples and superstition). Comp. *C. F. H. Marx*, Origines Contagii, (Original Causes of Contagion) Carlrühe and Baden 1824.

material substance, whatever it may be, that communicates infection, into all this they could hardly be expected to initiate investigations, [1] deficient as they were in every sort of aid and assistance for the task. For I ask, have we, in spite of all our researches, thus far attained to any satisfactory and certain results? Could the Anti-Contagionists ever have come forward at all, if we had been successful in demonstrating the contagion to be perceptible to the senses?

Besides all this, we actually find to the present day that in the countries in question the contagion exhibits but a low degree of virulence, and only under epidemic influence, as at the epoch of the Athenian Plague, did it assume a virulent character at all,—a fact that will be made yet clearer in our Continuation of the History of Venereal Disease. But wherever the contagion did exhibit this virulence of character, the ulcers that were set up passed over as a rule into gangrenous mortification, or else the physicians either exterminated it altogether by the actual cautery or removed it along with the part in which it had established itself. Thus

[1] As a rule they ascribed the origin of the contagion to *σῆψις* (putrefaction), and from their point of view septic, or putrefactive, diseases were pretty much the same as infectious (*Galen*, De febr. diff. I. 4.), Hence it would seem probable the *ἕλκεα σηπεδόνα* (putrefying ulcers) were at any rate partly looked at in the same light,—a circumstance of the highest importance as bearing on ulcers of the genitals, as in that case these latter are manifestly represented as being infectious. It is to be hoped that experts will give their decision as to this. At any rate as early as *Galen's* time (De locis effect. bk. VI. ch. 5., edit. Kühn Vol. VIII. p. 422.) the action of contagion was regarded as analogous to that of the electric ray-fish (*νάρκη θαλάττιος*) and the magnet, and the conclusion was drawn: *ταῦτά τε οὖν ἱκανὰ τεκμήρια τοῦ σμικρὰν οὐσίαν ἀλλοιώσεις μεγίστας ἐργάζεσθαι μόνῳ τῷ ψαῦσαι.* (these then are sufficient evidences of the fact that a small creature may produce very great variations by contact alone).

any further spread of the contagion in its original form was not to be expected, as in patients of the sort there can be no doubt all desire for coition must have been destroyed.

If we now bring together the results of our discussion so far, we shall find reason to believe that, speaking generally, the ancient physicians,—that is physicians properly so called,—possessed but scanty opportunities, especially in the case of women, [1] of observing with any precision the origin and course of affections of the genital organs, for it was mostly only the malignant forms of these that came under their notice, and these were of their very nature, except when epidemic conditions were at work, necessarily of infrequent occurrence. Their pathological views stood in the way of unprejudiced observation, *conspicuous* characteristic symptoms were as little to be found then as they are nowadays, any adequate knowledge of the material *substrata* of contagions was lacking to them in these as in other forms of disease, and thus they felt no direct inducement to class the *primary* affections of the genitals as formiug a special category of disease.

Then again with regard to the *secondary* symptoms, the ancient practitioners in the cases treated by them made the occurrence of such all but impossible, for scalpel and cauterizing iron either entirely eradicated the contagion along with its material *substratum*, or else removed it with all speed before it could be reabsorbed into the system. Even when these did nevertheless appear, in some instances too great an interval of time intervened, in others the parts attacked were too remote from the spot primarily

[1] These were treated by the female physicians(*αἱ ἰατρίναι*), *Galen*, De loc. effect. VI. 5., Vol. VIII. p. 414.) and the midwives, who had to examine the female genitals in cases of disease affecting them, and report the results to the Physicians. *Σκέψασθαι κέλευσον τὴν μαῖαν ἁψαμένην τοῦ τῆς μήτρας αὐχένος*, (bid the midwife examine by touch the neck of the womb), *Galen* says, loco citato p. 433.

affected for it to have been possible for them to be referred to any direct inter-communication. Indeed this was made an actual impossibility in most cases, as it was just those very spots that are the usual seat of the secondary affections which were attacked primarily in consequence of the different modes of *Venus illegitima* (abnormal love) with such extreme frequency as to make it barely practicable for the keenest eye at a diagnosis to discover any actual distinction between the two,—and this without taking into account the circumstance that in view of the pronounced tendency conditioned bv climatic causes for the morbid process to strike outwards to the external skin, mischief in the mucous membranes and bones must necessarily have fallen to a considerable extent into the background.

If circumstances put it out of the power of the ancient Physicians to unite under one whole the separate forms of Venereal disease, to look at the morbid process in its entirety, it is no less self-evident that for the same reasons they could have found no occasion to invent a *special name* for a thing that was simply invisible to them. Hence the conclusion drawn that, because no such special name is found, *therefore* Venereal disease cannot have existed, strictly speaking requires no further consideration. Still, granting for the sake of argument that they had recognized at any rate the generic difference of the primary affections, were they therefore bound to introduce a special name for them? *Galen* shall supply the answer. He says, mentioning [1] that the old Physicians possessed no special name for depression of the skull in conjunction with fissure of the bone: "It is better to give a clear description than to fall back miserably on barbarous names, which the younger physicians have invented in great plenty." In another place [2] he finds fault with the different

[1] *Galen*, De morborum causis, ch. 9., edit. Kühn Vol. VII. p. 39.

[2] *Galen*, Methodus medendi bk. II. ch. 2., edit Kühn Vol. X. p. 84.

designations given to ulcers, and then proceeds: "If I consented to enumerate all the names, I should be running the risk of deliberately teaching what I recommend others to avoid, when I say that the true searcher after truth must needs withdraw his attention from the nomenclature that has grown up, and fix his eyes on the actual fact."

While these expressions of opinion demonstrate the uselessness of the names, they show at the same time that no inconsiderable number of such names must no doubt have been in existence. So far as affections of the genitals are concerned, not only is this indicated by the Greek **φθινὰς,**—wasting disease and the Latin *robigo,*—ulcerous sore, not to mention the ambiguous **ἄνθραξ,**—carbuncle, malignant pustule, but *Celsus* expressly declares the fact, saying (Bk. VI ch. 18) at the beginning of his description of Diseases of the sexual parts: "Proxima sunt ea, quae ad partes obscoenas "pertinent, quarum apud Graecos vocabula et toler-"abilius se habent et accepta iam usu sunt, cum "omni fere medicorum volumine atque sermone "iactentur, apud nos foediora verba, ne consuetudine "quidem aliqua verecundius loquentium commendata "sunt." (Next come such words as apply to the parts of shame, the Greek names for which are at once less offensive and are now sanctioned by usage, as they are constantly occurring in every medical book and medical discussion, whereas our native (Latin) names are coarser and are not even recommended by any custom on the part of those who speak with some regard to modesty). Celsus himself communicates but few of these words, for he wrote *simul et pudorem et artis praecepta servans,* (observing at once the laws of modesty and the rules of his art); while between him and the writers of the Hippocratic school medical Literature is all but a blank to us. The same is the case between *Celsus* and *Galen*; and of a period so important for our purpose as that of the licentious Emperors, likewise not a single independent medical Writer has come down to us. In fact even the Fragments of the Compiler Oribasius, lately made known to the world by Mai, contain, alas! nothing more than the headings of the Chapters most interesting to us.

In such a condition of things it is really verging on the borders of folly to hope to give a dogmatic and decisive judgement as to the knowledge of Venereal disease possesed by the Physicians of Antiquity,—the more so as the extant medical Works have never once been adequately ransacked, as *Naumann* only the other day proved in the case of *Galen*. But of a surety it is easier to maintain the Ancients knew nothing of Venereal disease, than to devote the best part of a man's life-time to the investigation, how much the Ancients did actually know about it!

§ 40.

If we turn now from these discussions to the statements of the ancient Physicians themselves, there are two different ways in which we may regard them ourselves and present them to the reader's eyes. *Either* we put down consecutively everything that has been said by one and the same Author and examine each single datum we owe to him by itself, *or* we bring together the data given by different writers on one and the same subject, and then compare these one with another. The first way, the one generally followed by historians of Venereal disease hitherto, gives us it is true the general results of the knowledge possessed by the several writers on the different forms of Venereal disease; but, seeing on the one hand we do not in most instances actually possess all the works of our Author, while on the other even when we do, we are not justified in looking upon his report as embodying a *résumé* of all the knowledge of his time, the advantages of such a way of dealing with the subject are on the whole but slight, while it has the *dis*advantage of rendering considerably more difficult the general survey of the information possessed by Antiquity as to Venereal disease, which nevertheless is really our immediate and capital concern, and cannot fail moreover to occasion a host of contradictions.

The second way not only relieves us from this disadvantage, but also ensures us that general Survey which is peculiarly necessary, and to the absence of which the circumstance is chiefly to be ascribed that it has been possible hitherto to convince the opponents of the antiquity of Venereal disease only in the most incomplete manner of its actual existence in those times at all, as the exposition of the contrary view, in itself incomplete, was bound in its fragmentary presentment to seem even more incomplete still. Of course, in following the second way of exposition, there is an unavoidable dislocation of the data communicated by each individual writer, but this is a thing of but little moment, more particularly as its inconvenience is minimised by our giving the passages, when quoted for the first time, *in extenso*, so as to have on subsequent occasions merely to refer back to them. Again the want of a clear marking of dates, a point undoubtedly of great importance in historical researches, is readily obviated by our laying down the available fixed points of our chronology in the general Survey that forms a necessary conclusion to our exposition.

No doubt *Hensler* and *Alex. Simon* had already struck out this second way of exposition; but the latter writer merely examined the data of the several Writers by themselves without making any effort to build them up into one whole. To do this was, it is true, a proceeding quite foreign to the method adopted by the Ancients, but for our own time, accustomed as we now are to demand a systematic exposition of a subject, it seems absolutely indispensible. *Hensler* on the other hand in his treatment of the question fixed his particular attention solely on the Middle Ages, and made it his immediate aim merely to prove that previously to the ninetieth year of the XVth Century local affections of the genital organs were already well known, and had been subjected to treatment.[1]

Now with regard to the actual exposition that follows, we shall refrain in it as much as possible from going into particulars, such as the text itself or the views of the Authors might seem to make obligatory, as the needful space fails us, at any rate for the present. Moreover the matter coming under review has been discussed already by many others, while as for critical elucidations, let them be as pressingly required as they may, we lack all the necessary *apparatus criticus*. In fact in the case of several Writers, the translation, let alone the original text, was with difficulty accessible, for which reason many a passage of those already known may perhaps have been passed by unregarded. A complete collection of all passages, including those still unknown,—for the harvest as was mentioned above has by no means been all reaped,—will certainly not be demanded by any reasonable reader from a Student of thirty, for hardly even a greybeard Enquirer surely could boast of having read all printed works of the ancient Physicians. For the rest, our present object is not at all to give an exhaustive exposition of all the ideas and observations of ancient Physicians as to affections of the genital organs; it only concerns us here to bring together what is true and directly

[1] *Hensler*, History of Venereal Disease Vol. I. p. 191. He says explicitly: "However I do not propose to follow up to its original cause the history either of gonorrhœa, valuable as the results might be, nor that of any other complaint liable to occur. It is sufficient for my purpose to elucidate my Authorities for Venereal disease at its first appearance from the circumstances of their epoch, though no doubt incidentally the eye must sometimes take a wider sweep and look further and higher.

available for our task. Under this head wonld certainly seem to come the following seven points:

1. Gonorrhœa (*Clap*).

Nimia profusio seminis,—excessive flow of seed (Celsus), *γονόῤῥοια*.

Gonorrhœa, the name of which is compounded of *γονή* (badly made semen) and *ῥεῖν* (to flow), [1] consists in an affection of the seminal vessels, not of the private parts themselves, which merely serve as the road for the excretion of the seed. [2] *Two kinds* of gonorrhœa must be distinguished, according as the malady is, or is not, combined with erection of the penis. [3]

[1] *Galen*, De loc. affect. bk. VI. 6. (VIII. p. 439.), *τὸ δὲ τῆς γονοῤῥοίας ὄνομα προφανῶς ἐστι σύνθετον ἐκ τῆς γονῆς καὶ τοῦ ῥεῖν· ὀνομάζεται γὰρ τὸ σπέρμα καὶ γονός.* (Now the name of gonorrhœa is evidently compounded from the words *γονὴ* and *ῥεῖν*. For the semen (*σπέρμα*) is also known as *γονός*.

[2] *Galen*, loco cit. p. 441., *γονόῤῥοια μὲν οὖν τῶν σπερματικῶν ὀργάνων ἐστὶ πάθος, οὐ τῶν αἰδοίων, οἷς ὁδῷ χρῆται πρὸς ἔκρουν ἡ γονή·* (Gonorrhœa accordingly is an affection of the seminal organs, not of the privates, which the seed merely uses as its passage for excretion).—De usu partium bk. XIV. ch. 10. (IV. p. 188.), *κατὰ δὲ τὰς γονοῤῥοίας αὐτῶν μόνων ἐστὶ τὸ πάθημα τῶν σπερματικῶν ἀγγείων.* (But in gonorrhœas the affection is one solely of the seminal vessels).

[3] *Galen*, De symptom. caus. bk. II. ch. 2. (VII. p. 150.), *ὥσπέρ γε καὶ τῆς γονοῤῥοίας ἡ ἑτέρα διαφορά· εἰ μὲν γὰρ μετὰ ἐντάσεως τοῦ αἰδοίου γένοιτο, οἷον σπασμός ἐστιν, εἰ δὲ χωρὶς ταύτης, ἀῤῥωστία τῆς καθεκτικῆς δυνάμεως.* (As is the case too with the second variety of gonorrhœa. For if it be combined with tension of the private, it is a sort of spasm, but if without this, a weakness of retentive force). — Bk. III. ch. 11. (p. 267.), *καὶ μὴν καὶ αἱ γονόῤῥοιαι, χωρὶς μὲν τοῦ συνεντείνεσθαι τὸ αἰδοῖον,*

Gonorrhœa with erection of the penis is called sometimes *Satyriasis* or *Satyriasmus* sometimes *Priapism*, [1] and is a species of cramp, [2] which however only attacks the penis, belongs to the category of

ἀρρωστίᾳ τῆς καθεκτικῆς δυνάμεως τῆς ἐν τοῖς σπερματικοῖς ἀγγείοις· ἐντεινομένου δέ πως, οἷον σπασμῷ τινι παραπλήσιον πασχόντων ἐπιτελοῦνται. (Moreover also gonorrhœas, if not combined with a state of tension of the private, are from a weakness of retentive power in the seminal vessels; but if there is any tension, they are marked by a sort of spasm resembling that of spasmodic patients).

[1] *Galen*, De tumoribus praeternat., ch. 14. (VII. p. 728.), καθάπερ καὶ τὰς κατὰ φύσιν ἐντάσεις τῶν αἰδοίων μὴ καθισταμένας τινὲς ὀνομάζουσι σατυριασμὸν, τινὲς δὲ πριαπισμόν. (Precisely as tensions of the privates not originating in a natural way are called by some Satyriasis, by others Priapism). The latter, as we gather from *Galen*, Method. XIV. ch. 7. (X. p. 968.), by the younger physicians.

[2] *Galen*, De usu partium bk. XIV. ch. 10. (IV. p. 187.), πηλίκην γὰρ ἔχει δύναμιν εἰς τὴν τῶν περιεχομένων ἔκκρισιν ὁ οἷον σπασμὸς τῶν μορίων τοῖς ἀφροδισίοις ἑπόμενος, ἔνεστί σοι μαθεῖν ἔκ τε τῶν ἐπιληψίων τῶν μεγάλων κἀκ τοῦ παθήματος, ὃ δὴ καλεῖται γονόῤῥοια· κατὰ μὲν γὰρ τὰς ἰσχυρὰς ἐπιληψίας, ὅτι τὸ πᾶν σῶμα σπᾶται σφοδρῶς, καὶ σὺν αὐτῷ τὰ γεννητικὰ μόρια, διὰ τοῦτο ἐκκρίνεται τὸ σπέρμα· κατὰ δὲ τὰς γονοῤῥοίας αὐτῶν μόνων ἐστὶ τὸ πάθημα τῶν σπερμάτικῶν ἀγγείων· ὁποίαν οὖν τάσιν ἐν τοῖς εἰρημένοις νοσήμασι πάσχει, τοιαύτην ἴσχοντα ταῖς συνουσίαις ἐκκρίνει τὸ σπέρμα. (for how great a force in the way of stimulating the secretion of the surrounding glands is exerted by the species of spasm of the parts that follows on amatory action, you may learn from the seizures in the more serious forms of epilepsy, as also from the affection which is known as gonorrhœa. For in violent epileptic seizures, because the whole body is strongly convulsed, and with it the procreative parts, for this reason the semen is secreted; whereas in gonorrhœas the affection is one solely of the actual seminal vessels. Accordingly whatever tension these parts undergo in the diseases mentioned is the same in degree as they experience on secreting semen in acts of sexual intercoorse). Comp. Note 2.

the emphysemata, or inflations, [1] and is conditioned by an afflux of the humours, particularly of conspissated or badly compounded humours. [2] However this last phænomenon is only a symptom of that morbid lasciviousness which *Paulus Aegineta* entitles Priapism, while he designates the condition connected with it by the name of Satyriasis, this having its origin in an inflammatory affection of the seminal vessels. [3]

[1] *Galen*, Method. medendi bk. XIV. ch. 7. (X. p. 967.), *αὐτίκα γέ τοι πάθος ἐστὶ τὸ καλούμενον ὑπὸ τῶν νεωτέρων πριαπισμὸς, ἐπειδὴ τὸ αἰδοῖον ἀκουσίως ἐξαίρεται, τῶν οὕτω διακειμένων· ὃ θεασάμενός τις τῶν ἐν τοῖσδε τοῖς ὑπομνήμασι προγεγυμνασμένων ἑτοίμως γνωριεῖ τοῦ τῶν ἐμφυσημάτων ὑπάρχον γένους·* (The immediate complaiut is what is called by the younger school Priapism, when the private part is erected involuntarily in patients so afflicted; and if any of my readers who have been prepared beforehand in the present memoranda see this, he will readily recognize the phænomenon to belong to the class of the emphysemata, or inflations). De sympt. caus. bk. III. ch. 11. (VII. p. 266).

[2] *Galen*, De causis morb. ch. 6. (VII. p. 22.), *καὶ ὡς ἐνίοτε μὲν εἰλικρινὴς ἐπιῤῥεῖ τούτων ἕκαστος τῶν χυμῶν, ἐνίοτε δ' ἀλλήλοις ἐπιμίγνυνται· καὶ ὡς αἱ τῶν οἰδούντων — μορίων διαθέσεις ἐντεῦθεν ἐπὶ πλεῖστον ποικίλλονται . . . καὶ σατυριάσεις ἐκ τούτου τοῦ γένους εἰσι.* (And so sometimes each of these humours is secreted pure, while at other times they are mixed one with the other; and so from this circumstance the conditions of the parts suffering swelling vary in the highest degree . . . . Now cases of satyriasis are of this kind). Comp. Method. med. bk. XIV. ch. 7.

[3] *Paulus Aegineta*, bk. III. ch. 56., *ἡ σατυρίασις ἐστὶ παλμὸς τοῦ αἰδοίου φλεγμονώδει τινι διαθέσει τῶν σπερματικῶν ἀγγείων ἑπόμενος μετ' ἐντάσεως· καὶ εἰ μὴ παύσαιτο ὁ παλμός, κατασκήπτειν εἴωθεν εἰς πάρεσιν τῶν σπερματικῶν ἀγγείων ἢ σπασμόν, καὶ ἀπόλλυντας ὀξέως οἱ σπασθέντες· τελευτῶντες δὲ φυσῶνται γαστέρα καὶ ὑδροῦσι ψυχρόν.* (Satyriasis is palpitation of the private part following on an inflammatory condition of the spermatic vessels and accompanied with tension. If the palpitation do not cease, it commonly passes into paresis of the spermatic vessels or spasm, and patients attacked by the spasm quickly succumb; and in their last moments they

No proof is needed that both these views are right so far as this, that gonorrhœa is both spasmodic and inflammatory, and in either case may be accompanied by priapism. Nothing, or only very little, is evacuated of a nature to make the patients experience relief; and if there is, they are again attacked by the evil, until the original cause of the erection is eliminated, on which the penis relaxes of itself and subsides. [1] According to *Paulus Aegineta* paresis of the spermatic vessels,—the second form of gonorrhœa, [2]—supervenes, if the disease is not

have the abdomen distended and suffer from cold sweats.

[1] *Actuarius*, Method, med. bk. I ch. 22., Priapismus vero est permanens constansque colis extensio. — Corripit hic affectus cum calidus crassusque spiritus in colem decumbit, qui ubi non facile egredi permittitur, penem vi extendit. Hi exiguum vel nihil seminis eiaculantur, sentiunt tamen quod spiritus una excludatur et levari quidem aegri ita quadamtenus videntur: verum denuo eodem malo corripiuntur, donec intensionis causa fuerit sublata. Coles resolvitur, aut quod nervi illius aliqua intemperie debilitentur aut quod spiritus confluens deficiat vel meatus eius obstruantur dissecenturve. (Now priapism is a permanent and chronic state of erection of the member.—This complaint attacks a patient, when a hot and heavy spirit descends into the member, which not being suffered to readily escape, violently erects the penis. Such patients ejaculate little or no semen, yet feel that the spirit is voided along with it, and so far as there *is* any emisson, appear to be relieved thereby; but they are again attacked afresh by the same evil, until the cause of the tension has been removed. Then the member is relaxed, either because its muscles are weakened by some morbid condition, or because the spirit converging to it fails or its passages are blocked and become dried up).

[2] *Aretaeus*, Morb. chron. sympt. bk. II. ch. 5., *ἀπὸ σατυριήσεως ἐς γονοῤῥοίης ἀπόσκηψιν ἡ κατάστασις.* (The established tendency after satyriasis is towards a determination of gonorrhœa). *Caelius Aurelian*, Acut. morb. bk. III. ch. 18., Omnibus tamen in ultimo conductio nervorum fit, quam Graeci spasmon vocaverunt et voluntarius seminis iactus. (Yet in all cases eventually a certain action of the muscles takes place, which the Greeks call spasm, and a voluntary ejaculation of semen).

relieved, or else general spasms. Patients attacked by such spasms succumb rapidly, suffering from cold sweats and tympanitic distension of the abdomen. *Alexander of Tralles* (IX. 10) saw the erection even continue after the death of the patient. This form is not a common one; it occurs pre-eminently among young people, [1] and according to *Themison's* observations, who frequently saw the complaint in Crete, where however it was probably very often a result of pederastia, is subject to epidemic influence.

The *treatment* of this form of gonorrhœa demands according to *Paulus Aegineta* (loco citato) immediate general blood-letting,—this *Galen* [2] also recommends, and practised with advantage,—local cupping or leeching, simple clysters, cooling and composing embrocations and poultices of solanum (nightshade) or cicuta (hemlock) in the lumbar region, of litharge, Cimolian earth, psymithium (white-lead) with vinegar, water or sweet wine, on the perineum. Internal remedies are a decoction of mallows, mercury and birch-bark, sap of rue, decoction from the root of

[1] *Galen*, Method. med. bk. XIV. ch. 7. (X. p. 970.), *γίνεται δὲ οὐ πολλοῖς μὲν τὸ πάθος τοῦτο, νεανίαις γε μεν μᾶλλον ἢ κατ' ἄλλην ἡλικίαν·* (Now this complaint does not attack many, and young men are more liable than any other age). *Caelius Aurelian*, Acut. morb. bk. III. ch. 18., Sed antecedentes ipsius passionis causae sunt epota medicamina — *ἐντατικὰ* —, item immodicus atque intemporalis usus veneris. Est autem communis passio viris atque feminis, quae solet accidere aetatibus mediis atque iuventuti. (But the antecedent causes of the actual complaint are the taking of drugs, viz. aphrodisiacs, as also immoderate and unseasonable indulgence in love. And the complaint is common both to men and women, and regularly attacks persons in middle life as well as the young).

[2] *Galen*, Method. med. bk. XIV. ch. 7. (X. pp. 969 sqq.). Comp. De Composit. medicam. secund. locos, bk. IX. ch. 9. (XIII. p. 318.). *Caelius Aurelian*, Acut. morb. bk. III. 18., Chron. morb. bk. II. 1. V. 9. *Actuarius*, Method. med. I. 15. *Nonnus*, Epitom. ch. 194. *Priscian*, bk. II. ch. 11.

the iris, nymphaea (water-lily) and adianthum (maidenhair). Diuretics are injurious. Patients should at the same time be put upon a low, vegetable diet, and the supine posture avoided. *Galen* (loco citato) recommended in addition emetics, but not purgatives, also embrocations of *ceratum rosaceum*, friction and subsequently gymnastic exercises. *Alexander of Tralles* insists particularly on the patient avoiding [1] all wanton scenes and thoughts, and forbids the use of any cold, specially astringent things, whereby the resolution of the contraction is made more difficult (**πάϑος δυσδιαφόρητον γενέσϑαι**,—the affection is rendered hard to be resolved).

Gonorrhœa without erection of the penis, that is to say gonorrhœa proper, exhibits a persistent, involuntary discharge of the seed, [2] has some analogy

[1] *Caelius Aurelian* bk. III. ch. 18., Prohibentes etiam hominum ingressum et magis iuvenum feminarum atque puerorum. Pulchritudo enim ingredientium admonitione quadam provocat aegrotantes; quippe cum etiam sani saepe talibus usi statim in veneream veniant voluptatem, provocati partium effecta tentigine. (Forbidding the entrance even of men, much more that of youths, women and boys. For the beauty of those entering excites the patients by calling up remembered images; for even healthy subjects frequently enjoying such sights straightway fall in lustful love, incited by a certain tension of the parts being produced). He also recommended shaving the hair of the pubis.

[2] *Galen*, De loc affect. VI. 6. (VIII. p. 439.), *ἡ μὲν οὖν γονόῤῥοια σπέρματος ἀπόκρισίς ἐστιν ἀκούσιος, ἔξεστι δὲ καὶ ἀπροαίρετον ὀνομάζειν, ὥσπερ καὶ σαφέστερον, ἀπόκρισιν σπέρματος συνεχῶς γιγνομένην, χωρὶς τῆς κατὰ τὸ αἰδοῖον ἐντάσεως... ὥσπερ δὲ καὶ τ' ἄλλα πάντα τὰ ἐκ τοῦ σώματος ἡμῶν ἐκκενούμενα κατὰ διττὸν τρόπον τοῦτο πάσχει, ποτὲ μὲν ἐκ τῶν περιεχόντων αὐτὰ σωμάτων ἐκκρινόμενα, ποτὲ δὲ αὐτομάτως ἐκρέοντα δἰ ἀῤῥωστίαν τῶν αὐτῶν σωμάτων οὐ κατεχόμενα, οὕτως καὶ τὸ σπέρμα·* (Now gonorrhœa is an involuntary discharge of semen, or we may call it unintentional, if we prefer, as being a clearer term, the discharge of semen taking place continuously, without erection in the member..., And just as other parts of our body when evac-

with *incontinentia urinae*, and usually depends like the latter on weakness or failure in the retentive power of the spermatic vessels. [1] Very often an inflammatory stage supervenes, making the complaint approximate to the first form; patients secrete copious and hot semen, which provokes them to ejaculation,—an ejaculation however that is followed by great exhaustion. If they avoid copulation, headache is established, pains in the stomach and nausea, while nocturnal pollutions cause them similar inconveniences to those they incur from coition. The ejaculation is accompanied by heat and smarting pain,—and this not solely among men but with women as well; for one of these patients, *Galen* writes, [2]

uated, suffer this in one of two ways, sometimes being discharged by the bodies that surround them, at others flowing out automatically, as failing to be retained through some weakness in the bodies themselves, so is it also with the semen.—*Paulus Aegineta*, bk. III. ch. 55., *ἡ γονόῤῥοια σπέρματος ἐστὶν ἀκούσιος ἀπόκρισις σανεχῶς γινομένη χωρὶς τῆς κατὰ τὸ αἰδοιõν ἐνστασεως, διὰ τὴν τῆς καθεκτικῆς δυνάμεως ἀσθένειαν γινομένη*. (Gonorrhœa is an involuntary discharge of seed going on persistently without erection in the member, being due to feebleness of the retentive power). *Nonnus*, Epitome ch. 193., says the same.

[1] *Galen*, loco citato p. 441., *ὥσπέρ γε καὶ τὴν τῆς γονοῤῥοίας, ἀνάλογον οὔρων ἐκκρίσεσιν ἀκουσίοις, ὅταν ἡ κατέχουσα δύναμις αὐτὴ παραλυθεῖσα τύχῃ*. (Similarly too the discharge of gonorrhœa, analogous to the involuntary discharges of urine, whenever the retentive power itself has come to be paralysed). *Actuarius*, Method. med. bk. I. ch. 22., Causa autem eius est, seminalium vasorum fluxus facilitas, aut impotentia aut quod ob enatam intemperiem semen continere nequeant, aut quod humor quispiam mordax ibi abundans stimulet. (Now the cause of it is the facility of flow from the seminal vessels, either from impotence or because they are unable to retain the semen in consequence of a morbid condition that has arisen, or else because some *acrid* humour is there in over-abundance, stimulating the flow).

[2] *Galen*, De sanitate tuenda Bk. VI. ch. 14. (VI. p. 443.), *Μοχθηροτάτη δὲ σώματός ἐστι καὶ ἡ τοίαδε· σπέρμα*

told me that not only himself, but also *the women with whom he had accomplished coition*, experienced during the discharge a biting, burning pain. On the contrary, according to *Aretaeus*, [1] it would

πολὺ καὶ θερμὸν ἔνιοι γεννῶσιν, ἐπείγει γὰρ αὐτοὺς εἰς ἀπόκρισιν, οὐ μετὰ τὴν ἔκκρισιν ἔκλυτοί τε γίγνονται τῷ στόματι τῆς κοιλίας, . . . ἀσθενεῖς γίγνονται, καὶ ξηροὶ καὶ λεπτοὶ, καὶ ὠχροὶ, καὶ κοιλοφθαλμιῶντες οἱ οὕτω διακείμενοι· εἰ δὲ ἐκ τοῦ ταῦτα πάσχειν ἐπὶ ταῖς συνουσίαις ἀπέχοιντο μίξεως ἀφροδισίων δύσφοροι μὲν τὴν κεφαλὴν, δύσφοροι δὲ καὶ τῷ στομάχῳ, καὶ ἀσώδεις· οὐδὲν δὲ μέγα διὰ τῆς ἐγκρατείας ὠφελοῦνται· συμβαίνει γὰρ αὐτοῖς ἐξονειρώττουσι παραπλησίας γινεσθαι βλάβας, ἂς ἔπασχον ἐπὶ ταῖς συνουσίαις· ὡς δέ τις ἐξ αὐτῶν ἔφη μοι, δακνώδους τε καὶ θερμοῦ πάνυ τοῦ σπέρματος αἰσθάνεσθαι κατὰ τὴν ἀπόκρισιν, οὐ μόνον ἑαυτὸν, ἀλλὰ καὶ τὰς γυναῖκας αἷς ἂν ὁμιλήσῃ· (However the most troublesome condition of body is the following: some patients produce copious and hot semen, and this provokes them to ejaculation, then after its ejaculation, they grow relaxed at the neck of the belly, . . . and become weak, and dried up, and thin, and pale, and hollow-eyed, — the patients that find themselves so affected. And if after suffering in these ways, they then indulge in the intercourse of sexual love, they are afflicted in head and in stomach, and with nausea. Nor on the other hand do they get any great benefit from continence; for they come, by having pollutions in dreams, to undergo similar inconveniences to those they incurred in sexual intercourse. And as one of them said to me, *he experienced a biting and exceedingly hot sensation from the semen in its ejaculation, — and not himself only, but also such women as he had intercourse with*).

[1] *Aretaeus*, De morbor. chronic. symptom. bk. II. ch. 5., Ἀνώλεθρον μὲν ἡ γονόῤῥοια, ἀτερπὲς δὲ καὶ ἀηδὲς μέσφι ἀκοῆς· ἢν γὰρ ἀκρασίῃ καὶ πάρεσις τὰ ὑγρὰ ἴσχῃ καὶ γόνιμα μέρεα, ὅκως διά ψυχρῶν ῥέει ἡ θορὴ, οὐδὲ ἐπισχεῖν ἐστὶ αὐτὴν οὐδὲ ἐν ὕπνοισι· ἀλλὰ γὰρ ἤν τε εὕδῃ, ἤν τε ἐγρηγορέῃ, ἀνεπίσχετος ἡ φορὴ, ἀναίσθητος δὲ ἡ ῥοὴ τοῦ γόνου γίγνεται· νοσέουσι δὲ καὶ γυναῖκες τήνδε τὴν νοῦσον, ἀλλ' ἐπὶ κνησμοῖσι τῶν μορίων καὶ ἡδονῇ προχέεται τῇσι ἡ θορή· ἀτὰρ καὶ πρὸς ἄνδρας ὁμιλίῃ ἀναισχύντῳ· ἄνδρες δὲ οὐδ' ὅλως ὀδά-

seem the only symptoms found in conjunction with the complaint are itching of the privates, a voluptuous feeling and a violent inclination to sexual intercourse. This datum admits of ready explanation if we consider the fact that in southern countries the inflammatory stage that makes its appearance is very brief and as a rule hardly noticeable, provided,—though no doubt this condition was pretty often broken,—coition was not indulged in during its course.

As a matter of fact in the great majority of

ξονται· τὸ δὲ ῥέον ὑγρὸν λεπτὸν, ψυχρὸν, ἄχρουν, ἄγονον· πῶς γὰρ ζωογόνον ἐκπέμψαι σπέρμα ψυχρὴ οὖσα ἡ φύσις· ἢν δὲ καὶ νέοι πάσχωσι, γηραλέους χρὴ γενέσθαι πάντας τὴν ἕξιν, νωθώδεας, ἐκλύτους, ἀψύχους, ὀκνέοντας, λωφούς; ἀσθενέας, ῥικνούς, ἀπρήκτους, ἐπώχρους, λευκοὺς, γυναικώδεας, ἀποσίτους, ψυχροὺς, μελέων βάρεα, καὶ νάρκας σκελέων, ἀκρατέας, καὶ ἐς πάντα παρέτους· ἥδε ἡ νοῦσος ὁδὸς ἐς παράλυσιν πολλοῖσι γίγνεται· πῶς γὰρ οὐκ ἂν τῶν νεύρων ἥδε ἡ δύναμις πάθοι τῆς ἐς ζωῆς γένεσιν φύσιος ἀπεψυγμένης. (Gonorrhœa is not indeed a dangerous thing, but it *is* a disagreeable one, and one that is *in the highest degree unseemly in repute.* For if incontinence and *paresis* attack the soft procreative parts, the semen flows all the same even though the organs are cold, nor is it possible to stop it even in sleep; for whether a man sleep, or wake, the running is continual, and the flow of the seed goes on unconsciously. *And women also are subject to this complaint;* but in their case the discharge of the semen is accompanied with itchings and with pleasurable feeling, as well as with shameless intercourse with men, whereas men are not in any way excited. And the moisture that is discharged is thin, cold, colourless, unfruitful; for how should its nature, that is cold, send forth fertile semen? And if young men suffer from it, they are bound to grow old in constitution and condition, sluggish, relaxed, lifeless, hesitating, dull of hearing, weak, shrunken, ineffectual, pallid, white, womanish, without appetite, chilly, heavy of limb, and stiff of leg and palsied in every part. This complaint is the avenue to paralysis for many; for how should this power of the nerves not suffer when the natural parts pertaining to the generation of life are chilled).

instances the Physician had only the chronic form to treat. Generally speaking a patient first notices the complaint, when the discharge begins; and then the latter, when once the inflammatory stage is over, proceeds day and night undisturbed and without special voluptuous feeling, without wanton dreams, [1] often without any particular sensation at all. The actual discharge is a thin, cold, pale, sterile flux. Towards the end of the illness it becomes thicker, assumes an acrid quality, and eventually ceases altogether to flow. [2] But if the malady persists, especially in young people, then according to *Aretaeus*, the whole visage of the sufferers assumes a greyish look; they grow sluggish, atonic, spiritless, faint-hearted, indolent, dull, weak, emaciated, incapable of effort, unhealthy-looking, [3] pale, womanish, have

[1] *Celsus* De re med. bk. IV. ch. 21., Est etiam circa naturalia vitium, nimia profusio seminis, quod sine venere, sine nocturnis imaginibus sic fertur, ut interposito spatio, tabe hominem consumat. (There is another complaint connected with the private parts, viz. excessive discharge of semen, which apart altogether from love, and apart from nocturnal pollutions in dreams, is so persistent that, given a sufficient interval of time, it destroys a man by wasting).

[2] *Alexander of Tralles*, bk. IV. ch. 9., *δέονται γὰρ οὗτοι τῶν ἐπικιρνώτων καὶ ἐμψυχόντων πάνυ καὶ λουτρῶν εὐκράτων· ὥστε παχυνθεῖσαν ἠρέμα τὴν γονὴν καὶ εὔκρατον γενομένην, μηκέτι φέρεσθαι.* (For these patients require compound and very cooling drugs, and lukewarm baths; so that the seed growing quietly thicker and well-conditioned, may no longer flow away).

[3] *Galen*, Definit. medic. n. 288. (XIX. p. 426.), *Γονόῤῥοιά ἐστιν ἀπόκρισις ἐπιφέρουσα σπέρματος νόσημα μετὰ τοῦ τήκεσθαι τὸ σῶμα καὶ ἀχρούστερον ἀποτελεῖσθαι· γίνεται δὲ ἀτονησάντων τῶν σπερματικῶν ἀγγείων, ὥστε τρόπον τινὰ παρειμένων αὐτῶν μὴ κρατεῖσθαι τὸ σπέρμα.* (Gonorrhœa is a discharge producing a diseased state of semen accompanied by wasting of the body and an unhealthy-looking complexion; and it arises through the semen vessels having become atonic, so that, these being in a way paralysed, the semen is not retained).

no appetite, feel chilly, complain of heaviness in the limbs, are weak-loined, feeble and unfit for anything. According to *Galen*, the abdomen falls in, besides all the rest of the body collapsing more or less and withering; while patients become lean, of a yellowish pale complexion and hollow-eyed. In this way the complaint not unfrequently paves the road to paralysis, or else sufferers die of *tabes* or wasting. [1] Specifically and in itself the disease is not dangerous, but it provokes various other complaints, and represents a highly disagreeable, ill-reputed affection (Aretaeus), [2]

[1] *Actuarius*, Method. med. bk. I. ch. 22., Et in seminis quidem profluvio, neque coles intenditur, neque aeger eadem qua sanus afficitur voluptate, sed perinde ac si superfluum quiddam excerneretur, sensu privatur. Quod si morbus moram traxerit, necesse est ut aeger in colliquationem collabatur ac pereat; quod pinguior humoris portio eiiciatur ac vitalis spiritus non parum una effluat. (Moreover in this excessive flux of semen, neither is the member erected, nor does the patient experience the same pleasure as he does in health, but exactly as though something superfluous were being eliminated, he is robbed of sensation. But if the malady runs a more protracted course, the sufferer cannot but fall into collapse and succumb, inasmuch as the richer portion of the humour is ejaculated, and the vital spirit must escape along with it). As early as *Hippocrates*, De morbis bk. II., edit. Kühn Vol. II. p. we read: *ἡ νωτιὰς φθίσις ἀπὸ τοῦ μυελοῦ γίνεται· λαμβάνει δὲ μάλιστα νεογάμους καὶ φιλολάγνους . . . καὶ ἐπὴν οὐρέῃ ἢ ἀποπατέῃ, προέρχεταί οἱ θορὸς πουλὺς καὶ ὑγρὸς, καὶ γενεὴ οὐκ ἐγγίνεται, καὶ ὀνειρώσσει, κἂν συγκοιμηθῇ γυναικὶ, κἂν μή.* (Spinal consumption arises from the marrow; and it attacks particularly newly married men and lascivious subjects . . . . And every time the patient makes water or evacuates, semen flows from him copious and wet, and he does not succeed in generating, and has nocturnal pollutions, whether he sleep with a woman or no). Ought this not to be referred to gonorrhœa?

[2] *Aretaeus*, p. 424. loco citato; also De curat. morb. chron. bk. II. ch. 5., *καὶ τοῦ ἀτερπέος τοῦ πάθεος ʼεἵνεκεν καὶ τοῦ κατὰ σύντηξιν κινδυνώδεος καὶ τῆς ἐς διάδεξιν γένος χρείης λύειν χρὴ μὴ βραδέως τὴν γονόῤῥοιαν πάντων κακῶν οὖσαν*

that almost always follows a chronic course,[1]—for which reason Aretaeus and Caelius Aurelianus actually treat of it under the head of chronic diseases.

Gonorrhœal pus is infectious, as is implied by the Mosaic Laws of Purification (Leviticus Ch. XV.), and the malady is communicated by coition, as is seen from the words of *Galen*,—p. 428. But as early as the Fourth Century the idea was prevalent that the *conjunction of the stars* was not devoid of influence, as such or such a conjunction might from a man's very birth determine that *the individual was to die of gonorrhœa.* This at any rate is maintained by *Julius Firmicus Maternus*,[2] who lived in the time of

αἰτίην· (Equally on account of the disagreeable nature of the malady as on account of the risk of *tabes* or wasting and for the sake of the needful maintenance of posterity, gonorrhœa should be rapidly cured, being the cause of very many evils). Truly if not another passage remained to us from the Ancient writers besides these two of Aretaeus', they alone would suffice to convince us of the existence in his time of virulent gonorrhœa brought on by sexual intercourse; and it is quite inconceivable how *Simon*, Versuch einer krit. Gesch. (Essay towards a Critical History), Bk. I. p. 24., can say: "Thus for instance *all* the symptoms, which Aretaeus mentions in his Chapter on Gonorrhœa, speak for *true seminal flux!*"

[1] *Theodorus Priscianus*, bk. II. logic. ch. 11., Satyriasis, gonorrhœa vel priapismus, quibus similis est sub immoderata patratione molestia, his accidentibus disterminantur. Gonorrhœa sine veretri extensione vel usus venerii desiderio, spermatis affluentissima sub effusione corpora debilitat et per chronica tempora producitur. (Satyriasis, gonorrhœa or priapism, maladies involving similar inconvenience as in immoderate copulation, are distinguished by the following particularities. Gonorrhœa without erection of the member or desire for the enjoyment of love, debilitates the body by a most copious discharge of semen, and is protracted over chronic periods of time).

[2] *Julius Firmicus Maternus*, Astronomica bk. III. chs. 7 and 8., In loco octavo ♀ ab horoscopo constituto . . . si ☿ cum ea fuerit vel cum ☿ Venerem in hoc loco positam, malevola

Constantine the Great. The disease has to be carefully distinguished from the nocturnal pollutions, [1]

stella respexerit, vel per quadratum vel diametrum, vel si cum ipsis, in hoc loco fuerit inventa, omne eius qui natus fuerit patrimonium dissipatur vel qualicunque proscriptione nudatur, mors vero illi per gonorrheam, id est defluxionem seminis, aut contractionem vel spasmum aut apoplexin fertur. (In the eighth place determined by the horoscope stands ♀ Venus.... If ☿ (Mercury) be in conjunction with it, or if Venus standing in this place with ☿ (Mercury) be faced by an evil star, whether by quadrate or diameter, or if such star is found in conjunction with them in this place, all the patrimony of him who has been born under this conjunction is wasted, or is lost utterly by some proscription or another, and *his death is brought about by gonorrhœa, that is to say a flux of the semen*, or cramp or spasm or apoplexy.

[1] Caelius Aurelianus, Morb. Chron. bk. V. ch. 7., Item antecedens causa supradictae passionis, quam seminis appellamus lapsum, fuisse probatur, a qua discernitur, si quidem illa passio etiam per diem vigilantibus aegris fluere facit semen, nulla phantasia in usum venereum provocante. (Such is proved to have been another antecedent cause of the above named malady, which we call *discharge of semen;* but a distinct cause has to be assigned, if it so be that the malady in question makes the semen flow even by day and when the patients are awake, and though no dream provokes to the exercise of love). *Philagrius* appears to have made this distinction quite correctly, when as quoted by *Aëtius* (Tetrab. III. serm. 3. ch. 34.), De seminis in somno profluvio, Philagrii (On the discharge of semen in sleep, according to Philagrius), he says: Semen in somnis profundere dicuntur quicumque dum dormiunt, naturae genitale semen emittunt, quod ipsum eis ut plurimum ob vitiati humoris materiam, aut materiae multitudinem aut ob partium seminalium robur contingit. Iam vero quidam et ob animi moestitiam aut inediam, per somnos praeter consuetudinem semen excreverunt, atque id materiae acrimonia irritati, non ob partium seminalium robur, pertulerunt etc. (They are said to discharge semen in sleep, whoever during slumber, ejaculate *the genital seed of nature*, because they possess it in the greatest degree of abundance either on account of the constituting material of the semen being vitiated or on account

that are at times one of the sequelae of gonorrhœa.

The treatment is, according to *Aretaeus*, at the commencement that for an ordinary rheum or flux, by keeping the parts affected cool, in order to counteract the flow of the humours to them; by degrees going on to a heating and at the same time desiccating procedure, then the application of fresh wool to the part, the employment of friction, embrocations of *ceratum rosaceum* or *oinanthinum* with white wine, olive oil with melilot, marjoram, rosemary, poultices of barley-meal, saltpetre and dyll, but above all rue, with the addition of honey or, according to *Celsus*, vinegar; as further treatment, stimulating cataplasms, of a strength to redden the skin or even to bring out pustules on it, so as to draw off the afflux of the humours, or else as an alternative, plasters of the nature of the *emplastrum viride* (green plaster), of *baccae lauri* (laurel berries). As for internal treatment, the patient should drink decoctions of: *semen lactucae* (lettuce juice), *cannabis* (hemp), *rad. orcheos* (orchis root), *nymphaeae* (waterlily), *halicacabi* (bladder-wort), etc.; and take *castoreum* (beaver oil), or the antidotes of *Symphon*, *Philo*, or *Bestinus*, which are prepared from *viper's flesh*. In case of very profuse discharge, the patient should be directed to drink hard red wine; if he is acrid with bile (**χολωδέστερον καὶ δριμύτερον**,—over-bilious and

of the copiousness of this material, or else on account of the vigour of the seminal organs. But there are also many cases where men have emitted semen in sleep contrary to their wont in consequence of sadness of spirits or fasting, having done so because irritated by the acridness of the material, and not through any vigour of the seminal organs, etc.). The only pity is that Aëtius has not preserved for us his (Philagrius') opinion as to gonorrhœa, and has not shown clearly exactly what belongs to Philagrius in the Chapter; for a great deal, as indeed is stated, is from Galen and referred by the compiler to gonorrhœa. Philagrius in fact only lived in the latter half of the Fourth Century,—AD. 364 according to Sprengel, 300 according to Lessing.

acrid), lukewarm baths are brought into requisition (Alexander of Tralles). On one point all authorities are agreed, that the main thing to depend on is diet. Both food and drink, says Celsus, must be cold, a precaution Themison also recommended in satyriasis, whereas Caelius Aurelianus denounces it. The patient must not indulge in semen-forming matters, such as cause flatulency, but take nourishing food, flesh of animals but not fish, a little light wine with it, for the constant ejaculation is weakening; he should be careful as to resting, [1] lie on a cool bed, either on the right side or the left (Paulus Aegineta), not on the back (Celsus).

Where the complaint is of longer continuance, exercise in the open air and the use of cold baths is to be recommended, which latter *Celsus* [2] it appears prefers to see resorted to, as well as cold aspersions, almost at the very commencement; a mode of treatment that is even now coming into fashion again among ourselves, as the water-cure mania makes

[1] *Actuarius*, Meth. med. bk. IV. ch. 8., Convenit ad haec reliqua victus ratio, quae ad siccitatem declinet, sed non sit calidior, verum frigida. Insuper nutriendus aeger est, viresque modice reficiendae; namque ob continuam excretionem languet corpus et imbecillum est. Quies apta est, et balnea quae humectent tamen alioqui non sunt idonea. Animalia agrestia, quae refrigerantibus exsiccantibusque condiantur, sunt accommodata et vinum pauculum tenueque. (Consistent with this are the remaining rules of diet. This should incline towards dryness, but must not be at all hot, but cold. Further the sufferer must be adequately nourished, and his strength fairly well kept up; for owing to the constant ejaculation of semen the body grows languid and weak. Rest is desirable, and baths, in other circumstances used for moistening the body, are not here advisable. Game, seasoned with cooling and desiccating condiments, is appropriate, and a little thin wine.

[2] *Celsus*, bk. IV. ch. 21. In hoc affectu salutares sunt vehementes frictiones, perfusiones natationesque quam frigidissimae. (In this complaint violent frictions are advantageous, also aspersions and plunge baths as cold as they can be borne).

further and further progress. *Galen* [1] recommended,

[1] *Galen*, De sanitate tuenda bk. VI. ch. 14. (VI. p. 444.), —The best illustration in reference to the statements made in this connection by *Aëtius* (Tetrab, III. serm. 3. ch. 33.), which indeed is superscribed as Galen's and draws most of its material from him and from Aretaeus, showing however in many ways that it was based on personal observation or that the author had before him some better and older authority. Unfortunately the passage, previously glanced at, was subsequently mislaid by us, and so we are able merely to give it in a Footnote, with the request that the reader will complete from it what is said in the text. Profluvium igitur seminis, vasorum seminariorum affectio est, non pudendi, quae dolorem quidem non ita valde inferre solet, molestiam autem non vulgarem et pollutionem exhibet ob assiduum et invitis contingentem seminis fluxum Oboritur autem aliquando etiam ex seminariorum vasorum fluxione, quandoque etiam satyriasi praecedente profluvium seminis succedit. Contingit autem affectio maxime pubertatem transgressos citra decimum quartum annum, imo aliis etiam aetatibus. Est autem semen quod profluit, aquosum, tenue, citra appetentiam coeundi et ut plurimum quidem citra sensum, quandoque vero cum voluptate quadam promanans. Corrumpitur affectis sensim universum corpus ac gracilescit, praesertim circa lumbos. Consequitur et debilitas multa, non ob multitudinem seminis profluentis sed ob locorum proprietatem. Non solum autem viris sed et mulierculis hoc accidit, et in feminis sane aegre tollitur. Ceterum cura communis est cum ea quae in omni fluxione adhibetur. Primum igitur in quiete et pauco cibo ac aquae potu affectos asservare oportet; deinde etiam lumbos et pubem contegere lanis vino et rosaceo aut oenanthino aut melino madefactis. Neque vero ineptae sunt spongiae posca imputae. Sequentibus vero diebus cataplasmatis ex palmis, malis, acacia hypocisthide, oenanthe, rhoe rubro et similibus. Insessibus item adstringentibus utendum est, ex lentisci, rubi, myrti et similium in vino austero sive mero sive diluto decocto. Cibis autem utendum qui aegre corrumpantur et difficulter permutantur et resiccandi vim habent. Dandum etiam cum potu et cibis, viticis ac cannabis semen praesertim tostum. Rutae item semen ac folia, lactucae semen et cauliculi ac nymphaeae radix. In potu vero quotidie pro com-

muni aqua, aqua in qua ferrum saepe extinctum est praebeatur. Quidam vero corticem radicis halicacabi ex aqua eis bibendum praebuerunt, neque ineptum fuerit huius aliquando periculum facere. Antidotus etiam haec magnae celebritatis tum ad hoc modo semen profudentes, tum ad assidua in omnis profluvia commode exhibetur. Seminis salicis ʒvjj calaminthae ʒvj seminis viticis albae ʒv rutae ʒjv seminis cicutae ʒjj cum aqua in pastillos digerito et ex eis ad Ponticae nucis magnitudinem cum poscae cyathis tribus praebeto. Omnem vero acrium rerum esum et multi vini potum et olerum exhibitionem vitare oportet, diaetam vero universam resiccatoriam et adstringentem constituere. Post prima autem mox tempora ad unctiones et exercitatricem diaetam transeundum, per quam totum corpus et praesertim affecta, ad sanitatem perducantur, et plurima quidem tempora circa unctiones immorandum, paucies vero lavandum, si aut lassitudini aut cruditati mederi velimus. Bonum fuerit etiam, si nihil prohibuerit, ad frigidae lavationem defugere, quae omnem morbum ex fluxione obortum depellere consuevit, maxime si medicamentaria qualitate aqua praedita sit, velut sunt in Albulis aquae, quae etism in potu acceptae eis summe prosunt. Sunt autem sapore subsalso et tactu lactei teporis. Convenit item per intervalla quaedam illitionibus et epithematis et malagmatis uti, quae rubefacere et emollire possint, atque ea quae in profundo haerent ad superficiem transferre. Decubitus porro frequenter in latus fiat, calaminthae foliis et rutae et viticis substratis. Epithema autem in eis usu venit hocce. Capillum Veneris multum contundito et terito cum aceto aut apii succo aut seridis aut psyllii eoque cochlearum carnes coctas excipito et simul in linteolum infarta coxendicibus imponito. Utendum vero et praescripto ad priapismum cerato et iis quae paulo mox ad seminis in somno profluvia dicentur. Omnem autem de rebus venereis cogitationem excludere oportet. (Thus we see excessive discharge of semen is an effection of the seminal vessels, not of the member. *This complaint does not indeed as a rule cause any very great pain, but it does occasion no ordinary degree of inconvenience* and defilement in consequence of the constant involuntary discharge of semen. However sometimes it may arise from a flux in the seminal vessels, and *occasionally on an antecedent attack of satyriasis profuse discharge of semen supervenes.* The malady particularly attacks those who have passed the period of puberty but are under fourteen, but other ages are also liable. And the semen that is discharged is watery, thin, the discharge being unaccompanied with any desire for coition, and indeed as a rule without any feeling whatever, though at times taking place with a certain voluptuous sensation. The whole body of those attacked suffers and becomes wasted, especially in the lumbar region. There follows great weakness, not so much owing to the amount of the semen discharged as to the nature of the parts affected. *Again, this disease is not peculiar to men, but assails young women as well, and in the case of females is eliminated with very great difficulty*. However the treatment is the same as that applied in all fluxes. First of all therefore patients must observe rest and a scanty diet both in food and drinking water; then the loins and pubis should be covered with cloths moistened with wine, and *rosaceum* and oenanthinum and melinum (oil of roses, of young vine buds, of melilot). Sponges soaked in posca (acid drink of vinegar and water) are also appropriate. Then on the succeeding days cataplasms of palms, apples, acacia, hypocisthis (parasitic plant growing on the cisthus), wild vine, red wild-poppy, and the like. Embrocations moreover should be employed of an astringent character, consisting of a decoction of the mastic, bramble, myrtle and the like, in hard wine, whether unmixed or diluted. Diet should embrace such foods as resist corruption and deterioration, and possess a desiccative quality. Along with the food and drink should be administered the juice of the agnus castus and of *hemp*, especially after boiling. Also the juice and leaves of rue, the juice of lettuce and colewort and the root of nymphaea (water-lily). As to drink for daily use, instead of ordinary water, water should be given in which *iron has been repeatedly tempered*. Some practitioners indeed have administered the bark of the root of the bladder-wort in water as a beverage for such patients, and it will not be inappropriate to make trial of this on occasion. Another *antidote of great renown* is exhibited with advantage both for sufferers from this discharge of semen, as well as for constant fluxes of all kinds. Take of juice of the sallow ℥vjj, of calamint ʒvj, of juice of the white agnus castus ℥v, of rue ʒjv, of juice of hemlock ℥jj; compound with water into small cakes or lozenges, and administer one of these of the size of a hazel-nut along with three cups of posca (vinegar and water). *But the patient must avoid all eating of acrid*

besides diet and medicine, that with a view to retarding the preparation of semen, gymnastic exercises, particularly such as bring the upper part of the body into activity, e.g. ball-playing both with great and little balls and the casting of leaden disks, be resorted to. After bathing, patients must rub and wash over the hips with desiccative ointments, oil expressed from red, coarse olives, roses or quinces, wax-salves with the juices of *sempervivum* (evergreen house-leek), *solanum* (nightshade), *umbilicus Veneris* (navelwort), *portulaca* (purslain), linseed boiled in water, etc. I once saw, he says, the Intendant of a Gymnasium

things and the drinking of much wine and the use of vegetables; the diet must be generally of a desiccative and astringent type. Moreover presently after the earlier stages embrocations and an active mode of life should be adopted, whereby the whole body and particularly the parts affected are brought into a healthy state; the embrocations should be persevered in for long periods of time, but washing on the other hand sparingly employed, if we wish to remedy the lassitude and acrid habit of body. It will be of advantage moreover, *if there is nothing to prevent, to have recourse to cold bathing*, which has the property of expelling all diseases arising from flux, more especially if the water is endowed with a healing quality, such as the waters of Albulae, which also are of the greatest use in these cases when taken as a drink. They are of a slightly salt taste, and of a milky warmth to the touch. Further, it is suitable to employ at intervals lotions and poultices and plasters, such as will redden and soften the skin, and bring to the surface those matters that lie latent underneath. Again, *rest should frequently be taken lying on the side*, the leaves of calamint and rue and agnus castus being spread as a couch. A poultice employed in these cases is as follows. Pound a quantity of Venus-hair and rub it up with vinegar or parsley juice or that of endive or fleabane, add to it the cooked meat of snails, pack all together in a linen cloth and lay upon the hips. Also the wax plaster prescribed for priapism should be employed, and the remedies to be mentioned presently for discharges of semen during sleep. Lastly *all thinking about love ought to be avoided.*

Athletes lay a leaden disk on the lumbar region of an athlete as a measure against nocturnal pollution,—a means *Caelius Aurelianus* prescribed *also* for gonorrhœal patients,—and afterwards recommended the same treatment to another sufferer from these, who was thankful for the advice. Others again found lying on the *agnus castus* beneficial to them, as well as the taking of its juice along with rue. Violently active refrigerants in the form of ointments, prepared from poppy and *atropa mandragora* should not be employed, and this equally applies to sleeping on these plants when they are in bloom, for they act injuriously on the kidneys. On the other hand sleeping on roses was advantageous,—Caelius Aurelianus added to the list the leaves and flowers of *vitex* (agnus castus, Abraham's balm). "Besides these I have excogitated many other specifics for patients of the sort, and found their utility confirmed in practice. For instance those afflicted with such a condition of body should pay particular attention to this. When the accumulation of semen that has to be ejaculated is at its greatest, they should during the day take a nourishing yet moderate meal, and then when they lie down to sleep accomplish sexual intercourse. [1]

[1] Similarly *Aretaeus*, Morb. chron. therap. bk. II. ch. 5., says: *εἰ δὲ καὶ σώφρων ἔοι ἐπὶ τοῖσι ἀφροδισίοισι καὶ λούοιτο ψυχρῷ, ἐλπὶς ὡς ὤκιστα ἀνδρωθῆναι τὸν ἄνθρωπον*, (And if he indulge with moderation in love and bathe in cold water, there is good hope that the man will rapidly recover manly vigour). This need surprise us the less, if we remember that the notion of a superfluitas seminis (superfluity of seed),—this was why Diogenes practised onanism, *Galen*, Vol. VIII. p. 419.),—was all the time in the background, and gonorrhœa according to Caelius Aurelianus and other authorities actually arose from too great self-continence. Si igitur Venerem exercere consueverit et crebriore uti concubitu, nunc autem continentius et purius innocentiusque degat, sine dubio a copia id sustinet cum partes illam ferre nequeunt. (If therefore a man is in the habit of practising love and indulging in fairly frequent cohabitation, well and good; but if on the contrary he live a too con-

But on the following day, after taking their fill of sleep, they should on rising chafe themselves till the skin is reddened. Next they should rub the body all over with oil; then soon after take some well-leavened, pure bread, baked in the baking-pan, and mixed with wine, after which they may then go about their customary business. Between the rubbing with oil and the meal of bread patients may go for a walk, if there is a spot convenient for the purpose in the neighbourhood, *except in the colder time of the year, for at that season it is better for them to stay indoors.*"

With regard to *gonorrhœa in women*, it is all but impossible to arrive at any accurate knowledge of what the Ancient Physicians knew concerning it. The reason of this is that the views held as to the effect of deteriorated menstrual blood and of the **ῥοῦς γυναικεῖος** (female discharge), by means of which the whole body was supposed to purge itself of evil humours, [1] absolutely precluded the possibility

tinent, pure and innocent life, without a doubt he endures this evil from the over-copiousness (of semen), as the parts cannot tolerate it.) This idea owed its origin partly to the confusion of gonorrhoea with nocturnal pollutions,—a confusion found even in the passage from Galen quoted a little above, and in especial was revived in the XVth. and XVIth. Centuries under the auspices of the monks and nuns. It at the same time gave occasion to the practice of resorting to copulation with a maiden as a cure for gonorrhœa. At any rate it was an opinion already found in Hippocrates, that copulation was a desiccative measure which in diseases arising from the phlegmatic humour (*Hippocrates*, Epidem. bk. VI. Vol. III. p. 609., *Galen*, XVII. A. p. 284.) is of advantage to hot and moist constitutions (*Galen*, Vol. VI. p. 402.)

[1] *Galen*, De sympt. caus. bk. III. ch. 11. (VII. p. 265.), *ἀλλὰ καὶ τὰ μοχθηρὰ διὰ τῶν ὑστερῶν ῥεύματα, καλεῖται δὲ τὸ σύμπτωμα ῥοῦς γυναικεῖος, ἐκκαθαιρομένου κατὰ τοῦτο τὸ μόριον ἅπαντος τοῦ σώματος γίγνεται.* (Besides there are the troublesome fluxes by way of the womb; and the *symptom* of these is known as "female discharge", and takes place as the whole body purges

of any unprejudiced observation, in precisely the same way as down to quite modern times the *fluor albus* (white flux, blenorrhœa) conditioned the extremely imperfect knowledge possessed by the faculty of female gonorrhœa. We purpose to leave over the inquiry into the points which differentiate the two (male and female gonorrhœa) to another opportunity; and will only note here that gonorrhœa in women, strictly so called, was by no means utterly unknown,—in fact there is no doubt whatever as to its being distinguished from the **ῥοῦς γυναικεῖος** (female discharge), as is shown by the passage of *Galen* quoted above, and still more clearly by *Aretaeus*, [1] who speaks of **γονόῤῥοια γυναικεῖα**

itself by this part). *Nonnus*, ch. 204. *Paulus Aegineta*, bk. II. ch. 63. *Rufus* of Ephesus, bk. I ch. 44.

[1] *Aretaeus*, De sign. chron. morb. bk. IV. ch. 11., *ἄλλος ῥόος λευκὸς ἡ ἐπιμήνιος κάθαρσις λευκὴ δριμεῖα καὶ ὀδαξώδης ἐς ἡδονήν. ἐπὶ δὲ τοῖσι καὶ ὑγροῦ λευκοῦ, πάχεος, γονοειδέος πρόκλησις· τόδε τὸ εἶδος γονόῤῥοιαν γυναικείαν ἐλέξαμεν· ἔστι δὲ τῆς ὑστέρης φύξις, οὕνεκεν ἀκρατὴς τῶν ὑγρῶν γίγνεται· ἀτὰρ καὶ τὸ αἷμα ἐς χροιὴν λευκὴν ἀμείβει.* (Another white discharge is the menstrual purging, white, acrid, and provoking a pleasurable itching. But in addition to these forms there is also a calling out of a moist, white, thick, semen-like discharge; and this species we have named "*female gonorrhœa*"; and it is an escape from the womb, because this cannot retain the moist humours. Further, it actually changes the blood to a white colour.) Perhaps too what *Galen*, De semine bk. II. ch. 1. (IV. p. 599.), says is pertinent in this connection: *ταῖς δ' ἄλλαις ἔλαττόν τε καὶ ὑγρὸν ἐκπίπτον φαίνεται πολλάκις ἔσωθεν ἐξ αὐτῶν τῶν ὑστερῶν, ἵναπερ οὐρεῖ.* (but in other women there appears to be a smaller and moist discharge very often, inside, coming from the womb itself, in micturition). Again *Theod. Priscianus*, bk. III. 10., says: Aliquando etiam spermatis spontanei et importuni fluxu feminae fatigantur, quod Graeci gonorrhœam appellant. (Sometimes too women are troubled with a discharge of involuntarily and unexpectedly emitted semen, a complaint the Greeks call gonorrhœa.) Comp. the passage quoted above from Aëtius.

(female gonorrhœa) distinctly as **ἄλλος ῥόος λευκὸς,** another species of white flux. Whether perhaps this knowledge was first accumulated at the epoch of Tiberius and his fellows cannot indeed be positively determined; but certainly the word **ἐλέξαμεν** (we have named it) of the text of Aretaeus may very well leave room for such a conjecture, and as a matter of fact Aretaeus would appear to have lived under Domitian, and was therefore a contemporary of Martial's!

2. Ulcers and Caruncles in the Urethra.

We have already seen from Hippocrates, Celsus and Galen that the ancient Physicians had observed the inflammation and subsequent matteration of the small mucous glands of the urethra evidenced by the symptoms of painful micturition, and seeing that mere tenesmus, as well as dysentery, are denominated **ἑλκώσις** (ulceration) by them, it is by no means improbable that many a urethral ulcer and many a case of gonorrhœa may have been treated under the name of ischuria (retention of urine). This is the more likely, as we learn from a passage of *Celsus* [1], one usually misinterpreted in several respects,

[1] *Celsus*, De re medica bk. VI. ch. ch. 18., Solet etiam interdum ad nervos ulcus descendere; profluitque pituita multa sanies tenuis malique odoris, non coacta at aquae similis, in qua caro recens lota est; doloresque is locus et punctiones habet. Id genus quamvis inter purulenta est, tamen lenibus medicamentis curandum est... Praecipueque id ulcus multa calida aqua fovendum est, velandumque neque frigori committendum. (Moreover the ulcer is wont sometimes to descend to the *cords;* and then there is discharged a quantity of phlegm, a thin *sanies* of an ill odour, not congealed but like water in which a piece of fresh meat has been washed; and the place experiences pain and a pricking sensation. This sort, though it comes under the head of purulent complaints, should nevertheless be treated

that the urethral discharge was explained as due to

with mild drugs.... And above all this form of ulcer should be fomented with copious warm water, and should be covered and not exposed to cold). From the last sentence it may be concluded that it is not the acute form of blenorrhœa of the urethra that is in question here (bk. IV), but the chronic. The words *ad nervos* (to the cords) have given occasion to some very extraordinary explanations. *Simon*, Krit. Gesch. Vol. I p. 23., considers it would be most natural to refer this to the inside of the member, to the urethra in fact, though as a matter of fact gonorrhœa of the glans penis might just as likely be intended in the passage. But in the latter case the interpretation is absolutely impossible, as the glans penis is never called *nervus*. The corpora cavernosa it is true are described in several places by *Galen*, e.g. De loc. aff. bk. VI. ch. 6., as "a pipe-like cord, for the body is cord-like in form, the whole being hollow like a pipe", but he adds χωρὶς τῆς καλουμένης βαλάνου (always excepting the glans penis, as it is called, and indeed that *nervus* generally signifies the penis is evident at once from Horace, Epod. XII. 19.; even the plural *nervos* is found in *Petronius*, Sat. 129., 134.,—so the Greeks similarly use νεῦρον (nerve, cord) for the penis, sometimes with the addition σπερματικὸν (spermatic, seminal), as Eustathius points out,—Comm. on the Iliad, X. 1390. However Celsus had no idea of this in his mind; everything shows that with him the *ad nervos* points to nothing but the *vasa deferentia* or spermatic cords, as he distinctly declares himself in bk. VII. ch. 18: Dependent vero (testiculi) ab inguinibus per *singulos nervos*, quos κρεμαστῆρας Graeci nominant. (But the testicles hang from the groin by separate cords, which the Greeks call κρεματῆρες,—suspenders). Similarly *Columella*, De re rustic. bk. VI. ch. 26., Testium nervos, quos Graeci κρεμαστῆρας ab eo appellant, quod ex illis genitales partes dependent. (The cords of the testicles, which the Greeks name κρεμαστῆρες, — suspenders, because the genital parts hang by them); again *Pollux*, Onomast. bk. II. ch. 4., κρεμαστῆρας δὲ λέγονται τὰ νεῦρα, τοὺς διδύμους ἀνέχει. (κρεμαστῆρες,—suspenders, is the name of the cords; and they support the testicles). The possibility of the suppuration extending to the seed reservoir and the spermatic cords is proved by the case lately observed and made known by *Ricord*.

an extension of the ulcer to the spermatic cords (*vasa deferentia*,—seed-bringing vessels). Yet further confirmation is afforded by a passage of *Actuarius*, [1] already cited by Simon, and our own conjecture expressed on a previous page thus justified.

Ulcers however also occurred in the urethra [2] un-

[1] *Actuarius*, Method. med. bk. IV. ch. 8., Caeterum non est ignorandum, nonnunquam in interna penis parte exiguum tuberculum oboriri, quod dum disrumpitur, sanguinem aut exiguum puris effundit; quare quidam arbitrantur ex profundo ea prodire, citraque rationem metuere coeperunt. Verum res ex penis dolore deprehenditur. Venae autem sectione sola, victuque frigidiusculo aegrum a molestia vindicavimus. Quod si vitium moram traxerit et vulnus (ἕλκος?) altius pervenerit, enemata morsus expertia, qualibus in lippitudine utimur, infundimus. Balneo ac omni mordenti evidenterque calefaciente tum cibo tum potione abstinemus, ita namque promptius aeger valetudinem recipit. (However it must not be forgotten that sometimes a small tubercle is established in the internal part of the penis, which on bursting discharges blood and a small quantity of pus; for which reason some suppose these symptoms to proceed from a deep-seated evil, and have been unreasonably alarmed. But the truth may be gathered from the pain in the penis. However by the mere opening of a vein and a cooling diet we have saved a patient from ali inconvenience. On the other hand if the mischief has followed a protracted course and the sore (ἕλκος?,—ulcer) has penetrated farther in, we introduce clysters free from biting acridity, such as we make use of for blear-eyed patients. We forbid the bath, and everything acrid and manifestly heating whether in food or drink, for in this way the sufferer recovers his health more rapidly).

[2] *Paulus Aegineta*, bk. III. ch. 59., εἰ δὲ κατὰ τὸν καυλὸν ἔνδον τῆς τοῦ αἰδοίου τρήσεως ἀφανὲς ἕλκος γένηται, γινώσκεται ἐκ τοῦ πύον ἢ αἷμα κενοῦσθαι χωρὶς οὐρησέως. Θεραπεύεται δὲ πρῶτον μὲν ὑδαρεῖ μελικράτῳ κλυζόμενον, ἔπειτα δὲ γάλακτι, κἄπειτα μίξαντες τῷ γάλακτι τὸ τοῦ ἀστήρος κολλύριον, ἢ τὸν λευκὸν τροχίσκον, ἢ τὸν διὰ λωταριῶν ἐν μολυβδαίνῃ θυΐᾳ παραπέμπειν, ἤγουν καὶ πτερὸν βάψαντες διαχρίειν, εἶτα λεπτὸν στρεπτὸν χρίσαντες ἐνθῆναι· κάλλιστον δὲ ἐστὶ καὶ τὸ λαμβάνων κηκίδος καὶ πομφόλυγος, ἀμύλου τε

connected with tubercular swellings (ἀφανὲς ἕλκος,—invisible ulcer); these not unfrequently occasioned bleeding,[2] and made their presence known by the accompanying pain, while synchronously small irregularly-shaped particles (ἐφελκύδες) were ejected. The appropriate treatment of these ulcers has been described by *Paulus Aegineta* (loco citato); it consisted in injections of honey and milk (*Aëtius*, IV. 2. 19., and *Actuarius* also recommended *enemata morsus expertia*,—clysters free from biting acridity), introduction of lotus pounded in a leaden mortar by means of a feather or a twisted piece of lint (**λεπτὸν στρεπτὸν**, —light material twisted,—an anticipation

καὶ ἀλόης ἴσα, λειωθέντα ῥοδίνῳ καὶ χυλῷ ἀρνογλώσσου. (But if in the canal within the perforation of the member an invisible ulcer arise, it is recognized from the fact of matter or blood being discharged without micturition. And it is treated first by being *rinsed* with a weak honey-mixture, and then with milk and afterwards by mixing with the milk the salve of the *aster atticus*, or the white lozenge, or a preparation of lotus pounded in a leaden mortar; *a feather* should be dipped in this and it should be rubbed on, or else *a piece of thin material made into a twist* should be smeared with it and the drug introduced by this means; but the best of all is by taking equal parts of gall-apple, flowers of zinc, starch-flour and aloes smeared with rose-sap and plantain-sap).

[1] *Caelius Aurelianus*, Morb. chron. bk. II. ch. 8.. In iis enim qui ulcus habuerint, cum mictum fecerint, sanguis fluet attestante mordicatione et dolore et aliquando egestione corpusculorum, quae ἐφελκύδας Graeci vocaverunt. (In patients who have got an ulcer, whenever they make water, blood will flow and the fact be attested by accompanying biting sensation and pain and sometimes by the ejection of small particles which the Greeks have named ἐφελκύδες).

[2] *Galen*, De loc. affect. bk. I. ch. 5., εἰ γοῦν ὑμενώδους χιτῶνος ἐκκριθείη μόριον, ὅτι μὲν ἕλκωσίς ἐστί που, δηλώσει. . . . εἰ δ' οὐρηθείη τῆς οὐρήθρας αὐτῆς. (If for example a small portion of the membranous coat be shed, this will show there is ulceration somewhere . . . . And if in micturition particles of the urethra itself be passed). Comp. Paulus Aegineta, loco citato.

of the bougie ?) along with a mixture of gall-apple, flowers of zinc (oxide of zinc), starch-flour and aloes smeared in equal parts with rose-sap and plantain-sap.

Not unfrequently such ulcers give rise to the establishment of *caruncles in the urethra*, particularly *in the neighbourhood of the neck of the bladder*, though they occur[1] also in the ear, nose, as well as in connection with the privates and anus, in the latter case presenting the symptoms of ischuria (retention of urine), interfering as they do with the outflow of the urine. The presence of these caruncles may be diagnosed by the preceding symptoms, as also by the circumstance that the urine is evacuated by the introduction of a *catheter*, that this occasions pain at the seat of ulceration and breaks through the

[1] *Galen*, De symptom. caus. bk. III. ch. 8., *ἴσχονται μὲν γὰρ ἢ ἀδυνατούσης ἐκκρίνειν τῆς κύστεως, ἢ στεγνωθέντος αὐτῆς τοῦ στομάχου· ταυτὶ μὲν οὖν ἄμφω τὰ νοσήματα τῆς κύστεως ἓν κοινὸν ἔχει σύμπτωμα, τὴν ἰσχουρίαν· — αἱ μὲν οὖν στεγνώσεις τοῦ στομάχου δι' ἔμφραξίν τε καὶ μύσιν ἀποτελοῦνται· καὶ γίνεται ἡ μὲν ἔμφραξις ὑπὸ θρόμβου τε και πύου παχέος καὶ λίθου καὶ πώρου καὶ διὰ βλάστημά τι κατ' αὐτὸν ἐπιτραφὲν τὸν πόρον ὁποῖα κἀν τοῖς ἄλλοις ἅπασιν ἐκτὸς ὁρᾶται γινόμενα κατά τε τὰ ὦτα καὶ ῥῖνας αἰδοῖά τε καὶ ἕδραν· ἡ δὲ μύσις ἤτοι δι' ὄγκον ἐπὶ φλεγμοναῖς ἀποτελεῖται καί σκίῤῥοις καὶ τοῖς ἄλλοις οἰδήμασιν, ὅσα τε τὸν τράχηλον ἐξαίροντα τῆς κύστεως εἰς τὸν ἐντὸς πόρον ἀποχεῖ τὸν ὄγκον.* (For they suffer either because the bladder is unable to secrete or because its orifice is stopped; but both these complaints of the bladder have one symptom in common, viz. retention of urine .,.. Now the *stoppages* of the orifice are produced by *blocking* or by *closing up;* and stoppages are caused by a clot or dense matter or a calculus or chalk-stone or some growth that has formed in the actual passage, as is also observed to occur in other, external, organs, the ears, the nostrils, genitals, or fundament; but closure is due either to a tumour following on phlegmonous affections or by indurations or other swellings which dilate the neck of the bladder and discharge the tumour into the internal passage). Comp, *Caelius Aurelianus* bk. V. ch. 4.

caruncle, causing the urine to pass mixed with blood and the remains of the caruncle. It is necessary to know if a thrombus (blood-clot) or calculus blocks the urethra; but as to whether we pronounce the mischief to be situated in the urethra itself and the cause of the ischuria to be there as well, this is a distinction of no practical or scientific value.[1] For

[1] *Galen*, De loc. affect. bk. I. ch. 1. (VIII. p. 12.), *οὕτω δὲ εἰ καὶ σάρκα τινὰ δι' ἕλκωσιν ἐπιτραφεῖσαν ἡγούμεθα τὸν τράχηλον τῆς κύστεως ἐμφράττειν, ἔκ τε τῶν προηγησαμένων τοῦ ἕλκους σημείων ἔκ τε τοῦ κενωθῆναι τὸ οὖρον ἐπὶ τῷ καθετῆρι συλλογιούμεθα· καί ποτε καὶ γενόμενον οἶδα τοιοῦτόν τι πάθημα· διαβαλλομένου γοῦν τοῦ καθετῆρος, ἤλγησεν κατ' ἐκεῖνο τοῦ πόρου τὸ μέρος, ἔνθα καὶ πρότερον ἐτεκμηράμεθα τὴν ἕλκωσιν εἶναι· θλασθείσης δὲ τῆς σαρκὸς ὑπὸ τοῦ καθετῆρος, ἠκολούθησε μὲν μετὰ τὴν τῶν οὔρων ἔκκρισιν αἱματός τέ τι καὶ θρύμματα τῆς σαρκός·... τὸ δ' εἴτε πάθος εἶναι λεκτέον τοῦ πόρου τὸ γεγονὸς, εἴτε αἴτιον ἰσχουρίας ἐν τῷ πόρῳ περιέχεσθαι, τῶν ἀχρήστων εἰς τὴν τέχνην ἐστίν.* (Accordingly if we suspect some accretion of tissue, the result of ulceration, to be blocking the neck of the bladder, our diagnosis will depend both on the foregoing signs of the existence of an ulcer and also on the fact of the urine being voided on the introduction of a *catheter*. Sometimes moreover I have noted the following case to occur; on turning the catheter about pain was experienced at the part of the canal where we had previously conjectured the ulceration to be situated, and the tissue being broken down by the catheter, there followed after the evacuation of the urine some blood and particles of tissue.... Whether in this case we ought to describe the mischief as something affecting the urethral canal, or say that the cause is something lying in the same canal, is scientifically unimportant). For the catheter must always have the shape of the passage leading to the bladder (Method. med. bk. IV. ch. 7. X. p. 301.); accordingly it must be bent into the shape of the letter "S" (Introduct. ch. 19. Vol. XIV. p. 788). The inventor of it was Erasistratus (ibid. p. 751.). The employment of the catheter is well described by *Paulus Aegineta* bk. VI. ch. 59., who adds that different catheters must be used according to age and sex.

as a rule it was solely as being the excretory duct of the bladder that the urethra had some little attention directed to it; while any signs it exhibited were generally regarded simply as symptoms connected with the urinary bladder and the kidneys. Partial *growing up, or morbid extuberance, in the urethra* (**συσσάρκωσις**,—a growing together) following on a previous ulceration is described by *Heliodorus*, as given in Oribasius, [1] occasioning either a narrowing of the urethral passage in one spot or its being filled up over its entire superficies with morbid outgrowths of tissue. Partial narrowing causes dysuria or strangury (difficulty of micturition), the narrowing of the whole canal by morbid outgrowths, ischuria (impossibility of micturition, retention of urine). The outgrowth must be removed by means of a small lancet. The mode of procedure is then as follows. The patient is placed on his back, the penis straight out; then with the fingers of the left hand the operator compresses it behind the spot where the growth is found, in order to prevent the blood from flowing inwards when the incision is made; next he takes the knife in the right hand, pushes the point into the urethra, divides it as far along as the base of the morbid growth, but not so as to go beyond it. This done, he proceeds to cut out the growth by means of a circular incision, and compresses the urethra between the fingers, causing the growth to spring forwards. Supposing it now projects but does not actually spring out, it is extracted by means of a *mydion* (boat-shaped instrument). After the removal of the growth the urethra must be protected from contact with the urine, which during the first few days is best done by applying an *ipoterion*, or compress, [2] made of papyrus. The mode of preparing

[1] *Oribasius*, Bk. L. ch. 8. (Mai's Classicor. auctor. e Vatican. codd. edit.—Classical Authors edited from the Vatican MSS.), Vol. IV. p. 187.

[2] The word **ἰποτήριον** is also found written **ἰπωτήριον** in *Galen*, De comp. medic. sec. gen. bk. IV. ch. 7. (XIII. p. 725.), who gives it as a

this is described in detail later on, and a sort of elastic catheter indicated. Catheters of copper and tin might also be used, or a quill taken for the purpose. The tin or lead catheters are not to be inserted till after the third day, and carry in front a projecting shield. The application of a bandage described is declared to be of great advantage. Scirrhosities of *the neck of the bladder*, abscesses and the like, are mentioned by *Galen* (loco citato) as occurring occasionally. With regard to *diseases of the prostates* subsequent investigations must authenticate the amount of knowledge possessed of these by the physicians of Antiquity.

Inflammation of the testicles [1] is usually characterized according to *Paulus Aegineta* [2] by pain under strong pressure by the fingers, while only a slight pressure causes no uneasiness. Redness and heat are slight externally, but the latter is perceptible deep in by an investigating finger. Sometimes fever is associated with it, and if the inflammation is not quickly combated, the pain, *Celsus* tells us, [3] extends to the inguinal and lumbar regions, the parts swell, the spermatic cord grows thicker and at the same time indurated. Both authorities make the treatment consist at first in blood-letting at the ankle, [4] and the use of soft poultices of bean-meal, [5] pounded

φάρμακον (remedy) invented by Heraclides of Tarentum, but which is not described in detail. The word is missing in our Lexicons, though Castellus gives it.

[1] *Galen*, In Hippocrat. de diaet. in acut. (XV p. 759.), *γίνεται δ' ἔντασις ὄρχεως ἐνίοτε μὲν ὑπὸ τῆς καθ' ἑαυτὸν φλεγμονῆς, ἐνίοτε δὲ ὑπό τινος τῶν ἄνω φλεγμαινόντων ἑλκομένου.* (Now tension of the testicles occurs sometimes owing to inflammation in the testicles itself, at other times owing to one of more inward parts that are inflamed becoming ulcerated).

[2] *Paulus Aegineta*, Bk. III. ch. 54.

[3] *Galen*, De prognost, ex puls. bk. IV. ch. 10. (IX. p. 416.). Synops. de puls. ch. 31. (ibid. p. 540).

[4] *Celsus*, Bk. VII. 18. VI. 18.

[5] *Hippocrates*, de Nat. Homin. edit. Kühn. Vol. I. p. 364. *Galen*, Vol. XV. p. 131.

cumin, linseed, etc. to which in cases of induration is added later on a mixture of crocus and wine. In obstinate instances poultices are used of *rad. cucumeris agrestis* (root of the wild cucumber); *Paulus Aegineta* under these circumstances prescribes grapes, peas, cumin, brimstone, nitre and resin, made into a cataplasm with honey, besides sundry wax-salves. A considerable list of remedial agents is found enumerated in *Marcellus* (ch. 33.) intended to combat the *tumores et dolores testiculorum* (swellings and pains in the testicles); of these we will only mention the salves of mutton-suet and nitre, the sea-water compresses, the poultices of *rad. cicutae* (hemlock root), white of egg, frankincense and ceruse (white lead). *Aretaeus* [1] gives us an interesting piece of information

[1] *Galen*, Vol. XI. p. 877., XII. p. 50.

[2] *Aretaeus*, De sign. chronic. bk. II. ch. 8., *θῶυμα δὲ τουτέων μέζων, εἰς ὄρχιας καὶ κρεμαστῆρας ἀδόκητον ἄλγος ἐπιφοιτῇ· πολλοὺς τῶν ἰητρῶν ἥδε ἡ ξυμπαθείη λήθει· καὶ γάρ καὶ ἐξέταμόν ποτε τοὺς κρεμαστῆρας, ὡς ἰδίην ἔχοντας αἰτίην·* (And there is another thing more surprising than this, when the pain suddenly shifts to the testicles and spermatic cords. Now this sympathy between the different organs escapes many physicians; and sometimes they actually cut out the spermatic cords as if these contained the special cause of the suffering). In the edition due to Kühn's industry the word *κρεμαστῆρες* is translated by *musculos cremasteres dictos* (the muscles called cremasteres). The expression is also found in the "De sign. acut." II. 6., and *Petit* in his Commentary on the first named passage declares in all seriousness that the sympathy was sufficently well known to anatomists, arising from the connection of the cremasteres muscles with the peritonaeum and its processes, which statement appears to rest on the datum of *Galen*, De usu partium bk. XIV. ch. 11. (IV. p. 193.) and De semine bk. II. ch. 5. (IV. p. 635.), where the cremasteres certainly are called *μυώδη σώματα* (muscular bodies) and compared with the round ligaments of the womb. Still *Galen* says distinctly in the latter passage that they contained arteries, veins and the spermatic ducts, in the Isagoge ch. 11. (XIV. p. 719.) *ὅς (γόνος) φέρεται ἐπ' αὐτοὺς διὰ τῶν κρεμαστήρων* (it,—the seed,—is

to the effect that in order to counteract neuralgia of the testicles and spermatic cord, accompanied at the same time by intestinal colic, the spermatic cord was *cut out*, being looked upon as the cause of the suffering. Important too is the case related by *Hippocrates*, [1] where a patient at Athens suffered from *prurigo* (itch) of the whole body, but above all of the *testicles* and the forehead, his skin having grown thick and hard as it does in leprosy, so that nowhere could it be pulled up above the general surface.

Induration of the testicles is mentioned by *Galen*, [2] who assigns it as one cause of sterility. The same author [3] likewise speaks of the testicles being affected

conveyed to them through the cremasteres). On the other hand in the "De musc. sect. Vol. XVIII. B. p. 997., the musculi cremasteres properly so called are clearly described, and the statement added: Τὸ δὲ ἔργον αὐτῶν ἀνατείνειν τὸν ὄρχιν· ὅθεν ἔνιοι κρεμαστῆρας αὐτοὺς ὀνομάζουσι (but their duty is to hold up the testicles, for which reason some name them the cremasteres,—suspenders). Neither Blancard-Kühn nor yet Kraus's Lexicon give under the word "Cremaster" any meaning but that of the muscles; the same is true of Schneider. Comp. *Paulus Aegineta* bk. VI. ch. 61., where the spermatic cords are also called παραστάται (supporters), as also by Galen, Defin. med. XIX. p. 362. and De semine bk. I. Vol. IV. p. 565., where they are spoken of as κιρσοειδῆς παραστάται (varicose parastatae). A denomination Herophilus first made use of (Galen IV. p. 582.) and which according to *Athenaeus* Deipnos. bk. IX. p. 396. was likewise given to the testicles.

[1] *Hippocrates*, Epidem. bk. V., edit. Kühn Vol. III. p. 548. Besides Hippocrates mentions almost exclusively the sympathetic swellings of the testicles that occur in cases of interruptions of the respiration, particularly in coughs. Sextus Placitus Papyriensis likewise, ch. 92. 4., ch. 101. 2., speaks of prurigo veretri (itching of the privates).

[2] *Galen*, De semine ch. 15. (IV. p. 564).

[3] *Galen*, De medic. sec. loc. bk. IX. ch. 8. (XIII. p. 317.). *Paulus Aegineta* bk. III. ch. 54. Both authors also make mention in this connection of *sarcosis testium* (swelling of the flesh of the testicles).

with *aphthaec* (**διδύμους ἀφθῶντας**), which he says should be treated with *terra cimolia* (Cimolian chalk) and myrtle-berries.

§ 41.

3. Ulcers of the Genitals.

φθινάς, ἄνθραξ, ἔσχαρα,—robigo, cancer. (Wasting ulcer, malignant pustule, scab,—ulcerous sore, eating, suppurating ulcer).

Though we cannot exactly subscribe to Alexander Simon's declaration to the effect that it would fill whole volumes, if we wished to cite systematically and in full all that has been said by the oldest and earlier medical Writers on ulcerous affections that attack the sexual parts from the points of view of pathology and therapeutics, still the number of such passages is no doubt sufficiently imposing. Unfortunately their contents cannot be described as equally important; for the pathological side is sacrificed to the therapeutic,—in fact the great majority give nothing more than the general names **ἕλκος** (ulcer) or **φλεγμονὴ αἰδοίου** (inflamed tumour of the privates), and then at once pass on to discuss the remedial measures expedient. This mode of procedure

Rambach, Thesaurus Eroticus, a work which now for the first time is within our reach to consult, quotes under *ova* pro coleis (ova,—eggs, put for testicles):

Vel tantus ad ora veniret
Aut aliis causis ita computresceret ovum,
Ne fieri posset quin crudelis medicina
Ova recidisset, medici reprobabilis usus.

(In fact such foulness appeared, or from other causes the testicle was so rotten, that nought could be done but for cruel surgery to cut out the testicles,—the horrid habit of doctors), and assigns to it the name *Ovidius Pseud.* Is this perhaps a specimen of those old lines properly to be ascribed to some mediaeval monk?

is indeed quite consistent with the general character of medical science in those days, for it is always the case that the more medicine declines, the more practitioners think themselves bound to look for remedial means nowhere but in the prescription-books. Curiously enough we find that almost every thing given by the later physicians already has a place in the pages of *Celsus*; the latter probably utilized the Alexandrian physicians, on whose knowledge the later Writers appear to have made little advance.

Now with regard to ulcers of the genitals in general,—these are of frequent occurrence, as to begin with the parts are from their very constitution prone to putrefactive changes, as well owing to their moist nature, possessing as they do so many glands that draw moisture together, and being covered with hair, as because they are at the same time excretory organs [1]. The time of year exerts an influence on

[1] *Galen*, Method. med. bk. V. ch. 4. (X. p. 325.), *καὶ κατὰ τοῦτο ἐπ' αἰδοίων καὶ ἕδρας εἰς τὴν τοιαύτην ἀνάγκην ἀφικνούμεθα πολλάκις, ὅτι ῥᾳδίως σήπεται τὰ μόρια διά τε τὴν σύμφυτον ὑγρότητα καὶ ὅτι περιττωμάτων εἰσὶν ὀχετοί.* (And in this respect with regard to the privates and fundament we constantly come back to the same conditions of causation, viz. that these parts are readily affected by putrefaction, as well owing to their natural moistness as because they are channels for excretions). Commentar. in Hippocrat. De humor. (XVI. p. 414.), *ἀλλὰ καὶ ἡ φύσις τῶν τόπων οὐ μικρὸν πρὸς τὸ δέχεσθαι σηπεδόνας ποιεῖ· καὶ γὰρ τὸ στόμα καὶ τὰ αἰδοῖα πολλὴν ὑγρότητα τῇ φύσει κέκτηται· καὶ προσέτι τοὺς ἀδένας ἔχουσιν ἐγγὺς, ἅπερ πάντα τὰ περιττὰ εἰσδέχεσθαι πεφύκασιν.* (Moreover the nature of the localities has no small influence on their liability to putrefactive changes. For the mouth and the private parts possess much moisture of their very nature; and besides this they have the glands close by, all which circumstances tend naturally to make them the receptacles of excessive moisture). De usu partium bk. XI. ch. 14. (III. p. 910.), *ἤδε δὲ καὶ περὶ τὴν τῶν αἰδοίων φύσιν αἱ τρίχες ἅμα μὲν ἐξ ἀνάγκης ἐγένοντο, θερμὰ γὰρ καὶ ὑγρὰ τὰ χωρία.* (Now this quality and the fact of the privates being naturally surrounded with hair would seem to be necessary

the appearance of such ulcers, for they show themselves chiefly in the summer, [1] particularly when a South wind is blowing, [2] a wind that is moist and warm and fosters a tendency towards the resolution of fluid and solid parts alike. Thus ulcers of the genitals are likewise subject to epidemic influence, as has been clearly demonstrated on previous pages. They are acquired by coition, and that equally by natural coition, as the instance of Hero mentioned on a previous page shows without a shadow of doubt, as by the unnatural forms, and particularly by paederastia, which last caused the malady of Naevolus' slave also referred to in an earlier passage. Moreover in the hot regious of Asia and Africa want of cleanliness also, especially when men were uncircumcised, gave occasion, as in Apion's case, to the establishment of ulcers of the genitals. These were looked upon by the Ancient physicians in most instances as an outcome of the evil humours of the body,—an opinion which need cause us less surprise as even in much more modern times a large

consequences, because the localities are hot and damp).—*Cassius*, Problem. 2., Cur supremae corporis sedes ad nomas sunt opportunae, similiter et concavae? An quia noma putrefactio est quaedam et sensus interitus atque extinctio. Supremae autem partes ob alimenti penuriam calore facile destituuntur, ita ut hac de causa census ablationem incurrant. Concavae vero ob humidae in ipsis materiae affluentem copiam, cuius occasione putredine corripiunter. (Why are the extreme parts of the body liable to nomae (eating ulcers), and likewise the concave parts? It is because a *noma* is a form of putrefaction and a perishing and extinction of sensation? Now the extreme parts owing to the scantiness of the nourishment they get are easily robbed of heat, so that for this reason they incur loss of sensation. On the other hand the concave parts owing to the excess of moist matter that collects in them, which is the occasion of their being attacked by putrefaction). Comp. what was said above under the head of "Climate".

[1] *Hippocrates*, Aphorism. Vol. III. p. 724. *Galen*, Vol. XVI. p. 27.

[2] *Galen*, Comment in Hippocrat. De humor. Vol. XVI. p. 414.

number of physicians have endeavoured to explain the origin of chancres by an antecedent general infection, that manifested itself in this way, viz. by the appearance of these sores. Ulcers not unfrequently took the form of aphthae, particularly in women, [1] being in that case more superficial, but for that very reason readily eating their way over adjacent parts,—(*cancer*, eating ulcer). In many instances inflammation (**φλεγμονὴ, ἐρυσίπελας**,—phlegmonous inflammation, erysipelas) and swelling of the parts affected were accompanying circumstances. They were often painful,—sometimes moist, sometimes dry. In the majority of cases they assumed under favouring conditions a putrefactive character (**φαγέδαινα**,—phagedenic or eating ulcer), under which circumstances worms actually bred in the sores, or else they manifested from the very first a marked tendency to pass over into gangrene (**ἄνθραξ**, *carbunculus*,—malignant pustule, carbuncle), where as a rule merely an ulcer developing from a minute bladder (bleb) or **φῦμα** existed in the first instance. On the other hand its course was often very chronic, without phlegmonous ulcers at all, or if these were present, either they were callous, or else condylomatous outgrowths sprung from them.

In accordance with these varying factors did the *treatment of ulcers of the genitals* vary, though without any universally recognized special distinction from that adopted for ulcers in general. Speaking generally, purgings by the rectum are not indicated; but preferably in affections of the genitals revulsory treatment by emetics is employed. [2] If blood-letting

[1] *Hippocrates*, De nat. muliebr. Vol. II. p. 586., *ἀφθήσῃ τὰ αἰδοῖα* (the privates affected with aphthae). De morb. muliebr. bk. II. Vol. II. p. 614.

[2] Galen, Method. med. bk. XIII. ch. 11. (X. p. 903.), *ἀντισπᾶν γὰρ χρὴ τῶν ἀρχομένων ῥευματίζεσθαι παρρωτάτω τὸ περιττὸν, οὐχ ἕλκειν ἐπ' αὐτά· κατὰ τοῦτον οὖν τὸν λόγον οὐδὲ γαστρὸς οὐδ' ἐντέρων ἀρξαμένων φλεγμαίνειν ὑπηλάτῳ χρῆσθαι προσήκει· τὴν δ' αὐτην*

is resorted to, it must be either in the hollow of the knee or at the ankle. [1] As to local measures, fatty matters according to *Antyllus* are not good for the genitals, [2] whereas astringents and desiccatives are beneficial, if that is to say the phlegmonous condition is absent. [3] On the contrary if the latter is found, this must in the first place be combated, then a mixture applied consisting of sifted resin and pounded cumin, or alternatively a poultice of barley-meal, hydromel and vine-leaves reduced to a pulp, or else cumin with butter and tree-resin. [4] Above all Galen [5]

ἔνδειξιν ἔχει τούτοις μὲν μήτρα τοῖς ὀργάνοις αἰδοῖα· τό γε μὴν ἐμέτοις χρῆσθαι τῶν αἰδοίων πεπονθότων ἀντισπαστικόν ἐστι βοήθημα. (For what is necessary is to reject the excess as far as may be from the parts that are beginning to be congested, not to draw it towards them. Therefore in accordance with this reasoning neither in the case of belly nor of intestines, when these have begun to be inflamed, is it expedient to employ purging medicine; also the same indication as in the case of these organs holds good for womb, and private parts. The treatment when the privates are attacked is revulsory, viz. the use of emetics).

[1] *Galen*, loco citato p. 904., *ἐπὶ δὲ νεφρῶν καὶ κύστεως αἰδοίου τε καὶ μήτρας τὰς ἐν τοῖς σκέλεσι, μάλιστα μὲν τὰς κατὰ τὴν ἰγνύαν, εἰ δὲ μή, τὰς παρὰ σφυρόν.* (In complaints of the kidneys and bladder, of the privates and womb, bleedings on the legs, and particularly in the hollow of the knee, or otherwise at the ankle).

[2] *Oribasius*, Medicin. collect. bk. IX. ch. 24., Pudendis incommoda sunt pinguia, prosunt autem adstringentia. (Fatty matters are prejudicial to the privates, astringents on the contrary are of advantage).

[3] *Galen*, De medicam. sec. loc. compos. bk. IX. ch. 8. (XIII. p. 315.), *τὰ δ' ἐν αἰδοίοις ἕλκη καὶ κατὰ τὴν ἕδραν χωρὶς φλεγμονῆς ὄντα ξηραινόντων πάνυ δεῖται φαρμακων.* (Now ulcers on the privates and about the fundament, if free from the phlegmonous condition, require dessicative drugs above all). Method. med. bk. V. ch. 15. (X. p. 381.).

[4] *Galen*, loco citato pp. 317, 383.—*Oribasius*, Synops. bk. IX. ch. 38.

[5] *Galen*, Method. med. bk. X. ch. 9. (X. p. 702.).—*Aëtius*, Tetrab. II. serm. 1. ch. 91.

recommended in the early stages before the appearance of an eating or phagedenic ulcer (*κατὰ τῶν ἐν αἰδοίοις φλεγμονῶν ἐν ἀρχῇ, πρὶν ὑποφαίνεσθαι τινα νομώδη σηπέδονα,*—in phlegmonous affections of the privates at the commencement, before any eating ulceration appear) a *ceratum rosaceum* (wax-salve of roses), the preparation of which he gives *in extenso*, and Aëtius copying from him; its activity is enhanced by the addition of a little *oleum sabinum* (Sabine oil). If the ulcers are complicated with *swelling*, a compound of white-lead (*ψιμύθιον*) and triturated vine-leaves is applied, [1] sea-water compresses, [2] or poultices of boiled lentils and pomegranate rind. [3] For *painful* ulcers pompholyx (flowers of zinc) [4] was particularly recommended, or a decoction of linseed with the addition of myrrh; also woman's milk may be advantageously used as well, [5] especially with the addition of *anodynes*, and above all pompholyx or flowers of zinc. *Paulus Aegineta* (loco citato) prescribed the application of butter and resin melted together in equal parts, or linseed ground up with myrrh and resin. In *raw* and *dry* ulcers of the genitals the aloe was very generally prescribed; it was powdered and sprinkled over the sore, [6] or if a phlegmonous condition was already established, dissolved in water. [7]

[1] *Galen*, De compos.medic. sec. loc. bk. IX. ch. 8. (XIII. p. 316.). *Paulus Aegineta*, bk. III. ch. 59. *Oribasius*, De loc. affect. bk. IV. ch. 102.

[2] *Galen*, loco citato p. 316. *Paulus Aegineta*, loco citato. *Oribasius*, loco citato.

[3] *Galen*, loco citato p. 317.

[4] *Galen*, loco citato p. 316. De simplic. medic. temperam. ac facult. bk. X. (XII. p. 235.). *Paulus Aegineta*, loco cit. *Oribasius*, loco cit.

[5] *Galen*, De simplic. medic. temperam, ac. facult. bk. X. ch. 2. (XII. p. 268.).

[6] *Galen*, Method. med. bk. V. ch. 15. (X. p. 382.), De composit. medic. sec. loc. bk. IX. ch. 8. (XIII. p, 316.). *Paulus Aegineta*, loco cit. *Aëtius*, Tetrab. I. serm. 1. *Nonnus*, Epit. ch. 195.

[7] *Galen*, De simplic. medic. temperam. ac facult. bk. VI. (XI. p. 822.). *Aëtius*, loco cit.

In the second case *Oribasius* [1] prescribed likewise the use of lead,—and indeed it was a usual recommendation with regard to most of the recognized remedies that they should be pounded and triturated in leaden mortars with leaden pestles.

Superficial ulcers *of an aphthae-like character* were treated as early as in *Hippocrates'* time and indeed by him [2] with a decoction of myrtle-berries boiled in wine. As a remedy against *moist* ulcers a certain mixture of Crito's, compounded of frankincense and myrrh boiled in sweet wine, had a great reputation; [3] but above all the powder of *charta usta* (papyrus ash), anise and *cucurbita* (gourd) [4] was employed, after the ulcer had been washed with urine; further the *cortex pinus* (cork-tree), *lapis haematites* (bloodstone, haematite iron-ore), [5] to which frankincense was added in the case of more deep-seated ulcers, [6] also *cadmium ustum* (burnt calamine) (Paulus Aegineta); likewise washing with urine proved beneficial. [7] In *spreading or eating* ulcers (**νομῶδες ἕλκος**) a poultice was applied of lentils, pomegranates and oxymel [8] reduced to a pulp; but a still more usual remedy was to sprinkle verdigris over the sore, and especially

[1] *Oribasius*, De virtute simplicium bk. II., under word "Molibdos",—lead.

[2] *Hippocrates*, De natura muliebri Vol. II. p. 586.

[3] *Galen*, De composit. med. sec. loc. bk. VII. (XIII. p. 36.).

[4] *Galen*, loco cit. p. 316., Method. med. bk. V. ch. 15. (X. p. 382.), De simplic. medicam. temperam. ac facult. bk. VI. (XI. p. 832,). *Paulus Aegineta*, bk. III. ch. 59. *Oribasius*, De loc. affect. IV. 102. Collect. IX. 24. *Nonnus*, Epitom. ch. 195.

[5] Orpheus de lapidibus XVIII. 33.,

ἀνδρός τ' αἰδοίων ἄκος ἔσσεται, ὅς κε πίῃσι.

(And it shall be a cure of the privates of a man, whosoever shall drink thereof).

[6] *Galen*, Method. med. bk. V. ch. 15. (X. p. 363.).

[7] *Galen*, De simplic. medic. temperam. ac facult. bk. X. (XII. p. 285.).

[8] *Paulus Aegineta*, bk. III. ch. 59. *Oribasius*, Collect. bk. IX. ch. 24. *Nonnus*, Epitom. ch. 195.

[9] *Paulus Aegineta*, bk. IV. ch. 44. *Aëtius*, Tetrab. IV. serm. 2. eh. 17.

verdigris in conjunction with a salve made of *charta usta* (papyrus ash), sulphur, lead-slag, honey and *ceratum rosaceum* (wax-salve of roses); another remedy highly thought of was the *pastillus corax* (corax cake), the ingredients of which were verdigris, chalk, gall-nut, frankincense, turpentine, wax, oil of myrtles and beef-tallow; this was particularly beneficial in combating the carbunculous form of the disease. Very often however recourse to the cauterizing iron and the knife was unavoidable, especially if gangrene supervened, or if the callosity of the edges of the ulcer made cicatrisation impossible.

Such were the general methods of treatment employed for ulcers of the genital organs, but these naturally varied according to the various distinctions between the several sorts conditional on the situation of the sore. Thus it becomes our next business to indicate on what parts of the body ulcers were observed:—

A. Ulcers on the male Genital Organs.

It is invariably the case that forms of ulceration affecting the male genitals are the most familiar and best known, and this was equally true in Antiquity. Whatever information the Ancient physicians deemed it necessary to record on the subject is found as early as *Celsus* laid down with something approaching to completeness in his writings (VI. 18.).

a. *Ulcers of the Prepuce.*

According to Leonidas [1] fissures and cracks in the prepuce frequently occurred, in all cases of the latter being too tight and being forcibly drawn back. On these supervened pain and phlegmonous inflammation; and then if a cure were not speedily effected, the edges assumed a condition of callosity, necessitating

[1] *Aëtius*, Tetrab. IV. serm. 2. ch. 24. Collect. L. ch. 9.

the use of the knife for its removal. However, more often than not the wound broke out again, because as was noted as early as by *Hippocrates*, [1] wounds of the prepuce are as a rule obstinate in healing. To meet this eventuality *Galen* [2] provides an entirely suitable procedure. While ulcers of the glans penis demand desiccative remedies, those of the prepuce rather call for *epilotics*, [3] especially anise. Supposing the prepuce to become gangrenous, it must be cut away circularly, and the bleeding stopped by cauterization; if this treatment is not needful, a mixture of verdigris with honey, or pomegranate and vetch is applied. [4] Ulcers on the inner fold of the prepuce, as also on the skin of the penis generally, are mentioned by *Celsus* (VI. 18.), the latter likewise by *Galen*. Such ulcers on the inner fold of the prepuce, Celsus states, not unfrequently give occasion to the setting up of phimosis and paraphimosis; and yet another consequence, a morbid growing together of glans and prepuce was observed by *Oribasius* (loco citato, 5.) and *Paulus Aegineta* (VI. 56.), for which these authors prescribe appropriate medical and surgical treatment. Under the name of *cancer* (eating ulcer) of the prepuce Celsus, it would seem, describes the **νομὴ** (spreading ulcer) of the Greak physicians, which commences by the ulcer turning black. Occasionally too the ulcers developed out of themselves morbid growths, excrescences or condy-

[1] *Hippocrates*, Coac, praenot. Vol. I. p. 389., Aphorism. Vol. III. p. 752. *Galen*, Method, med. bk. III. ch. 1. (X. p. 161.).

[2] *Galen*, Method. med. bk, XIV. ch. 15. (X. p. 1001 sqq.).

[3] *Galen*, loco cit. bk. V. ch. 15. (X. p. 381.), De simplic. medic. temperam. ac facult. bk. VI. (XI. pp. 832, 806.).

[4] *Paulus Aegineta*, bk. VI. ch. 57.

[5] *Galen*, Method. med. bk. V. ch. 15. (X. p. 381.), *Aëtius*, Tetrab. III. 2. ch. 15., recommended drawing the prepuce forwards in micturition, so as to make the urine flow hetween the foreskin and glans penis, by which means the ulcers and fissures are readily cured.

lomata, particularly the form known as *thymion* (warty excrescence).

b. *Ulcers of the Glans Penis.*

These are, as pointed out by *Celsus* (VI. 18.), best described by taking their pathological and therapeutic aspects together; but it would serve no useful purpose to quote once more in this place the passages dealing with this part of the subject, which have been so often printed already. He makes a distinction, as does *Galen*, [5] between dry and clean, moist and suppurative, ulcers, the latter of which readily lead to phimosis and paraphimosis. The discharge is sometimes thin and watery, sometimes purulent, and on occasion becomes evil-smelling; the ulcerations both spread superficially and penetrate inwards, and may actually destroy the glans underneath the prepuce, so that it perishes altogether. When this happens, *Paulus Aegineta* (VI. 57.) has a leaden pipette inserted in the orifice of the urethra, to enable the patient to pass water. In other cases the prepuce grows into one with the ulcerated glans penis (*Celsus, Paulus Aegineta*, *Oribasius*). Ulcers *circa coronam glandis* (round the crown of the glans penis) are mentioned by *Aëtius.* [4]

A special kind is the *cancer colis* (eating ulcer of the member), probably the same as the **νομὴ** (spreading ulcer) of the Greeks, which Aëtius [1] delineates as a spreading, flaccid ulcer, which on pressure emits a thin bloody discharge, that subsequently becomes feculent. Hemorrhage is apt to supervene according to Celsus on the shedding of a cicatrix artificially produced by operation or the cauterizing iron. Another species of *cancer* is the **φαγέδαινα** (phage-

[1] *Galen*, Method. med. bk. V. ch. 15. (X. 381.). *Paulus Aegineta*, bk. III. 59. *Oribasius*, Synops. IX. 37. *Marcellus Empiricus*. ch. 33.

[2] *Aëtius*, Tetrab. IV. serm. 2. en 3.

[3] *Aëtius*, Tetrab. IV. serm. 2. ch. 17.

denic, eating ulcer) of the Greeks, which extends rapidly and penetrates to the bladder. It appears to be identical with **ἄνθραξ** (malignant pustule), though Celsus mentions the *carbunculus colis* (carbuncle of the member) in a special category; for the description he gives, bk. V. ch. 28., of carbuncle is equally applicable to the phagedaena. **Ἄνδραξ** (malignant pustule) begins with itching, later on a pustule, or else a number of little bladders or blebs resembling millet-seeds appear, which burst in much the same way as a blister due to burning does, leaving behind an *ulcus crustaceum* (scab-encrusted ulcer), resembling the cicatrix of a burn; this is firmly adherent and black in colour. The surrounding tissue is likewise black and violently inflamed, the inflammation not unfrequently having an erysipelas-like character. *Galen*[3] designates the process **ἀνθράκωσις**, and declares that buboes are an accompanying feature. He holds the ulcers of the genitals occurring under the special climatic conditions laid down by Hippocrates above to have been partly **ἄνθραξ**,[4] the disease to which Hero succumbed.

Another kind of ulcer affecting the male genitals is mentioned by *Pollux*[1] under the name of **θηρίωμα** (malignant sore), which *Celsus* (V. 28.) likewise speaks of, but without particularizing its situation. The same

[1] *Actuarius*, Method. med. II. ch. 12. *Aëtius*, Tetrab. IV. serm. 2. ch. 18. *Sextus Placitus Papyriensis*, ch. V. 2. V. 43. *Theodor. Priscianus* I. 25.

[2] *Galen*, Isag. ch. 16. (XIV. p. 777.).

[3] *Galen*, De temperam. 4. (I. p. 532.).

[4] *Pollux*, Onomast. bk. IV. ch. 26. 206., θηρίωμα, γίνεται μὲν ἕλκος περὶ ἀνδρῶν αἰδοῖα, ἔστι δὲ ὅτε καὶ περὶ δακτ ύ λ ο υ ς [read δακτυλ ί ο υ ς], καὶ ἀλλαχοῦ, αἷμα πολὺ καὶ μέλαν καὶ δυσῶδες ἀφιὲν μετὰ μελανίας τὴν σάρκα ἀνεσθίον. (θηρίωμα, —malignant sore, is an ulcer affecting men's privates, as well as sometimes the fingers (? the anus). and other parts, discharging much black evil-smelling blood, accompanied with black colour and eating away the flesh).

fact applies to ulcers of the glans penis as to those of the prepuce, viz. that many forms of morbid outgrowths arise from them; in other instances callosities on the edges of the ulcers are built up, leaving behind a callous protuberance, which the Greeks appear to have called ἧλος (a nail), the Romans *clavus* (a nail).[1] The proper treatment to be followed in each of these special cases is given by Celsus and the Writers he cites.

B. Ulcers of the Female Genital Organs.

In this connection, as indeed in the discussion of the female genital organs generally, we once again meet with the difficulty due to the indefiniteness of the names given to the several parts. Not only do the Greeks constantly make use of the general expression **αἰδοῖα, μόρια** (privates, parts), but they likewise employ **ὑστέρον** and **μήτρα** (the womb) sometimes as meaning the vagina, sometimes the uterus, though it is true the later Writers like *Galen*[2] designate the vagina **ἡ ὑστέρα,** the uterus **ὁ ὑστέρος,** yet without keeping consistently to the distinction.

[1] *Sextus Placitus Papyriensis*, XV. 3.

[2] *Galen*, Isagog. ch. 11. (XIV. p. 719.), **ταῖς δὲ γυναιξὶν ἡ ὑστέρα ἔοικεν ὀσχῇ ἀνεστραμμένῃ,** (but in women the vagina is like a scrotum inverted), though in accordance with what comes next the uterus may also by understood to be here intended. Commentar. in Hippocrat. De Alimento (XV. p. 326.), **περὶ δὲ τῆς ὑστέρας ὀλίγα ῥηθήσεται· καὶ πρῶτον μὲν, πότερον ὑστέρον ἢ μήτραν κλητέον ἐστὶ τὸ μόριον ἐκεῖνο, ὃ πρὸς τὴν κύησιν ἔδωκε φύσις ταῖς γυναιξὶν, οὐδὲν διαφέρει.** (Now about the vagina we shall not say much. However first of all we may remark as to the question whether we should name the part which nature has given to women for connection ὑστέρος or **μήτρα,** that this is a matter of indifference). Moreover the Physicians use **κόλπος** (fold, bosom), e.g. *Galen*, De tumoribus praeter naturam ch. 4. (VII. p. 717.) for the vaginal canal, as the Romans did *sinus* (fold, bosom) in Latin,

The same applies to the use in Latin of *locus* (place), *pars* (part), and *vulva* (womb), which last word stands for the uterus in *Celsus*, *Pliny* and most of the later Writers.

Passing over the indefinite expressions *dolores* (pains), *inflammatio* or *phlegmoné* (inflammation) of the genitals, although the treatment prescribed for them clearly implies that very often ulceration was concurrently present, we find the various kinds of ulcers of the female genitals most fully and systematically described by *Aretaeus*,[1] *Paulus Aegineta* (III. 65—68.) and *Aëtius*[2] following Archigenes, Soranus and Aspasia.

Abscesses Aëtius says (loco citato, ch. 110.) occur on the female *labia*; if these extend in the direction of the anus, they must not be opened with the knife, as fistulas are liable to be set up, but there is no fear of this when they extend towards the urethra. The same author (p. 109.) speaks of *pustulae scabrae* (scabrous, scurfy pustules) in the vagina and orifice of the womb, which throw off bran-like scales, as also (ch. 108.) of *tubercula miliaria* (miliary tubercles) in the same localities. These may no doubt be recognized by touch, but are better diagnosed by means of the uterine speculum, or *Dioptra*, and *ex coitus affrictu* (in consequence of friction in coition) interfere with menstruation and conception. Obviously what is here pointed to is the swollen mucous glands,

[1] *Celsus*, bk. V. ch. 25. *Marcellus*, De medic. ch. 7. 17. *Sextus Placitus Papyriensis* II. 7., XV. 2., XXXI. 12. *L. Apuleius* De herb. XLIX. 1., LXXIV. 3., CXXI. 2.

[2] *Celsus*, bk. V. 28. 25. *Galen*, Vol. II. p. 150., X. p. 993. XI. p. 9. 1001., XVI. p. 180., XVII. B. pp. 274, 855., XIX, p. 428. *Oribasius*, De virt. simpl. bk. II. 1. under word "Leucoion", De loc. affect. bk. IV. ch. 112. *Aëtius*, Tetrab. I. serm. 1. under word "Leucoion", Tetrab. IV. serm. 4. ch. 83. *Actuarius*, Method. med. bk. VI. chs. 8, 9.

[3] *Aretaeus*, De sign. chron. bk. II. ch. 11.

[4] *Aëtius*, Tetrab. IV. serm. 4. chs. 88—94.

which in our modern practice likewise are frequently observed in gonorrhœal cases. Often the ulcers take a form characterized by *fissures* (ῥαγάδες, *fissurae*,—fissures, *rimae*,—cracks), particularly at the orifice of the uterus. [1] Sometimes they become callous, at others give rise to morbid outgrowths; as a rule the discharge is a thin watery juice, and pain is felt during coition.

Ulcers strictly so called, says Aretaeus, are either superficial, in fact rather excoriations than ulcers, and far-spreading; they itch as though salt had been sprinkled on the surface, give off a small quantity of thick pus, free from smell, and are not malignant. To this class probably belong the aphthae-like ulcers of Hippocrates. [3] In other cases they are more deep-seated; being then painful, discharging an evil-smelling pus, and having a less mild character than the former, but still not such as to be described as malignant. If they penetrate yet deeper, the edges then become rough, the discharge takes the form of a malodorous juice, while the pain is more severe than in the other kinds. The actual tissue of the womb is partially destroyed in the latter case, while morbid outgrowths form, which make cicatrization extremely difficult. This last kind was known also as *phagedaena*, (eating ulcer); it is dangerous, especially if the pain increases and the patient falls into low spirits. An offensive juice is discharged, so foul that the patient herself is hard put to bear it; the ulcer is highly intolerant of being touched for the application of remedial means; it may end fatally,

[1] The uterine speculum is mentioned by *Aëtius* also chs. 86, 88. and its use described; as also by *Paulus Aegineta*, bk. III. ch. 65., bk. VI. ch. 73., and for the examination of the rectum, bk. VI. ch. 78.

[2] *Galen*, De loc. affect. bk. VI. ch. 5. (VIII. p. 436.). *Paulus Aegineta*, bk. III. chs. 59, 75. *Aëtius*, Tetrab. IV. serm. 2. ch. 15., serm. 4. ch. 107.

[3] *Hippocrates*, De natura muliebri Vol. II. pp. 586, (588), 591., De morbis mulier. bk. II. Vol. II. 878.

and is known under the name of "Crab-ulcer". *Νομὴ* (spreading ulcer),[1] carbuncle and *sordida ulcera* (foul ulcers) of the uterus are mentioned by *Aëtius* (loco citato), who shows the mode of investigating them by means of the uterine speculum and a treatment consisting mainly of injections[2] and pessaries prepared of a number of different remedies. Not unfrequently unskilful treatment of ulcers of the vagina occasioned morbid outgrowths, which according to *Celsus*' teaching,[3] must be removed by surgical means. Lastly the fact that ulcers of the genital organs of women were prejudicial to men who consummated coition with them and were for that reason dreaded by them, is clearly implied in the narrative of *Cedrenus*.[4]

[1] *Nonnus*, Epitom. ch. 206., distinguishes between *ῥυπάρον ἕλκος, νομὴ μετὰ φλεγμονῆς* (foul ulcer, eating sore with inflammation) and *ἄνευ φλεγμονῆς νομή* (eating sore without inflammation); as does *Paulus Aegin.*, bk. III. ch. 66.

[2] By means of the uterine syringe, *μητρεγχύτης*. *Galen*, Synopsis medic. sec. loc. IX. ch. 8. (XIII. p. 316.). *Oribasius*, Collect. medic. bk. X. ch. 25.

[3] *Celsus*, bk. VII. ch. 28. *Pliny*, Histor. nat. XXX. 4. *Sextus Placitus Papyriensis*, XXXII. 2. *Paulus Aegineta*, bk. III. ch. 73.

[4] *Cedrenus*, *Σύνοψις ἱστορικὴ* (Historical Survey), edit. J. Goar and H. Fabrot, Paris 1647. fol., p. 266. In Diocletian's time when persecutions of the Christians were general, a fair and modest maiden was charged with having spoken disrespectfully of the gods; for punishment she was sent to a brothel with the order that she must reimburse the brothel-keeper three shillings a day. The latter was to make her serve as a prostitute, and she was to receive all who wished to go with her, Account however was taken of the fact that she declared *she had an ulcer on her privates*, and this obliged them to wait till it was cured (*προσφασιζομένη ἕλκος ἔχειν ἐπὶ κρυπτοῦ τόπου καὶ τούτου ἀπαλλαγὴν ἐκδέξασθαι* (pretexting she had an ulcer in a secret place, and must wait for its removal). The same story is told by *Palladius*, Hist. lausiac. ch. 148., as having happened at Corinth, who calls the ulcer an evil-smelling one, that might easily stir the repugnance of her visitors against the girl, (*λέγουσα, ὅτι ἕλκος ἔχω τι*

4. Ulcers of the Fundament.

We have already seen how fissures and ulcers of the fundament were a not unusual consequence of the vice of the pathic, yet not the faintest indication of the fact is to be found in the medical Writers. The knowledge possessed by the Ancients as to affections of the fundament have been collected with a very considerable degree of completeness by *Aëtius*, [1] especially as copying Galen; the remaining authorities treat them as a rule in conjunction with the corresponding affections of the genitals, and mostly recommend the same remedies for them. So far therefore as they are concerned we refer back to the information given in connection with the latter. At the same time there mark may be permitted that this juxtaposition of the two seems to point to the Ancients having held, as we maintain they did, the view that affections of the genitals and affections of the anus arose from like causes and were of like character, as is shown by their dealing with the one and the other class of diseases on the same general lines.

Ardentes dolores (burning pains) [2] and *pruritus*

εἰς κεκρυμμένον τόπον, ὅπερ ἐσχάτως ὄζει, καὶ δέδοικα μὴ εἰς μῖσός μου ἔηθητε τῷ ἀποτροπαίῳ τοῦ ἕλκους· ἔνδοτε οὖν μοι ὀλίγοις ἡμέρας καὶ ἐξουσίαν μου ἔχετε καὶ δωρεάν με ἔχειν,—(saying "I have an ulcer in a secret part, which smells very ill, and I fear you may come to feel repugnance towards me owing to the foulness of the ulcer; grant me therefore a few days, then may work your will of me and I undertake to give myself freely). The last sentence shows clearly that the ulcer was easy to cure. Comp. Nicephorus, Hist. eccles. bk. VII. chs. 12, 13.

[1] *Aëtius*, Tetrab. IV. serm. II. chs. 1, 2, 3, 9, 10. *Galen*, Synops. med. sec. loc. bk. IX. ch. 7. (XIII. p. 315.). *Oribasius*, De loc. affect. bk. IV. ch. 93. *Paulus Aegineta*, bk. III. ch. 59.

[2] *Galen*, Euporist. bk. I. ch. 14. (XIV. p. 382.), Synops. med. sec. loc. bk. IX. ch. 7. (XIII. p. 315.), *Oribasius*, De loc. affect. bk. IV. ch. 93. *Paulus Aegineta*, bk. III. ch. 59.

(itching)[1] of the anus are not uncommon. *Inflammations*[2] often supervene as a consequence of fissures, morbid growths and ulcers. *Rhagades* (cracks) and *fissures*[3] are found either in the sphincter muscle or in the rectum, and are an accompaniment of condylomata, whenever the latter become inflamed and spread, causing the surrounding tissue to rupture; the edges frequently assume a callous condition, and then require to be broken down and thus transformed into a simple ulcer. Often abscesses are set up[4] as a result of the inflammation, and these are liable to lead to fistulas. The ulcers[5] on occasion assume the character of the **νομὴ φαγέδαινα** (eating and spreading ulcer). Supposing them situated on the sphincter ani, they must neither be cut nor cauterized, as severance of the muscle makes it impossible for the patient to retain the faeces. This loss of retentive power may also occur apart from any operation, if the **νομὴ** (spreading ulcer) destroy the muscle. Supposing on the contray the **νομὴ** to be below the sphincter, knife or cauterizing iron may either of

[1] *Galen*, Euporist. bk. I. ch. 14. (XIV. p. 382.). *Oribasius*, De loc. affect. bk. IV. ch. 94.

[2] *Galen*, Synops. med. sec. loc. bk. IV. ch. 6. (XIII. p. 309.), ch. 7. (p. 314.), Synops. med, sec. gen. bk. V. ch. 12. (XIII. p. 837.). *Oribasius*, De loc. affect. bk. IV. ch. 92. *Paulus Aegineta*, bk. III. ch. 59. *Nonnus*, Epit. ch. 198.

[3] *Celsus*, bk. VI. ch. 18., bk. VII. 30., bk. V. 20. *Galen*, Synops. med. sec. loc. bk. IX. ch. 6. (XIII. p. 309.), Synops. med. sec. gen. bk. V. ch. 13. (XIII. p. 840.), De simplic. med. temp. ac facult. bk. IX. chs. 3, 23. (XII. p. 231.), bk. XI. ch. 1. (XII. p. 333.), *Paulus Aegineta*, bk. III. ch. 59., bk. VI. ch. 80. *Oribasius*, De loc. affect. bk. IV. ch. 95. *Dioscorides* bk. I. ch. 34., ch. 94. *Sribonius Largus*, De compos. med. ch. 223. *Marcellus*, ch. 31. *Nonnus*, Epitom. ch. 196. *Isidorus*, Origin. bk. IV. ch. 7.

[4] *Aëtius*, loco citato ch. 9. from Leonidas. *Paulus Aegineta*, bk. VI. ch. 78.

[5] *Celsus*, VI. 18. *Galen*, Method. med. bk. V. ch. 15. (X. p. 381.), Synops. med. sec. loc. bk. IX. ch. 6. (XIII. p. 307.), De simplic. temperam ac facult. bk. VI. (XI. p. 821.). *Paulus Aegineta*, bk. III. ch. 59.

them be employed. In some instances ulcers lead to a morbid growth at the orificium ani, that must be obviated by means of pipettes of lead. [1] In other cases *rhagades* (cracks) and ulcers lead eventually to morbid outgrowths.

5. Buboes.

Bubo, panus (swelling resembling the thread wound on bobbin of a shuttle), paniculus (diminutive of same), inguen (swelling in the groin).

Under the name of *bubo* the ancient Physicians understood any form of inflammation of the lymphatic glands. Now such inflammation occurs above all other places in the inguinal region, and thus inflammation of the inguinal glands came to be especially indicated by the word, as well as the inguinal region itself. Similarly the Romans used *inguen* (the groin) both for the region and for the disease. Subsequently many distinctions were drawn; a phlegmonous affection combined with swelling was called a **βουβὼν** (bubo), while the name **φῦμα** (swelling) was appropriated to a swelling of the glands characterized by its rapid establishment and its tendency to suppuration (bubo with suppurative pustule in the centre), and **φύγεθλον** (burning swelling) to one conjoined with (cutaneous) inflammation of an erysipelas character, [2] which last form, if it passes on into induration, is known as **χοιρὰς** or *struma* (scrofulous or strumous swelling). The best exposition from the points of view equally

[1] *Paulus Aegineta*, bk. VI. ch. 80.

[2] *Galen*, Method. med. ad Glaucon. bk. II. ch. 1. (XI. p. 77.), De tumor. praet. nat. ch. 15. (VII. p. 729.), Comment. in Hippocrat. Aphorism. (XVII. B. p. 636.).—*Paulus Aegineta*, bk. IV. ch. 22. *Actuarius*, bk. II. ch. 12. *Cassius*, Problem. 42. *Nonnus*, Epitom. 247. *Heliodorus*, in Mai's Class. auctor. e Vatic. codd. edit. Vol. IV. p. 13. note 3.

of pathology and therapeutics is found in *Galen.*[1] The glands in virtue of their spongy structure are peculiarly liable to take up rheums or fluxes of all descriptions; accordingly the glands of the groin, armpits and neck swell, directly ulcers are set up in the toes, fingers or head. The body being overloaded with evil humours is another reason for the establishment of buboes, and in this case they are more difficult to cure. Further, *Hippocrates*[2] derived buboes in women from interrupted menstruation, and maintains[3] that the most part owe their origin to some affection of the liver.

The majority of Writers however are agreed that among other occasioning causes ulcers hold the first place,[4] though none of them speak expressly of ulcers of the genitals, unless indeed we see good to make the passage of Hippocrates discussed a little above refer to these. No doubt in this passage the words **ἑλκώματα, φύματα ἔξωθεν ἔσωθεν τὰ περὶ βουβῶνας** (ulcerations, tumours external and external in the inguinal region) might admit of such an explanation, in which case the words must be taken not as referring to each single patient, but rather held to mean that ulcers and glandular swellings with a tendency to suppuration were set up, the latter occurring in some patients in the urethra, in others in the groin. Such an interpretation is favoured

[1] *Galen*, Method. med. bk. XIII. ch. 5. (X. pp. 180 sqq.). Comp. *Celsus*, bk. V. ch. 28. *Oribasius*, Sympos. bk. VII. 31., De morb. curat. bk. III. ch. 46.

[2] Hippocrates, De natura pueri Vol. I. p. 390.

[3] Hippocrates, Epidem. bk. VI. Vol. III. p. 619.

[4] In reference to **ἄνθραξ** *Galen* says, Isagog. ch. 16. XIX. p. 777.): *ἀνθράκωσις δέ ἐστιν ἕλκος ἐσχαρῶδες μετὰ νομῆς καὶ ῥεύματος καὶ βουβῶνος ἐνίοτε καὶ πυρετῶν γινομένων περὶ τό ἄλλο πᾶν σῶμα, ἔστι δὲ ὅτε καὶ περὶ ὀφθαλμούς*. (But *ἀνθράκωσις* (malignant ulcer) is a scabby ulcer conjoined with eating ulcer and *discharge* and *bubo*, as also with fevers sometimes affecting the whole body and at other times the eyes in particular).

by the case of the Eunuch discussed in § 20, for there can be no doubt the metathesis of buboes into fistulous ulcers was noted by Celsus and other observers. Still it is highly improbable that ulcers on the feet should have afforded the sole and only cause of buboes; it is much more natural to suppose that this, as being the more rare case, was for that very reason brought into special prominence by the ancient Physicians. Besides we have seen above that the old Physicians seldom or never really had an opportunity of seeing the sympathetic buboes, as patients treated the ulcers themselves, and the buboes then disappeared spontaneously. Oribasius no less than other Writers holds buboes following on an ulcer to be without danger.

Lastly the cases are very rare in which secondary buboes under the prevailing tendency and course of the disease are thrown out on the skin, and if they do arise, the ulcer as a rule heals up. This being so, the Physician is consulted, only supposing the buboes refused to disappear. On the contary if the ulcer was still there, the Physician sought actually to stimulate it to enhanced activity, as is distinctly implied by what *Galen* says (loco citato). Lint smeared with *tetrapharmacum* (compound of wax, tallow, pitch and resin), liquified by the addition of *oleum rosaceum* (oil of roses) was applied and warm poultices over that; while on the actual bubo was laid in the first instance wool moistened with oil, to which when the pain and swelling of the part were relieved, was added an admixture of salt. Plethoric or cacochymic (generating evil humours) subjects are to be bled or cupped. If the bubo is inflamed and inclined to suppurate, it must be scarified, the patient having first been purged. Dispersion is then attempted, in this case by means of pulp and honey poultices, but not by plasters, as these are apt to provoke inflammation. If pus appears, recourse must not be had at once, as some advise, to opening with the knife; rather the poultices should be persevered with till the inflammation is relieved. Acrid poultices are suitable only when the metathesis to induration has already begun.

If dispersion does not follow and the matter has collected in greater quantities, then the most elevated spot, the same where the skin is the thinnest, should be opened. Should a part of the skin be discoloured, it must be cut away. Some advise always cutting out a piece in the shape of a myrtle-leaf, others make very long incisions; but this not only causes a disfiguring scar, but often also interferes with the movement of the part. As a general rule a single incision is sufficient, which should be made diagonally across the inguinal region, not parallel with the direct diameter of the thigh, as then the edges are brought actually into contact when the limb bends. [1] After the opening of the abscess, it should be treated by preference with finely sifted frankincense, as should all forms of ulcer. We may mention further that according to Sextus Placitus Papyriensis [2] the wearing

[1] *Galen*, loco citato p. 887., *ἐχούσης δὲ τῆς τοιαύτης τὸ μῆκος μεῖζον τοῦ πλάτους, ἐγκάρσιον ἔστω τὸ μῆκος ἐπὶ τοῦ βουβῶνος, οὐ κατ' εὐθὺ τοῦ κώλου· καὶ γὰρ κατὰ φύσιν οὕτως ἐπιπτύσσεται τὸ δέρμα ἑαυτῷ, καμπτόντων τὸ κῶλον*. (But such an incision having greater length than breadth, the length should be diagonally to the groin, not in the line of the direct diameter of the limb. For in this way the skin is naturally folded over itself, when patients bend the limb).

[2] *Sextus Placitus Papyriensis*, De medicamentis ex animal. ch. 1. note 14., Cervi pudenda si tecum habueris, inguina tibi non tumebunt, et si tumor antiquus fuerit, velociter recedet. (If you carry with you a stag's genitals, your groin will never swell, and if you have a long-standing swelling, it will quickly disappear). We must further note supplementarily that *Prophylactics against female gonorrhœa* appear also to have been known and used; at any rate *Galen*, Euporist. bk. II. ch. 26. note 37. (XIV. p. 485.), cites measures against humidity of the genital organs during coition (*πρὸς τὸ μὴ καθυγραίνεσθαι τὸ αἰδοῖον ἐν ταῖς συνουσίαις τῶν γυναικῶν*;—(to guard against the humidity of the genitals in coition amongst women), consisting in fact in unripe gall-apples,

of a stag's genitals was considered a *prophylactic* against buboes.

6. Exanthemata on the Genitals.

Long ago *Hensler* endeavoured in the Graduation Theme of his mentioned in the list of Historical Authorities to prove that certain eruptions occurring on the genitals were communicated and acquired as the result of coition. In particular did this apply above all to *herpes* (creeping eruption), under which name must be understood, as is distinctly implied in a passage of *Galen*, [1] a form of eruption accompanied by ulceration. It is true the passages of *Hippocrates* [2] cited by Hensler in regard to the *herpes esthiomenos* (eating herpes) would appear to be open to some doubt and obscurity, while the interpretations given by *Pollux* (Onomast. IV. 25. 191.) **φλυκτίς, φλύκταινα ἐπιμήκες, μάλιστα περὶ βουβῶνας καὶ μασχάλας. φύγεθλον, φῦμα περὶ βουβῶνα μετὰ πυρετοῦ,** (**φλυκτίς,** a long-shaped blister, particularly in the groin and armpits. **φύγεθλον,** a tumour in the groin accompanied by fever) refer probably only to bubonic swellings; still these objections hardly apply to the **φύματα** (swellings) described in § 32,—the less so as *Celsus* himself (VI. 18.) explains: "Tubercula etiam, quae "**φύματα** Graeci vocant, circa glandem oriuntur, "quae vel medicamentis vel ferro aduruntur; et cum "crustae exciderunt, squama aeris inspergitur, ne "quid ibi rursus increscat; (Tuberculous swellings also, which the Greeks call **φύματα,** arise *about the glans penis,* and are burned away either by caustic drugs or by the actual cautery. Afterwards when

ashes and wine as a lotion, or infusion of gall-apples with sulphurated wool as a vaginal-plug, honey and nitre as an embrocation!)

[1] *Galen*, Method. med. bk. II. ch. 2. (X. p. 83).

[2] *Hippocrates*, Aphorismor. Vol. III. p. 742., De liquidorum usu Vol. II. p. 163.

the scabs have fallen off, the sore is dusted with slag of bronze, to prevent any second growth later on). Moreover it is possible the passage of *Galen*, [1] **πρὸς δὲ τὰ ἐν αἰδοίοις φυόμενα ἀπίου σπέρμα ἐπίπασσε καὶ τραγείᾳ χολῇ περιχρῖε.** (But for growths on the privates sprinkle pear-juice and rub in goat's gall) may refer to these cases, though no doubt it may also be held to apply to the tubercles occurring in the female vagina (§ 41,—3. B.).

Again *epinyctis* (night-pustule), [2] which Hensler also mentions but declares to be equally open to suspicion as to interpretation, would seem hardly pertinent in this connection, for the violent pain experienced at once tells against the likelihood of its being an affection of this class. Its appearance *in eminentibus partibus* (on prominent parts, on the extremities) finds a clear explanation in the words added by *Pollux* (loco citato, 197.) **περὶ κνήμας καὶ πόδας ἐν νυκτὶ γενομένη** (appearing on legs and feet during the night); while it is proved that Celsus meant to indicate nothing else by it from his words in describing **φλυζάκιον** (little blister), which he says occurs *raro in medio corpore, saepe in eminentibus partibus*,—rarely on the trunk, frequently on prominent parts, extremities. Still we do not for a moment wish to dispute the fact that the male genitals were at any rate among the Ancients counted as belonging to the *partes eminentes*, and as chancious blebs do usually appear suddenly and often during the night, it is quite possible these may have been all along intended by *epinyctis*,—especially as on Hippocrates' authority [3] creeping eruptions (**ἕρπητες**) arise from night-pustules (**ἐκ τῶν ἐπινυκτίδων.** However

[1] *Galen*, Synops. medic. sec. loc. bk. IX. ch. 8. (XIII. p. 317).

[2] *Celsus*, bk. V. ch. 28. *Oribasius*, De morb. crat. bk. III. ch. 54. Synops. bk. VII. ch. 37, ch. 42., Collect. bk. XLIV. ch. 11. Mai loco cit. p. 31. *Aëtius*, Tetrab. IV. serm. 2. ch. 61. *Paulus Aegineta* bk. IV. ch. 9.

[3] *Hippocrates*, Prorrhet. bk. II. Vol. I. p. 204.

Pollux (loco citato, 206.) likewise again mentions the legs and feet (*κνήμαις καὶ ποσίν*), declaring these eruptions attack those of elderly people. From this we may conclude the epinyctis of the Ancient writers to have been very likely nothing else but that form of *impetigo* (scabby eruption) which is vulgarly known as the *salt-flux*.

Aëtius[1] mentions *pustulae spontaneae in pudendis* (pustules spontaneously set up on the privates), provoking *phimosis*, and describes[2] *scabies scroti* (scab of the scrotum) with metathesis into ulceration and scaliness, after the disappearance of which very often acute *pruritus scroti* (itch of the scrotum) is left behind. *Galen* (XIX. p. 449.) defines *psoriasis scroti* (itching of the scrotum) as a form of induration of the scrotum accompanied by itching, as well as in some instances by ulcers.

Under exanthematic types come also the various *condylomata*. These when they appeared on the genitals and in other localities of the body, were called by the Greeks **σῦκος, συκώσις, σύκωμα, συκώδης ὄγκος,** (fig, figlike excrescence, figlike swelling, figlike lump), by the Romans *ficus* (fig), whereas the same disease when it showed itself on the fundament, received the name of condyloma[3] *par excellence.* At the same time this distinction was by no means strictly observed; in particular the larger forms of *thymus* (warty excrescence) were designated by the name **σῦκος** (fig), albeit it would seem that *thymus* was used as specific name for all protuberances on the fundament and genitals. **Σῦκος** or *ficus* is according to *Galen*[4] an ulcerative tubercle secreting moisture,—the *varus* (blotchy eruption) on the contrary being dry, according to *Oribasius*[5] of circular shape

[1] *Aëtius*, Tetrab. IV. serm. 2. ch. 15.

[2] *Aëtius*, Tetrab. IV. serm. 2. ch. 20.

[3] *Galen*, Definit. medic. Vol. XIX. p. 446.

[4] *Aëtius*, Tetrab. IV. serm. 2. ch. 3.

[5] *Oribasius*, Synops. medic. sec. loc. bk. V. ch. 4. (XII. p. 823.). *Aëtius*, Tetrab. II. serm. 4. ch. 14.

and reddish colour, hardish and rather painful. It is found above all on the hairy parts of the body, the head, chin, fundament and genitals, [1] as the passages quoted above in § 13 from Martial show. They occurred, as it would seem, most frequently on the female genitals, in which situation they are described so long ago as by *Hippocrates* [1] under the name of **κίων** (pillar, pillar-like excrescence) and said to be evil-smelling. *Aspasia* [2] says, "condyloma est rugosa "eminentia. Rugae enim circa os uteri existentes "dum inflammantur, attolluntur et indurantur, tumor-"emque ac crassitudinem quandam in locis efficiunt. (a condyloma is a wrinkled protuberance. For when the wrinkles surrounding the orifice of the uterus grow inflamed, they become prominent and indurated, occasioning a swelling and thickening in the parts). *Paulus Aegineta* (III. 75., VI. 71.) describes them under the name of *hemorrhoids* as painful, reddish, excrescences suffused with blood, which break (**διαλείμμασι**), and give off a pale discharge in drops. Much more common was the appearance of *condylomata on the fundament*, [4] particularly in male

[1] *Oribasius*, Synops. bk. VII. ch. 40. *Aëtius*, loco citato. *Paulus Aegineta*, bk. III. ch, 3.

[2] *Marcellus*, De medic. ch. 31., gives prescriptions "ad ficos qui in locis verecundioribus nascuntur, (for fig-like swellings that occur in the more private parts). *Nonnus*, Epit. 214.

[3] *Aspasia*, De natura mulier. Vol. II. p. 588., De morb. mulier. bk. II. Vol. II. p. 879. The Etymologicum Magnum under the word explains κίων by ἀπὸ τοῦ κίειν καὶ ἀνίεναι εἰς ὕψος (so called from its going upwards and rising to a height). Comp. *Phil. Ingrassias*, De tumor. praet. natur. p. 273.

[4] *Aëtius*, Tetrab. IV. serm. 4. ch. 106.

[5] *Celsus*, bk. VI. ch. 18. *Aëtius*, Tetrab. IV. serm. 2. ch. 3. *Paulus Aegineta*, bk. III. ch. 59., bk. IV. ch. 15., bk. VI. ch. 80. *Sextus Placitus Papyriensis*, XI. 7. *Apuleius*, De herb. LXXX. 8. A large number of remedies against then are given by *Galen:* Vol. XIII. 309, 312, 422, 447, 512, 560, 715, 738, 781, 787, 824, 828, 831, 833, 837, 840.

subjects; in which case they were specially ascribed to pederastia, as we have already seen. This makes it impossible to decide definitely which condylomata were of primary and which of secondary character; but the fact in no way authorizes us to deny altogether the occurrence of the latter in Ancient times.

7. Morbid Outgrowths on the Genital Organs.

σαρκώδη βλαστήματα, verrucae. (fleshy outgrowths, warty excrescences).

The general name **θύμος** (*thymus*,—warty excrescence), or according to Celsus perhaps more correctly **θύμιον** (small warty excrescence), appears to have been used by the Greeks to designate all morbid outgrowths, and particularly those of the genitals and fundament, while they appropriated the expressions **σῦκος, ἀκροχορδὸν,** and **μυρμήκια** (fig or figlike excrescence, wart with a neck, wart growing directly on the skin) to signify the different subordinate species. The **θύμιον,** which *Celsus* [1] is the first Writer to delineate in detail, is a warty, reddish,—

[1] *Celsus*, bk. V. ch. 28. Comp. *Galen*, Defin. med. (XIX. p. 444.). *Oribasius*, Synops. VII. ch. 39., Collect. bk. XLV. ch. 12., bk. L. ch. 7. (in Mai loco cit. p. 43, p. 186). *Aëtius*, Tetrab. IV. serm. 2. ch. 3., serm. 4. ch. 105. *Paulus Aegineta*, bk. III. ch. 59., bk. VI. chs. 58, 71. *Nonnus*, Epit. ch. 197. *Pollux*, Onomast. bk. IV. ch. 25. sect. 194., **θύμος, ὑπέρυθρος ἔκφυσις, τραχεῖα, ἔναιμος, οὐ δυσαφαίρετος, μάλιστα περὶ αἰδοῖα καὶ δακτύλιον καὶ παραμήρια· ἔστι δ' ὅτε καὶ ἐπὶ προσώπῳ.** (**θύμος,**—*thymus*, a reddish outgrowth, rough, suffused with blood, not difficult to remove, occurring chiefly on the genital organs and anus and insides of the thighs; but sometimes on the face too). *Marcellus*, ch. 33. *Myrepsus*, XXXVIII. ch. 157.

according to Paulus Aegineta white too in some cases, and as a rule painless,—fleshy outgrowth, slender at the base, broader above, rather hard and rough at the top. Thus it bears a certain resemblance to the flower of the thyme, from which circumstance comes the name. The upper part is easily split, and then bleeds,—more than might be expected Aëtius says from its size; the same also sometimes happens spontaneously. Usually it has the size of an Egyptian bean, though occasionally it is quite small. Sometimes one such growth appears, at others several are found together, now on the palms of the hands, now on the soles of the feet; but the worst are always those on the genital organs.

According to *Aëtius*, who calls the larger sorts **σῦκος** (fig), *thymus* is also found on the fundament and on the face, in women on the *labia*, in the entrance to the vagina and in the vagina itself, spreading thence to the fundament and even over the thighs. This is confirmed by *Oribasius*, who as well as Paulus Aegineta and perhaps Celsus, distinguishes a *malignant* and a *non-malignant* form. The non-malignant growths generally disappear of themselves; but if they are amputated, there remains behind, so says Celsus, a circular root which penetrates deep into the flesh; and not only do they grow again, but further take the character of the malignant form, become painful and filled with a bloody ichor. The malignant show themselves both with and without ulceration, as well as after the disappearance of the non-malignant growth; they are harder, rougher and larger, have a dirty livid hue, and are painful, particularly on being touched. Thymus on the glans penis is more dangerous than when affecting the prepuce, [1] more especially if it assume a carcinomatous character. If of the non-malignant type it should be lightly scarified with the point of a scalpel, then

[1] *Hippocrates*, De ulcer. Vol. III. p. 319., shows a knowledge of them very uncommon so early as his time.

some mild escharotic employed, for which the Writer just named gives several prescriptions. If of the malignant type, it is according to Paulus Aegineta either tied with a horse-hair and then removed by knife or cautery, or according to what Oribasius says the latter is at once resorted to. But seeing thymus on the prepuce is often found affecting the inner and outer surfaces simultaneously, cautery must not be employed on both at once, for in that way the foreskin would be destroyed altogether. The better plan is to begin with those situated on the inner surface, first cutting them away, then cauterizing, and finally when they are cicatrized proceeding to the treatment of the others. But not a few are incurable.

Ἀκροχορδὸν [1] is a smooth, circular, fleshy protuberance, having a slender circular base, so that it looks as though it hung on a string, whence the name. It is painless and callous, usually has the same colour as the skin, while its dimensions seldom exceed those of a bean. As a rule several occur together, but disappear again of their own accord, especially if they are only small, though on occasion they get inflamed and suppuration follows; they leave no root behind on amputation. According to *Galen* and *Aëtius* they occur on the fundament, according to Philumenes, as given in the latter author, likewise on the female genitals. They are removed either by means of a thread or with the lancet, though escharotics and other acrid remedies are also employed.

A highly inveterate form is the **μυρμήκια,** or *formica* (ant) of later Writers, which is almost always

[1] *Celsus*, bk. V. ch. 28. ch. 1. *Galen*, Defin. med. (XIX. p. 444.) *Oribasius*, Collect. bk. XLV. ch. 11. ch. 14. (Mai loco cit. 41, 43. *Aëtius*, Tetrab. IV. serm. 2. ch. 3., serm. 4. ch. 105. *Paulus Aegineta*, bk. IV. ch. 15., bk. VI. ch. 87. *Actuarius*, bk. II. ch. 11., bk. IV. ch. 15., bk. VI. ch. 9. *Pollux*, Onomast. bk. IV. ch. 25. sect. 195.

discussed by medical Authors concurrently with **ἀκροχορδόν.** It is, Celsus tells us, less prominent and harder than the **θύμιον,** has deeper roots, is more painful, broad at the bass and slender at the top, less suffused with blood and seldom larger than a lupin-bean. The colour according to Aëtius is blackish. On its being touched, the patient has the sensation of having been bitten by an ant. As an exactly similar growth appears on the hands, most Writers, e.g. Celsus and Oribasius, speak only of this latter; but Aëtius describes it expressly as occurring on the fundament and on the female genitals; and it was observed in the latter situation by Philumenes, or Aëtius (loco citato, ch. 105.) in the case of *his own wife,* whom he cured by three days' fumigation with *origanum.* (wild-marjoram). Not to mention the usual escharotic remedies, for which Aëtius in especial gives several formulæ, the following modes of treatment recommended by the medical Writers evidently apply to warts on the hands only,—by extirpation with a myrtle-leaf shaped scalpel called a *scolopomachaerion* (small pointed surgical knife), squeezing off by means of a quill or metal pipette, and above all sucking with the lips and gnawing off. This last was in *Galen's* time especially [1] a very fashionable treatment and is described by him as a new discovery made at Rome.

§ 42.

Retrospect.

If we now turn back again and make a brief survey of the various forms of affections of the genitals described on preceding pages, comparing them with those of the present day, such as we have opportunity to observe in modern times, we think every unprejudiced reader will be found ready to

[1] *Galen,* Method. med. bk. XIV. ch. 17. (X. p. 1011.).

admit that they agree with these latter in *very nearly every* respect whatever, and that *every* doubt would be removed, if only the medical Writers had appended to the records of their observations in each case the words, "got by infection in coition." But to what cause do we refer such cases as a matter of fact, notwithstanding the denial on the part of the patient that he has exposed himself to any infection? Do we not take it for granted as a certainty that such infection did actually precede? Are we in the habit of noting down in every instance in our day-book of cases the antecedent act of coition that occasioned the chancre or what not; and does this omission in any way imply that this did not first occur? To our mind at any rate the fact suffices that non-professional observers and even a professional one like Galen have supplied irrefutable evidence that some of these affections were acquired by coition. Amongst others, morbid outgrowths for example are manifestly shown to have been so set up by the statement that they occurred on the fundament of pathics; and it needs no great perspicacity to draw the conclusion that if (unnatural) coition produced them in the pederast, the same maladies occurring on the genital organs owed their origin to the same cause.

But granting these maladies originated in coition, there must necessarily have been some other factors active as well, besides the mere act. Thus when patients are found explaining to the physician (Galen) that the women with whom they had accomplished coition suffered from the same evil as themselves (gonorrhœa), no one surely can suppose anything but that a transmission of the disease took place in virtue of a contagion. Such affections of the genitals as are transmitted in coition by contagion we are wont to regard as primary forms of Venereal disease; and those acquired and disseminated in the same way in Antiquity must accordingly be designated by the same name. But these primary forms extended not only to the genitals; they were equally and in the same way acquired through the various modes of *Venus illegitima* (abnormal Love) in the anus and the mouth, localities where we are accustomed nowadays to see the secondary symptoms chiefly appear. Consequently it was impossible for the Ancients,—and is really and truly no less so down to the present moment for the Moderns,—to make a definite distinction between primary and secondary forms. It is equally impossible to deny outright the former existence of the latter in these localities, the more so as, however wide the dissemination of vicious practices of various sorts, no very large number of men suffering from a diseased member are likely to have misused mouth or anus.

But if we are forced in considering the secondary forms to leave mouth and anus almost entirely out of the question,[1] then only cutaneous diseases and those affecting the bones are left us, for *ozaena* (fetid polypus), which was regarded as incurable by the Ancient physicians,[2] cannot any more than the

[1] Perhaps some weight should be attached to the fact that the ancient physicians recommend as remedies against ulcers of the nose and mouth exactly the same means as they employed in cases of ulcer of the genitals. Comp. *Celsus* bk. VI. ch. 18.

[2] *Celsus*, bk. VI. ch. 8., bk. VII. ch. 11. *Galen*, Synops. med. sec. loc. bk. III. ch. 3. (XII. 678.). *Oribasius*, De loc. affect. Vol. IV. chs. 45, 46. *Aëtius*, Tetrab. II. serm. 2. chs. 90, 91, 93. *Paulus Aegineta* bk. III. ch. 23. *Alexander of Tralles* bk. III. ch. 8. *Caelius Aurelianus* morb. chron. bk. II. ch. 1. *Actuarius*, Method. med. bk. II. ch. 8., bk. VI. ch. 4. *Nonnus*, Epit. ch. 93. *Pollux*, Onomast. bk. IV. ch. 25. sect. 204. The remark of *Galen*, Isagog. ch. 20. (XIV. p. 792.), is interesting that *falling way of the nose* from the palate gives sufferers an apelike look, (*ἀλλὰ κἂν ἐξ ὑπερῴας μεσίζῃ ἡ ῥὶς, ὥς φησι, σιμοῦνται ἀθεραπεύτως*,—(but if the nose separates from the palate, they get flat-nosed, as they say, like monkeys,—incurable.) A special *nasal syringe*, rhynenchytes, is mentioned by *Caelius Aurelianus*, Chron. bk. I. ch. 4., bk. III. ch. 2. Comp. *Calmasius*, Ad Solin p. 274.

others be taken into account in connection with primary affections of the mouth, unless indeed we are prepared to look upon the **ῥέγχειν** (snorting) of the men of Tarsus as a secondary complaint of pathics.

With regard to *cutaneous affections*, we have seen how the forms of *lichen* and *mentagra* passed over into *psora* and *lepra* (§§ 23, 25), and how the conclusion to be drawn from this is plain, viz. that the secondary cutaneous forms of Venereal disease were formerly assigned as belonging to leprosy. This seems to be confirmed by a passage of *Johannes Moschus*[1] that has only just been brought under our notice, in which it is related how a monk of the Monastery of Penthula could no longer master the appeals of the flesh, travelled to Jericho to get relief from the "superfluity of his naughtiness" in a brothel in that

[1] *Johannes Moschus*, Pratum spirituale (Meadow of the Soul) ch. 14. in Magna Bibliotheca veterum Patrum (Great Library of the Ancient Fathers) Vol. XIII. Paris 1644. fol., p. 1062., Ὁ Ἀββᾶς Πολυχρόνιος πάλιν ἡμῖν διηγήσατο, ἡμῖν λέγων, ὅτι ἐν τῷ κοινοβίῳ τοῦ Πενθουκλᾶ, ἀδελφὸς ἦν πάνυ προσέχων αὑτὸν καὶ ἀσκητής· ἐπολεμήθη δὲ εἰς πορνείαν, καὶ μὴ εἰσενεγκὼν τὸν πόλεμον, ἐξῆλθεν τοῦ μοναστηρίου καὶ ἀπῆλθεν εἰς Ἱεριχὼ πληρῶσαι τὴν ἐπιθυμίαν αὐτοῦ· καὶ ὡς εἰσῆλθεν εἰς τὸ καταγώγιον τῆς πορνείας, εὐθέως ἐλεπρούθη ὅλως· καὶ θεασάμενος ἑαυτὸν ἐν τοιούτῳ σχήματι, εὐθέως ἐπέστρεψεν εἰς τὸ μοναστήριον αὐτοῦ, εὐχαριστῶν τῷ Θεῷ καὶ λέγων, ὅτι ὁ Θεὸς ἐπήγαμέν μοι τὴν τοιαύτην νόσον, ἵνα ἡ ψυχή μου σωθῇ. (The Abbot Polychronius again related an incident to us, telling us how in the Monastery of Penthula there was a brother well self-disciplined and ascetic. But he was sorely tempted to fornication, and unable to fight the temptation, he went forth from the Monastery and departed to Jericho to fulfil his desire; and when he *entered into the common house of fornication, straightway he became leprous all over.* And when he saw himself in such a case, straightway he returned to his Monastery, blessing God and saying, "God hath brought down this disease upon me, that my soul might be saved").

place; how when he had entered the house, he was suddenly attacked by leprosy, whereupon he speedily returned to his Monastery. How much Venereal disease has in common with elephantiasis must be determined by later investigations. At any rate it is worth while to note its frequent occurrence in Egypt, its establishment in Italy along with the various forms of *lichen*, its infectiousness, as well as the statement of Celsus (III. 25.), who calls it an *ignotus paene in Italia morbus* (a disease almost unknown in Italy), and that even the bones would appear to be affected by it.

Lastly, inasmuch as the tendency of the morbid process to strike outwards to the skin was conditioned by the influence of climate, while cutaneous forms of Venereal disease were amongst the most common of occurrences, it follows that not only were affections of the mucous membranes bound to fall proportionally into the background and appear with less frequency, but those of the bones as well. Still the mucous membranes *were* sometimes attacked, and *affections of the bones* did also undoubtedly occur, though with incomparably greater rarity,—such affections being, as is well known, at the present day of rare occurrence, and especially so in hot climates. Corrosion of the tibia is mentioned by Plutarch, and peculiar pains of the periosteum, which are so deep-seated and stable as to make the patient believe the bones themselves to be the seat of the mischief, are spoken of as early as by *Archigenes* cited by *Galen*, [1] the latter adding that

[1] Galen, De locis affect. bk. II. ch. 8. (VIII. pp. 91, 104.). τοὺς δὲ ἀπὸ τῶν περὶ τὰ ὀστέα προστυπεῖς εὑρήσεις, ὡς αὐτῶν δοκεῖν τῶν ὀστέων ὄντας· ... ὅτι δ' οἱ τῶν περικειμένων τοῖς ὀστοῖς ὑμένων πόνοι βύθιοί τ' εἰσὶν, τοῦτ' ἔστι διὰ βάθους τοῦ σώματος ἐπιφέροντες αἴσθησιν, αὐτῶν τε τῶν ὀστῶν ἐπάγουσιν φαντασίαν ὡς ὀδυνωμένων, οὐδὲν θαυμαστόν· ὀνομάζουσι γοῦν αὐτοὺς ὀστοκόπους οἱ πλεῖστοι, γίνονται τὰ πολλὰ μὲν ἐπὶ γυμνασίοις, ἔστιν ὅτι δὲ καὶ διὰ ψύξιν, ἢ πλῆθος. (Now

these pains were commonly known as **ὀστοκόποι** (racking the bones). If further we ought to count in this connection those forms of *exostosis* (morbid excrescence) *of the bones of the skull* described above in § 26, which it seems were so prevalent among the inhabitants of Cyprus as to have gained for the island according to some authorities its name of ***Κεραστία*** (horned), [1] we should actually have to hand

you will find patients suffering from pains in the parts surrounding the bones inclined to suppose they are suffering from the bones themselves.... And it is not at all surprising that pains in the membranes that lie about the bones being deep-seated, that is giving a sensation of being deep-seated in the body, make patients imagine it is the bones themselves that suffer. In fact they call them generally bone-racking pains; and they are set up as a rule after bodily exercises, but also sometimes as a consequence of cold or heat).

[1] *Natalis Comes*, Mythologia bk. III. p. 383., Deinde dicta (Cyprus) C e r a s t i a, ut inquit Xenagoras in libro secundo de insulis, quod illam homines habitarent, q u i m u l t o s t u m o r e s, t a n q u a m c o r n u a q u a e d a m i n c a p i t i b u s h a b e r e viderentur, cum cornua *κέρατα* dicta sint a Graecis et *κεράσται* aornuti. (Then it (Cyprus) was also named *Cerastia*, as Xenagoras says in his second Book "On Islands", because its inhabitants *often had protuberances that looked like horns on their heads*, for horns are called *κέρατα* in Greek, and those having horns *κεράσται*. Comp. *Stephanus*, De urbibus, under word *Κύπρος*, and *Σφήκεια*. *Tzetzes*, in Lycophron. Cassandr. 474. p. 173., *ἐκαλεῖτο δὲ καὶ Κεραστία, ὡς μὲν Ἀνδροκλῆς ἐν τῷ περὶ Κύπρου λέγει, διὰ τὸ ἐ ν ο ι κ ῆ σ α ι α ὐ τ ῇ ἄ ν δ ρ α ς, ο ἳ ε ἶ χ ο ν κ έ ρ α τ α· ὡς δὲ Ξεναγόρας ἐν τῷ περὶ Νήσων, διὰ τὸ ἔ χ ε ι ν π ο λ λ ὰ ς ἐ ξ ο χ ὰ ς, ἃς κέρατα καλοῦσι, Κεραστία ὠνομάσθη*. (And it was also called *Κεραστία*, according to Androcles in his Book "On Cyprus", *because men lived in it who had horns;* but according to Xenagoras in his "On Islands", because they had many protuberances, which they call horns, for this reason it was named *Κεραστία*). Even supposing the etymology to be a fable, is the fact therefore on which it was based bound to be mythical too? Again *Pollux*, Onomast. bk. IV. ch. 25., says, *Κέρατα, ἐν τῷ τόπῳ τῶν κεράτων περὶ τὸ μέτωπον π ω ρ ώ δ ε ι ς ἐ κ-*

proofs of the existence in Antiquity of *all* the symptoms that at the present day constitute Venereal disease. All we need to do is to unite these into one general picture and give the name that is now sanctioned by custom, in order to arrive at the final result,—that *Venereal Disease*, though not recognized and described as such by the Ancient Physicians, *was as a matter of fact existent in Antiquity.*

φύσης, (horns,—*a sort of callous outgrowths* at the place where horns grow on the forehead). The words succeeding περὶ τὸ δέρμα (on the skin) are so doubt more appropriately taken with ἕρπης (creeping eruption) that comes next after them. In *Sextus Placitus Papyriensis*, ch. XI. 5. we read: Elephantis stercus illitum omnes tumores emendat, et *duritias, quae in fronte nascuntur*, mire tollit, (Elephant's dung rubbed on cures all swellings, and removes in a wonderful way the *callosities that grow on the forehead*), but this really and truly can only be held applicable to cutaneous tubercles.

CONCLUSION.

Having reached this general result at the conclusion of the first Part of our Investigations, we would now seem only to have to co-ordinate the various pieces of evidence thus far brought together without reference to time and place, but merely on the principle of similarity of contents, under local and temporal conditions, in order to obtain a general exposition of *the development of Venereal Disease in Antiquity*. Willing as we may be to undertake the task, and necessary as its performance is,—for it is precisely this that constitutes the History properly so called of the Disease,—still we must freely admit that for the present the fixed data indispensable for the work are too few to enable us to do more than offer suggestive hints. At the same time to supply these missing data by hypotheses that must necessarily lack all positive grounds, is not, at any rate in our opinion, consistent with the dignity and duty of a Historian.

As to the *local* determinations, those defining the places, to which such or such information given us belongs, are extremely scanty, and such as they are, we owe them mainly to the non-professional Authors. Among the Physicians, who from the nature of the case must be chiefly considered here, they are all but entirely wanting; true they are almost all Greek instances, still in the majority of cases it is left absolutely undetermined whether the observations, the mere results of which moreover are given us, were made in Greece, at Rome or in Asia Minor. But even supposing knowledge amounting to certainty *were* available on this point, yet the local range as compared with the whole Ancient world is too limited to entitle us to use it successfully as evidence in drawing up a general History of the Disease.

The *temporal* determinations are in no better case. This is especially so where the Physicians are concerned; not to mention the general uncertainty as to the epoch at which most of them lived and made their observations, they are for the most part bad witnesses for this reason if for no other, that they have obviously copied one from another, or at any rate so far as their works are extant for our examination, utilized,—with the possible exception of Galen,—certain common sources of information, which unfortunately have been completely lost. The loss is the more to be deplored as the authorities in question belonged just to the most flourishing period of scientific Medicine, that of the Alexandrian physicians.

Yet another drawback is that up to the present we are entirely without information as to the consecutive order of the series of epidemics in Antiquity, by the indirect help of which alone do the historical factors conditioning Venereal disease become discernible; while so far as appears, there is no reasonable hope of our ever attaining any clearer light on the point. Nay! even if we did possess the information, it could only apply to Greece, Rome and Asia Minor, for as previously pointed out, in countries situated in the hot Zone the *genius epidemicus* (general consensus of epidemic conditions) is but rarely as a rule strong enough to override the *genius endemicus* (general consensus of endemic conditions). As much therefore as can in such a state of things be predicated with some basis of reason as not entirely hypothetical may be pretty well summed up as follows:—

Diseases of the genital organs developed little by little among nearly all the Peoples of Antiquity known to us at all intimately under the favouring conditions detailed in preceding pages. At the same time in virtue of the large number of counteracting influences they seldom attained to any high degree of intensity, and remained mostly local, taking the form of mucous discharges and superficial ulcers, without provoking any general reaction of the organism. Even when such reaction did occur, it was the skin that felt it, in such a way as to throw off the effects of morbid activity in the form of cutaneous maladies. These conditions lasted usually as long as the different Peoples continued to cultivate mutual exclusiveness; directly they abandoned this, and individual members of different foreign stocks began to combine to gratify an unbridled licentiousness, affections of the genitals not only increased in frequency, but over and above this a malignant character was stamped upon them, with which both the development and the intensity of any particular contagion stood in direct ratio.

Examples are to be found in the Plague of Baal Peor among the Jews at Shittim (§§ 8. and 9. above), in the introduction of the cult of Dionysus at Athens (§ 98.) and of Priapus at Lampsacus (§ 7.), both of which latter are connected with the March of Bacchus to and from India, as well as lastly in the introduction of the Lingam-worship in India itself (§ 6.). All these phænomena point to the conclusion that a remarkable frequency and malignity of affections of the genitals was connected with influences conditioned from without, amongst which we have to reckon the general epidemic conditions. This becomes the more interesting and important from the fact that we meet with the same thing again in the XVth. Century, a period when the incorrect view taken of the circumstances led to the most contradictory opinions being held. However both influences and effects were merely transitory, as is proved by the unanimous consensus of authorities that the phænomena provoked by the conditions disappeared again after a certain interval of time, an interval that seems among the Jews only to have lasted somewhat longer under endemic influence.

Still under no circumstances does this justify us in arguing to a total absence of all affections of the genital organs,—as is proved, no doubt after an interval of more than a thousand years, (if indeed we are to admit the occurrences just mentioned to count at all as actual historical facts), by (1) the general weather conditions laid down by Hippocrates and their consequences, and (2) an event that probably was connected with the same conditions, the Plague of Athens described by Thucydides. Here we find indisputable proof given us that affections of the genitals, as also most likely the contagion conditioning them, increased under favourable epidemic influence in frequency, malignity and intensity, while concurrently the secondary forms manifested themselves pre-eminently by symptoms of an exanthematic type.

For close on five hundred years onwards we are again left without information; but the statements contributed by Celsus show that meantime there had been ample opportunities of observing and treating affections of the genitals. In the time of Pompey the Great, when Themison made his observations on the wide prevalence of satyriasis in Crete, there was developed, it would appear, though from what causes is not known, a general consensus of predominantly exanthematic conditions, that seems to have continued for a long period of time, no doubt as was to be expected with sundry interruptions intervening. Under favour of these conditions was developed in the first instance elephantiasis, and later on under the Emperor Claudius *mentagra*, which above all in Martial's time afflicted the Romans, while caricous tumours (*ficus*) became an every-day complaint. From that epoch onwards, direct historical evidences more and more tend to disappear, till eventually it is only in the prescription-books of Physicians that we gather any inkling of the continued necessity for medical aid and concurrently of the existence of Venereal Disease.

INDEX

OF

GREEK AND LATIN WORDS

EXPLAINED IN THE TEXT,

AND OF THE

SUBJECTS DISCUSSED

IN BOTH VOLUMES

INDEX

OF AUTHORS EXPLAINED OR EMENDED.

INDEX

OF GREEK WORDS EXPLAINED.

INDEX

OF LATIN WORDS EXPLAINED.

INDEX OF SUBJECTS.

A.

B.

C.

D.

E.

F.

G.

H.

I.

J.

K.

L.

M.

N.

O.

P.

R.

S.

T.

U.

V.

W.

Z.

Finished
Printing Five
Hundred Copies of
this Book in two Vols. August
MDCCCXCVIII at Nymeguen, Holland, at the
Printing-House of G. J. Thieme,
Oriental Printer, for
Charles Carrington
of Paris.

Zeitfracht Medien GmbH
Ferdinand-Jühlke-Straße 7
99095 Erfurt, Deutschland
produktsicherheit@kolibri360.de